# The Dark Thread

THE EARLY MODERN EXCHANGE

**Series Editors**

Gary Ferguson, University of Virginia;
Meredith K. Ray, University of Delaware

**Series Editorial Board**

Frederick A. de Armas, University of Chicago; Valeria Finucci, Duke University; Barbara Fuchs, UCLA; Nicholas Hammond, University of Cambridge; Kathleen P. Long, Cornell University; Elissa B. Weaver, Emerita, University of Chicago

**Titles in the Series**

*Involuntary Confessions of the Flesh in Early Modern France,* Nora Martin Peterson

*The Enemy in Italian Renaissance Epic: Images of Hostility from Dante to Tasso,* Andrea Moudarres

*Retelling the Siege of Jerusalem in Early Modern England,* Vanita Neelakanta

*Advertising the Self in Renaissance France: Lemaire, Marot, and Rabelais,* Scott Francis

*Women Warriors in Early Modern Spain: A Tribute to Bárbara Mujica,* edited by Susan L. Fischer and Frederick A. de Armas

*The Dark Thread: From Tragical Histories to Gothic Tales,* edited by John D. Lyons

# The Dark Thread

## From Tragical Histories to Gothic Tales

*Edited by John D. Lyons*

UNIVERSITY OF DELAWARE PRESS
*Newark*
Distributed by the University of Virginia Press

University of Delaware Press
© 2019 by John D. Lyons
All rights reserved
Printed in the United States of America on acid-free paper

*First published 2019*

ISBN 978-1-64453-162-4 (cloth)
ISBN 978-1-64453-163-1 (paper)
ISBN 978-1-64453-164-8 (e-book)

9 8 7 6 5 4 3 2 1

Library of Congress Cataloging-in-Publication Data is available for this title.

*Cover art:* Stained page from the *Boston Gazette and Country Journal.* (Tracy W. McGregor Library, American History Collection, Albert and Shirley Small Special Collections Library, University of Virginia)

# Contents

Acknowledgments   vii

Introduction   1

The Death of Tragedy and the Birth of the Gothic
JOHN D. LYONS   15

Metamorphoses of the *Histoires tragiques*
HERVÉ-THOMAS CAMPANGNE   30

The Real of the Tragic Tale in Sixteenth-Century France
DAVID LAGUARDIA   45

Doubtful Readings in Rosset, Nodier, and Potocki
TIMOTHY CHESTERS AND JOHN D. LYONS   65

The Beauty of Violence in Rosset and Barbey d'Aurevilly
KATHLEEN LONG   82

Solution and Dissolution: Zayas's Darkening Threads
MARINA S. BROWNLEE   104

Evil Mothers: From Devouring Witches to Deadly Ghosts
MARÍA TAUSIET   116

On Specters and Skulls: Rosamund and Alboin in Seventeenth-Century French Tragedy
MICHAEL MEERE   129

"Autre fait arrivé au château de Nicklspurg, en Moravie": Diderot and the Horrid Case Study
CAROLINE WARMAN   149

At the Dark Edge of Enlightenment: Early Modern Vampires
GUY SPIELMANN                                                           160

Darkness at Noon: Sade's Way to Terror
PHILIPPE ROGER                                                          174

Anachronism, Heterotopia, and Gender in Anglophone Gothic
ALISON BOOTH                                                            197

Inassimilable: Gothic Francophobia in "The 'Haunted House' in Royal Street"
JENNIFER TSIEN                                                          211

Houses That Live and Die: From Greek Tragedy to the Gothic
JOCELYN MOORE                                                           225

Selected Bibliography                                                   241
Notes on Contributors                                                   247
Index                                                                   251

# Acknowledgments

Most of the studies gathered in this volume were initially presented at a colloquium held on the grounds of the University of Virginia on March 25–26, 2016, with generous funding from the Florence Gould Foundation of New York and from the Buckner W. Clay Endowment for the Humanities at the University of Virginia. The organizers and participants wish to express their gratitude for this indispensable support. The administrative staff of the Department of French at the University of Virginia, Margaret Stein and Kathleen Halvorsen, worked tirelessly to make the colloquium a success. Particular thanks are due to Antoine Guibal and Casey Shannon, who provided advice, organization, design work, and material assistance both in the planning stages and at every moment of the colloquium itself.

# The Dark Thread

# Introduction

What became of the tragic? In a world that no longer, after the early nineteenth century, produced many new dramatic works designated as "tragedy," is the tragic dead? In early modernity, in the sixteenth, seventeenth, and even eighteenth centuries, a very large number of literary works were printed and performed under the name "tragedy," "tragical history," *Trauerspiel*, and *histoire tragique*. This is the period so often said to be the second great period in which tragedies were created and performed, after the fifth century BCE.[1] Yet by the end of the eighteenth century, when Friedrich Schiller published a play that seems very much to contain the sort of dramatic dilemma and incidents that were up until then called "tragic," the playwright published his *Die Räuber* (1781) as a *Schauspiel* (simply "a play") rather than as a tragedy. The dramatic tragedies of antiquity, works of Aeschylus, Sophocles, and Euripides, continued to be read and performed, as were the plays of Shakespeare and some of his contemporaries such as Marlowe, Hardy, Webster, Garnier, and Ford, but tragedy no longer seemed writable after 1800. With regard to performance, only a small proportion of Renaissance and seventeenth-century dramatic works remained, and with regard to the narrative genre of "tragic tales," few survived in print—the rare outcroppings of a vast literary repertory, most of which has vanished from the sight of everyone save a few scholarly specialists. It seems safe to say that very few literate people today are aware that in Shakespeare's day "tragic" stories in great quantity appeared not only on stage but as narratives available in printed collections. If such popular narratives are remembered at all, only a handful are cited as sources for such plays as Shakespeare's *Romeo and Juliet* and *Hamlet*, both of which draw on the continental *novella* tradition.[2]

To the question, "What became of the tragic?" the present volume proposes the answer that the rich, popular, and aesthetically uneven constellation of tragic stories of early modernity did not go out of existence but changed name and continues to fascinate viewers and readers of plays, films, television shows, and novels without being designated as "tragedy" or "tragic." We call this strand of literary culture, often ignored in mainstream accounts of tragedy, the "dark thread," consisting of dramas and narratives that manifest the fearful, homicidal, familial violence that typifies tragic plots in antiquity and early modernity. If this hypothesis is correct, and if the "disappearance" of tragedy (from among contemporary literary creations) at the end of the eighteenth century is primarily a change in nomenclature, then the topic far exceeds the capacity of a single volume. Here, then, we limit ourselves to connecting two points in the timeline of popular engagement with the tragic: on one hand, the popular narratives of the late sixteenth and early seventeenth centuries and, on the other hand, the popular fiction that emerges in the eighteenth and nineteenth centuries under such varied names as the "Gothic"—tales, romances, and novels—*Schauerromane*, shilling shockers, sensation literature, and so forth. The examples considered are largely drawn from the French literary tradition, but the contributors generally suggest that a similar enterprise of connecting early modernity and Romantic culture could bear fruit across a wide spectrum of languages and national cultures.[3]

### The Tragic Home

At the outset, however, we need to set forth some explanation of what we are calling the "tragic," because if we claim that it continues to exist, under different names, we must say how we propose to recognize it. The concept of tragedy reemerged in Europe at the end of the fifteenth century, when the Greek text of Aristotle's *Poetics* was translated into Latin by Giorgio Valla (1498) and soon after published in Greek by Aldus Manutius (1495).[4] Increasing numbers of other editions in various languages appeared, and, crucially, many book-length commentaries were published, so that by the early seventeenth century the idea of tragedy was widely connected with this slender book of descriptive remarks about ancient Greek drama. Aristotle proposed a plot-centered view of tragedy ("it is evident that the poet should be a maker of his plots more than of his verses").⁵ But these plots should be of a specific kind. The acts depicted

> are necessarily the work of persons who are near and dear (close blood kin) to one another, or enemies, or neither. But when an enemy attacks an enemy there is nothing pathetic about either the intention or the deed, except in the actual pain suffered by the victim; nor when the act is done by "neutrals"; but when the tragic acts come within the limits of close blood relationship, as when brother kills or intends to kill brother or do something else of that kind to him, or son to father or mother to son or son to mother—those are the situations one should look for.⁶

Alongside this conceptual or theoretical rediscovery, of course, came also the publication, in Greek, and then the translation of the three Greek tragedians, starting with the first Aldine edition of Sophocles in 1502, Euripides in 1503, and Aeschylus in 1518.⁷ So playwrights and authors of tales seeking to locate or invent tragic stories could also observe what actually happened in ancient texts called tragedies. Even without knowledge of or agreement with Aristotle's teachings, early modern writers could see that one set of elements of the tragic plot stood out: violence against and even murder of family members, often not initially recognized as such. It is easy to see why the stories of Oedipus, of Hippolytus and Phaedra, of Thyestes, of Agamemnon, and of the madness of Heracles could encourage the choice of stories of treachery and mistaken homicide that abound on the Renaissance stage, where kin, friends, and guests prove unexpectedly deadly. This core of domestic violence is what we are here identifying as the "tragic." This central characteristic of ancient Greek tragedy has been brilliantly explored by Elizabeth Belfiore in *Murder among Friends. Violation of "Philia" in Greek Tragedy*.⁸ It is clear that in early modernity homicidal violence continued to be a major component of tragedies and tragic stories. Neither guests (in *Macbeth*), lovers (in *Le Cid*), sons (in *Rodogune*), sisters (in *'Tis Pity She's a Whore*), wives (in *The Tragedy of Mariam*), mothers (in *Britannicus*), nor in fact any form of kin are spared in early modern dramatic tragedy. Similar inventories could easily be made for nondramatic narratives in both "tragical histories" and Gothic tales and novels.

## Idealism and the Great Cultural Divide

Despite the obvious centrality of violence among friends and kin in Greek tragedy, many readers will be surprised by the insistence on the events that are constitutive of ancient and early modern tragedy. Generations of students have been taught that the "tragic" and by extension dramatic "tragedy" is in its essence concerned neither with violence nor with the family. Here is a relatively typical twentieth-century description of tragedy: "Tragedy is an action in which the hero's greatness leads inexorably to suffering. Tragedy contrasts what is substantial and great with the negative consequences of this greatness. By substantial I mean that which is aligned with virtue, both primary virtues such as goodness and justice and secondary or formal virtues such as courage, loyalty, or discipline. The substantial requires that the self abandon limited desires and interests for the sake of what transcends the self, the universal."[9] And here is another from a standard reference work: "Tragedy, branch of drama that treats in a serious and dignified style the sorrowful or terrible events encountered or caused by a heroic individual."[10] It is easy to see why many works designated as "tragical histories" in early modernity would not pass muster as "tragic" by prevailing standards. Even by the relatively less demanding standards of this second definition, the story of *Hamlet* would not qualify by itself as tragic. Suppose a man and a woman conspired to kill the woman's husband so that they could marry and take possession of all the dead man's wealth. And that the murdered man's son, though anxious to avenge his father, cannot make up his mind to kill the murderers. Such a plot only becomes, on this view, tragic if it is told in a "serious and dignified style." Otherwise it would be merely squalid.

Clearly something drastic happened between the time of Shakespeare and his contemporaries who wrote *histoires tragiques* and the early nineteenth century, when such pivotal authors as Victor Hugo disavowed the term "tragedy." In Hugo's case, what changed was very specifically the *word*, because Hugo in fact admired Shakespeare immensely. But Hugo could no longer use the word "tragedy" to refer to *Hamlet* or *Macbeth*. Instead, he called them "dramas" (*drames*): "Shakespeare is the drama."[11] What happened to shift the common understanding of tragedy in such a major way? And how does that shift relate to the avoidance of the generic designation "tragedy" for literary works written in the nineteenth century and later?

The crux of the issue seems to be the emergence of the *philosophical*—in fact, Idealist—concept of the "tragic" (*das Tragische*) at the end of the eighteenth century, followed by the application of this new view of the "tragic" as the standard by which to judge those dramatic works called "tragedies." As Peter Szondi has said: "Since Aristotle, there has been a poetics of tragedy. Only since Schelling has there been a philosophy of the tragic."[12] Once Schelling, Schiller, and Hegel had promoted this new quintessence of the tragic—the true, modern tragic that is so much better than anything the Greeks could have understood—it became apparent that many ancient tragedies are simply not "tragic." In order to construct the "tragic," philosophers had to discard ancient tragedy, which was inferior and impure. Friedrich Schiller wrote of the effect required by the experience of the dénouement of a pure tragedy in his essay "On the Tragic Art":

> [The] knot is untied, and with it vanishes every shade of displeasure, at the highest and last step to which man perfected by morality rises, and at the highest point which is attained by the art which moves the feelings. This happens when the very discontent with destiny becomes effaced, and is resolved in a presentiment or rather a clear consciousness of a teleological concatenation of things, of a sublime order, of a beneficent will. Then, to the pleasure occasioned in us by moral consistency is joined the invigorating idea of the most perfect suitability in the great whole of nature. In this case the thing that seemed to militate against this order, and that caused us pain, in a particular case, is only a spur that stimulates our reason to seek in general laws for the justification of this particular case, and to solve the problem of this separate discord in the centre of the general harmony. *Greek art never rose to this supreme serenity of tragic emotion, because neither the national religion, nor even the philosophy of the Greeks, lighted their step on this advanced road.* It was reserved for modern art, which enjoys the privilege of finding a purer matter in a purer philosophy, to satisfy also this exalted want, and thus to display all the moral dignity of art.[13]

The process of purging the tragic canon has been wonderfully described by Joshua Billings, and there is no need here to summarize his detailed analysis.[14] Suffice it to say that the Idealists, in the full flush of Enlightenment enthusiasm for progress and liberty, selectively read tragedies, both ancient and early modern, with a view to finding there examples of the assertion of such triumphant human will. Billings's summary description of this modernizing conception of tragedy is quite damning: "Idealism is ahistorical in its understanding of literature, willful and appropriative in its readings, selective in its canon, alternatively naive or reactionary in its politics, and fatally imbued with idiosyncratic Christian theologies."[15]

It is difficult to resist the thought that the rise of this new Idealist doctrine led to—or at least, was involved in—the parting of the ways between high culture and low culture with regard to tragic stories. As Billings writes, "Around 1800, tragedy's way of meaning underwent a major shift, with broad consequences for thought on literature and philosophy."[16] When this shift occurred, and when, as a consequence, "tragedy" and the "tragic" were appropriated for "serious" literature and drama, popular fiction did not follow. Why did much of the somber, deathly, domestic violence appear in a current of literature called the "Gothic"? This particular question of nomenclature largely exceeds the scope of the present volume, though one hypothesis (traced in the first essay) concerns the theme of the return of the dead, linking a particular kind of horror to the ghostly persistence of the past and of earlier generations, something for which gothic architecture could be a metonym. Since the Idealists were modernizers and sought in their preferred tragic plots a progressive vision of human freedom, it is not hard to see why anything suggestive of visible pastness would make a convenient marker for a literature that exploited nonmodernity and bondage—this is a fairly standard genealogy of the "Gothic" as an outgrowth of the Enlightenment. But already in early modern tragedy and tragical histories there are similar settings of violence in castles, manors, and tombs. The "Gothic" can also be seen as manifesting a tension that exists in the sixteenth- and seventeenth-century tragic between the desire to assure readers and views of the utter realism and factuality of the events portrayed, on one hand, and the desire to place the horrifying events at a safe remove from the audience, on the other. Several contributions in the present volume discuss these paradoxical impulses throughout the tradition that we are calling "the dark thread."

## The Dark Thread

The fourteen essays of the present volume attempt to help readers recognize the profound continuity in the constellation of the tragic, a continuity that can be described once we accept the historical fact that high culture, with its transcendent, purified "tragic," parted ways with low culture. The latter preserved those elements of ancient Greek and Latin tragedy that Schiller and other philosophers rejected. Renewed attention to the popular tradition of the tragic has many very practical advantages. For one thing, it can help us deal with one of the most common reactions of young readers when they first encounter early modern tragedy, for example in the works of Corneille and Racine. What college teacher has not heard the objection, "This play isn't really tragic, because . . .": What usually follows is an example of a "real" tragedy chosen from among the very select canon that survived the Idealist purge around 1800 and then was promoted intensively by Nietzsche, A. C. Bradley, and Freud, among other major modern authors.[17] For another thing, the studies presented here help to show that the popular literature of the nineteenth century did not simply emerge from—and in reaction to—the Enlightenment but rather has roots in an uninterrupted fascination with the terror that accompanies a certain category of violent actions.[18]

In tracing the "dark thread" that links early modern tragic narratives and dramas to their later avatars, the fourteen essays of our volume emphasize different aspects. Because there are so many ways to approach this topic—focusing on the early period, the later period, the intertextual and allusive linkages between the two, or even going back to antiquity to show how Romantic authors can be influenced by ancient Greek themes—the essays are presented in an entirely arbitrary sequence. It may be worthwhile, however, to mention some of the principal concerns linking the present studies together.

## Connections through Time and Space

Marina Brownlee, Hervé-Thomas Campangne, and David LaGuardia evoke for us the vital, interconnected sixteenth- and seventeenth-century cultural universe of the novella collections that flourished in Italy, Spain, and France with somber tales of mayhem, often within families or among friends or trusted figures of institutional authority. Brownlee, in particular, shows how stories circulated across linguistic and national boundaries. Plots from Boccaccio and Bandello in Italy made their way to Marguerite de Navarre and François de Belleforest in France and Maria de Zayas in Spain. This influence can take many forms, explicitly acknowledged by the authors or unacknowledged. The same plot, once it is made available in a new language for a new national audience, can change significance, depending on the cultural climate at the moment of publication. Even the simple fact of selecting one earlier story, while making a translation of a collection, could alter the overall impact on the reader and even move into new generic territory. Indeed, there seems to have been a process of increasing concentration on the tragic—the violent, the frightening—aspect of novellas as the genre moved west from Italy. Matteo Bandello's *Novelle* (1554–73) contained 214 stories, many of which were facetious and in no way violent.[19] Yet when Pierre Boaistuau and his successor François de Belleforest translated and adapted a selection of the *Novelle* into French, they concentrated exclusively on the violent and even hyperviolent ones, and titled their series of volumes not *Nouvelles* but instead *Histoires tragiques*. Campangne describes in detail this process of transformation and the new departures that occurred when Belleforest branched out and added stories of his own creation or that he found in other sources. In an epoch when other published sources of news scarcely existed, such stories often insisted on their basis in reality, however far-fetched some of them seemed. This is the aspect of the tragic tale on which LaGuardia concentrates, showing that in addition to the tales collected into books, there were also lurid stories printed and sold as broadsheets. It is perhaps no accident, as LaGuardia suggests, that such publications circulated widely at a time of civil war and widespread atrocities in France during the civil (or religious) wars of the sixteenth century, also a period when religious doctrines insisted heavily on the weight of original sin and the fallen human condition.

The connection between these sixteenth- and seventeenth-century texts and those of the nineteenth century is the concern of several essays, including those by Timothy Chesters, John Lyons, and Kathleen Long, who show that later authors rewrote or otherwise made extensive use of earlier models, sometimes acknowledging this influence explicitly. In the first essay, Lyons shows that already in *The Castle of Otranto* (1764), Horace Walpole explicitly seeks literary status for his narrative by reference to famous seventeenth-century works, both English and French. Chesters and Lyons discuss the way one of the most grotesque of the seventeenth-century tales by François Rosset was reworked by the Romantic author Charles Nodier, whose use of the same names and places signals the filiation, the "dark thread," that connects him to the genre of the tragic tale. The supernatural elements of both Rosset's and Nodier's versions of the story relate in important ways to the issues raised by LaGuardia: the relation between prodigious, scarcely believable incidents and a narrative style that presents these things as actually occurring. Here the more recent critical concept of the literary "fantastic" comes into play. In "fantastic" narrative the reader is left uncertain whether to believe or not to believe the reality of what is related. Was it all a mirage? And even if supernatural influences are at work, are they not also sources of illusion and deception? The fascination with boundaries of knowledge in the tradition of the tragic tale (which was often associated in early modernity with *histoires prodigieuses*—tales of marvels) is closely connected with questions about the boundaries of good and evil. The aesthetic allure of evil characters is often discussed with regard to the better-known dramatic tragedies of the seventeenth century. Pierre Corneille is perhaps the playwright and commentator best known for probing the boundaries of crime and virtue in relation to aesthetics. His choice of "monsters" as the center of some of his plays (figures such as Medea, Attila, and the Cléopâtre of *Rodogune*) surely influenced Jean Racine's choice of the perverse emperor Nero, whom Racine himself called "un monstre naissant" (an emerging monster) as the focus of his *Britannicus*. The main female character of Corneille's best-known play, *Le Cid*, was criticized by some contemporaries as a moral monstrosity. Long, in her essay on the nineteenth-century author Barbey d'Aurevilly, addresses precisely the topic of the relationship between aesthetic pleasure and moral transgression. She also shows that Barbey found his story material in François Rosset's *Histoires tragiques*, where the incident described already seems recounted with the awareness that it will provoke an uneasy sense that beauty triumphs over moral and social law. Perhaps it is not a coincidence that the transgressive element in both versions of the story is linked to the woman protagonist.[20]

## The Tragic Woman

Michael Meere and Maria Tausiet also describe numerous examples of plots in which the women characters take a large portion—probably a disproportionate share—of blame for the violences committed. The Rosamund and Alboin mythos that Meere explores dates back to late antiquity, but it exploded in popularity on the early modern stage, where the theme of vengeance for domestic murder and the narrative and dramatic technique of the ghostly apparition very much suited the taste for the macabre exploited also by the tragic tales—in fact, Belleforest published a narrative version. As is the case in the "fantastic" narratives, the different versions of the Rosamund and Alboin story leave uncertainty about objective existence of the ghosts. The stagings of the story are also interesting for their use of a visual device that is almost a signature of early modernity—of the "baroque" aesthetic—the skull. Hamlet's dialogue with Yorick's skull is almost universally known, and skulls are strewn around the seventeenth-century stage quite liberally (e.g., *The Revenger's Tragedy*, 1606). But they are also frequent motifs in the novella tradition, where, as in the Rosamund and Alboin story studied by Meere, they are often part of a gender-specific scenario: the woman drinking from the skull of a deceased loved one.[21] Tausiet writes about another female-centered form of horror, the interrelated figures of the witch and the mother, a theme that has a long history in the tragic repertory, as exemplified by Medea, the murderous mother and sorceress. After reviewing a number of ancient and widespread legends of malevolent and homicidal mothers, Tausiet describes the late medieval and early modern configuration of the infanticidal witch. As LaGuardia showed, much of the fascination of the tragical tales resided in their perceived proximity to contemporary reality, and in the texts Tausiet describes, there is a two-directional influence of the narratives about evil women—from legendary narratives to social action and back to further narratives. Women were condemned to torture and death on the basis of the belief in witches, and then the "documented" reality of witches—the reports of their trials and condemnations—fed popular narratives in a cycle of fear.

### Enlightenment and After

It is tempting to believe that popular superstitions of this sort belong principally to the "dark ages" prior to the Reformation and Renaissance, but as Guy Spielmann shows in his essay on early modern vampires, the earliest documented reports of vampire activity come from the late seventeenth century. The Enlightenment was apparently not as enlightened as we might think, or—perhaps a more troubling explanation—superstition may exert a greater fascination as the world becomes more disenchanted, more rational, more scientific. And the interest in vampires exhibits a characteristic that is extremely widespread throughout early modern dramatic tragedies and tragic tales: xenophobia, the fear of the foreign. As Spielmann shows, western Europeans saw vampires as a phenomenon indigenous to the eastern limits of Christian civilization, the marches in which Ottoman Muslims and Christian Kingdoms fought for dominance. Is this not reminiscent of the way tragedy so frequently locates the violence in some other land, if not some other era? As the novella stories moved from Italy, to France, Spain, and England, the locations of the plots did not always move. The Italy of Bandello's *Novelle* and the France (and Italy) of Belleforest's *Histoires tragiques* remained the preferred settings for later English-speaking writers, happy to outsource or distance horror. So often, in the English "Gothic," the evildoers were non-English and usually non-Protestant.

This "otherization" of tragic violence becomes especially apparent when the early tragic tales reappear in their Gothic form, beginning with Walpole's *The Castle of Otranto*. If Gothic literature is "gothic," it is largely because of Walpole's choice of an Italian and medieval setting for his over-the-top plot of multigenerational mayhem and revenge, which takes place in a gothic castle with subterranean tunnels—the surrealists, as Philippe Roger notes, understandably considered Walpole their precursor. The horrors are, from the point of view of the English author and his English-speaking readers, multiply distanced, taking place in an Italian-speaking, Catholic (thus superstitious), and outdated culture. It is not surprising that the conventional account of the origins of Gothic fiction see this cultural fashion as an Enlightenment reaction against all that is not rational and modern.[22] John Lyons argues, however, that *Otranto* conforms in multiple respects to a paradigm that greatly preexists the eighteenth century, in fact, precisely to the ghost-haunted revenge tragedies described by Meere and also evidenced by *Hamlet* and a myriad of tales of hauntings such as those studied by Timothy Chesters in his important *Ghost Stories in Late Renaissance France*.[23]

The Gothic representation of horrors that happen far from the place of the author and the reader and thus among people who are in an important sense different and therefore fearful is the focus of Alison Booth's and Jennifer Tsien's studies of some British and American examples of the genre. In the cases Booth studies, the incidents recounted take place in what she calls "anachronistic heterotopias," places that deploy the double displacement so typical of tragedy and tragic tales in early modernity, but here we see the extendibility of these notions, when Booth places *The Castle of Otranto* side by side with Stevenson's *Dr. Jekyll and Mr. Hyde*. She shows how both narratives work to provide the reader with a warrant of authenticity and realism while also giving evidence that this supposed truthfulness has no grounding in the world outside the fiction. Tsien brings the horror in question closer to home, as she describes a heterotopia within a real, historical city, the New Orleans of George Washington Cable's story "The 'Haunted House' in Royal Street," in whose very title we can perceive the division between the ordinary and the bizarre, potentially supernatural and thus fantastic. The text Tsien analyzes looks in many ways like those found in early seventeenth-century collections like François Rosset's, but in keeping with the "othering" that functions so powerfully in the modern Gothic tradition, the evil within the house is located in the Creole culture (actually a mixture of non-Protestant, non-English-speaking ethnicities: Spanish, Creole, and Irish) that separates that evil, inner world from the United States anglophone and Protestant culture that surrounds it.

In the present volume there are essays that concern not only the view of Anglo-American writers looking at the exotic French or Creole culture but also French writers looking at the British. Thus, the complexity of eighteenth-century French relations to the "dark thread" is evoked by Philippe Roger, in his detailed and lively account of the Marquis de Sade's rejection of the English Gothic. If Ann Radcliffe's Gothic derives from an "enlightened" British horror of (and fascination with) French and Italian Catholic perversity, Sade, as Roger shows, rejects such a literary mode because it is unreal and because there are more fearful events in the actual, contemporary world than in such imaginary re-creations of an unseen world. Although today many in France and elsewhere claim Sade for the Gothic, Roger makes a convincing case that the author of the *120 Days of Sodom* himself rejected any such affiliation. Caroline Warman looks at Sade's contemporary Denis Diderot within the framework of literary horror and finds that the encyclopedist shared with Sade a focus on horrible things that happen in the contemporary world. Diderot's materialist, atheist text, is about "monsters" within nature and about our ability to perceive the material world. The boundaries of belief and disbelief, of male and female, normal and abnormal—or even impossible—are challenged in the Diderot texts Warman describes in ways that recall the overlapping earlier genres of the *histoires tragiques* and the *histoires prodigieuses*. Diderot was fascinated with the bizarre, and particularly when it was also real.

The volume ends with an essay that ties together the earliest tragedies of Greek antiquity with nineteenth-century America. In Jocelyn Moore's discussion of Edgar Allan Poe's "The Fall of the House of Usher," we see how a central trait of the tragic tradition in its purely canonical form remains in the Gothic: the terrifying house, which, of course, is not only a building of stone but also the family itself, the "house of" Usher or Atreus, their *oikos*. While the physical role of houses expands considerably in the ever more lavish physical descriptions that progress in detail from the sixteenth-century to the nineteenth-century Gothic, the close relationship between doomed house and its inhabitants is one of the clearest, most consistent strands of the "dark thread." Both Agamemnon's palace and Usher's manor are redolent with fear, perceptible to visitors who arrive. In both cases the protagonists inherit their doom, just as many—though not all—characters in the tragic histories and other dramatic tragedies do. But in almost every case the idea of safety or protection that is normally—or at least ideally—attached to the concept of home is overturned, so that what should be safe is precisely the source of danger.

In short, the studies presented here are an invitation to rethink the relationship between high-cultural, canonical ideas of tragedy, and the vast literary realms of popular literature that the concept of the tragic has generated in European and American modernity.

## Notes

1. For a typical comment of this sort, see Albert Camus, "On the Future of Tragedy (1955)," in *Lyrical and Critical Essays*, ed. Philip Thody, trans. Ellen Conroy (New York: Vintage, 1970), 298 and 296.

2. *Romeo and Juliet* is said to root itself in Italian stories going back to Masuccio Salernitano's *Il novellino* (1476), Luigi da Porto's "Giulietta e Romeo" (1524), before it then appeared in Matteo Bandello's "Giuletta e Romeo" (1554) and was translated into French by Pierre Boaistuau in his 1559 *Histoires tragiques* (François Belleforest and Pierre Boaistuau, "Histoire troisième de deux Amans, dont l'un mourut de venin, l'autre de tristesse," in *XVIII. Histoires Tragiques* [Turin: Cesar Farine, 1670], 38–77), and then into Arthur Brooke's *The Tragical History of Romeus and Juliet* (1562). The story of *Hamlet* also appeared in a collection of *Histoires tragiques* by François de Belleforest in 1570 under the title "Avec quelle ruse Amleth qui, depuis, fut roi de Danemark, vengea la mort de son père Horwendille, occis par Fengon son frère et autre occurrence de son histoire." For an accessible text of the French version, see Christian Biet, ed., *Théâtre de la cruauté et récits sanglants en France: XVIe–XVIIe siècle* (Paris: R. Laffont, 2006), 506–45.

3. For a more detailed development of this argument, see John D. Lyons, *Tragedy and the Return of the Dead: Rethinking the Early Modern* (Evanston, Ill.: Northwestern University Press, 2018).

4. Bernard Weinberg, *A History of Literary Criticism in the Italian Renaissance* (Chicago: University of Chicago Press, 1961), 361.

5. Aristotle, *The Poetics of Aristotle: Translation and Commentary*, trans. Stephen Halliwell (Chapel Hill: University of North Carolina Press, 1987), 34, chap. 11.

6. Ibid., 40–41, chap. 14.

7. See Martin Sicherl, "Die Editio Princeps Aldina des Euripides und ihre Vorlagen," *Rheinisches Museum für Philologie* 118, no. 3/4 (1975): 205–25; and Marsh McCall, "The Source of the Aldine Edition of Aeschylus' 'Supplices,'" *Bulletin of the Institute of Classical Studies*, no. 32 (1985): 13–34.

8. Elizabeth S. Belfiore, *Murder among Friends: Violation of "Philia" in Greek Tragedy* (New York: Oxford University Press, 2000).

9. Mark William Roche, *Tragedy and Comedy: A Systematic Study and a Critique of Hegel* (Albany: State University of New York Press, 1998), 49,

10. *The New Encyclopaedia Britannica* (Chicago: Encyclopaedia Britannica, Inc., 1987), 11, 888.

11. Victor Hugo, "Préface," in *Cromwell* (Brussels: Meline, Cans et Compagnie, 1637), v–lxxxi. English text from "Preface to Cromwell" (1827) in *The Project Gutenberg EBook of Prefaces and Prologues to Famous Books*, ed. with introductions and notes, Charles W. Eliot (Project Gutenberg: 2004).

12. Peter Szondi, *An Essay on the Tragic*, trans. Paul Fleming (Stanford, Calif.: Stanford University Press, 2002), 1.

13. Friedrich Schiller, "On the Tragic Art," in *Aesthetical and Philosophical Essays* (New York: Harvard Publishing, 1895), 381, emphasis added.

14. Joshua Billings, *Genealogy of the Tragic: Greek Tragedy and German Philosophy* (Princeton, N.J.: Princeton University Press, 2014).

15. Ibid., 3.

16. Ibid., 1.

17. Friedrich Wilhelm Nietzsche, *The Birth of Tragedy out of the Spirit of Music*, trans. Michael Tanner (London: Penguin, 1993); Sigmund Freud, *The Interpretation of Dreams*, trans. A. A. Brill (New York: Macmillan, 1913); A. C. Bradley, *Shakespearean Tragedy: Lectures on Hamlet, Othello, King Lear, Macbeth* (London: Macmillan, 1904).

18. On recovering an idea of early modern tragedy, see Blair Hoxby, *What Was Tragedy?: Theory and the Early Modern Canon* (Oxford: Oxford University Press, 2015).

19. Matteo Bandello, *Novelle*, in *Tutte le opere di Matteo Bandello* (Milan: Mondadori, 1952).

20. Friedrich Schiller, in his essay "On the Tragic Art," specifically criticizes some major tragedies in which transgressive women appear, such as Shakespeare's *Macbeth* and Corneille's *Rodogune* (*Aesthetical and Philosophical Essays* [New York: Harvard Publishing, 1895], 379).

21. François Rigolot, "Magdalen's Skull: Allegory and Iconography in Heptameron 32," *Renaissance Quarterly* 47, no. 1 (1994): 57–73.

22. Fred Botting, "'In Gothic Darkly': Heterotopia, History, Culture," in *A Companion to the Gothic*, ed. David Punter, Blackwell Companions to Literature and Culture (Oxford: Blackwell, 2000), 3.

23. Timothy Chesters, *Ghost Stories in Late Renaissance France: Walking by Night* (Oxford: Oxford University Press, 2011).

JOHN D. LYONS

# The Death of Tragedy and the Birth of the Gothic

Standard accounts of the emergence of what we call the "Gothic" in literature begin with the Enlightenment and with the Gothic revival in architecture. "The Enlightenment," writes one scholar, "which produced the maxims and models of modern culture, also invented the Gothic."[1] Occasionally such accounts mention a few other antecedents, such as the Reformation and the Quarrel of the Ancients and the Moderns, finding in the Gothic turbulent confrontations of progressive reason and tyrannical obscurantism.

Yet perhaps it would be worthwhile to envision an even bolder hypothesis that springs from the association of Renaissance tragedy and "tragic" stories. Could it be that the "Gothic" is a modern form of tragedy, though it is rarely conceived as such, and that it is part of a tradition that goes back over two millennia?[2] I think that it can be seen as the *return* of tragedy into a modernity that tried unsuccessfully to reject that ancient tradition. Such a supposition unsettles many literary-historical and cultural notions that underpin the already-mentioned standard account by which the Gothic was created by the Enlightenment. I say "unsettle" rather than "refute" because I, too, believe that a parting of the ways occurred in the late eighteenth century and that leads us to have an incomplete and anachronistic vision of both tragedy and the Gothic. To pursue this idea, I would like to first sketch a historical overview, then explore one thread of the connections between tragedy and

"Gothic" narratives—namely the plot of returns—and finally look at a single example of Gothic fiction, namely Walpole's *The Castle of Otranto*.

Historically, let us think, for a moment, of the tragic tradition—the dark thread—in terms of five moments: (1) the three Greek tragedians (Aeschylus, Sophocles, and Euripides); (2) Aristotle's *Poetics*; (3) the sixteenth-century revival of the terms "tragedy" and "tragic"; (4) German Idealism and its sublime conception of the tragic; and (5) the Gothic as the heir of the pre-Idealist idea of tragedy.

Aeschylus, Sophocles, and especially Euripides wrote tragedies that were plotted around nonheroic or postepic events (e.g., the return from Troy), including infanticide and other intrafamilial killing, incest, premature burial (the burial of the living), failure of burial (the nonburial of the dead), misrecognition of family members, angry ghosts, and madness. The characters of their plays were most often of heroic stature, such as Agamemnon, but they were not represented at their best moments and did not die noble deaths. We need only think of Agamemnon in his bath.

Aristotle's *Poetics* gave a selective reading of the work of the tragedians. The *Poetics* was, of course, of no significance in antiquity, since it was written after the tragedies of Aeschylus, Sophocles, and Euripides, but it became a central text for the sixteenth- and seventeenth-century French and Italian literary culture that produced the first Aristotelian tragedies (Aristotelian and neo-Aristotelian are in this context synonymous, since there are no tragedies conceived in terms of the *Poetics* prior to the sixteenth century).[3] Much of the *Poetics* concerns the structure of plots, type of persons to be represented, the relationships among those persons, and the emotional effect on the audience. The events that form the plots concern suffering. Killing or not killing and recognizing or not recognizing are central, and these events specifically concern family members or friends. Moreover, the major source of such events is said to be a set of families (legendary or historical) within which sufficient suffering has occurred (chap. 14). And where there is the most horrible outcome, there we find what Aristotle called "the most tragic":

> Though the poets began by accepting any tragic story that came to hand, in these days the finest tragedies are always on the story of some few houses, on that of Alcmeon, Oedipus, Orestes, Meleager, Thyestes, Telephus, or any others that may have been involved, as either agents or sufferers, in some deed of horror. The theoretically best tragedy, then, has a Plot of this description. The critics, therefore, are wrong who blame Euripides for taking this line in his tragedies

and giving many of them an unhappy ending. It is, as we have said, the right line to take. The best proof is this: on the stage, and in the public performances, such plays, properly worked out, are seen to be the most truly tragic; and Euripides, even if his execution be faulty in every other point, is seen to be nevertheless the most tragic certainly of the dramatists.[4]

In short, Aristotelian tragedy centers on killing among friends—as Elizabeth Belfiore's excellent book, *Murder among Friends*, reminds us.[5]

In the sixteenth and seventeenth centuries, the rediffusion of the texts of pre-Aristotelian tragedy (Aeschylus, Sophocles, and Euripides), and of Seneca's tragedies, along with the *Poetics* led to a massive production of theatrical and nontheatrical texts in France and England designated by their creators as "tragedy" or "tragic." Since tragedy was something new to mid-sixteenth-century audiences and readers, printed versions of tragedies sometimes included an explanation of what tragedy was. Toward 1570, Jean de La Taille explained to his readers that tragedy concerned unexpected death and suffering and *not* suffering brought about by an enemy, "et non point de choses qui arrivent tous les jours naturellement et par raison commune, comme d'un qui mourroit de sa propre mort, d'un qui seroit tué de son ennemi, ou d'un qui seroit condamné à mourir par les loix et pour ses demerites" (and not things that happen every day naturally and for ordinary reasons, like someone simply dying, or someone killed by his enemy, or someone condemned to death according to the law and for his crimes).[6] In the boom of treatises and prefaces that followed, it is clear that theorists were casting around for some clear idea of what was actually tragic. Writers of tragedies and tragic narratives seem to have been much less conflicted than theorists, though they shared with La Taille a preference for unusual, unexpected, extremely horrible, highly pathetic killings. Very frequently, as one would expect on the basis of the *Poetics*, family members and friends cause each other's deaths. Certain elements that had appeared in ancient— that is, in pre-Aristotelian tragedy—became more frequent and central: ghosts, failed burials, burial of the living, and murders and tortures motivated by religious difference and/or by revenge.

Toward the end of the seventeenth century, in the course of the Quarrel of the Ancients and the Moderns in France, Greek and Roman tragedy was increasingly rejected as crude and uncivilized. Tragedy, opined the Moderns, needed to be refined and to reflect the religious, moral, and cultural progress of western Europe. As Saint-Evremond wrote, during Racine's lifetime, modernity must reject classical tragedy in favor of a new, more refined, and less horrifying kind.

> Pour vous dire mon véritable sentiment, je croi que la Tragédie des Anciens auroit fait une perte heureuse en perdant ses Dieux avec ses Oracles et ses Devins. C'étoit par ces Dieux, ces Oracles, ces Devins, qu'on voyoit régner au Théâtre un esprit de superstition et de terreur, capable d'infecter le genre humain de mille erreurs, et de l'affliger encore de plus de maux. Et à considérer les impressions ordinaires que faisoit la Tragédie dans Athènes sur l'ame des Spectateurs, on peut dire que Platon était mieux fondé pour en défendre l'usage, que ne fut Aristote pour le conseiller: car la Tragédie consistant, comme elle faisoit, aux mouvemens excessifs de la Crainte et de la Pitié, n'étoit-ce pas faire du Théatre une école de frayeur et de compassion, où l'on apprenoit à s'épouvanter de tous les périls, et à se désoler de tous les malheurs?[7]

> (To tell you my true opinion, I believe that the tragedy of antiquity would have done well to lose not only its gods but also its oracles and its soothsayers. Because of these gods, these oracles, and these soothsayers, theater was dominated by superstition and terror that could spread a thousand fallacies among mankind and afflict it with even more evils. And when we consider the impact of Athenian tragedy on the soul of the audience, we can assert that Plato was more correct in forbidding tragedy than Aristotle was to recommend it: for since tragedy consisted of excessive movements of fear and pity, didn't this make theater a place to learn fright and compassion, where one could learn to be afraid of all dangers and to bewail all misfortunes?)

At the end of the eighteenth and the beginning of the nineteenth century, the process of "refinement" was intensified, the importance of reason and conceptual alternatives emphasized, and anything physical deemphasized. Tragedy became less "yucky" and more philosophical. As Peter Szondi writes: "Since Aristotle, there has been a poetics of tragedy. Only since Schelling has there been a philosophy of the tragic."[8] In this simple observation we can see the perception of a split between something old (tragedy) and something new (the tragic), and with this division comes a radical shift in the cultural hierarchy. Henceforth the "tragic" of the philosophers, by a kind of *coup d'état*, will occupy the position of prestige, and philosophers will collectively control the power to certify which works are worthy of the epithet "tragic," thus distinguishing between true tragedies and tragedies in name only. For Schiller, Shakespeare's *King Lear* and *Macbeth* appear to be very faulty, as does Corneille's *Rodogune* because there is too much horror.[9] Tragedy reaches its perfection in the realization of human freedom and in reconciliation with the world:

> This happens when the very discontent with destiny becomes effaced and is resolved in a presentiment or rather a clear consciousness of a teleological concatenation of things, of a sublime order, of a beneficent will. Then, to the pleasure occasioned in us by moral consistency is joined the invigorating idea of the most perfect suitability in the great whole of nature. In this case the thing that seemed to militate against this order, and that caused us pain, in a particular case, is only a spur that stimulates our reason to seek in general laws for the justification of this particular case, and to solve the problem of this separate discord in the center of the general harmony.[10]

With this idealized form of tragedy, the canon is overturned, and henceforth the inferiority of Greek tragedy is apparent. As Schiller writes further: "Greek art never rose to this supreme serenity of tragic emotion, because neither the national religion, nor even the philosophy of the Greeks, lighted their step on this advanced road. It was reserved for modern art, which enjoys the privilege of finding a purer matter in a purer philosophy, to satisfy also this exalted want, and thus to display all the moral dignity of art."[11]

At the time Schiller was writing, fewer and fewer new plays were being written, published, and performed with the designation "tragedy," and more and more were called "dramas" or, like Schiller's own *Wallenstein*, "dramatic poems" (*dramatische Gedichte*). Hegel followed Schiller's path and drove the conception of the tragic even further into transcendence and abstraction. His characterization of tragedy would have been difficult for an early modern playwright or reader to recognize. Hegel wrote, "*Tragedy* consists in this, that ethical nature, in order not to become entangled with its inorganic nature, separates the latter from itself as a fate and opposes itself to it; and by acknowledging this fate in the struggle against it, ethical nature is reconciled with the divine being as the unity of both."[12] The Idealist influence on the view of tragedy was influentially disseminated in the English-speaking world by A. C. Bradley's *Shakespearean Tragedy* (1904).[13] Twentieth-century German philology and stylistics continued at least until midcentury to perpetuate Idealist assumptions, as we see in the work of Leo Spitzer.[14]

If, after Schiller and Hegel, tragedy consisted of reconciliation with destiny and the separation of the inorganic and ethical natures, what was to become of the whole inventory of literary motifs that had, with varying dosages and emphases, furnished the stuff of both theatrical and narrative tragic works both in the canon of antiquity and in early modernity? It certainly does seem to be the case that tragedy "died," as the title of George Steiner's book has it.[15] But all the things that happened in tragedy and tragic narrative continued to happen in literary fiction (and also in life), and only eight years after Edmund Burke's great essay on the aesthetics of fear appeared—his *Philosophical Enquiry into the Origin of Our Ideas of the Sublime and Beautiful* (1756)—Horace Walpole published *The Castle of Otranto* (1764).

Burke's essay deserves a moment of attention not only because of its publication at the very moment when the philosophical Idealists were promoting an intellectual conception of the tragic. Although tragedy is not the central focus of Burke's fear-centered sublime, his use of the example of a theatrical tragedy makes it clear that for him the high road of a tragic founded on ethics and admiration has nowhere near the powerful emotional and aesthetic effect of physical pain and death. For Burke, tragedy provided the public with pleasure by displaying the suffering of others. He used the term "delight" to designate this particular enjoyment. To examine the effect of tragedy in a proper manner, he writes: "We must previously consider how we are affected by the feelings of our fellow creatures in circumstances of real distress. I am convinced we have a degree of delight, and that no small one, in the real misfortunes and pains of others."[16]

Burke proposes to his readers the following thought experiment, meant to isolate the core attraction within tragedy:

> Choose a day on which to represent the most sublime and affecting tragedy we have; appoint the most favorite actors; spare no cost upon the scenes and decorations; unite the greatest efforts of poetry, painting, and music; and when you have collected your audience, just at the moment when their minds are erect with expectation, let it be reported that a state criminal of high rank is on the point of being executed in the adjoining square; in a moment the emptiness of the theatre would demonstrate the comparative weakness of the imitative arts, and proclaim the triumph of the real sympathy.[17]

The "real sympathy," a term easily misunderstood—Burke uses it for situations that produce "delight"—locates the affect of tragedy not in admiration (in the sense of esteem) but rather in the spectacle of a person being killed. Now, why is this example important? It seems that Burke points in an entirely different direction for the tragic from that taken by the German Idealists. And in Ann Radcliffe's essayistic dialogue "On the Supernatural in Poetry" (written to accompany a novel published in 1826, though it remained unpublished until after the author's death), the novelist who is so central to the establishment of Gothic fiction cited Edmund Burke as a kindred spirit.

## Returning

After this very rapid overview of the tradition of tragedy and the tragic, up to the end of the eighteenth century, let us consider a thematic feature that appears with great frequency in ancient tragedy, in Renaissance and early modern tragedy and tragic tales, and in Gothic fiction: the theme of returning. It is clear that those who write historically and critically about the Gothic are well aware of this thematic and plot feature because it is presented energetically in a twentieth-century essay that is cited in almost all writing about the Gothic, Freud's suggestive and highly influential (though perhaps unconvincing and incoherent) essay "Das Unheimliche" (1919) for which we in English use the unfortunate translation "The Uncanny"—thus losing a major clue to its pertinence for our topic, the persistent tragic and Gothic concentration on violence within families (that is, within the home, or *Heim*). Actually, if Freud had called this phenomenon the "Gothic," it would have been perfectly apposite. There is a particular passage in Freud's text that strikes me as significant, and this is the only example that the author gives of his *own* experience of the "uncanny," a sensation to which he says he is not inclined. This is the passage in which he describes the uncanny produced by repetition: "The factor of the repetition of the same thing will perhaps not be acknowledged by everyone as a source of the sense of the uncanny. According to my own observations it undoubtedly evokes such a feeling under particular conditions. . . . One may, for instance, have lost one's way in the woods, perhaps after being overtaken by fog, and, despite all one's efforts to find a marked or familiar path, one comes back again and again to the same spot."[18] The discussion of the repetition of the same event or place appears just after the description of the "double," or *Doppelgänger*, as a trait of the uncanny, and it is easy to see that the general category in question is repetition.

Later in "The Uncanny," Freud mentions the return of the dead as *reve-*

*nants*, and thus we can see that there is a broad thematic at work here, one that can be characterized with a set of words all beginning with the same morpheme: return, resemblance, revenant, repetition.[19] We could add to that, revenge, and we would have a set of terms very useful for describing tragedy and tragic narratives, particularly in a period known by another word in this family, the Renaissance.

What so often happens in the tradition of tragedy, from Aeschylus up to Racine, is that someone returns, sometimes expected but often unexpected. Perhaps, if a single type of event had to be chosen, other than murder, as central to tragedy, it would be this category of return and repetition. Agamemnon's return, in Aeschylus's play, is the necessary condition for Clytemnestra and Aegisthus to kill him in return for his having consented to the killing of his own daughter Iphigenia. And we know that Aegisthus, in killing Agamemnon, the son of Atreus, was also revenging (i.e., returning the evil of) Atreus's murder of Aegisthus's half brothers, sons of Thyestes. Atreus had killed Thyestes's sons when Thyestes had unwisely returned home. And Agamemnon's son Orestes returns home to kill his father's killer and also his mother, but the murder of his mother returns to haunt Orestes in the form of the Eryinnes. And so it goes in the endless spirals that René Girard has described as mimetic violence.[20] The problem posed by such family murders is that death alone is never sufficiently definitive. There seems to be a will-o'-the-wisp of an opportunity to make the cycles cease at the time of burial, and tombs and visits to tombs are prominent features of many ancient tragedies. Aeschylus's *Libation Bearers* opens as the slave women set forth to pacify the spirit of the dead Agamemnon in hope of preventing his return, yet as they go, they sing what they heard from the soothsayers,

> ... they who read the dream meanings
> and spoke under guarantee of God
> told how under earth
> dead men held a grudge still
> and smoldered at their murderers.[21]

In one of the earliest forms of a question that echoes through the millennia of the tragic tradition, they ask, "What can wash off the blood once spilled upon the ground?"[22] The persons of many a tragic story are heavily invested in this prophylactic attempt to prevent the return of the angry dead, who have already been mistreated in life but are often furthermore mistreated in death, as was the corpse of Polyneices in *Antigone*.

# THE DEATH OF TRAGEDY AND THE BIRTH OF THE GOTHIC

These inopportune returns home of the living and of the dead continue in early modern dramatic tragedy as in tragic narratives. Attentive as we often are to the love stories that have an increasingly important place in seventeenth-century tragedy, we sometimes overlook the persistent motif of the return of the dead. In Racine's *Phèdre* the predicament of the living seems absorbing enough, but we may forget that the two crucial turning points are Thésée's reported death and then the astounding news that he has *returned* as if from the dead! And we may be so caught up in the obstacles to young love in the story of Romeo and Juliet (whether in Bandello's or Boaistuau's or Shakespeare's version) that we forget that Juliet returns from the dead, surrounded by rotting corpses, at the very wrong moment.

There are many ways in which the dead return. Sometimes they are hazy specters as in *Hamlet* or in Jean-Pierre Camus's "Le fantôme."[23] Sometimes they are, like Thésée, thought to be dead but are not really dead. Oedipus, after all, had been meant to be exposed as a baby on Mont Cithaeron. As far as his parents knew, he was dead (and we could, if time permitted, make a substantial list of these *revenants*, including Joas in Racine's *Athalie*, etc.). Sometimes the dead return in their genetic replicas, their descendants. And sometimes they return in spectacular apparitions.

## *Otranto* and Tragic Returns

Walpole's *Castle of Otranto* is often designated as the first or foundational "Gothic" novel, and in it repetition and resemblance are emphasized almost to a parodic extent. The unhappy dead return metonymically in the form of the gigantic helmet that falls from the sky, killing Conrad of Otranto, and in the form of the gigantic sword that matches the scale of the helmet; the dead return in the form of the apparition that springs from the painting of Alfonso the Good, rightful possessor of the fief of Otranto; Alfonso also returns in the form of a descendant who resembles the dead Alfonso to such an extent that he seems to be a *Doppelgänger* of this ancestor. The young stranger Theodore's visible replication of the appearance of Alfonso, though not fully understood until the last paragraphs of the novel, is remarked upon obsessively by the other characters. And then, in spectacular fashion (perfectly suited to a seventeenth-century machine play, a *pièce à machines*, or to modern cinema), the ghost of Alfonso appears at the novel's end, much larger than life, destroying a portion of the castle itself and designating his living likeness, Theodore, as his rightful heir.

*The Castle of Otranto* is the probably the clearest evidence of the link between early modern tragedy and the Gothic novel, because Walpole very openly transposed a "revenge tragedy" into a narrative, nontheatrical form.[24] The underlying cause of the events (which take place during a time span very close to the ideal twenty-four hours of Cornelian or Racinian tragedy and are divided into five chapters that neatly correspond to the five-act structure of French classical tragedy) is Alfonso's incomplete burial, as that rite is understood from Aeschylus to Corneille. The former ruler of Otranto cannot rest in peace because his death has not been avenged; there is still unfinished business. The nature of the unfinished business is explained to the reader, and to the principal characters of the novel itself, only after the apparition of the giant: Alfonso had not died of natural causes or from wounds sustained in the crusades, but he was poisoned by the usurper Ricardo, grandfather of the current possessor of the castle, Manfred.

At this point everything becomes clear. The principle that the dead do not separate themselves from the living until their earthly business is finished is set forth shortly before the giant's arrival. Walpole was obviously refreshing the reader's understanding of this tragic tradition when he had the ghost of a saintly hermit appear to give a scolding to the lecherous old man who represents a branch of the Alfonsine clan, Frederic. The latter had heard a prophetic revelation from the dying hermit in the Holy Land that permitted Frederic to find the gigantic sword, inscribed with an enigmatic message concerning his daughter's rescue ("Alfonso's blood alone can save the maid").[25] When Frederic is on the verge of cutting a deal with the usurper Manfred, whereby the two old men would marry each other's daughter, Frederic encounters a reminder of the need to do things for the dead. Seeing before him a talking skeleton in a monk's habit, Frederic asks, "Can I do aught for thy eternal peace?"[26] And then further asks, "What remains to be done?" Theodore's father, the count of Falconara, likewise demands "sacred vengeance" for the "unsatisfied shade."[27]

We can recognize in *Otranto* bits and pieces of innumerable early modern tragedies. There is the ghost of the elder Hamlet calling for the death of the brother who murdered him. There is Chimène in Corneille's *Le Cid*, whose father's corpse remains both unavenged and unburied at the end of the play, sending the action of the play into a repeating loop of duels that would in principle never end if royal authority did not step in and set an arbitrary limit. And we recognize the *deus ex machina* of ancient, pre-Aristotelian tragedy, which returned in the seventeenth century in the example of the talking statue of the dead commander in Molière's *Dom Juan*, who comes to take the eponymous protagonist to hell.

Walpole himself points the reader toward French or Italian theater as the model for his story, and the paratextual fiction that the novel is merely a translation from the Italian retraces the steps of the Bandello-Boaistuau-Belleforest-Paynter conduit by which the plots of so many *histoires tragiques* and then English dramatic tragedies arrived.[28] The fictitious translator of *The Castle of Otranto* praises the precision and register of the "original" Italian and deplores the defects of English for this purpose, and then writes that he regrets that the Italian author "did not apply his talents to what they were evidently proper for, the theatre."[29] In the preface to the second edition, in which the pretense of translation is abandoned, Walpole cites as his models not previous narrative writers but rather dramatists. The contrast between the "coarse pleasantries" of the servants and the "dignified tone" of the major characters comes, he writes, from Shakespeare: "The great master of nature, Shakespeare, was the model I copied. Let me ask if his tragedies of Hamlet and Julius Cæsar would not lose a considerable share of their spirit" if the minor characters were omitted.[30] He then pursues this matter of the contrast of tones by citing Voltaire's edition and commentary of Corneille and then discusses Voltaire's own theater, specifically his *Enfant prodigue*, from the preface of which Walpole gives a lengthy quotation, in the original French, before saying, "Surely if a comedy may be *toute serieuse*, tragedy may now and then, soberly, be indulged in a smile."[31]

Walpole's presentation of theatrical tragedy as the foundation of his writing is a reminder that the "tragic," which is often said to be a creation of nineteenth-century German philosophers, is, in fact, historically, a quality or a set of characteristics that transcends what we are accustomed to call literary genre.[32] Romeo and Juliet in Boaistuau's French narrative version is no less "tragic" than in Shakespeare's stage version. The English playwright is simply a better writer, but what makes the play a tragedy is not the diction (as Aristotle's *Poetics* reminds us) but the set of events and relationships that lead to the death of the principal characters. "Tragic" plots move from narrative to dramatic and from dramatic to narrative.

But they have at their core a set of frequently occurring combinations of actions and personal relationships, such that an "actantial" model similar to the one Propp derived for the Russian folktale or that Greimas distilled still further in various semiotic configurations is more useful and faithful to the history of "tragic" works than is a generic model. I do not mean to pretend that a novel by Ann Radcliffe and a tragedy by Euripides are strikingly similar, or that a story by Claude Malingre and one by Wilkie Collins could ever be mistaken one for the other.[33] Ideologies, economies, political regimes, languages, religious conflicts, and technologies all condition the texts that the authors of different centuries produce. But there is across the centuries a matrix of events and relationships calculated, within the social horizon of the specific period, to create a kind of fear—terror, horror—that is different from the fear of epic confrontation, the battle of foe against known foe. Within the tragic matrix, people are killed by their kin, their friends, their neighbors. There is a reason why we call the Holocaust "tragic" and not "epic."

Repetition and resemblance are only one strand of this matrix, and they alone are not necessarily distinctive marks of tragedy. The tradition of resemblance is forever marked as a comic motif since Plautus (though there was a tragedy by Sophocles called *Amphytrion*). And repetition figures as a comic device in theories—such as Bergson's—as well as in practice, as *Groundhog Day* shows, or Hitchcock's *The Trouble with Harry*, where Harry's corpse is repeatedly buried and repeatedly exhumed. Although repetition and resemblance are both forms of returning, and although the second is a source as well of confusion, in tragedy these returnings, resemblances, repetitions, and confusions are of a particular type. Although I find it difficult to generalize on this matter—and that is why I am happy to have such insightful colleagues to help me puzzle this out—it does seem to me that Freud is right to find that repetition as unaccountable return is a source of the uncanny (or unhomey). And if we consider *The Castle of Otranto* as a repository of tragic motifs that have taken on the particular garb of the Gothic, it seems to me that it helps us see that in tragedy a certain form of progress that excludes returns has been frustrated in favor of an arrangement in which boundaries have been effaced so that reversibility is possible. Put in its starkest form, there is a boundary between the living and the dead that should be passable in only one direction. Tragedy, in antiquity and early modernity, and the Gothic, more recently, display norms violated, and the refusal of the angry dead to stay dead (itself the result of the violation of the norm of family and allies: Alfonso the Good was poisoned by his chamberlain) is the most potent and fearful of those non-unidirectional, time-sequential returns. But the disorder that is manifested by the dead returning to threaten the living appears in *Otranto* in less spectacular but equally sinister violations of sequence. As soon as the gigantic helmet has killed Conrad, Manfred's only male heir to Otranto, Manfred decides to take the place of his son by marrying his fiancée, Isabella. Her flight to avoid this fate occupies the rest of the novel and includes Manfred's proposition to her father, who was believed to be dead but who returns from the crusades: Manfred will marry Isabella, and Fredric will marry Manfred's daughter Matilda. This grotesque mismatching shows that the orderly sequence of generations has been thrown out of kilter and set into some kind of backward looping in which fathers are marrying their daughters, a kind of delegated incest.[34]

So, while Freud seems to be right that repetition can produce the "uncanny," it seems that repetition and return need to be combined with something else to move out of the comic register, and the return of the dead, or of their nondeparture, seems to be one important element. The linear progression of inheritance from parent to child, the nonconfusion of generations, the burial of the dead by the living, and the nonreturn of the dead seem to be ideals or norms that are horribly threatened in works that, before the nineteenth century, were called "tragic." It almost seems as if Walpole in *Otranto* was restaging *Oedipus Rex*. There, too, as in so many other dramatic tragedies, the return of someone dead or believed to be dead causes a horrendous nonsequential pairing in which the generations of a family interbreed.

In a literary-allegorical mode as well, the "Gothic" stages the return of a living thing, a tradition that was more than once presumed dead. Tragedy returned in the Renaissance, but this "return" was not, particularly in France, an untroubled one. Even during the decades of what is widely viewed as the golden age of dramatic tragedy, controversy swirled around the most prominent dramatists as they attempted both to bring tragedy back to life and yet make sure that it did not come back to life the way it had been. Tragedy, along with Homeric epic, fueled the Quarrel of the Ancients and the Moderns, and the latter wanted to have as little as possible to do with the crude and savage Greeks.[35] A similar spirit of modernity fires up Schiller and Hegel, who would like to bury the past so that modernity can begin. They do not like the smell of corpses, the hands stained with blood, the shrieks in the night, the cannibalistic feasts, the sound of rats scurrying in the dungeons, the desperate scratching of hands pushing from inside the buried coffin. And so Schiller theorized a truly modern tragedy that would leave the past with its guilt and horror behind. But at the same moment emerged the Gothic, or should I say, at the same moment the past continued to return, as it always does in the tragic, but now that the "tragic" had been appropriated for a soaring, noble, heroic struggle with the gods and with fate, all the corpses had to go somewhere else, into the Gothic crypt.

## Notes

1. Fred Botting, "'In Gothic Darkly': Heterotopia, History, Culture," in *A Companion to the Gothic*, ed. David Punter, Blackwell Companions to Literature and Culture (Oxford; Malden, Mass: Blackwell, 2000), 3.

2. For instance, in *A Companion to the Gothic*, ed. Punter, there seems to be no mention of any of the Greek or Roman tragedians and no mention of tragedy.

3. Bernard Weinberg, *A History of Literary Criticism in the Italian Renaissance*, chap. 9, "The Tradition of Aristotle's *Poetics*: I. Discovery and Exegesis" (Chicago: University of Chicago Press, 1961), 349–423.

4. Aristotle, "Poetics," in *The Complete Works of Aristotle: The Revised Oxford Translation*, ed. Jonathan Barnes, trans. I. Bywater, vol. 2 (Princeton, N.J.: Princeton University Press, 1984), 1453a18–29, p. 2325.

5. Elizabeth S. Belfiore, *Murder among Friends: Violation of "Philia" in Greek Tragedy* (New York: Oxford University Press, 2000).

6. Bernard Weinberg, *Critical Prefaces of the French Renaissance* (Evanston, Ill.: Northwestern University Press, 1950), 226.

7. Charles de Saint-Evremond, "De la tragédie ancienne et moderne," in *Œuvres en prose*, ed. René Ternois, STFM (Paris: Librairie M. Didier, 1962), 4, 177. All translations from French are mine unless otherwise noted.

8. Peter Szondi, *An Essay on the Tragic*, trans. Paul Fleming (Stanford, Calif.: Stanford University Press, 2002), 1.

9. Friedrich Schiller, *Aesthetical and Philosophical Essays* (New York: Harvard Publishing, 1895), 379.

10. Ibid., 381.

11. Ibid.

12. Qtd. in Szondi, *An Essay on the Tragic*, 15.

13. A. C. Bradley, *Shakespearean Tragedy: Lectures on Hamlet, Othello, King Lear, Macbeth* (London: Macmillan, 1904).

14. Leo Spitzer, "The 'Récit de Théramène' in Racine's 'Phèdre,'" in *Leo Spitzer, Essays on Seventeenth-Century French Literature*, ed. David Bellos (Cambridge: Cambridge University Press, 1983), 209–51.

15. George Steiner, *The Death of Tragedy* (London: Faber and Faber, 1961).

16. Edmund Burke, *A Philosophical Enquiry into the Origin of Our Ideas of the Sublime and Beautiful* (Oxford: Oxford University Press, 1990), 42.

17. Ibid., 43.

18. Sigmund Freud, *The Uncanny*, trans. David McLintock (New York: Penguin, 2003), 143–44.

19. Ibid., 148.

20. René Girard, *Deceit, Desire, and the Novel* (Baltimore: Johns Hopkins University Press, 1965).

21. Aeschylus., *The Libation Bearers*, in *Aeschylus I*, trans. Richmond Lattimore (Chicago: University of Chicago Press, 1942), vols. 37–41, p. 94.

22. Ibid., vol. 48, p. 94.

23. Jean-Pierre Camus, "Le fantôme," in *Divertissement historique* (Rouen: Vaultier, 1632), 76–83.

24. One scholar has even attempted to pinpoint the *specific* revenge tragedy that

Walpole had in mind (see Paul Lewis, "The *Atheist's Tragedy* and *The Castle of Otranto*: Expressions of the Gothic Vision," *Notes and Queries* 223, no. 25 [1978]: 53).

25. Horace Walpole, *The Castle of Otranto: A Gothic Story*, ed. Nick Groom (Oxford: Oxford University Press, 2014), 76.

26. Ibid., 98.

27. Ibid., 87.

28. See the selected bibliography of this volume.

29. Ibid., 7.

30. Ibid., 10.

31. Ibid., 12.

32. Clara F. McIntyre notes that "the rise of the Gothic novel coincides, roughly, with a distinct revival of interest in Elizabethan drama. Both in published collections and on the stage, during the last half of the eighteenth century, the public had an opportunity to become acquainted with plays which had been little known for many years" (McIntyre, "Were the 'Gothic' Novels Gothic?," *PMLA* 36 [1921]: 646).

33. Claude Malingre, *Histoires tragiques de nostre temps* (Rouen: Ferrand et Daré, 1641). Cf. Wilkie Collins, *The Woman in White*, ed. John Sutherland (Oxford: Oxford University Press, 2008).

34. Avril Horner and Sue Zlosnik point out the violation of boundaries in Gothic narratives: "Gothic writing always concerns itself with boundaries and their instabilities.... Serious Gothic writing manifests a deep anxiety about the permeability of such boundaries [e.g. living/dead; natural/supernatural]" ("Comic Gothic," in *A Companion to the Gothic*, ed. Punter, 243).

35. See Larry F. Norman, *The Shock of the Ancient: Literature and History in Early Modern France* (Chicago: University of Chicago Press, 2011).

HERVÉ-THOMAS CAMPANGNE

# Metamorphoses of the *Histoires tragiques*

François de Belleforest's anthologies of *Histoires tragiques*, published between 1559 and 1583, met with unprecedented commercial and literary success throughout Europe.[1] One of Belleforest's stories, which recounts the tragic destiny of Prince Hamlet of Denmark, provided a source for Shakespeare's famous play.[2] The Bard of Avon was not the only one who found inspiration in the French writer's prose: from the early seventeenth century to the 1750s, these tales of murder, passion, and revenge were reprinted, translated, and rewritten by countless authors and playwrights.

This essay will show how three of these writers, Simon Goulart, Jean-Pierre Camus, and Aimé-Ambroise-Joseph Feutry, carefully took into account what they perceived to be the tastes and expectations of readers of successive generations as they adapted three of Belleforest's *Histoires tragiques*. In order to conform to new times and to fulfill specific ideological objectives, they focused on selected details in these dark and bloody tragedies while rejecting others, and in some cases, completely transformed the plots and meaning of Belleforest's narratives. The French writer's tales sometimes underwent such a metamorphosis that they were virtually unrecognizable. Yet, beneath these reinventions of material found in the popular *Histoires tragiques* series, emerges a dark thread that takes us from the late French Renaissance to the age of Enlightenment. The presence of this dark thread shows that in spite of shifting mentalities and sensibilities, the reading public's taste for sensational and tragic tales remained virtually unchanged.

The French *Histoires tragiques* were themselves re-creations of older material. With his collaborator Pierre Boaistuau, who published the first volume in the collection, François de Belleforest originally translated and adapted novellas selected from Matteo Bandello's Italian *Novelle*. Yet with his *Quatriesme tome des histoires tragiques* (1570), Belleforest decided to give the series a new departure. No longer content with translating tales borrowed from Bandello, he provided stories that he allegedly invented. Some were actually selected, translated, and embellished from various French and foreign authors, especially those he read as he was preparing his *Cosmographie universelle* (1575). Others were based on oral sources, and several even staged Belleforest as an eyewitness.[3] Many related sensational crimes, such as, for example, the story of Saint Jean de Ligoure, a counterfeiter who set his castle on fire and murdered his wife and children in an attempt to escape justice.[4]

The first novella that interests us appeared in Belleforest's *Septiesme tome des histoires tragiques*, originally published in 1582. In this story,[5] we meet a gentleman who falls in love with the wife of his companion in arms. After the faithful spouse rejects his advances, he becomes spiteful and takes revenge by telling his friend that she has betrayed him with a young man who often visits their household. The jealous husband mistreats his wife, who dies of sorrow and despair. A few years later, the slanderer reappears and confesses his terrible lie; he presents his old friend with a dagger and asks him to kill him. When the gentleman refuses, the slanderer commits suicide by drinking from a poison vial before anyone can stop him. In view of these strange circumstances, the dead man's widow undertakes legal action against the surviving gentleman, who is soon arrested and accused of having poisoned his friend, as well as his own wife. Seized by despair, the gentleman confesses to these two murders. The judges condemn him to death by decapitation, but in a dramatic turn of events, the slanderer's manservant appears in court and tells his master's tragic story: after the death of his friend's wife, the slandering gentleman was overwhelmed with anguish and hopelessness and had told his servant about his decision to confess and to put an end to his days. He even ordered him to purchase a vial of deadly poison from a local apothecary. In view of this testimony, the court releases the gentleman, banishes the slanderer's manservant for a period of five years, and sentences the apothecary to the galleys.

With its complex plot and unexpected twists, Belleforest's tale is designed for readers who seek variety and novelty, in keeping with the author's stated intention throughout his volumes of *Histoires tragiques* to provide what he calls "un Theatre diversifié d'occurences" (a theatre of diversified events).[6] His narrative sometimes borders on the fantastic, conjuring up the *Histoires prodigieuses*, a novella genre that Belleforest knew firsthand as the continuator of Pierre Boaistuau's collection of stories relating strange events and phenomena:[7] when the slanderer appears at his old friend's house after many years, he is described as someone who resembles "un spectre, ou l'idée de quelque fantosme[, ] ... si deffigurée qu'on eut plustost estimé que ce fut une anatomie, ou le corps d'un trespassé que quelqu'un jouissant, et de mouvement, et de vie" (a specter, or the idea of a ghost, ... so disfigured that one would have thought he was an écorché, or a dead corpse).[8] Accompanied by a servant who looks just as ghostly, he provokes an uncanny effect as he tells his strange story of desperation and revenge in front of all those who are gathered at the gentleman's castle.

Belleforest's *Histoire tragique* is a moral tale that warns readers about the devastating consequences of slander and jealousy, as well as a psychological study of the different characters in a narrative that the author describes as a "tragédie" or a "furieuse et sanglante histoire" (furious and bloody story).[9] In keeping with the code of passions as they were understood in sixteenth-century Europe, we follow the travails of love felt by a man who falls for his best friend's wife, we discover all the symptoms of the choler of the gentleman who believes he has been betrayed, we observe the melancholia that slowly kills a young woman who has been wrongfully accused of the worst debauchery. In the manner of André du Laurens and other doctors of his day,[10] Belleforest describes, analyzes, and gives diagnoses, as well as possible remedies for the ravages of passion.[11]

Most importantly, however, Belleforest's story is a *nouvelle à clef* that chronicles sensational court proceedings. The two protagonists of the tale, we are told, are gentlemen who fought in the company of the Marquis of Villars, and who both owned neighboring land in the province of Auvergne. The events at hand allegedly took place right after Villars became admiral of France, in 1572. Although several details show that Belleforest did not know firsthand about the trial of the unfortunate gentleman who was accused of being a murderer,[12] he constructs a suspenseful and captivating judicial narrative. His *Histoire tragique* provides a tightly knit courtroom drama that highlights the hesitations of the judges in view of the slight evidence presented by the accusing party,[13] the Parlement's order to the magistrates to obtain statements from all potential witnesses, the complications of the appeal made by the accused gentleman's daughter, and the spectacular last-minute appearance of an unexpected witness. When Belleforest states that his *Histoire* contains a series of "actes tragiques" (tragic acts),[14] he does not simply mean that it depicts gruesome, shocking, and bloody events in keeping with a Senecan view of tragedy; he implies that pathos will arise from his chronicle of a court trial gone wrong, and invites readers to empathize with a wrongly convicted man.

Unsurprisingly, Belleforest's sensational *Histoire tragique* inspired several imitators. In 1614, Protestant pastor Simon Goulart included a version of the story of the wrongfully accused gentleman in a collection of anecdotes titled *Thresor des histoires admirables et memorables de nostre temps*. Goulart, who claims to have read the story in the "memoires d'un personnage honorable, docte, et tres-digne de foy" (memoirs of an honorable, learned and trustworthy personality),[15] provides a skeleton version of Belleforest's narrative. While most of the recounted events are the same as in his predecessor's *Histoire tragique*, Goulart gives the tale a completely different ending. In his version, there is no last-minute testimony by an unexpected witness; the accused gentleman is sentenced to death and promptly beheaded. Only a few years later will the truth surface, as the wrongly accused gentleman's son requests the Parlement de Paris to reopen the case.

Goulart mainly reads this story as an example of delayed divine vengeance, echoing the Plutarchian notions that vice is its own punishment.[16] Rather than describing the sensational events of a trial, he is interested in showing that fallible human beings, because of their imperfect knowledge, cannot understand why God inflicts punishment when he does. Goulart does not even address the irony of the condemnation of an innocent man. In keeping with his stated intention in the introduction to his collection of stories, Goulart relates events that are as memorable as they are miraculous in the etymological sense of the word: they are astonishing, amazing objects of wonder.[17] He shares Belleforest's intent to moralize, but, unlike the *Histoires tragiques* author, he does not indulge in the pleasure of storytelling and entertaining readers, writing: "Comme aux bons estomacs il ne faut point de saupicquets, les esprits robustes aussi se contentent de lecture simple, laquelle ils ruminent, pour la convertir en substance vivifiante" (Just like good stomachs do not need spicy sauces, good spirits content themselves with simple reading, which they ponder in order to convert it into an invigorating substance).[18]

Bishop Jean-Pierre Camus, who also gave a version of the slanderer's story in his 1630 *Spectacles d'horreur*, could not have agreed more. In his rendering of the tale, titled "La force du regret" (The power of regret), the protagonists are named Didime, Rotilde, and Fredoard. The events at hand, we are told, took place not far from the Alps, not so long ago. Unlike Goulart, Camus is careful to insist on the jealous husband's excessive reaction as he learns of his wife's alleged infidelity: "Ce n'estoit plus un mary, c'estoit un demon . . . qui la tourmentoit tous les jours de quelque nouveau supplice" (He was no longer a husband, but rather a demon . . .who persecuted her every day with some new torment).[19] Camus thus justifies the punishment of the jealous husband who, in his version of the story, as in Goulart's, is finally beheaded. This ghastly ending adds to Belleforest's version of the tale a chilling effect that transforms it into a true "spectacle of horror." Didime's fate shows that a guilty conscience is like "un bourreau, ou plustost un enfer" (an executioner, or rather, hell),[20] for in Camus's narrative, the "power of regret" does not only concern the slanderer but also the jealous husband, who, out of remorse, confesses to have poisoned his wife, as well as his old friend, even though he is not guilty of these crimes. Like his Protestant predecessor, the Catholic bishop is mainly interested in describing the tragic fate of those who err, not in constructing a suspenseful narrative in the manner of Belleforest's *Histoire tragique*. He tells his readers: "Comme je ne vise en ces Histoires racourcies qu'au recit des faicts simples et sans ornement, je ne m'amuse pas beaucoup à la description des causes, et beaucoup moins à representer la mauvaise conduite des pecheurs en leurs pernicieux desseins" (Since my only aim in these abridged stories, is to recount simple facts without embellishment, I don't waste time describing reasons, and even less representing the improper behavior of sinners in their pernicious intent).[21] A fervent supporter of the Tridentine ideology,[22] Camus created brief and shocking narratives for readers who might busy themselves with many other matters besides sin, guilt, and hell. His "spectacle of horror" was designed to remind them of their importance and significance. Camus's narrative is also evocative of the *canard* genre,[23] in contrast with Belleforest's *Histoire*, which is more reminiscent of *factum* and pardon tales that circulated in *ancien régime* France.[24] Camus, like the authors of popular *canards* who reported horrible crimes and extraordinary events, is especially interested in the culprit's spectacular punishment, in the guilty conscience and unbearable regrets that bring the slanderer to suicide. Belleforest's argumentative narrative, on the other hand, reads like one of the *factum* that were written in order to show the innocence of a defendant.[25] As much as the slanderer's destiny, the accused gentleman's legal ordeal is clearly, as we have seen earlier, at the center of his *Histoire tragique*.

More than a century after Jean-Pierre Camus, a translator, novelist, and sometimes poet named Aimé-Ambroise-Joseph Feutry also gave a version of Belleforest's *Histoire tragique*.[26] Like Belleforest, Feutry presents his story as a *nouvelle à clef*: since it concerns a well-known family that deserves the greatest respect, he explains that he will use pseudonyms, although he gives the events at hand a specific timeline, beginning in 1634.[27] Feutry's tale, however, only follows Belleforest's and Camus's version until its midpoint. In his narrative, the slanderer, now called Alceste, falls in love with his friend D'Orval's wife, Elmire. When she rejects his advances, Alceste tells D'Orval that Elmire has been involved with the knight of Castro, an Italian gentleman who often visits his household. Like the protagonist in Belleforest's tale, D'Orval is seized by jealousy and rage; like him also he mistreats his wife, who is soon exiled to a faraway castle. The darkest and most tragic details in Belleforest's and Camus's *histoire*, however, have vanished from Feutry's narrative. There is no poison, no trial with spectacular twists, no beheading. Instead, Feutry develops one of the minor subplots in Belleforest's story to give his tale a surprise ending. In the original *histoire*, the jealous husband learned a few years after the death of his wife that his presumed rival had been castrated following a childhood accident. That is how he understood that his friend's accusations against his wife were unfounded. A skillful narrator, Belleforest actually gave readers a clue as to this peculiar detail, emphasizing the presumed rival's feminine traits as soon as he appeared at the beginning of the story: "Un jeune gentil-homme fort beau, et qui n'avoit un seul poil de barbe et d'une face si mollette et douillette qu'on l'eut plustost pris pour une femme que pour rien qui ressentit son homme: et de fait s'il eut esté acoustré en fille, on l'eut plustost pris pour une belle damoiselle que pour un guerrier et vaillant gendarme" (A young gentleman who was very handsome, and who did not have one hair of beard on his face that was so smooth and soft that you could have thought he was a woman; and in fact, had he been dressed as a girl, you would have thought he was a pretty maiden rather than a warrior and brave soldier).[28] In 1753, Feutry goes one step further. As Elmire is in exile and "aux portes de la mort" (at the gates of death),[29] the Knight of Castro returns and reveals his true identity: he is in fact a young woman, who, after becoming a widow, resorted to cross-dressing in order to follow her lover without suffering the scorn of her entourage. Alceste the slanderer is ridiculed and cast out, D'Orval and Elmire are reunited, and Castro marries her lover: the darkness of the Renaissance *Histoire tragique* gives way to melodrama and eighteenth-century sentimentalism.

Feutry, who wrote in the introduction to his anthology that he would rather move his readers by providing *exempla* than repulse them by offering precepts,[30] imitated several other tales by Belleforest. Two of them give us further insight into the reception of the *Histoire tragique* genre in mid-eighteenth-century France.

The first of these stories was originally included, like the slanderer's tale, in Belleforest's seventh volume of *Histoires tragiques*.[31] It takes up a well-known theme: a jealous husband has his wife's lover executed. During a meal, he presents her with the severed head of the dead man on a plate. When she refuses to acknowledge her faults and change her behavior, the woman is jailed in a sinister tower and condemned to look at the severed head every day thereafter. The story's topic is reminiscent of the thirty-second tale in Marguerite de Navarre's *Heptameron*, as well as of a narrative by Bandello that Boaistuau translated with Belleforest's help for the original volume of *Histoires tragiques* published in 1559.[32] However, Belleforest reexamines this familiar tale in several creative ways.

Like the slanderer's story, he presents it as a *nouvelle à clef* based on true events, claiming that the main protagonist is still alive at the time he is writing his text.[33] In order to renew a literary *topos*, Belleforest chooses, as he also did in the case of the slanderer's story, to present his narrative as a judicial chronicle. The story's narrator becomes an investigator, as well as a prosecutor who seeks to show the guilt of a woman whom he blames for her "madness and perversity," as well as the innocence of a gentleman who has been "blecé au plus sensible de son ame" (wounded at the most sensitive of his soul).[34] Legal vocabulary abounds in Belleforest's text: the man who has been sent to spy on the gentleman's wife is presented as a "tesmoing oculaire" (eyewitness) who "certifies"[35] that the woman has been unfaithful and advises his friend to bring the matter before a tribunal. The betrayed husband is about to take the law into his own hands, prepares to kill his wife and her maidservants, but realizes that by doing so "il couvriroit le tort de ces aduteres, et rendroit sa justice coupable" (he would cover up the guilt of the adulterers, and make his justice blameworthy).[36] Instead of choosing this path, he has his wife's lover arrested and brought to court, where his guilt is proven using "lettres, instructions et tesmoignages suffisans" (letters, investigations, and sufficient testimony).[37] This *Histoire tragique* thus provides a contrastive analysis on three forms of justice. Belleforest first shows the limits of private justice, which was authorized in a society where husbands who killed unfaithful spouses could obtain royal pardon through letters of remission,[38] but still remained exposed to the reproaches and suspicion of their relatives and neighbors. To this kind of justice, Belleforest prefers royal justice, which proves the philanderer's guilt with certainty and makes his punishment a public matter. The lover's execution is completed by the intervention of divine justice, which condemns a guilty wife to withstand eternal torment for having committed a sin that Belleforest views as "la cause des ruines des royaumes et grandes provinces" (the reason for the ruin of kingdoms and great provinces).[39]

In keeping with his goal to stick to the "faits principaux, et quelques réflexions morales" (main facts, as well as a few moral remarks) in the stories he anthologized,[40] Feutry did not retain Belleforest's considerations on justice in his 1753 version of the adulterer's tale. As an author especially critical of the novels of his day, which he describes as too long and overly complex, Feutry wants to write a short narrative that delivers a clear moral message to readers who live in a society that he deems to be profoundly corrupt. Whereas Belleforest dwelt on the *innamorento* that preceded the tragic events he described in his novella, Feutry emphasizes the deceitfulness of the woman he calls Henriette from the very beginning, giving her a lover even before she marries. In his version, Henriette is led further astray by a character who does not appear in the original story: she is a woman, or rather a "monster," Feutry writes, who poisons her father and brother in order to inherit a large estate,[41] and who becomes Henriette's model. In Belleforest's tale, the unfaithful wife was a perfect tragic character, in keeping with the Aristotelian definition of a protagonist of the *metaxu*, a figure who is not completely evil or entirely good.[42] She simply surrendered to the advances of one of the numerous followers who took advantage of her husband's repeated absences. Feutry, on the other hand, is more interested in staging for his readers a woman who is debauchery incarnate, an *exemplum* to be avoided at all costs. Although his wife is rewarded with the same ghastly punishment as in Belleforest's tale, the betrayed husband in Feutry's story does not bring the woman's lover to the royal authorities but kills him with his own hands. The intricate reflection on various forms of justice that was the focus of Belleforest's narrative does not interest Feutry, who mainly seeks to explain dark and tragic events and to justify the husband's cruelty in view of his wife's extreme dissoluteness. Belleforest challenged some of the conventions of the *Histoire tragique* in his version of the story: the husband actually went as far as forgiving his unfaithful wife before she resumed her debauchery. Feutry, on the other hand, reverts to a more traditional vision of the genre. His version is based on a structure described by Sergio Poli, who explained that *histoires tragiques* generally entail a simple progression that takes readers from the statement of a law, to a transgression, to a final punishment.[43]

Another one of Belleforest's *Histoires tragiques* underwent equally significant transformations in Feutry's 1753 anthology. This tale, which was widely disseminated in the sixteenth century,[44] recounts the ordeal of a young woman who was allegedly stranded on a desert island during a voyage to the

Americas. The *damoiselle*, as Belleforest calls her, took part in the expedition to the New World undertaken by her brother. Here again, the novelist presents his story as a *nouvelle à clef*, and we can easily identify this brother and captain as Jean François de la Roque de Roberval, who had been commissioned by King Francis I to settle the province of Canada. During the crossing, the young woman fell in love with one of the gentlemen in Roberval's company, secretly married, and became pregnant. Her brother, who soon found out, was outraged by the couple's behavior and by his sister's failure to ask him permission to marry. He disguised his wrath but prepared to take a terrible revenge: using the pretext of a provisioning stop, he abandoned the wife and husband on a desert island. The couple survived as it could, the damsel gave birth, but her child died of hunger. The gentleman soon met the same fate, leaving the young woman alone until she was rescued by a passing ship after a few years.

Simon Goulart also gave readers of his *Thresor* a version of this well-known story, emphasizing some of the stranger and tragic elements it contains: on the island, the couple is tormented by evil spirits; the *damoiselle* is forever distressed by the "frayeurs et horreurs" (fear and horror) of her ordeal.[45] However, unlike Belleforest, who embellished his *Histoire tragique* with long monologues, as well as with poems supposedly written by the gentleman who married the *damoiselle*, Goulart sticks to describing a chain of unfortunate events. In true humanist fashion, he leaves it to his readers to comment or interpret the story he recounts.[46]

Belleforest and Goulart focused on what Aristotle described in his *Poetics* as a "tragic incident that occurs between those who are near or dear to one another," in this case, between a brother and sister.[47] As in the best tragedies, harm occurred among *philoi*.[48] Moreover, Belleforest's and Goulart's versions centered on a "banissement," the type of exile that Jean de La Taille highlighted in his *Art de la tragédie* as one of the situations most likely to bring about the passions and emotions peculiar to tragedy.[49] In his 1753 rendering of the tale, Feutry took a very different stance: he transformed the *damoiselle*'s tragic ordeal into a Robinsonade. In his version of the story, the island is no longer "un desert espouvantable" (terrifying desert);[50] its small lake and lush forest provide abundant nourishment for the stranded couple, who soon build a dwelling that resembles a palace more than a cabin made out of driftwood and branches. In his *Histoire tragique*, Belleforest speculated as to the language that would be spoken by a child born in complete isolation, referring to Egyptian Pharaoh Psamtik's famous experiment as related in Herodotus's *Histories*.[51] Unfortunately, in his version the story, the child died too soon to prove or disprove such a hypothesis. Feutry takes the experiment further: he seeks to describe the mind-set of a child born on a desert island. In his narrative, although the husband of the young woman, now called Elise, dies after a few months on the island, their child survives. Laïda grows up with no other interlocutor but her mother, who handles her education according to the principles of nature rather than culture. Giving her a general idea of laws and society, Elise favors a philosophy that teaches her daughter that "le bonheur étoit plus facile à trouver dans la retraite, que parmi les hommes" (happiness is found in retreat more easily than among men).[52] After their rescue and return to civilization, Laïda never forgets this lesson, nor the taste for solitude that her years on the desert island imprinted upon her: after she meets a young man and marries, they retire to an isolated piece of land where they live far away from society, according to the principles of nature. Although he keeps the moral message of the *Histoire tragique*, Feutry adapts Belleforest's tale to what he perceives to be his readers' tastes. As the translator and continuator of Daniel Defoe's *Robinson Crusoe*,[53] he understands that readers thirst for exotic adventure novels. As a critic of Enlightenment philosophy, he opts for sentimentalism and reflects on what he deems to be the defects of the civilization of his day.

Several conclusions can be drawn from the transformations undergone by Belleforest's *Histoires tragiques* in Goulart's, Camus's, and Feutry's collections of short stories. As Michel Simonin has shown, Belleforest's tales succeeded the *Amadis de Gaule* as the bestseller of their time,[54] finding their way into the libraries of aristocratic men and women, as well as into those of people of varied stations in sixteenth-century society. In spite of their author's repeated claim that his only goal was to extol virtue and blame vice, the *Histoires tragiques* were also entertaining stories that provided readers with dark and captivating plots, as well as with long love monologues and erotic scenes. With Goulart and Camus, these narratives were stripped of their courtly elements, in accordance with the Protestant ideology of the first author, and the Tridentine objectives of the second. Yet the dark and tragic elements in Belleforest's *Histoires* remained untouched in their versions of his tales.

In the mid-eighteenth century, the *histoires tragiques* received a more complex treatment. Feutry retells Belleforest's stories but often strips them of some of their more shocking elements. In his anthology, the *histoire tragique* is fused with elements borrowed from the sentimental novel genre and rewritten according to the precepts of anti-Enlightenment ideology. It actually might be claimed that in Feutry's volume, Belleforest's *tragic* stories are watered down in order to simply become *stories*, as the title of his anthology indicates: *Choix d'histoires tirées de Bandel, de Belleforest, de Boaistuau's*. One could also conclude that the 1750s rang the death knell of the *histoires tragiques* genre. After all, François de Rosset's *Histoires mémorables et tragiques de nostre temps*, a volume that enjoyed success comparable to Belleforest's collection, were last reprinted in 1758. Nevertheless, Feutry's adaptation of the *Histoires tragiques* points to another conclusion: the alleged morality and sensibility of his time forbade him to tell the dark and gruesome stories imagined by his ancestors exactly as they had. Yet these tales were there to be exploited, "ni traduites, ni exactement imitées" (neither translated, nor exactly imitated),[55] Feutry wrote, but renewed by skillful authors.

Antoine-René de Voyer d'Argenson de Paulmy, whose library comprising a hundred thousand volumes would later become the Bibliothèque de l'Arsenal, provides more insight into the ambivalence with which the *Histoire tragique* genre was viewed in the later part of the eighteenth century. In his 1781 *Mélanges tirés d'une grande bibliothèque*, he reviews, one by one, the 104 tales comprised in Boaistuau's and Belleforest's seven volumes of *Histoires tragiques*. Many of them are presented as "ghastly," "revolting," "scary and unpleasant,"[56] yet Paulmy tirelessly summarizes each *Histoire tragique* and obviously finds pleasure in recounting some of the darker and more disturbing events in these tales. However, when it comes to Belleforest's story of the severed head, Paulmy claims that indignation prevents him from writing further: "La vingtieme [histoire] est encore une de ces horreurs qui ne mérite pas que nous nous y arrêtions: il s'agit d'une femme de mauvaises mœurs, horriblement punie par son mari jaloux" (the twentieth tale is too horrible for us to even give it consideration: it is the story of a debauched woman, who is dreadfully punished by her husband).[57] For many readers, Paulmy's rhetorical half silence certainly may be construed as an invitation to look for the original volumes of *Histoires tragiques* in order to read them as they were conceived and written by Belleforest, an author who did not hesitate, Paulmy writes, "to deploy all the horror he is capable of imagining."[58]

## Notes

1. Boaistuau's and Belleforest's *Histoires tragiques* were often reprinted between 1559 and 1616. They were also translated into German, Dutch, Spanish, and English, becoming a truly pan-European phenomenon. For studies of the *histoires tragiques* genre and its literary and cultural impact, see Richard Carr, *Pierre Boaistuau's Histoires tragiques: A Study of Narrative Form and Tragic Vision* (Chapel Hill: University of North Carolina Press, 1979); Sergio Poli, *Histoire(s) tragique(s): Anthologie/Typologie*

*d'un genre littéraire*, Biblioteca della ricerca (Fasano: Schena, 1991); and Thierry Pech, *Conter le crime: Droit et littérature sous la contre-réforme: Les histoires tragiques (1559–1644)* (Paris: Honoré Champion, 2000).

2. For recent articles on Belleforest as a source of *Hamlet*, see Julie Maxwell, "Counter-Reformation Versions of Saxo: A New Source for 'Hamlet'?," *Renaissance Quarterly* 57, no. 2 (2004): 518–60; and András Kiséry, "'I Lack Advancement': Public Rhetoric, Private Prudence, and the Political Agent in 'Hamlet,' 1561–1609," *ELH* 81, no. 1 (2014): 29–60.

3. See, for example, stories 7 and 8 in Belleforest's 1572 *Le cinquiesme tome des histoires tragiques*, ed. Hervé-Thomas Campangne, Textes Littéraires Français (Geneva: Droz, 2013).

4. Ibid., story 8.

5. Belleforest, *Le septiesme tome des Histoires tragiques, contenant plusieurs choses dignes de mémoire, et divers succez d'affaires, et evenements, qui servent à l'instruction de nostre vie* (Paris: Emmanuel Richard, 1583), story 12.

6. Belleforest, *Le cinquiesme tome des histoires tragiques*, 540. All translations are mine except where otherwise noted.

7. Boaistuau's *Histoires prodigieuses* were first published in 1560. Belleforest's continuation appeared in 1571.

8. Belleforest, *Le septiesme tome des histoires tragiques*, 381r.

9. Ibid., 366r, 392r.

10. See, for example, André Du Laurens, *Discours de la conservation de la veue: Des maladies melancholiques: Des catarrhes: & de la vieillesse* (Tours: Jamet Mettayer, 1594); and Jean Aubery, *L'Antidote d'amour, avec un ample discours contenant la nature et les causes d'iceluy, ensemble les remèdes les plus singuliers pour se préserver et guérir des passions amoureuses, par Jean Aubery* (Paris: C. Chappelet, 1599).

11. Belleforest writes about the love-stricken gentleman: "Il est bien vray qu'il fut si discret, que jamais il ne se declaira à personne des ceste sienne affection: ce qui depuis cuida causer une suite de malheur, et un plus grand nombre d'actes tragiques en ceste histoire: ainsi que pourrez entendre par le discours d'icelle" (Truly he was so discreet that he never told anyone of his ailment: which is what caused a series of sad events, and a greater number of tragic acts in this story) (Belleforest, *Le septiesme tome des histoires tragiques*, 366r).

12. See, for example, Belleforest, *Le septiesme tome des histoires tragiques*, 392r: "Quoy qu'il en soit, le valet fut banni pour cinq ans, et l'Apoticaire jugé et condemné aux galeres, la vie leur estant donnée et sauvée, ne sçay pour quelle raison et consideration" (In any case, the servant was banished for five years, and the apothecary was tried and condemned to the gallows; their lives were spared, I don't know for what reason and consideration).

13. Belleforest, *Le septiesme tome des histoires tragiques*, 386r.

14. Ibid., 366r.

15. Simon Goulart, *Le troisiesme et quatriesme volume du Thresor des histoires admirables et memorables de nostre temps* (Cologny: Crespin, 1614), 89.

16. This concept is developed in Plutarch's *De sera numinis vindicta*, translated by Jacques Amyot as *Pourquoi la justice divine différe parfois la punition des maléfices*.

17. "Je les appelle admirables, à cause que les raisons d'une grand' part d'icelles sont fort eslongnées de mon apprehension, et qu'il y a du miracle, ce me semble" (I call them Admirable, because the reasons of many of them are far beyond my apprehension, to my judgement they are miraculous) (Simon Goulart, *Thresor d'histoires admirables et memorables de nostre temps* [Geneva: Paul Marceau, 1610], 5).

18. Ibid., 6.

19. Jean-Pierre Camus, *Les spectacles d'horreur: Où se descouvrent plusieurs tragiques effets de nostre siecle* (Paris: André Soubron, 1630), 181.

20. Ibid., 193.

21. Ibid., 174.

22. On Camus's Tridentine views, see Cécile Huchard, "Historical Studies—I Protestant Historiographies—History and Providence in the Works of Simon Goulart," *Bulletin: Études, Documents, Chronique Littéraire* 152, no. 2 (2006): 221.

23. On the history of *canards* in France, see Jean-Pierre Seguin, *L'Information en France avant le périodique: 517 canards imprimés entre 1529 et 1631* (Paris: Maisonneuve et Larose, 1964); and Maurice Lever, *Canards sanglants: Naissance du fait divers* (Paris: Fayard, 1993).

24. Davis gives an overview of these pardon tales in early modern France in *Fiction in the Archives: Pardon Tales and Their Tellers in Sixteenth-Century France* (Stanford: Stanford University Press, 1990). For a more recent presentation of the *factum* genre, see also Marie Houllemare, "Factums et jugement du public dans la seconde moitié du xvie siècle," *Histoire de la justice* 20, no. 1 (2010): 35–42.

25. Belleforest's intention to show the gentleman's innocence clearly appears in this monologue: "Ha pauvre damoiselle que ta langue a esté et trop sage et trop secrette, car si tu eusses dit ce qui estoit je t'eusse crue cognoissant ton integrité, et tu vivrois, et je serois en joye et repos, et ce malheureux n'auroit damné son ame. Au fort je suis innocent du tout, et n'ay failly que pour aymer mon honneur: et ores je n'ay voulu venger l'injure que cestuy m'a faite, ains suis marry de ce qu'il a faict, et me crains qu'il n'en advienne encor quelque scandale. Non obstant ne laissons pour cela de disner, louans Dieu que nos mains ne sont soullées en sang, ny nos desirs en vengeance, et si mon adversaire meurt, la faute en est sienne et la condemnation de sa mort tombera sur sa teste maudite, qui devoit attendre qu'on le tuast (ce n'eust pas pourtant esté moy) sans estre le detestable executeur de sa miserable vie." (Ah, poor maiden, your tongue has been too prudent and too secret, for if you had said what was true, I would have believed you, knowing your integrity, and you would live, and I would be happy and at peace, and this wretch would not have damned his soul. After all I am completely innocent, and my only fault came from cherishing my honor. And now I did not wish to take revenge for the affront that he did me, but am instead unhappy about what he did and I fear that some scandal may result. But in spite of all that, let us dine and praise God that our hands have not been sullied with blood nor our desires with vengeance. And if my adversary dies, the fault is his and the guilt for his death will be

on his cursed head, for he should expect to be killed by someone (though not by me), without that person being the detested executioner of his wretched life.) (*Le septiesme tome des histoires tragiques*, 387 r).

26. Feutry is presented as a member of the American Philosophical Society on the title page of the 1779 edition of his *Choix d'histoires tirées de Bandel, Italien; de Belleforest, Commingeois; de Boaistuau, dit Launai; Et de quelques autres Auteurs*. He was a correspondent and admirer of Benjamin Franklin, whom he describes as the "terror of tyrants" in his *Nouveaux opuscules poétiques* (1779).

27. Aimé-Ambroise-Joseph Feutry, *Choix d'histoires tirées de Bandel, Italien; de Belleforest, Commingeois; de Boaistuau, dit Launai; et de quelques autres Auteurs*, vol. 2 (Paris: Bastien, 1779), 297.

28. Belleforest, *Le septiesme tome des histoires tragiques*, 364r.

29. Feutry, *Choix d'histoires* (1779), 314.

30. "Les préceptes révoltent, l'exemple touche" (Feutry, *Choix d'histoires tirées de Bandel, Italien; de Belleforest, Commingeois; de Boaistuau, dit Launai; et de quelques autres Auteurs* [London and Paris: Durand and Pissot, 1753], ix).

31. Belleforest, *Le septiesme tome des histoires tragiques*, story 8.

32. The story is titled "D'une gentilfemme Piedmontoise, qui surprinse en adultere, fut punie cruellement par son mary."

33. Belleforest, *Le septiesme tome des histoires tragiques*, 222v.

34. Ibid., 248r.

35. Ibid., 241v.

36. Ibid., 242r.

37. Ibid., 242v.

38. On this question, see Davis, *Fiction in the Archives*, 36–50.

39. Belleforest, *Le septiesme tome des histoires tragiques*, 248 r.

40. Feutry, *Choix d'histoires* (1753), viij.

41. Ibid., 59.

42. See Aristotle, *The Poetics*, trans. W. Hamilton Fyfe (New York: Putnam, 1932), chap. 13, 1453a7.

43. Sergio Poli, *Histoire(s) tragique(s): Anthologie/Typologie d'un genre littéraire* (Fasano and Paris: Schena and Nizet, 1991), 7.

44. This tale appeared in Marguerite de Navarre, *L'Heptameron* (Paris: B. Preuost,1559), as well as in André Thevet, *La cosmographie universelle d'André Thevet, cosmographe du roy: Illustrée de diverses figures des choses plus remarquables veuës par l'auteur, & incogneuës de noz anciens & modernes* (Paris: Chez Guillaume Chandiere, 1575); and *Le grand insulaire et pilotage d'André Thevet, angoumoisin, cosmographe du Roi: Dans lequel sont contenus plusiers plants d'isles habitées, et deshabitées, et description d'icelles* (ca. 1586–87). On these different versions, see Arthur P. Stabler, *The Legend of Marguerite de Roberval* (Pullman: Washington State University Press, 1972); and Michel Bideaux, *Roberval, la demoiselle et le gentilhomme: Les Robinsons de Terre-Neuve* (Paris: Classiques Garnier, 2009).

45. Goulart, *Le troisiesme et quatriesme volume du Thresor des histoires admirables*, 430.

46. "Aussi n'ai-je pretendu proposer que les simples declarations des evenemens, sans m'estendre en applications, pour entreprendre de pousser le lecteur dedans le sentier de mes conceptions.... [C]e pourra estre assez, selon mon project, d'avoir monstré ce qui a esté dit ou fait que j'ai estimé memorable" (So I have only attempted to present simple expositions of the events without interpreting them, in order to move the reader in the path of my thoughts.... [I]t will be enough, according to my plan, to have shown the things said or done that I have found worth remembering) (ibid., 417).

47. Aristotle, *The Poetics*, chap. 14, 1453b9–23.

48. On harm to *philoi* as a central element in the plot structure of tragedy, see Elizabeth Belfiore, *Murder among Friends: Violation of "Philia" in Greek Tragedy* (Oxford: Oxford University Press, 2000).

49. "Tragedy then, is a type and kind of poetry that is not common, but as elegant, beautiful, and excellent as possible. Its only true subjects are the piteous fall of great princes, the mutability of fortune, exiles, wars, pestilency, famin, captivity, the heinous cruelty of tyrants." (La tragedie donc est une espece, et un genre de Poësie non vulgaire, mais autant elegant, beau et excellent qu'il est possible. Son vray subject ne traicte que de piteuses ruines des grands seigneurs, que des inconstances de Fortune, que bannissements, guerres, pestes, famines, captivitez, excecrables cruautez des Tyrans.) (Jean de La Taille, *De l'art de la tragedie*, in *Saul le furieux* [Paris: Frederic Morel, 1572], 2v).

50. Belleforest, *Le cinquiesme tome des histoires tragiques*, 167.

51. Ibid., 168.

52. Feutry, *Choix d'histoires* (1779), 281.

53. Feutry published a "free translation" of Defoe's book titled *Les avantures, ou la vie et les voyages de Robinson Crusoë* (Frankfort: Aux depens de la Compagnie, 1769).

54. See Michel Simonin, *François de Belleforest et l'histoire tragique en France au XVIe siècle* (Ph.D. diss., Université Paris-Est, 1985), 2:587.

55. Feutry, *Choix d'histoires* (1753), viij.

56. Antoine-René de Voyer de Paulmy d'Argenson, *Mélanges tirés d'une grande bibliothèque: De la lecture des livres françois: Romans du seizième siècle* (Paris: Moutard, 1781), 123.

57. Ibid., 196.

58. "Dans la quarante-sixieme histoire, notre Autheur déploie toute l'horreur qu'il est capable d'imaginer" (ibid. 172).

DAVID LAGUARDIA

# The Real of the Tragic Tale in Sixteenth-Century France

According to Jean-Pierre Seguin, in France the "fait divers," or news item, began to circulate in printed form at the end of the fifteenth century with the rapid development of print technology.[1] Throughout the sixteenth century, there was a growing interest among the reading public, which has to be understood in its historical specificity, in curious stories of all kinds. The *occasionnels* and *canards* that Seguin catalogued were probably printed in relatively large numbers throughout the century and described strange and extraordinary occurrences, weather events such as floods and lightning strikes, celestial anomalies and signs, bizarre hybrid animals, monstrous human births, thefts, duels, apparitions of demons, ghosts, and monsters, miracles, and finally bloody crimes and the even bloodier executions of their perpetrators. The criminal pamphlets among these, which Maurice Lever baptized *les canards sanglants*, often narrated what we might describe as the "tragic" turn that events took especially in families and marriages, resulting in stories meant to serve a didactic and exemplary purpose.[2] In keeping with the theme of this volume, I would like to examine the extent to which the increasing sixteenth-century French fascination with supposedly true accounts of murders, incest, rape, and infanticide that these pamphlets make manifest might be understood in relation to the idea of the tragic. Do the different kinds of descriptions of horrific crimes in these pamphlets conform to anything that the readers and listeners of the time could recognize as *une histoire tragique*?

Reading today, and knowing everything that we know ranging from Aristotle's *Poetics*, to Boaistuau's and Belleforest's *Histoires tragiques*, to Shakespeare, Racine, and Nietzsche, it is somewhat difficult to determine how much of an influence tragedy and the category of the tragic might have had on the telling of true stories from the real world in the form of these ephemeral pamphlets. Nevertheless, from examining a significant sample of *les canards sanglants*, it seems as though the idea of the tragic story began to structure the understanding of violent events in the real world at around the same time that Boaistuau used the generic term *histoire tragique* for his translations of Bandello in 1559.[3] Despite the persistence of a more archaic narrative style that I will discuss in a moment, the reality of criminal events began almost immediately to be influenced by an ancient cultural paradigm that initially seems to have been quite foreign to the narration of these kinds of news items. At the risk of restating the obvious, I would like to recall briefly some of the elements of tragic discourse and "the tragic," despite the dangers of disassociating these from actual performances, as John Lyons remarked in his introductory notes for "The Dark Thread" conference.[4]

In Aristotle's well-known description in *The Poetics*, tragedy was performed as part of a collective festival that represented or imitated events and characters within carefully organized plots. It also called upon spectators to participate actively and emotionally in staged events. The tragic functioned, therefore, within a complex assemblage of elements: a conventional and stylized manner of speaking to addressees; a limited scope of subjects and characters; an affective relationship between speaking actors and their listening public, which is a promise that is made but rarely fulfilled in the pamphlets that I will examine here; the anchoring of represented events in a strict moral code; a consistent referentiality to historical and mythological figures who would be immediately recognized by the audience. Most of the major studies concerning French Renaissance tragedy concentrate on the kinds of events that have to be represented in tragedies, and especially on the organization of those events into a plot that is recognizable as tragic.[5] The lengthy negotiations of French dramatists with Aristotle's seminal study hence are more concerned with performance practices than they are with the definition of what might constitute the idea of the tragic divorced from the exigencies of staging tragedies, as Lyons has remarked. In the next few pages I would like to examine the effects that the stylized narrative representation of violence in tragic stories might have had on the brute facts of crime and its punishments, which were initially catalogued in the *canards sanglants* in a more archaic clerical language.

In relation to a possibly conventional conception of what a tragic narrative should be, violence was a part of everyday reality in the sixteenth century. The *canards sanglants* represent a presumably real world in which sexual violence, murder, incest, and even fratricide, parricide, infanticide, and brutal executions could erupt at any moment into the burgeoning public consciousness represented by the printing press and its products. In the realm of this peculiar form of literature, death or the threat of death always seemed to be hovering in the background and could emerge as the inevitable consequence of the transgressions, errors, and moral flaws of its characters. In this light, the word "real" in my title might be understood in two senses: first, there was a reality of violent and murderous acts and events that generated the *canards sanglants* in the sixteenth and early seventeenth centuries, and that one might try to track down by reading other sources such as journals and criminal registers. Second, and without belaboring a potentially tiresome theoretical point, what Jacques Lacan calls "the real" of trauma and violence "is never missing from its place" in the *canards*, as he wrote in his seminar on "The Purloined Letter."[6] To express this point in the terms that one finds in the *canards* themselves, beneath the surface of everyday life at the end of the Renaissance in France, there always lurked a libidinal domain of "la concupiscence [des] désirs et [des] voluptés charnelles" (the lust of desires and carnal pleasures)[7] that included things like greed, anger, and lust, and that often erupted with mortal consequences for both those who acted on their desires and those who happened to be in the way when these drives sought their satisfaction in the symbolic order of religion, morality, a rigid class hierarchy, and patriarchy. Here I would like to focus on the relation between the highly conventional narrative representation of violence in tragic stories and the brute facts of crime and its punishments that we encounter in some of the *canards sanglants*, recounted in a very simple narrative style.

In the multiple titles that are used for the *canards*, it seems as though the people who wrote, retold, and sold these stories to an avid reading and listening public were hard-pressed to define exactly how these kinds of events from the real world were to be named. Surprisingly, the adjective *tragique* was rarely used to name the *canards* of the sixteenth century and even into the seventeenth century. Among the ninety extant pamphlets that are specifically accounts of criminal cases, which were printed between 1574 and 1637 and catalogued by Jean-Pierre Seguin in 1964, there are only nine that use the word *tragique* in their rather long titles. In fact, this key word is not used on a pamphlet's title page until 1597, while the generic designation of *histoire tragique*, which, as we have seen, had already appeared in Boaistuau's translation of Bandello's tales in 1559, is not printed on the title page of a *canard* until 1602 and is used only five times between then and 1625. In this small fraction of what we may assume to have been a mass of printed material that related criminal stories to a popular audience, it seems as though the sometimes extreme violence that characterized daily life between 1574 and 1625 was conceived primarily in terms other than the idea of "the tragic." The most common titles used in this corpus were *discours*, which appears thirty-three times, and *histoire*, used thirty-two times. The remaining twenty-five texts are named not using these generic terms but, rather, according to their contents. For example, the words *cruauté* and *cruel* appear eight times, that is, almost as often as the word *tragique* itself, in titles that begin with such phrases as *Cruel et estrange meurtres et massacres* (Cruel and strange murders and massacres); *Cruauté plus que barbare et inhumaine* (A more than barbarous and inhuman cruelty); *Cruauté d'une jeune demoiselle* (Cruelty of a young girl); *Cruauté horrible et espouvantable perpetree contre Jacques Puget* (A horrible and frightful cruelty perpetrated against Jacques Puget), etc. The adjectives used to modify a *discours* or an *histoire* cover a wide range of ideas, including *sanguinaire, cruelle, émerveillable, épouvantable, effroyable, horrible, vray, véritable, tres-veritable, merveilleux, admirable, lamentable, pitoyable, prodigieuse,* and *mémorable* (bloody, cruel, marvelous, horrifying, frightful, horrible, true, truthful, very truthful, marvelous, admirable, lamentable, pitiful, prodigious, memorable), all of which are used as often or even more than the word *tragique*. Each of these adjectives can be combined in any number of ways, as in the case of the first pamphlet that I will examine here, the *Histoire horrible et espoventable d'un enfant, lequel, apres avoir meurtry & estranglé son pere, en fin le pendit* (A horrible and horrifying story of a child, who, after having murdered and strangled his father, finally hung him), printed in 1574, or in the second pamphlet that I will analyze from the same year, the *Histoire du plus espouvantable et admirable cas qui ait jamais esté ouy au monde, nouvellement advenu au Royaume de Naples* (The story of the most horrifying and admirable case that has ever been heard in the world, which recently happened in the Kingdom of Naples). What seems to have been the case, at least in the naming of these crimes, is that they were viewed as horrifying, frightful, cruel, bloody, lamentable, pitiful, marvelous, prodigious, unbelievable, and even memorable more than they were thought to be tragic. In terms of the genealogy that we are tracing in this volume, the horror, cruelty, and fright elicited by these stories of bloody crimes appear to have been more important than a sense of their tragedy, at least as far as we can judge from their title pages, which we know to have been announced on the street by the ambulant salesmen or *colporteurs* who sold them.[8] Nevertheless, and as we will see in detail in a moment, the notion or even the "literary practice" of the tragic seems gradually to have influenced or perhaps even "infiltrated" the telling of these stories from very early on, even if their writers did not always appear to be explicitly aware of the fact that they were transcribing the elements of this ancient form of discourse.

The first pamphlet, the *Histoire horrible et espovantable d'un enfant*, describes a case of parricide, and was printed in Paris by Jean de Lastre in 1574, though there is no date on the title page other than the one attributed to the crime itself. The first significant details on the title page are related to the geographic and temporal specificity of the event, as well as the description of this case of parricide as "horrible and frightful." As in most of the *canards*, its didactic intentions are made clear in a double prefatory frame, while the telling of the story itself presents important differences with regard to what was already understood at the time as *une histoire tragique*. First, there is an "épistre au lecteur" from the printer and bookseller, who addresses himself directly to his potential readers and expresses his doubts whether he should tell this horrifying story: "J'ay esté en doubte (Lecteur François) si je te devois communiquer ceste Histoire de Suysse, touchant un cas de parricide (I was in doubt [French reader] whether I should communicate [to you] this story from Switzerland concerning a case of parricide)."[9] This hesitation derives from the nature of the crime recounted in the textual merchandise that the bookseller wants to sell to his audience, which he qualifies by using a classical reference: "Ciceron disoit, les loix antiques des douze tables n'avoir fait aucune mention de ce crime si execrable, que les Legislateurs ne se pouvoient persuader, qu'il peust jamais advenir" (Cicero said that the ancient laws of the twelve tables made no mention of this crime that was so execrable that the legislators could not be persuaded that it ever could happen).[10] Because of the horror and fear that it inspires, parricide is impossible from the perspective of the moral code that supported the rigid hierarchy of the patriarchal family. The narrator nonetheless proclaims that when it occurred in the ancient world, the Romans represented the magnitude of this crime by an exemplary and emblematic punishment:

> La punition estoit entre les romains, de mettre le criminel (apres avoir esté fouetté de verges, tant que le sang luy sortist de toutes parts) en un sac de cuir, & couldre & enfermer avecques luy un Serpent, un Singe, un Chien & un Coq, puis jetter le sac à val l'eau. Ce que aucuns ont estimé avoir esté inventé sagement, pour declarer

tel meurtrier de père ou mere, meriter d'estre exterminé de tous les elemens, comme ils l'en privoient de tous par ce moyen. Quant aux quatre bestes, dont ils l'accompaignoient, le discours en seroit trop long pour le present.[11]

(The punishment was among the Romans to place the criminal [who had already been whipped with rods until he was bloodied all over] into a leather bag, and to sew in there with him a snake, a monkey, a dog, and a cock, and then to throw the bag into the water. Some have thought that this was a wise invention, in order to declare that such a murderer of his father or mother deserved to be exterminated by all of the elements, just as they deprived him of everything by this method. As for the four beasts with which they accompanied him, the discourse concerning them would be too long for our present purposes.)

The printer's presentation of the *Histoire horrible et espoventable* of 1574 hence expresses to the reader a moral indignation that is supported by classical references and transcribes an uncertainty that raises a few intriguing questions: What is it that is being accomplished by the translation, transcription, printing, and sale of this anecdote to specifically French readers and listeners? What did it sound like to a French audience to hear this story announced or cried out, as it would have been, in the public sphere? What role did the extreme violence that it represents and retells play in the support of a given social structure? The bookseller's final remark concerning the example of ancient punishment confirms a limited or restricted oral usage of the pamphlet in the public realm: an interpretation of the animals used in the infliction of this punishment would be too lengthy for it to fit within the limited confines of the present text, conceived perhaps as a public enunciation that had to be accomplished within a certain limit of time. Here we recall that the pamphlets collected by L'Estoile were "criés" and "prêchés" on the street corners of Paris. During an age that loved rebuses of all kinds, the printer/author proclaims that, due to its length, the interpretation of this text's visual puzzle would be inappropriate to the elocutionary performance of this didactic story.

Aside from their performative and economic aspects, the earliest extant pamphlets printed in French to focus on crimes were also curiously associated with travel to neighboring countries, this first one to Switzerland, and the second one to the Kingdom of Naples. The printer's hesitation at the opening of the text asks whether the reader, defined by his belonging to the French kingdom, should be apprised of this unthinkable crime that happened in the neighboring country. As L'Estoile's *Registres-journaux* make clear, there was a complex usage of printed materials, manuscripts, and enunciated discourses in the public sphere during the wars of religion that was intended both to reinforce and to undermine different factions in a fractured political hierarchy. An important element of this usage was the enunciation of orthodox religious doctrines that either supported or sought to destabilize organizations of power within the kingdom, and that situated readers in their proper places within differently conceived social orders. In this sense the story provides a didactic example that promotes a certain idea of Frenchness, which is framed in such a way that this concept interacts with the ideas of travel, cultural otherness, the production of public discourse, moral codes of conduct, and the conception of criminality itself. Its sale and public enunciation disseminated these ideas, which I would argue contributed to the maintenance of the social order.

While it clearly shares some elements of the *histoire tragique*, the second *canard* that is my subject here, the *Histoire du plus espouventable et admirable cas qui ait jamais esté ouy au monde*, printed in Paris by Jean Ruelle in 1574, similarly begins with an address by a named author who speaks in the text to his friend, a bookseller from Lyon, to whom he offers the story that he heard or learned of during his travels to the Piedmont region of Italy. The public and collective mode of address that characterized ancient tragedy were hence replaced in the *canards* by the material realities of publishing and readership that were radically transformed by the increasing availability of printed matter, which in turn had a decisive impact on the conception of authorship. The pamphlet's convoluted description of the Trans Alpine provenance of the story is expressed in a lengthy liminal text that was characteristic of French Renaissance pamphlets in general, and of many of the bloody stories that began to appear shortly after the first *histoires tragiques* were translated into French and published:

> Guillaume de la Taissonniere, Gentil-homme Dombois, à Benoist Rigaut, marchand Libraire de Lyon. Partant dernierement de Lyon pour suivre Monsieur de Perès, Ambassadeur pour Monseigneur le Duc de Savoye en France, en son voyage de Piedmont, & ailleurs où l'honneur de ses commandemens me tireroit: je vous promis librement, comme vostre bon amy de long temps, vous donner advis de tout ce que je trouverois par deçà digne d'estre communiqué à noz François: pourveu que ce ne fust au prejudice d'aucun Prince.

Suivant laquelle promesse, estant venue en ceste court la certaine nouvelle d'une des plus piteuse & lamentable histoire [sic] du monde, fraischement advenue au Royaume de Naples, j'ay bien voulu desrober un quart d'heure à mon exercice courtizan pour la vous tourner en François, afin que vous en faites [sic] part aux curieux de nostre France, à laquelle je suis tant affectionné, pour l'honneur & bien que j'y ay receu & espere y recevoir, que je n'oublieray jamais telle obligation & redevance. Sur ce faisant fin je vous diray à Dieu. De Turin ce 26 de Febvrier, 1574. Vostre affectionné amy à jamais, G. DE LA TESSONNIERE.[12]

(Guillaume de la Taissonniere, a gentleman from the Dombes, to Benoist Rigaut, bookseller in Lyon. Lately having left Lyon in order to follow Monsieur de Perès, Ambassador of My Lord the Duke of Savoy in France, on his voyage to Piedmont, and wherever else the honor of his orders might lead me, I promised you freely, being your good friend for a long time, to let you know everything that I would see down there that would be worthy of being communicated to our Frenchmen, as long as it were not prejudicial to any Prince. Following that promise, having reached this court the certain news of one of the most pitiful and lamentable stories of the world, which newly occurred in the Kingdom of Naples, I wanted to steal away a quarter of an hour from my exercises as a courtier in order to translate it into French for you, so that you may allow the curious men of our France, to whom I am so affectionately attached, know about it, for the honor and goods that I have received and hope to receive from them, which is an obligation and debt that I will never forget. On this note I bid you God speed, from Turin this 26th of February 1574. Your affectionate friend forever, G. DE LA TESSONNIERE.)

The *translatio* of this kind of anecdote across the Italian peninsula and from Italy to France evokes the persistent cultural movement of ideas and stories across the Alps that fueled the French Renaissance. By the time this *canard* was printed, several generations of French noblemen had already been traveling to Italy for various reasons, as la Tessonière does here. The text also implies that there was an oral transmission of the anecdote that will be recounted here from the Kingdom of Naples in the south to the Piedmont in the north. Moreover, a certain kind of attention paid to stories that were told at court seems to be part of the author's "courtly exercise or performance," despite his claim that he "stole" fifteen minutes away from his duties in order to translate the story into French from an unnamed source.

The pamphlet describes this information as "a certain or true piece of news," using the generic term *nouvelle* in one of its senses as a news item, or *fait divers*. The real of the tragic story in sixteenth-century France in a much more material sense has to include the concrete realities of this form of transmission, inscribed within a mode of address that was familiar to readers of prefaces of this kind, in which the author offers this "pitiful and lamentable story" of multiple murders in a Neapolitan family to the bookseller as an act of friendship. One of the most intriguing elements in this introduction, then, which seems to be a letter to the bookseller that is merely reprinted here, is the idea that the delivery and dissemination of bloody anecdotes is part of the courtly duty that lesser noblemen traveling in the company of more important figures such as the ambassador would have had to fulfill or perform in order to be recognized as worthy courtiers. This familiar idea appears in a number of Renaissance sources, and especially in the novella tradition stretching directly from Boccaccio to Marguerite de Navarre, as well as in the introductory remarks of Castiglione in *Il Cortegiano*.[13] Why would specifically this kind of story have been "worthy of being communicated to our fellow Frenchmen," as the author proclaims to his friend the bookseller? He claims that there is something in this story related to a conception of the French as *curieux*, that is, as literal collectors of certain kinds of stories, and especially, in the case of diarists such as Pierre de L'Estoile, who calls himself a *curieux* on one of his title pages, as people who would stuff their libraries with pamphlets, *canards*, books, coins, political placards, *mémoires*, and all kinds of ephemeral texts, some of them on broadsheets, and many of them handwritten.[14] The collection and transmission of these stories participates, I would argue, in the preservation of a given status quo, which relied upon the usage and the threat of both symbolic and real violence for its continued existence.

The *Histoire horrible et espoventable* of 1574 tells its story in a very factual way after its didactic framing devices. There is an identical introductory paragraph in both of these pamphlets that speaks of the punishments meted out by God for those who have "stumbled into the trap of sin" after refusing to listen to the divine voice calling for their repentance. Given the vigorous condemnations presented in both of this first pamphlet's frames, it is surprising that the description of the crime itself is rather simple, especially after the emotional appeal of the writer to his readers and listeners that ends the second frame:

> Comme beste, ou animal non raisonnable, [le pécheur] despouillé de sa naturelle liberté, va errant parmy les bois environnez de poignantes espines, & finablement trebusche dans le piege, & se prend aux laqz de peché, d'où procede l'execution de la sentence tresjuste du tresredouté Roy des estoilles: comme veritablement il est advenu à ceux que je nommeray cy apres au pitoyable discours que vous entendrez.[15]

(Like a beast or irrational animal, [the sinner], stripped of his natural liberty, goes wandering into the woods surrounded by sharp thorns, and finally trips into the trap and falls into the pit of sin, from which results the execution of the very just sentence of our most feared Lord of the stars: as it truly happened to those whom I will name in the following pages, in the pitiful discourse that you will hear.)

After a conventional metaphorical description of the sinner's descent into a life of sin, the narrator proclaims that the punishment suffered by the criminal who is the protagonist of this work represents a form of divine justice. Nevertheless, it is clear from the end of the text that the brutal punishment imposed on the transgressor was carried out according to very human visual codes meant to indicate a maximum intensity of suffering on the part of the transgressor. What is most striking in the liminal text, however, is the apostrophe to the text's potential listeners, who are promised a *"pitoyable discours"* that they will "hear" or "listen to" in the following story, highlighting the oral usage of the pamphlet. According to Le Trésor de la langue française, the adjective *pitoyable* signifies "qui inspire de la pitié" (that which inspires pity) in French at least since the fourteenth century. As I have already noted in reference to the recurrent words used in the titles of these pamphlets, these kinds of discourses were meant to inspire fear, horror, and pity in their listeners, and this promise of strong emotions appears to have been one of their major selling points as commodities in the archaic public sphere, which is another partial answer to the questions I raised above. "Buy this pamphlet, oh listener and reader," it seems to say, "and your emotion will be a sign that you occupy your rightful place in a kingdom stratified from the lord of the stars down to the humblest peasant." Aristotle's notion that tragedy is supposed to establish this kind of affective link between the spectacle and its audience is echoed here, but in this example, any further notion that the pamphlet will tell its story in a tragic mode ends at this point.

In other words, in the telling of the story itself, this promise of an affective engagement of the listener in the story goes unfulfilled, and the straightforward narration of the crime contains no emotional evaluation of it whatsoever from this point onward. It is almost as if an account had been transcribed here from a criminal register, with its dry and almost clerical style, as in the much earlier *Registre criminel du Châtelet de Paris* of 1389, or in Pierre de L'Estoile's notes about crimes and executions that he had witnessed.[16] The text begins its account of the crime as follows:

> Au païs des Suysses, & en la ville de Lutzelflu, y avoit un homme fort aagé, lequel depuis l'aage de trente ans avoit esté toujours du Conseil d'icelle ville: Lequel ayant amassé sept cens florins, monnoye du païs, tant pour subvenir à sa debilité & foiblesse, que pour l'entretenement de sa femme & de ses enfans, iceux florins luy furent derobez, & apres fut trouvé pendu & estranglé. Or estimoit-on que par desespoir de l'argent perdu luy mesme se fust ainsi pendu.[17]

> (In the country of the Swiss, and in the town of Lutzelflu, there was an elderly man, who had been a member of the council of this town since the age of thirty: and who, having amassed seven hundred florins, the currency of this country, as much to help himself in his fragility and weakness, as to provide for his wife and children, had this money stolen from him, and afterward he was found hanged and strangled. Yet, it was judged that out of despair from the lost money he had hanged himself.)

This passage and the rest of the pamphlet contain a documentary language that belies the description of this case as a "discours pitoyable." This *canard* is unusual in that it illustrates every step of the crime and its punishment with very simple woodcuts, in a kind of multimedia style that prefigures the forensic television programs of today, which allow viewers to witness every step of horrific crimes and their punishments. The *Histoire horrible et espoventable* seems to share this desire to depict the crime visually and to allow its listeners/readers to serve as witnesses. The first three images represent the events recounted in the son's confession, in which he describes how he murdered his father by strangling, beating, and hanging him. As I have mentioned, the calm and matter-of-fact tone of this quoted discourse recalls the language of criminal registers and lacks entirely the emotional entreaty and the rhetorical figures of the second pamphlet that I will examine in a moment. The son's confession in the first pamphlet reads in part as follows:

Quand mon pere eut apperceu que je luy avois desrobé son argent, il se courrouça à l'encontre de moy, m'en demandant restitution: & un jour il s'en vint vers moy en l'estable où j'estois, me demandant icelle somme. Je luy respons que s'il vouloit venir avec moy, je luy monstrerois le lieu où estoit son argent: ce qu'il m'accorda. Ce pendant je preparay un licol, & lo menay sur une petite montee, comme si je luy eusse voulu monstrer son argent. Lors se voyant mocqué, & cuidant descendre de ladite montee, je luy jettay le licol au col, le renversant par terre, & le trainant au bas de ladite montee, dans une fosse: puis m'esloignay un peu, & appercevant qu'il desgainoit un cousteau qu'il portoit à sa ceinture, à fin de couper le licol, j'accouru à luy, & le luy ostant de la main, je le navray de telle façon, que par ce moyen le licol se trouva sanglant.[18]

(When my father saw that I had stolen his money, he was furious with me, and demanded restitution: and one day he came to me in the stable where I was, demanding the said sum of money. I responded that if he wanted to come with me, I would show him the place where the money was, to which he agreed. At this time I prepared a noose, and I led him up onto a little hill, as if I wanted to show him where his money was. Then when he thought that I was mocking him, and wanted to go down from the said little hill, I threw the noose around his neck, knocking him down, and dragging him to a pit at the bottom of the said hill; and then I stepped back a little, and seeing that he was trying to unsheathe a knife that he carried on his belt, so that he could cut the noose, I ran toward him, and taking the knife from his hand, I beat him in such a way that the noose became bloody.)

This is the language of the clerks who kept records at courts in criminal registers, which is a fact that is given away by the usage of two apparently insignificant linguistic tics that are still characteristic of the archaic legal language in English today. These have to do with the kind of self-referentiality and looping back upon itself of juridical discourse: the expressions "me demandant *icelle* somme," and "cuidant descendre de *ladite* montee" recall the constant and somewhat redundant terms "the aforesaid sum" and "the said hill" that pepper contracts to this day. Far from being a spontaneous and natural confession on the part of the criminal, this is a text that was transcribed by a scribe trained in the conventions of legal language, which bore none of the markers of the tragic discourse that we as readers were promised in the work's preface. The story told in this first criminal *canard* seems not to have been expressed in tragic terms at all, despite the promise that it makes to inspire pity in its audience. On the contrary, this story presents an archaic, almost medieval account of the brutal consequences of transgressing the order of property and rank within the family that structured early modern society. Since this text with its images may have served as the material basis for a kind of performance on the streets where the pamphlet was "advertised," sold, and "cried out," the "real" or the "reality" of this type of narrative has to include the material realities of buying, selling, and performing these works in public. The question as to what the "reality" of these stories may have been is hence shaped and perhaps deformed by the narrative conventions of enunciating this kind of discourse in front of an audience that was manipulated by this kind of performance and that would ultimately have its understanding of its lived reality transformed by the infiltration of "tragic" elements into collective media and methods of storytelling.

In contrast, the narrative style of the second pamphlet bears all of the hallmarks of tragic discourse, despite the fact that it uses an identical didactic introduction to prepare its readers for the events to come. In order to go to a banquet, a woman by the name of Flaminie leaves her eighteen-month-old son, Scipion, in the care of another son by the name of Giovan-Maria, who is seven years old. An accident ensues when the seven-year-old is rocking his brother's cradle and it tips over, suffocating the baby. The scene of the mother's return to this horrid scene is recounted in a discourse that we would clearly understand as "tragic":

> La mere retournee du malheureux banquet, trouve que Giovan-maria plouroit enfantinement la mort de son petit frere, & desirant sçavoir la cause de ses pleurs, comme font les meres, elle veoit son petit Scipion mort souz le berceau: parquoy ceste miserable mere voyant son fils bien aymé passé à l'autre vie, elle se donnant en proye au pleur & au desespoir, & se despouillant de toute maternelle pieté, apres plusieurs impertinentes parolles qu'elle prononçoit contre ledit Giovan-maria, comme mechant, traitre, detestable : « Comment peut permettre Dieu que j'aye tant de patience avecques toy que je ne t'arrache avec les maternelles mains le meschant cœur, origine & seulle occasion de la mort de ton frere! Je veux tout maintenant mettre fin à tels malheureux jours. » Sur cela ayant mis à part l'amitié maternelle, & destinee à se venger de son cher fils innocent, elle le print par les pieds & l'eslevant en l'air le tua, escarbouillant sa teste contre la muraille, de

manière que du sang de son second fils elle tacha & couloura la muraille de la chambre maritale : chose certainement digne de toute pitié, & d'estre insculpee en marbre pour exemple à la posterité.[19]

(The mother upon her return from the unhappy banquet finds Giovan-maria crying childishly at the death of his little brother, and wanting to know the cause of his tears, as mothers do, she sees her little Scipion dead beneath the cradle: for which reason this miserable mother, seeing her beloved son passed on to the other life, and giving herself over to tears and despair, and stripping herself of all maternal piety, she pronounced many impertinent words against the said Giovan-maria, such as, "Wicked, detestable traitor, how can God permit me to have so much patience with you that I do not rip out with my maternal hands your wicked heart, the origin and sole occasion of the death of your brother; I now want to put an end to your unhappy days." Thereupon, having set aside maternal friendship, and destined to avenge her dear, innocent son, she took him [Giovan-maria] by the feet, and lifting him up in the air she killed him, smashing his head against the wall such that she stained and colored the walls of her marital chamber with the blood of her second son, which is a thing that is certainly worthy of all pity, and of being inscribed in marble as an example for posterity.)

Unlike the other *canard* from 1574, the author/writer of this *Histoire du plus espouvantable et admirable cas* seems acutely aware of the tragic attributes of his self-conscious and perhaps clumsy literary language. The first of these are the names of the characters with their classical overtones, especially the unfortunate baby with his august Roman name, and the murderous mother whose moniker recalls the via Flaminia of ancient Rome. The second is a familiar poetic inversion of the normal order of adjectives and nouns in the passage, a catalogue of which highlights the semantic domain into which a terrible accident causes a murderous rage to erupt. From the *malheureux banquet*, to the *miserable mere*, to her lack of *maternelle pieté*, and the violence of her *maternelles mains* that put an end to Giovan-Maria's *malheureux jours* by ripping out his *méchant coeur*, there is an uncanny insistence on alliterations of the letter *m*. This phonetic repetition calls attention to the intersection in this scene of the maternal, the marital, and the murderous, but strangely when this link is explicitly stated in the text, the order of the adjectives returns to that of conventional speech: Flaminie forgets the *amitié maternelle* that she owes to her son and bashes out his brains against *la muraille de la chambre maritale*. Reading in a Tom Conleyesque manner, we realize that all of these *m*'s point not only to the marble in which this scene should be engraved, as well as to the stone walls of the marital chamber that serve as a murder weapon, but also to the horror of *la mort* that invades this noble house.[20] There is something stony and sculptural about the transcription of this scene, a motif that is continued in the intensification of violence and the multiplication of dead bodies that bring the story to a paroxystic climax in the manner of the best tragedies.

The phonetic repetitions in this passage prepare the terrain for a reference to one of the most famous figures in classical tragedy, that of the mother who kills her own children in *Medea*, which was continuously adapted and translated into modern languages beginning in the fifteenth century and continuing on into the eigthteenth century. After Flaminie's stylized and conventional lamentation over the misery of her life, her husband, Anselme, arrives home and launches into an almost Racinian apostrophe to his wife:

Flaminie, quel espouventable office & quelle severe demonstration se presente à mes yeux? quel exemple de pitié m'a ce jourd'huy preparé mon sort infortuné? pourquoy t'avoy-je laissee en la maison meschante ennemie de mon sang? indigne de comparoir devant les vivants? qui me tient que je ne t'arrache ce coeur ingrat? ô jour le plus infortuné de tous les autres & digne de perpetuele memoir? aujourdhui (femme trescruele) tu t'acquiers le nom de l'ingrate & perfide Medee![21]

(Flaminie, what horrifying rite and what severe demonstration do my eyes see? What example of pity has my ill-fortuned destiny prepared for me this day? Why did I leave you at home, wicked enemy of my blood, unworthy of appearing before the living? Who will keep me from ripping out your ungrateful heart? Oh most unfortunate day of all, worthy of perpetual memory! Today, oh cruel woman, you take on the name of the ungrateful and perfidious Medea!)

While it is here in the midst of the story that Flaminie acquires the name of Medea, it was already clear from her preceding actions, her outcries, and her lamentations that hers was a reincarnation of this ancient story, which makes us wonder about the verisimilitude of this particular anecdote, since it follows a bit too closely the rules and dictates of tragedy in order to be viewed as a true or real story. Another astounding detail a bit further on in the pamphlet reconfirms the idea of a sculptural or statuary quality to the narration of this story: "Et ainsi esloigné de toute pitié & de l'amour conjugal, il s'approcha de sa femme infortunee, avecques le poignart en la main, adjoustant, O digne de mille morts voicy la fin de ta vie. La dame cognoissant son mary avoir le cœur enflammé & allumé de courroux, s'oppose à luy, & luy empoigne la barbe à belles deux mains."[22] (And thus removed from all pity and conjugal love, he approached his unfortunate wife with a knife in his hand, crying out, "Oh worthy of a thousand deaths, here is the end of your life!" The lady, seeing her husband's heart enflamed and burning in anger, opposed him, and grasped his beard with two full hands.) Here Flaminie assumes the position of a supplicant grabbing the beard of her husband, which is a posture that seems to be depicted in at least one of the many engraved illustrations of Ovid's Medea story from the sixteenth century.[23] The entirety of the series of events recounted in the *Histoire du plus espouvantable et admirable cas* was influenced and perhaps even generated by the knowledge that the writer seems to have had of this ancient story and its various manifestations in the Renaissance, both in print and in graphic illustrations of Ovid's *Metamorphoses*.

In conclusion, the real of this type of story has to be understood in what might be called its "dimensional complexity." The *canards sanglants* are anchored in a dense reality and material volume composed of disparate elements that work together to form the complex conceptual paradigm from which these stories derived their meaning. As we have seen, the history of French noblemen traveling to Italy and Switzerland engendered a tradition of narrative transmission that eventually appeared in printed pamphlets throughout the sixteenth century. As the liminal text of the first *canard* makes clear, this tradition included the writing of letters intended for publication, which was common throughout the century, as well as the oral cultural practices and habits of the French and Italian courts, which required the collection, retelling, and circulation of diverse kinds of stories. This dissemination of oral accounts was intricately interwoven with the customs of patronage and aristocratic service, and participated as well in the formation of friendships among men who were called upon to "perform" narratively both at court and later in print. Finally, the everyday realities of printing, posting, selling, and performing pamphlets on the streets, combined with the necessity of translation for the sake of transmitting ideas from France's cultural interlocutors, make of this type of narrative a complex social, economic, and political phenomenon. The real of the tragic story is hence found not only in the violent contents of stories that apparently had to be told and retold repeatedly and that eventually made their way into print.

The facts of violence, death, and blood that fascinated sixteenth-century readers also were among the foundations of a narrative economy that was a concrete manifestation and performance of a hierarchical ideology and social structure, which these stories both supported and disseminated. The pamphlets that told criminal stories were embedded in these historically specific conditions and played a small yet significant role in the real manifestations of a dominant ideology that was in crisis throughout this period. The *canards sanglants* were a small but significant element of this distant and multifaceted reality, which they help us to understand and to describe.

Another significant aspect of these pamphlets that is at the heart of our project in this volume concerns the questions with which I began, which sought to understand the *canards sanglants* in terms of three senses of the word "tragic." The first of these is the conventional notion of what constitutes a "tragedy" in our sense of the word, such as the account of multiple accidental deaths and murders in a single family. The story of a woman who killed her son and was stabbed by her husband was horrifying, dreadful, frightful, and terrifying for sixteenth-century readers and listeners, but they probably would not have recognized it as "tragic" as we would. The second sense might be derived from the *histoires tragiques* that began to be in vogue in French letters shortly after the publication of Boaistuau's collection of 1559. The idea of the tragic at this time was colored by an archaic practice of disseminating horrific or appalling narratives in print, which reveal that the readers and spectators of the period had an appetite for stories of gruesome brutality that was quite distinct from the potential desire for tragedies as spectacles. The third notion would be a properly Aristotelian concept of the structure and effects of tragic performances on given audiences. The purgation and purification that the philosopher described as the effects of staging tragedies were perhaps echoed in the largely unfulfilled promise made in some of the *canards* that their readers and listeners would be moved and morally instructed by the horrors revealed to them in the pamphlet that they were about to purchase. The brutal stories told in the *canards sanglants* were hence hybrid products or even commodities that borrowed their elements from a number of different textual and discursive categories: criminal registers, legal documents, didactic encomia, exempla, letters, apostrophes to friends, travel accounts, reports of distant marvels and horrors, sales pitches from printers and booksellers, evocations of classical *topoi*.

Within this kind of "heteroglossia," our own or Aristotle's ideas of tragedy, both of which are potentially anachronistic, never seem to be far from the stories that the *canards* tell. Nevertheless, neither of the two examples that I examined ever adopted a truly tragic form, while their mode of expression at times demonstrated the influence of the ideas of the tragic that were circulating among a learned reading and writing public at the time of their printing. The "real" of the tragic tale, understood both in the Lacanian sense as a violent foundation for narrative production and as the material facts of printing, publishing, and storytelling during this period, might be delineated on the basis of the extant documents catalogued by Maurice Lever and Jean-Pierre Seguin. Within their hybridity, the *canards* perhaps elaborated upon or even unintentionally parodied some of the fundamental ideas and techniques of classical tragedy, at the same time that they maintained the distinctiveness of the multiple clerical, professional, mercantile, and literary languages in which they were expressed. As such, they provide us with a glimpse of a fascinating transitional period in the history of French letters, during which one of the dominant literary concepts of the following century began to emerge from a dense linguistic and enunciative multiplicity.

## Notes

1. Jean-Pierre Seguin, *L'Information en France avant le périodique: 517 canards imprimés entre 1529 et 1631* (Paris: Maisonneuve et Larose, 1964).

2. Maurice Lever, *Canards sanglants: Naissance du fait divers* (Paris: Fayard, 1993).

3. Pierre Boaistuau, *Histoires tragiques extraictes des oeuvres Italiennes de Bandel, & mises en nostre langue Françoise, par Pierre Boaistuau surnommé Launay* (Paris: V. Sertenas, 1559).

4. "During the seventeenth century the boundaries between these popular narratives and theatrical tragedy were quite permeable (both Shakespeare—e.g. *Romeo and Juliet*—and John Webster staged stories from Bandello), and Andreas Gryphius based a German *Trauerspiel* on a story in one of the French collections. Gradually, however, the institutions of high culture separated the respectable genre of 'tragedy' from its less favored kin. And, perhaps not surprisingly, tragedy itself, cut off from its sensational and experiential roots, fell out of favor, becoming the object of Romantic philosophical reflection that extracted from tragedy a new conceptual essence, 'the tragic'" (John D. Lyons, unpublished preliminary note for the conference "The Dark Thread," University of Virginia, March 25–26, 2016). On the complexities of defining tragedy and the tragic in early modern France, see John D. Lyons, *Kingdom of Disorder: The Theory of Tragedy in Classical France* (West Lafayette: Purdue University Press, 1999).

5. See, for example, Donald Stone Jr., *French Humanist Tragedy: A Reassessment* (Manchester: Manchester University Press, 1974); Gillian Jondorf, *French Renaissance Tragedy: The Dramatic Word* (Cambridge: Cambridge University Press, 1990); and

Elliott Forsyth, *La tragédie française de Jodelle à Corneille (1553–1640): Le thème de la vengeance* (1962; Paris: Honoré Champion Éditeurs, 1994).

6. "Pour le réel, quelque bouleversement qu'on puisse y apporter, il y est toujours et en tout cas, à sa place, il l'emporte collée à sa semelle, sans rien connaître qui puisse l'en exiler" (Whatever upheaval one might bring to the real, it is at any rate always in its place, and carries its place glued to the sole of its shoe, without knowing anything that might exile it from there [my translation]) (Jacques Lacan, "Le séminaire sur 'La lettre volée,' in *Écrits* [Paris: Éditions du Seuil, 1999], 25).

7. Lever, *Canards sanglants*, 69.

8. According to Pierre de L'Estoile, the "belles figures" of the Ligue propaganda pamphlets that he collected were "imprimées, criées, preschées et vendues publiquement à Paris par tous les endroits et carrefours de la ville" (printed, "cried out" or advertised, enunciated, and sold publicly in Paris in all of the spaces and intersections of the city), which gives us an idea of the wide dissemination of pamphlet literature at the time. See the recent edition of *Les belles figures et drolleries de la Ligue*, ed. Gilbert Schrenck (Geneva: Droz, 2016), 4–5, where L'Estoile's long title for his collection contains the passage quoted above.

9. *Histoire horrible et espovantable, d'un enfant, lequel apres avoir meurtry et estranglé son père, en fin le pendit: Et ce advenu en la ville de Lutzelflu, païs des Suysses, en la Seigneurie de Brandis, pres la ville de Berne, le iii jour du mois d'Avril*. 1574 (Paris: Jean de Lastre, s.d.), Ai verso (55). This pamphlet is reprinted in Lever, *Canards sanglants*, 55–59. All page references will be to the original pamphlet, using its system of numbering, and with page references to Lever's edition in parentheses following the original page number. All translations are mine.

10. Ibid., Ai verso (55).

11. Ibid., Ai verso (55–56).

12. *Histoire du plus espouventable et admirable cas qui ait jamais esté ouy au monde, nouvellement advenu au Royaume de Naples, par laquelle se void l'ire de Dieu n'estre encore appaisee, & nous tous humains subjets à son juste jugement* (Paris: Jean Ruelle, 1574), no pagination. The text is reprinted in Lever, *Canards sanglants*, 49–53. This quote is on pages 49–50 of Lever's text, to which I will refer for the sake of convenience.

13. In Castiglione's version of this *topos*, noteworthy, eminent, or qualified men were called upon to contribute to the "discussions" that went on at the court of Duke Guidobaldo of Urbino: "In these books we shall not follow any strict order or list a series of precepts, as is the normal practice in teaching. Instead, following many writers of the ancient world, and reviving a pleasant memory, we shall recount some discussions which once took place among men who were singularly qualified in these matters" (*The Book of the Courtier*, trans. George Bull [London: Penguin, 1967], 40).

14. On one of his manuscripts, Ms F. Fr. 6678 in the BnF, L'Estoile entitles his collection as follows: "Registre-journal d'un curieux de plusieurs choses memorables advenues et publiées librement à la françoise pendant et durant le regne de HENRI IIIè Roy de France [. . .]." See the remarkable catalogue of L'Estoile's collection in

Florence Greffe and José Lothe, *La vie, les livres et les lectures de Pierre de L'Estoile: Nouvelles recherches* (Paris: Honoré Champion, 2004).

15. *Histoire horrible et espoventable d'un enfant,* Aii recto-verso (56).

16. See the remarkable *Registre criminel du Châtelet de Paris du 6 Septembre 1389 au 18 Mai 1392,* 2 vols. (Paris: Société des Bibliophiles François, 1861). L'Estoile's account of the execution of Jean Dadon comes to mind here. See his *Registre-journal du règne de Henri III,* ed. Madeleine Lazard and Gilbert Schrenck, 6 vols. (Geneva: Droz, 1992–2004), 5:174–75.

17. *Histoire horrible et espoventable d'aun enfant,* Aii verso–Aiii recto (56–57).

18. Ibid., Aiii recto–B recto (57–58).

19. Lever, *Canards sanglants,* 51.

20. See Tom Conley, *The Graphic Unconscious in Early-Modern French Writing* (Cambridge: Cambridge University Press, 1992).

21. Lever, *Canards sanglants,* 52.

22. Ibid.

23. See, for example, one such illustration in Anonymous, *La vita et Metamorfoseo d'Ovidio* (Lyon: Giovanni di Tornes, 1559), 99, available on Gallica.

TIMOTHY CHESTERS AND JOHN D. LYONS

# Doubtful Readings in Rosset, Nodier, and Potocki

In 1890 Guy de Maupassant published what was to be the last collection of short stories to appear in his lifetime under the title *L'inutile beauté*. The eleventh and concluding tale, entitled simply "Qui sait?" (Who knows?), sums up the paranoid atmosphere of the volume as a whole, and indeed of its author's final years (Maupassant would die three years later, following a suicide attempt, in Esprit Blanche's sanatorium at Passy). "Qui sait?" begins as its solitary and world-weary Parisian narrator describes how he returned home late from the Opera one night to find his furniture walking out of his house. He watches in horror as his armchairs and piano prance and skip into the street outside, followed by "les canapés bas se traînant comme des crocodiles sur leurs courtes pattes, puis toutes mes chaises, avec des bonds de chèvres, et les petits tabourets qui trottaient comme des lapins" (the low canapés slithering like crocodiles on their short feet, then all my chairs, bounding like goats, and the little stools, scampering like rabbits).[1] He wrestles briefly with his writing desk, "un rare bibelot du dernier siècle" (a rare curio from the last century), full of prized letters and photographs, before that, too, breaks free. In an attempt to collect himself following this mysterious "theft," the narrator travels south to the Mediterranean and Africa. Then, two years later, while visiting Rouen he suddenly comes upon his missing possessions in a backstreet antique shop. He buys back a Louis XIII wardrobe and a Henri II table from the shop owner, a disquieting figure with a luminous bald head, before alerting the police, who promise to arrest him. But when they turn up at the premises the following day, the antique dealer has vanished, along with the furniture. The narrator receives a message from his servant back in Paris informing him that the "stolen" items had reappeared in his home that very morning, all in their proper place.

"Qui sait?" represents perhaps the acme of the nineteenth-century fantastic in France—if not the best-known, among the cleanest and possibly the very last major example of the genre. By "fantastic" here we have of course in mind Tzvetan Todorov's celebrated definition as "that hesitation experienced by a person who knows only the laws of nature, confronting an apparently supernatural event."[2] This vacillation between alternative categories is a central criterion for Todorov. The presence of supernatural elements alone is insufficient; only if these are accompanied by some uncertainty as to whether they are supernatural at all does a story qualify as fantastic. Sometimes this uncertainty is felt by the characters themselves, sometimes the readers, sometimes both. In "Qui sait?" the dimension of uncertainty is established in the framing device Maupassant lends the main account. We learn at the opening of the tale that the narrator is in fact telling his story from a sanatorium (maison de santé) and that, aside from us the readers, the only other party to whom he has related these events is the doctor who is treating him. Though he himself is convinced as to their veracity, doubt thus intrudes from the very first page: "Si je n'étais sûr de ce que j'ai vu, sûr qu'il n'y a eu dans mes raisonnements aucune défaillance, aucune erreur dans mes constatations, pas de lacune dans la suite inflexible de mes observations, je me croirais un simple halluciné, le jouet d'une étrange vision. Après tout, qui sait?" (If I were not sure of what I had seen, sure that there had not been any failure in my reasoning, any error in my perceptions, any gap in the rigorous sequence of my observations, I would believe myself to be hallucinating, the plaything of a strange vision. After all, who knows?")[3]

Here we find juxtaposed in its purest form the hesitation Todorov describes. The reader has to choose, but of course finally cannot, between two competing explanations for the events described—the demonic agency of the Rouen antiques dealer on the one hand, the paranoid delusions of the storyteller on the other. This is in fact only the first of many occasions on which the narrator has recourse to the title question, which quickly becomes a kind of refrain. "Qui sait?" might indeed be regarded as the signature of a genre that—even as it asserts supreme narratorial certainty—integrates the possibility of its own skeptical critique.

Todorov and those who have adopted his definition consider *la littérature fantastique* a resolutely modern (in the case of France, postrevolutionary) phenomenon. Todorov himself writes of the genre as "nothing but the bad conscience" of the positivist nineteenth century—a kind of atavistic Other lurking beneath the scientific consensus of bourgeois-industrial rationalism.[4] (E. J. Clery has argued something similar in the case of the English Gothic.)[5] Todorov also notes the marked intimacy between tales such as "Qui sait?" and realist fiction, which for the length of the nineteenth century embraced the fantastic like its own obscene shadow. Many practitioners of the fantastic were of course also leading lights of realist prose: Balzac, Zola, and especially Maupassant (Todorov might also have mentioned Flaubert's juvenilia or, for that matter, the blind beggar who haunts *Madame Bovary*).[6] The mysteriously animate furniture of Maupassant's story could be said to embody precisely this paradoxical dimension. As the armchairs, tables, and spoons escape their domestic prison, they enact a peculiarly apt revenge on bourgeois acquisitiveness. They also take to an absurd conclusion realism's ideal of descriptive vitality: here the bric-a-brac and "bibelots" of the realist interior no longer merely reflect its inhabitants (as they do, famously, in Balzac's Maison Vauquer); they have actually *become* its inhabitants.[7]

In what follows we would like to begin loosening this supposedly inevitable connection between the fantastic and its nineteenth-century context. More specifically we want to suggest how doubt was also a prominent feature of a much earlier body of texts—namely the French demonologies and *histoires tragiques* of the late sixteenth and early seventeenth centuries. This claim might once have appeared surprising to somebody unfamiliar with this corpus; from popular histories of the witchcraft persecution, one might suppose early modern demonologists to have been possessed of a kind of crazed certainty, with hesitation belonging wholly on the side of "modern," rationalist heroes, notably Montaigne. The work of Terence Cave and Stuart Clark in particular has now made such assumptions untenable, finding that doubt, especially over the evidence of the senses, to be not an opposing but integral element of "thinking with demons," up to and including in Descartes's *Meditations*.[8] We do not want to repeat these arguments here, especially as regards the close relations between demonology and Pyrrhonist skepticism. We limit ourselves to a few remarks on doubt—why it arises, how it functions, in late-century French demonology—and then examine some pertinent aspects of a *histoire tragique*.

The chief intellectual task of European demonology was not to prosecute witches but to establish clear dividing lines between natural, demonic, and divine agencies acting in the sublunary world. Distinguishing between the latter two categories was theologically straightforward, for both Catholics and

Protestants. With one or two notable exceptions (Jean Bodin being one), most demonologists accepted the orthodox distinction between demonic and divine interventions in human affairs.[9] Demons, being part of created nature, could manipulate only natural properties—of plants, animals, minerals. This they were able to do with remarkable subtlety, but there their power ended; in contrast, resurrecting the dead or transforming men into beasts, for example, lay strictly beyond Satan's influence. Here we encounter the well-known distinction between divinely wrought *miracula*, conducted above the course of nature (*supra naturam*) and demonic *mirabilia*, which operated preternaturally (*praeter naturam*). Meanwhile the business of discerning demonic events from natural ones was much more vexed. Precisely because demonic agency was simply an exaggerated, or supersubtle form of natural causality—nature speeded up—the distinction between these two categories was strictly one of degree rather than kind. As demonologists realized only too keenly, this created great scope for uncertainty over where any particular instance of aberrant phenomena fell.

Some drew the dividing lines between divine, demonic, and natural phenomena with great confidence; and it is against this epistemological optimism that demonology deploys its efforts again and again in the early modern period. Two certainties in particular became the target of sustained demonological critique. The first was what we might call Peripatetic or naturalist certainty ("naturaliste" being the term used in French, by Montaigne and others, for anyone who subscribed to the slogan "naturalia naturaliter"—natural things by natural means). Natural philosophical explanations for aberrant phenomena had gained increasing prestige over the course of the sixteenth century; and late-century demonologies devote considerable space to the naturalist arguments offered by writers such as Pietro Pomponazzi, Giarolamo Cardano, and Giambattista Della Porta.[10]

The trendsetter in this was Ludwig Lavater's 1570 treatise *De Spectris*, translated shortly afterward into French as *Trois livres des apparitions des esprits*.[11] A quick glance at the contents page of book 1 reveals the extent of Lavater's interest in natural causes:

> Chap. 1: "Les melancholiques et insensez s'impriment en la fantaisie beaucoup de choses dont il n'est" (Melancholics and those without sense accept in their fantasy many things that are not).
>
> Chap. 2: "Gens craintifs se persuadent de voir et ouir beaucoup de choses dont il n'est rien" (Fearful people convince themselves that they see and hear many things that are not).

Chap. 3: "Ceux qui ont mauvaise veue et ouye imaginent beaucoup de choses qui ne sont pas" (Those with poor sight and hearing imagine many things that are not).

Chap. 10: "On prend beaucoup de choses naturelles pour des esprits" (We mistake many natural things for spirits).

Aside from sickness or melancholy of the kind that afflicts Maupassant's narrator, Lavater acknowledges a host of everyday phenomena that might be mistaken for supernatural apparitions—glowworms, echo, cats, sleepwalkers, a loose window casement blowing in the wind, woodworm, the cry of owls or bitterns. But, as Lavater is at pains to stress, this is not to say that apparitions are *always* reducible to everyday causes. Pierre Le Loyer's sustained attack on Cardano in his *Quatre livres des spectres* (Four books of specters, 1586) makes this point especially clear.[12] A recurrent target of *Des spectres* is the blind conviction with which Cardano expands the scope of nature's subtleties, even in those cases where a simpler, demonic explanation lies at hand. At one point Le Loyer is discussing the ghostly apparitions reputedly common in Iceland: how much more plausible, he claims, to attribute these to demonic activity than to follow Cardano in ascribing them to the Icelanders' diet of root vegetables, or the presence of bitumen in the soil. Tellingly, Le Loyer refers to natural philosophers not as "naturalists" but rather as "dogmatists"—a term usually employed by sceptics to describe opponents too convinced of their position. Demonology is placed on the side of doubt or hesitation.

The second kind of certainty demonology had in its sights was superstition, especially that found among witches and their accusers. Superstitious certainty differs from naturalist certainty in crediting demons not with too little power but too much. A key passage in the preface to Nicolas Rémy's *Daemonolatreia* of 1593 sets out the implications of this for the demonological investigator, who must tread a narrow line between credulity and doubt:

> No one ... will think my narration unworthy on that account to be handed down to posterity, as long as it is free from all absurdity. For I know that there are many who, because of such reports, are ready to believe others which are utterly ridiculous: as that witches can by their spells change men from being men and turn them into beasts; that their souls at times depart from their bodies, and return again to them as if by right of postliminy.... But I have no more in common

with those who in this way let the reins of their credulity go loose, than I have with those who hold them in too tight. For both are in error.[13]

We might associate the image of the prudent horseman, holding the reins of assent neither too loosely nor too tightly, with a writer like Montaigne, but it is far from uncommon in demonological writing of the period. The existence of superstitious credulity requires that hesitation be engineered into the very fabric of demonological enquiry, especially given the centrality of witches' confessions as evidence.

This disjunction between the learned, measured investigator and popular superstition accounts for a good deal of the hedging in Rémy especially, whose own experience as a prosecutor had brought him face to face with any number of wild claims. This again from his preface:

> It may be that some will accuse me of being nothing but a retailer of marvelous stories, seeing that I speak of witches raising up clouds and travelling through the air, penetrating through the narrowest openings, eating, dancing and lying with Demons, and performing many other such prodigies and portents. But I would have them know first that it was from no scattered rumors, but from the independent and concordant testimony of many witnesses that, as I have said, I have reported these things as certain facts; secondly, that I have argued these matters not captiously but logically, and have always tried to adduce proofs which are in accordance with the spirit of the Christian religion; and finally, that all who wish to do so are perfectly free to disagree with me, for I do not profess to give utterance to infallible decrees.[14]

Notice here how the ecumenical last line ("all who wish to do so are perfectly free to disagree with me, for I do not profess to give . . . infallible decrees") suddenly undercuts Rémy's preceding talk of "concordant testimony," "certain facts," logical argument, proofs, and so on. In this he has something in common with Maupassant's narrator. If we look back at the second passage quoted from Rémy, he, too, adduces flawless "reasoning" and impeccable "perceptions," speaks of "the rigorous sequences of my observations," only then to fall back on the doubtful "who knows?"

Picking its way between naturalist certainty on the one side and superstition on the other, demonology was itself a hermeneutics of suspicion. In this regard we would like briefly to consider what that hermeneutics looks like when transposed into two ghost narratives of the period. The first is Le Loyer's influential story of Philinnion and Machates, which appears in a chapter of the *Quatre livres des spectres* entitled "De l'apparition des demons en cadavres ou charoignes de morts" (On the apparition of demons in the cadavers or corpses of the dead).[15] The story follows what is a fairly widespread folk template—that of the "revenant lover." Le Loyer took his account from Xylander's 1568 Latin translation of Phlegon of Tralles, a Greek paradoxographer—or collector of marvels—writing in the time of the Emperor Hadrian.[16] In Xylander the story takes the form of a letter written by Phlegon himself, in his capacity as a local administrator, to another unnamed official. Its general gist is this: A youth, Machates, is visiting the house of one Charito and Demostratos when one night he is visited by a beautiful young woman. The woman's nurse sees the couple through the bedroom doorway, cries out in horror, and informs the girl's parents. The next day Charito, the mother, quizzes Machates. He nervously admits that the woman who visited him—not only the previous night, but several nights before that—is Philinnion, the daughter of the household. Charito now begins to wail in disbelief: her daughter is long-dead, she tells him, and buried in a tomb. A stupefied Machates shows the mother two love tokens—a ring and a breast band—exchanged between the lovers the night before.

The following night Machates receives a further visit, this time under strict instructions to alert the girl's parents right away. Philinnion brings food and shares it with him. What happens next differs quite markedly between Xylander's Latin and Le Loyer's French versions. One important divergence is the emphasis Le Loyer places on uncertainty, here evoked from the perspective of Machates. Le Loyer shows him wondering: Is the girl I'm consorting with truly dead, as Charito claims? Or is she in fact alive, and her visitations susceptible to another, less sinister explanation? "Machates regardant de plus pres à la contenance, à la face, au corsage, et à la couleur aucunement vermeille de la fille, ne pouvoit se persuader que ce fust un corps mort, ou l'ombre et spectre d'un corps" (Machates, looking more closely at the expression, the face, the bosom, the somewhat rosy coloration of the maid, could not believe that this was a dead body or the shade and specter of a body).[17] Here Machates takes on the role of amateur demonologist (even goes as far as to adopt Le Loyer's own term "spectre," a near-neologism at the time the text was published). In another skeptical moment we see him engaged in an extraordinary piece of wishful thinking, imagining that Charito might have lied in an attempt to trap her daughter: "Il consideroit . . . que la fille, au desçeu de ses parens, venoit en cachettes à luy, à une heure propre pour ceux ou celles qui veulent negotier et traiter d'amour familierement, et que sa mere la feignoit morte, afin que par ceste ruze elle les trouvast sur le faict tous deux" (He thought . . . that the maid, without her parents' knowledge, came secretly to him, at a propitious hour for those who wish to discourse and treat intimately of love, and that her mother pretended to think her dead, so that by such a deceit she might find the two of them in the act).[18] Ultimately, the demonic hypothesis turns out to be the correct one. Demostratos and Charito come running, and the demon duly departs Philinnion's corpse, leaving it motionless on the bed. The parents grieve inconsolably; Machates grows despondent and takes his own life. The town elders order that the tomb be dug up; there they find—you guessed it—a breast-band and a ring.

Le Loyer's revenant narrative was repeated widely in the late sixteenth and especially early seventeenth century. Ghost stories in this period took a markedly more sensationalist turn, such that the kind of titillation it afforded—sex with strangers, the lingering attention paid to the girl's mysterious body, the spectacular denouement—proved irresistible to writers of *canards, histoires prodigieuses*, and also, as we shall see in a moment, *histoires tragiques*. But Philinnion's return also became a fixture in learned demonology, where we find it retold and discussed in Rémy, Martin Delrio, Pierre de Lancre, and many others.[19] André Valladier, in his Advent sermons of 1612—later published as *La sainte philosophie de l'ame* (The holy philosophy of the soul)—adduces it to show how the demon "entrera dedans un corps mort, le mouvera, et le fera marcher, mesme parler, non d'un parler propre à l'homme, mais battant tellement l'air qu'on ne pourra nullement recognoistre aucune difference" (will enter into a dead body, will give it motion, and will make it walk, even speak, not with a speech proper for a man, but compelling the air in such a way that one cannot at all recognize the difference).[20] Writers like Valladier are drawn to the story as ultimate evidence of Satan's power as *simia dei*—the ape of God—a natural magician so consummately subtle that all categories blur, all distinctions collapse. "One" here (*on* in Valladier's "*on* ne pourra nullement recognoistre aucune difference") occupies the place of both perplexed demonologist and the unfortunate youth who, in this and so many other stories like it, is made to feel the chill of fantastic hesitation.

The nineteenth-century authors of fantastic fiction Jan Potocki and Charles Nodier must have known of Le Loyer's tale.[21] They must have known it because they certainly knew François de Rosset's *Histoires memorables et tragiques de ce temps* (Memorable and tragic stories of this day).[22] Rosset cites the story of Philinnion and Machates in the conclusion of the tenth of his *histoires tragiques*, which itself tells the story of a Lyon nightwatchman, La Jacquière, who like Machates sleeps with a demon in the guise of a beautiful young woman.[23] Significantly, however, this reference to ancient authority comes only in the conclusion of Rosset's tale, which begins by stressing that the story he is about to tell is based on recent, well-known, events. The chapter title gives the reader the basic story line, "D'un démon qui apparaissait en forme de damoiselle au lieutenant du chevalier du guet de la ville de Lyon. De leur accointance charnelle, et de la fin malheureuse qui en succéda." (Of a demon who appeared in the form of a lady to the deputy head of the watch of the city of Lyon. Of their carnal knowledge, and of the unhappy end that followed.) The rather fussy specification of the exact title of the main male figure seems intended to assure the reader that the writer is extremely well-informed and scrupulous in his documentation: the protagonist, Thibaud de la Jacquière, is not simply part of the night guard but is apparently the second-in-command to the head of what we would call the police. We recognize here what Barthes calls the *effet de réel* (the effect of the real) by which apparently insignificant details (without any necessary causal relation to the events) can lull readers into the aesthetically pleasing sense that the story is true. The title recalls the premise of Rosset's work as a whole, which is to give an accurate representation of the world in which he and his readers live. These are said to be "histoires mémorables et tragiques de *ce temps*" (emphasis added) and thus to distinguish them precisely from Le Loyer's use of the Machates story. The commitment to recount recent real events was a generic marker of the broad category to which the *histoires tragiques* belongs and which David LaGuardia examines in another essay in this volume.[24]

At the end of a polemical introduction in which Rosset gives the epistemological and theological framework for the incident that he is about to narrate, he tells us that the events occurred only four or five years before his writing.[25] La Jacquière's occupation leads him to know the underside of urban life, the banal brutality of murders, robberies, and other violence. Yet even though he is charged with maintaining order in the world around him, La Jacquière is notorious for his own vice: he frequents prostitutes, despite being "grandement blâmé de ce vice" (greatly reproached for this vice). This initial presentation gives little hint of anything beyond a purely material or natural sphere of the sort that would, centuries later, be familiar to the readers of Balzac or Flaubert. Yet all changes in an instant, and this tipping point brings us to the dilemma of the fantastic. La Jacquière shares with his subordinates that he is, on this particular evening, feeling the urges of the flesh with particular acuteness: "Je ne sais mes amis, se dit-il, de quelle viande j'ai mangé. Tant y a que je me sens si échauffé que, si maintenant je rencontrais le diable, il n'échapperait jamais de mes mains que premièrement je n'en eusse fait à ma volonté." (I do not know, my friends, he said, what I ate. For I feel so hot that if I were to meet the devil himself he would not escape from me before I had my way with him.)[26] In these two sentences Rosset juxtaposes two domains of causality that for many of his readers (though not all) would appear to be entirely distinct. First, the lieutenant's sexual need is linked to the aphrodisiac effect of something he had eaten. Here, there is nothing spiritual or even mental but only the material, bodily functioning of the humors impelling La Jacquière toward sexual intercourse. The second sentence is a bridge to a more troubling and troubled imaginative, moral, and religious domain. La Jacquière's very condensed sexual fantasy links rape, homosexuality, and the doctrine of diabolical presence. Although the devil is traditionally assigned the role of leading mankind into temptation, in La Jacquière's wish the devil would be subordinated and would serve the mortal's pleasure: the devil would be coerced or raped. Secondly, even though the devil here has the traditional masculine gender ("*il* n'échapperait jamais"), this appears to cause the lieutenant no hesitation to engage with him sexually. The expansion of the protagonist's appetite from the female prostitutes he frequents (*garces*) is probably not an accidental detail on Rosset's part, for in his opening statement of purpose, he claims that those who deny the reality of demons and who insist that any such apparitions must have a purely material cause are "atheists and epicurians" (des athées et des épicuriens). We know that in early modernity atheism was routinely conflated with deviation from Christian sexual rules.[27] Moreover, in the concluding pages of the tale, the narrator sets forth what he claims to be an ineluctable progression of vice, one that is paradoxically sanctioned by God: "La paillardise attire l'adultère, l'adultère l'inceste, l'inceste le péché contre nature, et après, Dieu permet qu'on s'accouple avec le diable" (Lasciviousness leads to adultery, adultery to incest, incest to the sin against nature, and afterwards, God allows it to happen that one couples with the devil).[28]

La Jacquière's statement, or rather boast, of voracious and unbounded sexual appetite is immediately followed by the narrator's exclamation of a causal link between this boast and the sudden arrival of a well-dressed young woman: "O jugement incomparable de Dieu! A peine a-t-il achevé de proférer ces paroles qu'il aperçoit en une rue, qui est proche du pont de Saône, une damoiselle bien vêtue accompagnée d'un petit laquais qui portait une lanterne." (Oh, incomparable judgment of God! Scarcely had he finished saying these words than he saw, in a street that is near the bridge on the Saône, a well-dressed lady accompanied by a little lackey bearing a lantern.)[29] Even without the narratorial intervention attributing the connection between the protagonist's words and his immediate sighting of the young woman, the reader would surely recognize the phenomenon of wish-fulfillment, a concept or belief that stretches from antiquity into our own contemporary world, the *Lupus in fabula* tradition, in which words, and in particular, expressed wishes, determine outcomes in ways the speaker could not have foreseen.[30]

Rosset's story differs from Le Loyer's in that the reader, rather than the protagonist, is expected to perceive, or at least to wonder about, a shift from the realm of the purely material to that of the supernatural. La Jacquière is surprised (*émerveillé*) to see such a beautiful, apparently wealthy, woman in the street with only the escort of a small child servant, but his perception remains at the purely aesthetic level, the pleasure of an unusually charming adventure. Blinded first of all by his own physical needs, then by the visual attraction of the woman's beauty and adornment, and then by the ego-boosting thrill of finding himself placed in the flattering position of rescuing a woman in danger, La Jacquière escorts—the verb "is led" might seem to the reader to be more appropriate—the mysterious woman to her home, unaware of any looming disaster. The reader experiences the narrative in a very different way, and this would be the case even without the giveaway constituted by the story's title. Both the reader and La Jacquière know that there is something implausible about the woman's appearance in that time and place, but this implausibility functions in two registers. For the lieutenant, this has all of the natural magic of lust and love, the charm of an adventure, in which the unexpected is what gives every otherwise banal incident a heightened pleasure. For the reader, there is something exceedingly odd about everything that follows the woman's arrival. On one hand, the woman provides an account to motivate her presence—that is, for every point that seems strange (Where is she coming from so late? Why did she not spend the night at her friend's?), her explanations are entirely consonant with an ordinary, worldly causality.[31] The woman in effect becomes the second, the internal, narrator of the tale, offering an account that differs from what the general narrator (presumably Rosset) has told us about the need to doubt purely immanent, entirely material explanations of things. But beyond seeming too seamlessly explained, La Jacquière's experience contains elements that the reader, who is not caught up in the sexual frenzy, finds alarming.

The woman guides La Jacquière to her dwelling, far from the center of Lyon, a "maison fort écartée" (very isolated house).[32] Is this a significant detail? For readers of Gothic fiction (as well as of Sade), an isolated locality, particularly at night, is likely to create an atmosphere conducive to fear-filled suspense. La Jacquière enters the house with two of his men, sending the rest away. Oddly, at this moment a cold breeze arises, although it is July (in the South of France), and the lady has her lackey light a fire in the fireplace. Until they arrived at the house, there was no mention of cold or wind, suggesting another one of those signals dear to later writers of tales of fright (and to the directors of horror films). Moreover, the inside of the house is decorated improbably with an exceptional emphasis on the color yellow: there are a bed of yellow taffeta, a yellow bed canopy, and drapes of yellow twill. For readers of Rosset's day, more accustomed to color symbolism than are most of today's readers, yellow probably made them think of the color of sulfur, the traditional color of hell (with its associated stench).[33] To all of these clues, in which the alert reader will find the basis for a dramatic irony, La Jacquière and his associates are blissfully and lustfully blind. In short, the narrative progression builds climactically in the two separate registers. As the protagonist and his men have sex with the lady, the reader realizes that the naturalistic understanding of the sequence of events is becoming ever more untenable. La Jacquière obtains from the lady everything he desires. He seems to be living in some kind of erotic dream. And then, all of sudden, the dream collapses when the "woman" pulls up her beautiful dress to reveal a putrescent cadaver.

The naturalistic understanding (La Jacquière's) and the spiritualistic, demonological one are skillfully juxtaposed. In keeping with what we have come to call the fantastic, the naturalistic narrative has just enough possibility to remain within the realm of a verisimilar text (though one that requires considerable motivation, the incorporation of enough details to just push it over the threshold of believability) until the final demonic unveiling. And so, Rosset's denunciation of the doubters ultimately prevails. Or does it? Who witnessed all of what happened? After the demon revealed itself, the house disappeared with a clap of thunder, leaving only a dung-filled ruin. One of the three men was already dead when neighbors found them lying in filth. La Jacquière died the following day, and the third man lived three or four days—long enough to tell all the details. In short, the difference between a naturalistic, skeptical understanding of what happened (or what may have happened) and the Scriptural, supernatural one, hangs by a very slender thread: the confession of a traumatized survivor of a night of debauchery.

To guide us in our understanding, we do have, of course, the insistent, even hyperbolic, assertions of the general narrative voice that "Ceux qui nient l'apparition des esprits ne savaient que dire, se voyant confondus par un tel exemple. Mais les chrétiens et catholiques y remarquent les justes jugements de Dieu." (Those who deny the apparition of spirits remained speechless, put to confusion by such an example. But Christians and Catholics recognize the just judgments of God.)[34] Should we believe this? Or should we suppose that Rosset, not known as a theologian or even as a doctrinal polemicist but rather as a professional story writer, poet, and translator, simply packaged his salacious stories within an orthodox, official Catholic framework that would permit uncensored publication? We return to the hesitation that is the very core of the fantastic. We find ourselves indeed at an aporia.

One may very well object to this application of the descriptive term "fantastic," forged by theorists of literary genre to help describe nineteenth-century fiction. Not only is the epistemological horizon of the early seventeenth-century, at the very beginning of scientific modernity, vastly different from that of the nineteenth century, but the attendant political and religious institutions that constrained and also motivated Rosset's discourse were also quite different. What justifies, in our view, the perception of a continuity between the early modern genre of the *histoire tragique* and the nineteenth-century texts that have come to be identified as fantastic is the alacrity with which the later authors attached themselves to their early modern forebears.

Charles Nodier's reworking of the Rosset story is a case in point. Nodier's 1822 collection *Infernalia* includes "Les aventures de Thibaud de La Jacquière" (The adventures of Thibaud de La Jacquière), which is designated as a "petit roman" (little novel).[35] Nodier develops the character of Thibaud, making him the son of a rich and pious merchant and a member of the royal guard of King François. And he also expands markedly the role of the seductive, yet apparently very innocent, lady, giving her the name Orlandine (which itself could be an allusion to another early modern tale, the story of Rolandine in Marguerite de Navarre's *Heptaméron*).[36] Absent from this version are the prefatory and concluding discussions in which Rosset argued in detail that the devil could reuse corpses. But the theme of the magical efficacy of wishes is accentuated, in that Thibaud several times not only mentions the devil but actually calls for the devil to damn him. Having been sent home to Lyon by the king, who hopes that his sinful way can be corrected, Thibaud publicly raises a cup of wine and devotes himself to the devil, saying: "Sacré mort du grand diable! je lui veux bailler, dans ce vin, mon sang et mon âme, si jamais je deviens plus homme de bien que je le suis." (By the holy death of the great devil! May I give him, with this wine, my blood and my soul if I ever become more righteous than I am.)[37] He later calls upon the devil in a magic incantation expressive of his sexual needs: "Sacrée mort du grand diable! je lui baille mon sang et mon âme, que si la grande diablesse, sa fille, venait à passer, je la prierais d'amour, tant je me sens échauffé par le vin." (By the holy death of the great devil! I give him my blood and my soul, and if the great she-devil, his daughter, came near, I would make love to her—this wine makes me so hot.) We note in passing that Nodier recognized the gender issues raised in Rosset's text and has here "normalized" Thibaud's sexual orientation.[38] Where Rosset's Thibaud's single invocation of the devil seems simply to be a figure of speech, a way of expressing an exceptional sexual drive and macho virility, Nodier's protagonist seems deliberately defiant of the religious piety of his father and even the caution of his companions. He sends the latter away with the comment, "Vous voyez que celui que j'ai invoqué ne m'a pas fait attendre; ainsi, bon soir" (You see that he whom I invoked has not made me wait. And so, good evening).

In terms of the doubt that marks the fantastic as a genre, we can see that Nodier makes the interpretative task more complex than did Rosset. In Rosset, Thibaud perceived everything in an entirely naturalistic or materialist way, not suspecting a supernatural intervention, whereas the reader increasingly feels that something quite extraordinary is occurring. Thus there are in Rosset two registers, the protagonist's and the implied reader's. But Nodier's Thibaud is harder to fathom. Does he believe in the efficacy of these diabolic invocations? Or is he, as a libertine, simply mocking his society's norms? The latter is probably the case, and yet Nodier leaves us guessing about the protagonist's state of mind.

The suggestion that Thibaud himself may, mentally, be somewhere in between a belief in demonic intervention and a skeptical position is reinforced by Nodier's account of the nighttime walk from the center of Lyon to the isolated house. As the young woman, the black boy-servant (whose lantern is broken and no longer lights the way) and Thibaud wander around the city, "si long-temps, qu'à la fin il semblait à Thibaud qu'ils s'étaient égarés dans les rues de Lyon" (for such a long time, that finally it seemed to Thibaud that they had become lost in the streets of Lyon).[39] Meanwhile, the "belle égarée" (beauty who had lost her way) tells Thibaud a complex tale of her imprisonment by an older man who is apparently grooming her for marriage (like the Arnolphe of Molière's *Ecole des femmes*). This internal narration, too long and subtle to analyze in detail here, is like a spider web in its complexity. On one hand, it strengthens the apparently naturalistic view of the situation, casting into the background both Thibaud's diabolic invocations and his father's pious prayers for his son's salvation. On the other hand, it makes us wonder whether the protagonist is fully aware of what is going on. Are the nocturnal trek and the story both labyrinths that befuddle Thibaud so that he comes to resemble Maupassant's character in "Qui sait?" Such a state of mental confusion is strongly suggested by one detail of the arrival at Orlandine's house. Once there, Thibaud notices something about the boy-servant: "Thibaud s'aperçut alors que ce n'était pas un enfant, comme il l'avait cru d'abord, mais une espèce de vieux nain tout noir et de la plus laide figure" (Thibaud then noticed that it was not a child, as he had at first believed, but a kind of old dwarf, all black, and with the ugliest face).[40] Again, there are two possible explanations for this new perception. One is that the darkness outside had prevented Thibaud from seeing the servant clearly. The other is that the servant actually changed somehow on entering the house, just as Orlandine, in bed, suddenly becomes "un horrible assemblage de formes hideuses et inconnues" (a horrible concatenation of hideous and unknown shapes) and announces that she is Beelzebub.

The fantastic, as Todorov says, "met précisément en question l'existence d'une opposition irréductible entre réel et irréel. Mais pour nier cette opposition, il faut d'abord en reconnaître les termes" (questions precisely the existence of an irreducible opposition between real and unreal. But in order to deny an opposition, we must first of all acknowledge its terms).[41] Both the early modern *histoire tragique* and the nineteenth-century fantastic story are written within the ideological framework of an opposition not only between true and false but between possible and impossible. In one period the oppositions are dominated by theological doctrines and in the other by scientific ones, in particular by neurology and psychiatry. Both bodies of texts make strong gestures toward grounding the events in recognizable places and toward providing plausible character motivation. Both give the readers the *frisson* of something frightening and mysterious that may (or may not) breech the barrier that surrounds reality as we know it.

## Notes

1. Guy de Maupassant, *L'inutile beauté*, 3rd ed. (Paris: Victor-Havard Éditeur, 1900), 305–6.

2. Tzvetan Todorov, *The Fantastic: A Structural Approach to a Literary Genre*, trans. Richard Howard (Cleveland: The Press of Case Western Reserve University, 1973), 25.

3. Maupassant, *L'inutile beauté*, 305–6.

4. Todorov, *The Fantastic*, 168.

5. E. J. Clery, "The Genesis of 'Gothic' Fiction," in *The Cambridge Companion to Gothic Fiction*, ed. Jerrold E. Hogle (Cambridge: Cambridge University Press, 2002), 21–39.

6. Murray Sachs, "The Role of the Blind Beggar in 'Madame Bovary,'" *Symposium;* Syracuse, N.Y. 22, no. 1 (Spring 1968): 72–80.

7. Sigmund Freud, in *The Uncanny*, mentions stories of animated furniture as an instance of the "uncanny," a concept that has much in common with the fantastic. (*The Uncanny*, trans. David McLintock and Hugh Haughton [New York: Penguin, 2003], 151).

8. Stuart Clark, *Thinking with Demons: The Idea of Witchcraft in Early Modern Europe* (Oxford: Oxford University Press, 1997). Descartes, in both the *Discourse on Method* and the *Meditations of First Philosophy* not only practices doubt but entertains the possibility that he and others are mad.

9. Jean Bodin, *De la démonomanie des sorciers*, ed. Virginia Krause et al. (Oxford: Oxford University Press, 2016).

10. Pietro Pomponazzi, *Les causes des merveilles de la nature; ou, Les enchantements* (Paris: Rieder, 1930); Girolamo Cardano, *Les liures de Hierome Cardanus . . . intitulés de la subtilité, & subtiles inuentions* (Paris: L'Angelier, 1556); Giambattista Della Porta, *La magie naturelle: Ou les secrets et miracles de la nature* (Lyon: Jean Martin, 1565; repr., Le Prieuré: Les Editions du Prieuré, 1993).

11. Loys Lavater, *Trois livres des apparitions des esprits, fantosmes, prodiges & accidens merveilleux qui précédent souventes fois la mort de quelque personnage renommé [. . .]* (Geneva: Jean Durant, 1571).

12. Pierre Le Loyer, *Quatre livres des spectres ou apparitions et visions d'espirits, anges et demons, se monstrans sensiblement aux hommes* (Paris: Chez Gabriel Buon, 1586).

13. Nicolas Rémy, *Demonolatry*, trans. E. Allen Ashwin (London: J. Rodker, 1930), xiii.

14. Ibid., xii.

15. Le Loyer, *Quatre livres des spectres*, 375–415.

16. Wilhelm Xylander, ed. and trans., *Antonini Liberalis Transformationum Congeries: Phlegontis Tralliani de Mirabilibus & Longæuis Libellus* (Basil: T. Guarinum, 1568). The modern English translation is that of William Hansen, *Phlegon of Tralles' Book of Marvels* (Exeter: University of Exeter Press, 1996).

17. Le Loyer, *Quatre livres des spectres*, 387.

18. Ibid.

19. Pierre de Lancre, *Tableau de l'inconstance des mauuais anges et demons* (Paris: N. Buon, 1613); Martin Antoine Delrio, *Les controuerses et recherches magiques de Martin Delrio*, trans. André Du Chesne (Paris: Jean Petit-pas, 1611); Rémy, *Demonolatry*.

20. André Valladier, *La sainte philosophie de l'âme, sermons pour l'Advant preschez à Paris à St-Médric, l'an 1612* (Paris: P. Chevalier), 607.

21. Jean Potocki, *Manuscrit trouvé à Saragosse*, ed. René Radrizzani (Paris: Le Livre de Poche, 1993); Charles Nodier, "Les aventures de Thibaud de La Jacquière: Petit Roman," in *Infernaliana* (Paris: Goetschy, 1822), 95–111.

22. François de Rosset, *Les histoires tragiques de nostre temps* (Geneva: Slatkine Reprints, 1980).

23. François Rosset, "D'un démon qui apparaissait en forme de damoiselle au lieu-

tenant du chevalier du Guet de la ville de Lyon: De leur accointance charnelle, et de la fin malheureuse qui en succéda," in *Les Histoires mémorables et tragiques de ce temps* [1619], ed. Anne De Vaucher Gravili (Paris: Le Livre de Poche, 1994), 251–61.

24. See, in this volume, David LaGuardia's essay "The Real of the Tragic Tale in Sixteenth-Century France."

25. Anne de Vaucher Gravili notes that Rosset may have been inspired by a pamphlet, "Discours merveilleux et véritable d'un capitaine de la ville de Lyon que Sathan a enlevé dans sa chambre depuis peu de temps" (Paris: Fleury Bourriquant, 1613).

26. Rosset, "D'un démon qui apparaissait en forme de demoiselle," 253.

27. See, for example, in Frédéric Lachèvre, *Le libertinage devant le Parlement de Paris: Le procès du poète Theophile du Viau (11 Juillet 1623–1er Septembre 1625); Publication integrale des pieces inedites des Archives nationales* (H. Champion, 1909), the conflation of atheism and sodomy made by the Jesuit Garasse (176). See also Michel Jeanneret, *Éros rebelle: Littérature et dissidence à l'âge classique* (Paris: Le Seuil, 2003), esp. chap. 4, "Le fouët des paillards," 95–120.

28. Rosset, "D'un démon qui apparaissait en forme de demoiselle," 260.

29. Ibid., 253.

30. Freud, *The Uncanny*, trans. McLintock and Haughton, 154–55.

31. Gérard Genette, "Vraisemblance et Motivation," in *Figures II* (Paris: Éditions du Seuil, 1969), 71–99.

32. Rosset, "D'un démon qui apparaissait en forme de demoiselle," 255.

33. Ibid., 255, note by Anne de Vaucher Gravili.

34. Ibid., 259.

35. Nodier, "Les aventures de Thibaud de La Jacquière: Petit Roman."

36. Marguerite de Navarre, *The Heptameron*, trans. Paul A Chilton (Harmondsworth, Middlesex, England: Penguin, 1984), story 21, 236–54.

37. Nodier, "Les aventures de Thibaud de La Jacquière: Petit Roman," 96–97.

38. Ibid., 98.

39. Ibid., 100.

40. Ibid., 107–8.

41. Todorov, *The Fantastic*, 167–68.

KATHLEEN LONG

# The Beauty of Violence in Rosset and Barbey d'Aurevilly

Jules Amédée Barbey d'Aurevilly, best known for his complexly transgressive story collection *Les diaboliques*, stands among the most intriguing modern heirs of the *histoires tragiques* tradition.[1] His depictions of the fallen aristocratic class, mostly composed at the far end of the series of violent revolutions that shook nineteenth-century France and displaced the nobility from its domination of French society, combine an admiration of aristocratic decadence with that of the Nietzschean supermen and -women who upend social hierarchies and gender norms and refuse to restrain themselves within social codes.[2] This admiration tends to subvert the search for justice that characterizes many of the early modern *histoires tragiques*, particularly those of Pierre de Boaistuau[3] and François de Rosset. Barbey's representations of the acts committed by these various characters create an aesthetic of violence, or disgust, or sexual transgression that exceeds the moral complexities of the tales that inspire him. His retelling of the seventh tale in Rosset's *Histoires tragiques*,[4] a story of incest between brother and sister, in "Une page d'histoire"[5] creates an aesthetic of transgression and of violence that surpasses the moral complexities already evident in the original version, to express admiration for this pair's violation of social norms. Both versions rely heavily on the spectacle of punishment, but whereas Rosset's version lingers on the spectacle of the execution, Barbey's reworking is more impressionistic, creating a series of vignettes that neither add up to a coherent narrative nor explain the meaning of this tale. Nonetheless, some theatrical elements link the two versions. Barbey's version even goes so far as to express a sense of overwhelming loss caused by the death, centuries before, of this exceptional pair, as they stand in for a culture, noble and corrupt, violent and beautiful, that is gone forever. In the face of such loss, Barbey d'Aurevilly implies that literature writes more truly than history, revealing what history attempts to cover over. In this regard, then, literature is itself a transgressive act, one that mirrors the crime of the incestuous couple. This transgression is often underscored in the tale by an emphasis on the spectacle of crime and punishment, particularly a striking visual image that both represents the crime in some way and enables a reaction of admiration, the seeds of which were already planted in Rosset's story.

### Historical Background

Rosset's seventh tale already presents a morally complex account of crime and punishment, the story of an incestuous couple, brother and sister, based on a historical event, the execution of the incestuous brother and sister of this pair, Marguerite and Julien de Ravalet de Tourlaville. Their tale appears briefly in Pierre de L'Estoile's journals:

> Le mardi 2e de ce mois, furent décapités, en la place de la Grève à Paris, ung beau gentilhomme Normant, riche (ainsi qu'on disoit) de dix mil livres de rente, nommé Fourelaville, avec sa sœur, fort belle, aagée de vingt ans ou environ, et ce pour l'inceste qu'ils avoient commis ensemble: desquels le pauvre père s'estant jetté à genoux aux pieds du Roy, le jour de devant, pour demander leur grâce, Sa Majesté lui auroit refusé, aiant fait response que si la femme n'eust point esté mariée, il lui eust volontiers donné sa grâce, mais que l'estant, il ne pouvoit: bien lui donnoit-il leurs corps pour les faire enterrer.
> La Roine aussi s'y monstra fort contraire, et dit au Roy, qu'il ne devoit souffrir une telle abomination en son Roiaume.[6]

(Tuesday, the second day of this month, was decapitated at the Place de Grève in Paris a handsome Norman gentleman, wealthy and with ten thousand pounds of rent [so they said], named Fourelaville, with his sister, very beautiful, twenty years old or so, because of the incest they committed together; for whom the poor father had thrown himself on his knees at the King's feet, the day before, to beg for their pardon. His Majesty refused him, having responded that if the woman had not been married, he would have gladly given his pardon, but that given that she was, he could not. But he did give him their bodies to be buried.

The Queen also showed herself to be strongly opposed, and said to the King that he should not suffer such an abomination in his kingdom.)

Already, L'Estoile's brief account mentions the beauty of the brother and sister and underscores that it is adultery, not incest, that is the reason for their execution (it is the fact that she is married that dooms them). The basic outlines of this brief account are repeated in pamphlets written shortly after the event, among them the *Supplice d'un frère et sœur décapités en Grève pour adultère et inceste*,[7] which combines the theme of the couple's beauty with the horror of their crime, as well as the father's request for mercy (although, in the case, only for his daughter). The additional detail of the couple's beauty moving the spectators at the execution to pity enters into this account: "Les assistants leur ont départi leurs prières et la plupart de leurs larmes, à si piteux spectacle où leur tendre jeunesse et beauté émouvaient les plus durs cœurs à pitié" (The spectators devoted their prayers and most of their tears to this so pitiful spectacle in which their tender youth and beauty moved the hardest hearts to pity). This reaction is tempered by the "atrocité de deux crimes si énormes" (the atrocity of two such enormous crimes).[8] This double reaction of pity (si piteux spectacle) and horror at the *atrocité* also drives the narratives (and the narrators) of both Rosset's and Barbey d'Aurevilly's versions of this story, although to different degrees.

### The Role of Incest

The fact that it is the adulterous nature of the relationship that motivates the aversive response of the onlookers and the narrator in these contemporary accounts, much more than the incest, as the *Supplice* and L'Estoile's accounts focus on adultery as the primary crime, may reflect attitudes traced by historians like Sara McDougall, who notes a great deal of tolerance for incest in spite of prohibitions, particularly in marriages among the nobility.[9] But Rosset's and Barbey's narratives focus on the horror of incest more than the adultery. What the historical background might explain is the highly equivocal nature of both literary versions of the story, in which condemnation is matched with admiration of the exceptional couple. Their responses, and the complexity of historical responses to incest, may suggest that the subversive nature of incest may play a very different role in society, binding some families together even while pushing the limits of taboos.

Maureen Quilligan has built on feminist critical perspectives on the incest taboo to suggest incest as a zone of women's agency, their ability to effect change, in early modern literature and politics. Basing this critique on feminist anthropology of the past few decades, she points out the lacuna concerning women's feelings and their agency (their freedom to choose outcomes) in Lévi-Strauss's formulation of this taboo:

> As he concludes his seminal work, *Elementary Structures of Kinship*, Lévi-Strauss points out the endemically problematic position of women tabooed by the incest prohibition. This discussion is, in fact, the only time that he takes into account how the tabooed women might themselves experience their functional status as passive objects to be traded in the system of exchanges just analyzed.... Although Lévi-Strauss observes here that a girl might have some feeling about the particulars of the exchange, he emphatically insists that she cannot change its nature, which is to be, in Eve Kosofsky Sedgwick's useful shorthand, a "homosocial connection," a bond not between a man and a woman, but "between men."

Quilligan points out that Lévi-Strauss argues that the "system of exchange of women, enforced by the incest taboo, works like a language." He sees women in this system as functioning like signs. Quilligan points out the disruptive nature of women engaging in the system of signs and using it, rather than merely serving as signs: "While Lévi-Strauss never explores the implications of the fact that a woman's value-endowed ability to speak, that is, to manipulate signs herself, may come into conflict with her function as a sign in the system of the traffic in women, it is clear that female semiotic agency is potentially *very* problematic to this system."[10] Quilligan links this suppression of women's agency over language ("women cannot speak for themselves in the kinship system") with suppression of female desire.[11] She traces how the denial to woman of "the ability to manipulate the fully articulated system of signs with which men communicate with each other" persists through the work of Lacan, and a number of the feminists who attempt to move beyond Lacan's and Lévi-Strauss's formulations.[12]

Quilligan then uses the work of anthropologist Annette Weiner to develop a theory of women's agency in "the processes of civilization." This theory links women's participation to a different role, one of caring "for those objects that are never intended to circulate" and that are linked to a "social group's coherence and history," to what Weiner calls "sibling intimacy."[13] In fact, Quilligan links what she calls "their endogamous position" to the exercise of "immense political power."[14] She points to a number of examples of incestuous relations between brother and sister in mythology and folklore as an integral part of origin tales, suggesting that this relationship is foundational in these contexts.

The concept of women's language as disruptive in the context of the exchange of women between men will be useful for understanding the roles Marguerite (called Doralice in Rosset's story) plays in the two versions of the tale. The notion of her relationship with her brother as allowing her (and him) to exercise power is more complex, as this power resides more within the couple than in the larger context of society. However, the combination of Marguerite's control of language and of signs grants both her and her brother the power of emotional control over witnesses to the execution and over the narrators themselves. In part, this power is the result of her asserting control over the spectacle of her own death, and assuring specific reactions from those around her. Thus, this issue of the link between transgressive sexuality and feminine agency or power becomes significant in both Rosset's and Barbey d'Aurevilly's versions of the tale, and, in the end, this combination creates a vivid portrait of the brother and sister pair.

## The Spectacle of Death

Linked to this agency by means of the brother's and sister's beauty is the question of spectacle. Even in the anonymous pamphlet cited above (*Supplice* [. . .]), their beauty has a profound effect on the audience at the execution. As Mitchell B. Merback[15] and Paul Friedland[16] have described at length, capital punishment in Europe became increasingly a spectacle over the course of the early modern period. Merback notes that a "reconfiguration of the spatial relations between actors and audience, like the stepped-up presence of armed militias, distanced spectators physically from the scaffold and thus psychologically from the humanity of the suffering convict."[17] In tracing this evolution toward a more distanced spectacle, Friedland cites the fate of Marguerite and Julien as an early example of the increasingly theatrical nature of executions, discussing firsthand accounts and Rosset's version of events.[18] But Friedland notes that the sympathy of the audience is emphasized in these accounts, a sympathy that is largely absent from historical audiences of eighteenth-century executions. He sees the late sixteenth and early seventeenth century in France as a crucial period for the development of two new modes of responding to executions:

> The period from the 1550's until the first decade of the seventeenth century, therefore, witnessed the birth of two related but somewhat different ways of watching executions. One the one hand, a new, almost clinically detached way of watching them came into existence, which we saw in the diaries of Thomas Platter, and which enabled viewers to observe executions without participating in the traditional ceremony of repentance and healing. On the other hand, the French public was beginning to show an insatiable appetite for sensationalistic and dramatic accounts of crimes, criminals, and executions, a craving that could be satisfied either by attending executions or, increasingly, by consuming broadsides and other kinds of texts devoted to the subject.[19]

While Friedland is right to see this story as exemplifying the public's taste for a sensational performance, Marguerite's/Doralice's sincere repentance, which moves the spectators to tears, recalls the audience participation in the ceremony of repentance in earlier forms of execution, thus bridging a more intimate form of execution with the more modern spectacle of violence. Much of this response speaks to the power of her language in Rosset's version of the tale; for Barbey, it is the manipulation of the spectacle through her violence toward the executioner, thus asserting her rank and privilege as she is about to die, that gives her actions power. At any rate, in both versions, she is the dominant character, who creates the spectacle as a reflection of her agency, that is, of her own will.

### Rosset's Version

Rosset's narration of the seventh tale of his collection begins with the conventional denunciation of vice and sin that precedes most of his stories, and suggests that it will follow the formula of the commission of a horrible sin followed by swift and terrible punishment. But, as with a number of the tales in Rosset's collection, the devil is in the details, which convey on the part of the narrator an ambivalence toward the sinners that calls into question the morality of the punishment. The evil of this couple is mitigated by their beauty, a complication that is even more apparent in Barbey d'Aurevilly's reworking of the tale.

The narrator seems to give a potential justification for the sister's behavior toward the beginning of the tale: whereas Doralice had many meritorious suitors of an acceptable age ("Elle fut recherchée d'une infinite de cavaliers qui avaient beaucoup de mérite et qui étaient d'âge sortable" [She was courted by an infinite number of gentlemen of great merit and who were of a suitable age]), her father decides to marry her to a very rich but aging neighbor.[20] She justifies her resistance to this marriage, and then her love for her brother, using literary models as precedents, showing her command of the rhetoric of self-justification. Her command of language helps her to refuse the rules of exogamy. At her execution, her admirable self-control combined with her beauty permits her to play the role of the tragic heroine quite well, repenting and accepting her punishment with courage and constancy, and evoking the sympathy of the crowd. Barbey also depicts Marguerite's agency, her intentional and voluntary actions, and the theatricality of her behavior, but with some striking differences, as we shall see. Kris Vassilev has noted this complex relationship between theatricality and morality in one of Barbey's most famous stories, "Le bonheur dans le crime," from *Les diaboliques*: "Mais si ce véritable arsenal d'expressions aux accents explicitement moralisateurs nous autorise à évoquer les enjeux éthiques de la tragédie, l'écriture des *Diaboliques*, elle, donne à voir un rapport plus général entre théâtre et récit, en raison de l'importance décisive conférée, au sein de la narration, au concept de spectacle" (But if this veritable arsenal of expressions with explicitly moralizing tone authorizes us to evoke the ethical stakes of tragedy, the writing of *Les diaboliques*, reveals a more general relationship between theater and narration, because of the decisive importance conferred, at the heart of the narration, to the concept of the spectacle).[21]

The spectacle, particularly as managed by Marguerite/Doralice, is central to the plot of both stories and complicates the moral force of tragedy, which is repeatedly invoked by both narrations. As Vassilev points out in his analysis of "Le bonheur dans le crime," the plot depends entirely upon the roles the characters play: "L'intrigue repose ici entièrement sur le jeu de théâtre auquel s'adonnent les personnages" (The plot rests entirely here upon the theatrical role-playing to which the characters have given themselves over).[22] This complicates the ethical nature of the narration, since the characters offer the behavior and appearance of innocent (or at least not guilty-seeming), injured parties, even when they are confessing their sins, thus calling into question the justice of the sentence.

The narrator's ambivalence at certain moments seems to create a space for this feminine agency and power in the context of theatrical role-playing, as he clearly alternates between condemning the couple's crime and excusing it. After declaring in his opening diatribe that "je suis contraint de confesser que notre siècle est l'égout de toutes les vilenies des autres" (I am obliged to confess that our century is the sewer of all of the vile acts of the others), Rosset introduces the villains of the story: "une fille que nous appellerons Doralice et un fils, plus jeune qu'elle de quelque dix-huit mois que nous nommerons Lizaran. Cette fille et ce fils étaient si beaux qu'on eût dit que la nature avait pris plaisir à les former pour faire voir un de ses miracles" (a girl whom we will call Doralice and a boy, younger than she by some eighteen months, whom we shall call Lizaran. This girl and this boy were so beautiful that one would have said that nature had taken pleasure in forming them in order to make one of its miracles visible). This shift from a rhetoric of disgust, invoking the image of the sewer, to the admiration of such "miracles" of beauty creates a contrast that is difficult to resolve and that continues to jar the reader throughout the narration. This contrast is made even more dramatic by the implied comparison between this beautiful couple and corporeal monstrosities at the beginning of the story, as Astrée Ruciak has pointed out, when the narrator says: "Il ne faut plus aller en Afrique pour y voir quelque nouveau monstre. Notre Europe n'en produit que trop aujourd'hui." (One doesn't have to travel to Africa to see some new monster there. Our Europe produces far too many of them these days.)[23] Thus, the first few lines of the story create an atmosphere of moral ambivalence, hovering between repulsion and admiration: are the characters monsters or miracles?

The children are in fact admirable in a number of ways. The narrator insists upon their resemblance to each other: "Ils se ressemblaient si parfaitement que jamais la Bradamante de l'Arioste ne fut si semblable à son frère Richardet" (They resembled each other so perfectly that never did Ariosto's Bradamante resemble her brother Ricciardo so well). They receive the same education and prove to be gifted: "Le père fut soigneux de les faire instruire en leur âge plus tendre en toutes sortes d'exercices vertueux, comme à jouer de l'épinette, à danser, à lire, à écrire, et à peindre. Ils y profitaient si bien qu'ils surmontait le désir de ceux qui avaient la charge de les enseigner." (The father took care to have them taught from their tenderest youth in all sorts of virtuous pursuits, such as playing the spinet, dancing, reading, writing, and painting.)[24] They are represented as exceptional, and exceptionally worthy, but particularly in creative and performative pursuits. The narrative carefully nestles its description of them into a web of literary references that softens the confusions that their appearance and closeness create.

Their constant companionship leads to the forbidden relationship, bit by bit, in a manner that makes their love seem inevitable. First, "ces deux jeunes enfants nourris toujours ensemble s'aimaient d'une telle amour que l'un ne pouvait vivre sans l'autre" (these two young children always raised together loved each other with such a love that one could not live without the other). They are even allowed to sleep together as children, for too long it seems. Rosset takes this opportunity to warn mothers and fathers about this practice: "Je crois fermement que le mal procéda de cette trop longue accointance" (I firmly believe that the evil arose from this too long acquaintance). At every turn, he seems to be creating excuses for their excessive behavior, but he recalls himself with swift moral judgments, such as "Mais l'amour impudique et détestable y était déjà sans doute mêlée" (But the immodest and detestable love was without a doubt already mixed into it).[25] Thus, the ambivalent response is maintained throughout the narrative, even as their excessive love for each other becomes apparent.

The two are separated when Lizaran is sent off to school. He is clearly brilliant and returns home in triumph. His father is proud, "Mais ce ne fut rien au prix du contentement que sa sœur en reçut. Elle ne cessait de l'embrasser et de le baiser." (But this was nothing compared to the contentment that his sister received from it. She never ceased to hug and kiss him.) They try to restrain themselves out of shame and a sense of the gravity of the sin, but their passion gets the better of them: "Ni l'un ni l'autre ne pouvaient si bien refréner leur maudite passion qu'elle n'échappât parfois au frein de la raison" (Neither one nor the other could so well control their damnable passion as to prevent it escaping sometimes from the reins of reason).[26] This description of their love displaces the agency for their behavior onto the passion itself, so that it is no longer the characters who are in control and thus in some way excusing them from responsibility. It is the passion, and not the couple, that violates the limits of reason. Again, this rhetorical shifting of responsibility is reminiscent of the complaints of the powerless lover in Petrarch's *Rime*, who positions himself as defenseless and assaulted by Love, thus denying his own agency (his own free will), a recurrent theme throughout the sequence from the third poem on.

The supposedly guilty couple are further excused when their greedy father marries Doralice off to an older man, "fort riche mais déjà grison" (very rich but already gray-haired). This is classic exogamy, a mutually beneficial arrangement between two men that gives one the money he wants, and the other a bride he needs, while the object of the exchange, Doralice, remains voiceless in the context of this agreement. The narrator declares: "Ah! Maudite avarice, que tu causes du mal au monde! Celui qui t'appelle racine de tous vices avait bien connaissance de ce que tu es et de ce que tu produis." (Oh! Damnable avarice, how you cause evil in the world. He who calls you the root of all vices knows well what you are and what you produce.) But Doralice is not merely the passive object of this exchange, and in begging her brother to save her from this marriage, she deploys all of the vocabulary of the *mal mariée* of medieval romance: "Faut-il que je passe la fleur de mon âge avec une personne que je déteste plus que la mort meme? Mon père n'est-il pas bien cruel de me livrer entre les mains d'un mortel ennemi? Consumerai-je donc désormais mes jours en une servitude si contraire à mon âge?" (Must I spend the flower of my youth with a person I detest more than death itself? Is my father not truly cruel in delivering me into the hands of a mortal enemy? Will I consume henceforth my days in a servitude so contrary to my age?")[27] While this passage is also littered with denunciations of either the vice of incest or the crime of adultery (it is not always clear which one is in play) as an "exécrable péché" (an execrable sin), "un tel crime" (such a crime), "un péché si detestable" (such a détestable sin), repeated several times, it also seems to excuse the same sin in advance. Her father has exchanged her with another elderly man in order to improve the finances of the family (or his own personal finances), in an act of traditional but misguided exogamy. Both Doralice and the narrator see this act as the justification, if not the catalyst, for her refusal of traditional sexual norms. In short, her father's use of her as an object to be bartered triggers her agency in her own sexuality by causing her to take on a role in reaction, that of the medieval badly married young wife, calling up yet more literary models, such as Marie de France's "Guigemar," where the *mal mariée* is saved from a marriage to a cruel older man by the handsome young hero, that authorize her to transgress social norms. Her beauty and self-mastery throughout the story enhance this agency, insofar as she can control others, and cause the narrator to question the very social norms he claims to be upholding.

This ambivalence is clear in the narrator's repetition of this rhythm of denunciation and excuse throughout the tale, particulary when he even goes so far as to say: "A la vérité, s'ils n'eussent été si proches de sang, ils seraient plus excusables en leur folle passion: car elle était une des beautés les plus parfaites que j'aie jamais vue, et lui, l'un des plus beaux gentilshommes qu'on puisse voir. Mais quand je pense à leur vice si scandaleux, je suis contraint de m'étonner comme Dieu, qui voit tout, pouvait souffrir cette méchanceté sans la punir." (In truth, if they had not been so closely related by blood, they would have been more excusable in their insane passion: for she was one of the most perfect beauties that I had ever seen, and he was one of the handsomest gentlemen that one could ever see. But when I think of their scandalous vice, I am obliged to express astonishment at how God, who sees all, could ever have endured this evildoing without punishing it.)[28] Once again, the narrator begins by almost excusing the protagonists' behavior because of their beauty and excellence but then withdraws once more into the position of scandalized moralist. At the same time, however, he is shifting the blame onto God, who sees all, for not ending this behavior, in an echo of the earlier blaming of passion for their conduct. Of course, this later passage could be read as foreshadowing of the inevitable doom that this couple faces, since all of the misdeeds recounted in the *Histoires tragiques* are punished.

The couple escapes to Paris, but the husband finds out where they are and has them arrested. Although the father begs Henri IV to pardon them, they are condemned to death. Claire Esnault states that the narration of the execution scene in this story particularly underscores the pity inspired in the crowd by the punishment and the beauty of those punished. She notes possible sources for this scene, and for its effect: "La thématique de la beauté des exécutés vient peut-être de la tradition des martyrologes, que les guerres de religion ont ressuscité" (The theme of the beauty of those executed comes perhaps from the tradition of martyrologies, which the Wars of Religion had resuscitated).[29] She points to descriptions of the execution of Mary, Queen of Scots, which similarly emphasizes her great beauty. Then, she links this effect to theatrical effects theorized since Aristotle:

> La beauté des deux jeunes gens trouve son apogée pathétique dans l'évocation du spectacle punitive. À travers la prière et les larmes, le théâtre de la mort devient un lieu de communion entre suppliciés et spectateurs. Les notions aristotéliciennes de terreur et de pitié sont mobilisées: le public est conscient de l'"abominable passion" des condamnés, mais ne peut s'empêcher de compatir à leur sort et d'admirer leur constance.[30]

> (The beauty of the two young people finds its pathetic apogee in the evocation of the punitive spectacle. By means of prayer and tears, the theater of death becomes a place of communion between the condemned and the spectators. Aristotelian notions of terror and pity are mobilized: the public is aware of the "abominable passion" of the condemned, but cannot prevent itself from feeling compassion for their fate and admiration for their constancy.)

The narrator focuses on Doralice, who faces her punishment with dignity and courage (and beauty, of course), maintaining her rhetorical agency to the very end, in the sense that she controls the response of the spectators at her execution. She begs to take all the blame on herself, and that her brother be spared. Her self-control wins over the sympathy of all those present, as well as of the narrator: "Le premier qui parut sur cet infâme théâtre fut Doralice, avec tant de courage et de résolution que tout le monde admirait sa constance" (The first one to appear on this infamous stage was Doralice, with so much courage and resolution that everyone admired her constancy). The emphasis on the theatrical nature of this scene suggests that she is playing her role well: "L'on eût dit, quand elle monta sur l'échafaud, qu'elle allait jouer une feinte tragédie, et non une véritable" (One would have said, when she climbed onto the scaffold, that she was going to play in a feigned tragedy, and not a real one).[31] The spectators weep because of her beauty and composure in the face of death.

Her constancy in the face of death confirms her right to dignity in death, as an incident involving her body suggests. When one of her stockings is accidentally exposed by the executioner's assistant who is moving her body out of the way—"fit voir un bas de soie incarnat" (showed a red stocking)—the executioner reacts by kicking the assistant off of the scaffold in anger. The narrator exclaims at this exposure: "Une telle beauté, encore qu'elle eût mérité la mort, ne devait pas être si vilainement traitée" (Such a beauty, although she might have merited death, should not have been treated so villainously).[32] It is at this moment that the crime is erased by both her beauty and her composure: she should have been treated even after death like a lady, not like a criminal. Lizaran faces his death with similar elegance and bravery: "Il était le vivant portrait de sa sœur, comme nous avons déjà dit, et par conséquent doué d'excellente beauté" (He was the living portrait of his sister, as we have already said, and consequently endowed with excellent beauty). When he prays to God, the people "en ressentait une grande douleur" (felt a strong sorrow at this).[33] By the end of this scene, their compassion is directed entirely at the beautiful couple, whose beauty and courage have thus controlled the reactions to the scene of their death, as well as future narratives of these events. While Rosset ends with a moralizing ending about God's inevitable punishment, the noble and beautiful couple seem exceptional enough to be justified in their violation of social norms and taboos, and thus the function of the *histoire tragique* is no longer that of a moralizing example.

## "Une page d'histoire"

"Une page d'histoire" takes up the story of Julien and Marguerite Ravalet but does not retell it so much as deconstruct it in five acts. These five acts in turn rely on images that dominate each section and guide the tale in different directions. The first part is an exordium that places the narrator in his "terre natale de Normandie" (birthplace in Normandy), surrounded by the ghosts of all who had lived there, with him or before him. This links the narrator to the tale geographically, since the Ravalet family lived in the same region, and affectively, since the brother and sister are among the ghosts that haunt him. The second part hints at guilt and gestures toward a violent family history, linking the doomed family to that of the corrupt Valois line (and to their mother, Catherine de Medici) and using their warlike castle as the image of their cruelty. The third section continues the history with some brief allusions to horrible deeds committed by Ravalet ancestors, linking them to Marguerite and Julien's crime but also using them to demonstrate the relative lack of severity, even perhaps the ironic justice, of their actions. This section ends with the image of the red stocking, this time deliberately revealed by Marguerite as a provocation to the executioner. The fourth section begins with a discussion of the relationship between history and poetry, using the image of history as a tapestry that poetry pierces to reveal the truths that the weaving of history might cover. It continues with a discussion of the Ravalet castle, Tourlaville, and a portrait of Marguerite that the narrator places there and then "reads" as evidence of her mind-set, even though he has already labeled this history "impénétrable." The fifth section consists of a brief review of written evidence and ends with an image of two swans swimming on the castle's lake, evoking the doomed pair.

In this series of scenes, only a few elements of Rosset's story are repeated: the exceptional beauty of the couple, the scene of execution. He briefly mentions the adultery but reverses the severity of the two crimes: "Plus tard, on la força d'épouser ce messier Le Fauconnier, et c'est ainsi qu'elle introduisit l'adultère dans l'inceste; mais l'inceste dévora l'adultère, et des deux crimes fut le plus fort" (Later, they forced her to marry this Monsieur Le Fauconnier, and thus she combined adultery with incest; but incest consumed adultery, and of the two crimes incest was the stronger).[34] While Barbey gives pieces with which the story could be constructed, he does not offer a coherent narrative, choosing rather to give striking images and details of the story in a way that elicits both the reader's curiosity and suggests the distance between narrative accounts and any possible comprehension of events in this "histoire psychologiquement impénétrable."³⁵ Rosset tries to offer a well-organized, chronological narrative, one that nonetheless contains some dissonances, but Barbey's narration jumps back and forth in time, accumulates visual effects (the boudoir, the portrait, the swans) that do not exist in his intertext, and refuses any moralizing conclusion. In fact, the dénouement of the story, the execution, takes place in the third act, before the detailed description of the crime, which takes place in the fifth part.

In short, Barbey reworks the tragic form so as to transgress its rules and demonstrate the way in which tragedy constructs morality by organizing crime and punishment in chronological order, as if the latter is the inevitable result of the former. Vassilev raises the question of the potential effect of this theatricalization of the *nouvelle* form, relative to Barbey's story "Le bonheur dans le crime": "La question se pose de savoir si la théâtralisation de la nouvelle, présentée comme inhérente à l'intention d'édification, parvient à susciter le fonctionnement éthico-esthétique du système tragique, ou si elle l'enraye au contraire" (The question arises whether one can know if the theatricalisation of the *nouvelle*, presented as inherent to the intention to edify, succeeds in putting into play the ethico-aesthetique functioning of the tragic system, or if, on the contrary, it frustrates such functioning).³⁶ The problem with "Bonheur" is that no punishment follows the crime, thus raising the question of the universality of tragic moral structures. This violation of tragic norms is reflected in a narrative broken into what Vassilev calls "une pluralité de voix narratives" (a plurality of narrative voices) that blurs both the origins and the purpose of the narration.³⁷ The disrupted chronology and impressionistic collection of highly visually charged moments in "Une page d'histoire" mimic the plurality of narrative voices in "Bonheur" but also blur the tragic structures that are suggested but not adhered to with any consistency. Perhaps in the context of this uncertainty, only an affective response to aesthetic prompts is possible, thus distancing morality from the tale.

The effect of this series of scenes with their evocations of vivid visual moments is that of vignettes carefully stage-managed by the narrator, thus splitting the spectacle into at least two layers. On one level, the narrator presents us with what he wants us to see, not promising any truth or insights into events but commenting nonetheless on the scenes he offers. This gesture makes apparent the manipulations of the spectacles offered in order to evoke responses from the reader; it also calls into question the spectacles featuring Marguerite and Julien. These are often evoked by objects, not only the portrait but also the "petit lit de ce boudoir bleuâtre, dont le satin glacé était aussi froid qu'un banc de cimetière au clair de lune" (little bed in this bluish boudoir, whose glazed [or frozen] satin was as cold as a cemetery bench in the moonlight). In this same boudoir, the narrator sees the couple in the mirror but realizes that they will disappear when he is not present, thus suggesting the subjectivity of these spectral spectacles.[38] The reader cannot know whether an event as presented is true, only the effect it might have. Nonetheless, the effect is presented as having the force of a different sort of truth from that of historical events.

The separation of these narrative spectacles from the notion of historical truth or any meaning that might inform them also takes the ambivalence of Rosset's account in a slightly different direction, suggesting not that the beauty of the couple might excuse the crime but that the crime excuses itself by the very means of its own horror: "Cette histoire fut celle d'un amour et d'un bonheur tellement coupables que l'idée en épouvante ... et charme (que Dieu nous le pardonne!) de ce charme troublant et dangereux qui fait presque coupable l'âme qui l'éprouve et semble la rendre complice d'un crime peut-être, qui sait? Envieusement partagé" (This tale was one of a love and a happiness so guilty that the mere idea of it horrifies ... and charms—may God pardon us!—with that troubling and dangerous charm which makes the soul that feels it almost guilty and seems to render it an accomplice of a crime perhaps, who knows? Enviously shared).[39] Already the narrator seems to be seduced by the transgressive behavior of the beautiful couple rather than the beauty itself. Without the grounding in any notion of historical accuracy or higher meaning, the morality of the couple's actions is separated from their effect on the spectators, including the narrator. The monstrous becomes miraculous.

This transformation is written into the family history of the pair. As noted above, in the second and third sections of the story, Barbey d'Aurevilly emphasizes a family heritage permeated with sin and crime: "Le caractère le plus marquée de leur terrible race avait été une atroce impitoyabilité. . . . Quand ils s'avisaient d'être débauchés, c'était de la débauche qui va jusqu'au sang et jusqu'à la mort." (The most evident quality of their terrible race had been a horrifying pitilessness. . . . When they decided to be debauched, it was the debauchery that went as far as blood and as far as death).[40] One ancestor rapes and kills a young girl, another kills a priest, a third his own brother. Everyone in the region trembles at the thought of the monsters to come from this appalling family. "Mais cette horrible attente fut trompée. Les monstres qu'on attendait furent deux enfants de la plus pure beauté, qui sortirent tout à coup, un jour, comme deux roses, de cette mare de sang des Ravalet." (But this horrible anticipation was mistaken. The monsters that were awaited were two children of the purest beauty, who appeared all at once, one day, like two roses, in this pond of blood of the Ravalet family.)[41] They are the reverse of their ancestors: "Julien et Marguerite de Ravalet, ces deux enfants, beaux comme l'innocence, finirent par l'inceste la race fratricide de leur aïeul. Il avait été, lui, le Caïn de la haine. Ils furent, eux, les Caïns de l'amour, non moins fratricide que la haine." (Julien and Marguerite de Ravalet, these two children, as beautiful as innocence, ended through incest the fratricidal race of their ancestor. He had been, himself, the Cain of hatred. They were, themselves, the Cains of love, no less fratricidal than hatred).[42] Barbey lingers for quite some time on this irony of their crime, in that their love punishes their ancestors' hate.

Barbey mixes beauty and violence more eloquently and perversely than Rosset in his account of the execution (which he jumps to without going into long detail about the crime that led to such punishment):

> La grossière Tradition qui ne regarde pas dans les âmes, se trouve à bout de tout quand elle a écrit le mot indigné d'inceste et qu'elle a montré du doigt le billot où les deux incestueux couchèrent sous la hache leurs belles têtes, si belles, qu'elle-même, la brutale Tradition, les a trouvées belles, et que le seul détail qu'elle n'ait pas oublié, dans cette histoire psychologiquement impénétrable, tient à cette surprenante beauté.[43]
>
> (Crass Tradition, which does not see into souls, finds herself at the end of her rope when she writes the indignant word *incest* and when she points out the chopping block where the incestuous pair laid down under the axe their beautiful heads, so beautiful that even she, brutal Tradition, found them beautiful, and that the only detail that she did not forget in this psychologically impenetrable story, was this astonishing beauty.)

Here, the author repeats but also transforms a strategy used by Rosset: the indignation of Tradition at the criminal nature of this act is juxtaposed with the exceptional beauty of the pair, and beauty wins out over the traditional taboos, to the point of effacing the crime in favor of the beauty. The one detail carried down the generations by Tradition is an aesthetic one, which stands outside of the realm of facts or events.

In this context, Marguerite (the real name of the sister) also maintains some degree of agency to the very end in Barbey's version, using her beauty to manipulate not the outcome but the circumstances of her execution. One can only speculate about the relationship between her incest and her agency; once the laws of family and marriage are transgressed, perhaps she is free to reinvent herself as powerful, but the story offers only images without explanation. Nonetheless, she plays with the power of her beauty as she reveals her own red stocking, thus distracting the executioner, whom she then slaps to bring him back to his senses. This gesture suggests a level of control of the spectacle and self-control at the moment of death that both echoes and intensifies the effect of the confessions in Rosset's version, where, accepting death, the pair maintain a large degree of control over their audience. Death itself, in the form of the executioner, seems to be under the influence of her beauty and her anger.

The agency of beauty, or perhaps the beauty of agency, in the sense of having the power to rewrite the script in order to create a more emotionally striking outcome, is strongly linked to literature in this version of the story. For Barbey, this story is the domain of poets rather than of historians, whose knowledge is limited by the "facts" and documents they might be able to gather. After the anecdote of Marguerite slapping the executioner, which follows upon a series of imagined events on Barbey d'Aurevilly's part, he concludes the first, supposedly factual, portion of the story: "Et voilà tout ce que l'on sait de cette triste et cruelle histoire. Mais ce qui passionnerait bien davantage serait ce que l'on n'en sait pas!" (And there is everything that one knows about this sad and cruel story. But what would be much more enticing would be what one does not know!)[44] He imagines a Chateaubriand or a Byron telling this story: "C'est l'imagination des poètes qui perce l'épaisseur de la tapisserie historique ou qui la retourne, pour regarder ce qui est derrière cette tapisserie, fascinante par ce qu'elle nous cache" (It is the poets' imagination that pierces the thick tapestry of history, or that turns it over, to see what is behind this tapestry, fascinating because of what it hides from us).[45] In this passage, history is related to tradition in a way; it is about facts and laws and events; yet it does not reveal all but selects the details that fit its own agenda, that of chronology, progress, or whatever form of order deemed appropriate by the historian who weaves the tapestry. What is hidden from historical ordering of events, what remains incomprehensible—impenetrable—is penetrated by poetry. This image of literature as piercing the dense fabric of history, or turning it over to see what is underneath, links the transgressive nature of poetic imagination to the marvelously, beautifully, transgressive behavior of the incestuous pair.

From this moment on, Barbey inscribes a poetics of violence and loss into his fragmented retelling of the tale. He barely mentions the crime and is more focused on loss as he describes walking through the castle of Tourlaville, surrounded by the ghosts of a doomed family, observing the tattered remains around him "ces lambris semés d'inscriptions tragiquement amoureuses, et dans lesquelles l'orgueil d'une fatalité audacieusement accepté respire encore" (these panels covered with lovingly tragic inscriptions, and in which the pride of a destiny audaciously accepted still breathes).⁴⁶ He describes the portrait of Marguerite at some length: "Les cheveux sont blonds,—de ce blond familier aux filles de Normandie, qui a la couleur du blé mûr noirci par l'âpre chaleur solaire d'Août, et qui attend la faucille. Eux, ces cheveux mûrs aussi, mais pour une autre faucille, ne l'ont pas attendue longtemps!" (The hair is blond—of that blond common to the girls of Normandy, which has the color of ripened wheat darkened by the harsh sunny heat of August, and which awaits the scythe. This hair, also ripe, but for another scythe, which it did not await for long!).⁴⁷ This series of images oscillates between beauty and its loss, strangely imbuing the latter with the power of the former through juxtaposition, even while signaling the fragility of beauty by the images of its passing away.⁴⁸

Barbey focuses mostly on Marguerite and describes her as more admirable than the other "grandes Incestueuses de l'Histoire et de la Poésie.... Son crime, à elle, qui fut toute sa vie et qui date presque du berceau, elle le porte sans remords, sans tristesse et même sans orgeuil, avec l'indifférence d'une fatalité contre laquelle elle ne s'est jamais révoltée" (the great incestuous women of History and of Poetry.... Her crime, which was her entire life and which began almost in the cradle, she carried without remorse, without sorrow, and even without pride, with the indifference of a destiny against which she never revolted.)⁴⁹ Only some letters sent to her brother expose her passion. There is a sense of her agency, her willful participation in her own crime; she is not swept away by it or by any of the emotions that might have surrounded it but accepts it and her death deliberately.

The author turns this agency, this power to act, toward that of literature, which shapes its own version of events, not beholden to history or to ugly Tradition. Barbey finishes his account of this crime and its punishment with a description of the castle:

> Le château, dont alors on réparait les ruines, que j'aurais laissées, moi, dans leur poésie de ruines, car on ne badigeonne pas la mort, souvent plus belle que la vie, ce château a les pieds dans un lac verdâtre que le vent du soir plissait à mille plis.... C'était l'heure du crépuscule. Deux cygnes nageaient sur ce lac où il n'y avait qu'eux, non pas à distance l'un de l'autre, mais pressés, tassés l'un contre l'autre comme s'ils avaient été frère et sœur, frémissants sur cette eau frémissante. Ils auraient fait penser aux deux âmes des derniers Ravalets, parties et revenues sous cette forme charmante; mais ils étaient trop blancs pour être l'âme du frère et de la sœur coupables. Pour le croire, il aurait fallu qu'ils fussent noirs et que leur superbe cou fût ensanglanté.⁵⁰

(The castle, the ruins of which were being repaired, ruins which I would have left, myself, in their poetry of ruins, for one does not patch up death, often more beautiful than life, this castle has its feet in a greenish lake that the evening wind folded into a thousand pleats.... It was the hour of dusk. Two swans swam on the lake, where they were alone, not at a distance from each other, but pressed up against each other, even piled on top of each other, as if they had been brother and sister, trembling on the trembling water. They would have made one think of the two souls of the last of the Ravalet family, gone and returned in this charming form, but they were too white to be the soul of the guilty brother and sister. To believe this, they would have had to be black, and their haughty necks bloody.)

What color are the swans? When I ask my students this question and tell them they cannot look at the story, they always remember the swans as being black, with bloody necks. The internal "reality" of the story, itself a construct, is replaced with an imaginary one, more vivid than ordinary reality but also reminding us that reality is not always as present as poetic representation might lead us to believe. In this conclusion to the story, we are led to understand the effect of literature, which can lead us to see what is not even there, and thus which can raise the dead and give them power over us—even if they might not ever have really existed. Literature haunts us with beings that might not even be there but remain at our elbow, guiding us along. This is literature's transgression.

While "Une page d'histoire" seems to focus at certain moments on acceptance of fate or destiny, the figure of the narrator or author rewrites this understanding of agency, this ability to control perception, as he evokes the continual presence of the long-dead couple (as well as the dead in general at the beginning of the tale). As in Rosset's account, it is the pair's, particularly Marguerite's, acceptance of death that makes the spectators at the execution marvel. Their exceptional crime leads inevitably to their death, but that crime and that death immortalize them forever. This immortality has an aesthetic of its own that reinforces the beauty of the crime; the narrator offers images covered in darkness and shadow, darkness that enhances rather than effaces the striking beauty of the couple and of their crime. As he says, death is "often more beautiful than life." He prefers that the castle remain in ruins, just as the narrative exists only in pieces, as the sign of that which remains lost and cannot be recuperated by history, and perhaps not even literature.[51] But the horrible "crime" and the miraculous beauty of the pair remains. In this, Barbey d'Aurevilly seems to subvert the course of moralizing histories that promote tradition over individual freedom and agency.

Of course, Barbey is a perverse writer if one wants to think of him in conventional terms; after all, he is the author who proposes the possibility of "Happiness in Crime" in *Les diaboliques*,[52] refuting the moralizing tales of crime and punishment. But the terrifying beauty of "Une page d'histoire" presents the death and loss of Marguerite and Julien de Ravalet as far more alluring and poetic than any aspect of their life, including their crime, which is barely discussed in the story. The possibility of agency in the face of inevitable destiny, the acceptance of death, frees the couple to exercise limited and yet powerful agency over the staging of that death, making it harrowingly beautiful and inscribing it in the minds of both spectators and readers for centuries to come.

## Notes

1. This collection can be found in the *Œuvres romanesques complètes*, ed. Jacques Petit (Paris: Gallimard, 1966), vol. 2, 9–264. "Une page d'histoire," not a part of *Les diaboliques*, was first published in *Gil Blas*, December 26, 1882; it is also to be found in the second volume of the *Œuvres romanesques complètes*.

2. For an analysis of Barbey d'Aurevilly's representation of the aristocracy in the context of his larger body of work, see Alice de Georges-Métral, *Les illusions de l'écriture, ou la crise de la représentation dans l'œuvre romanesque de Jules Barbey d'Aurevilly* (Paris: Champion, 2007).

3. For more on this subject, see Jean-Claude Arnould, "La justice au banc d'essai des Histoires tragiques," *Cahiers des recherches médiévales et humanists (Journal of Medieval and Humanistic Studies)* 19 (2010): 287–97.

4. François de Rosset, *Les histoires mémorables et tragiques de ce temps (1619)*, ed. Anne du Vaucher Gravili (Paris: Livre de Poche, 1994), 206–21. All translations of this text in this essay are my own.

5. Also in the *Œuvres romanesques complètes*, 365–78.

6. Pierre de L'Estoile, *Mémoires-Journaux: 1574–1611*, vol. 8, *Journal de Henri IV: 1602–1607*, ed. G. Brunet et al. (Paris: Librairie des Bibliophiles, 1880; reproduction, Librairie Jules Tallandier, 1982), 108. All translations of this text in this essay are my own.

7. In Maurice Lever, *Canards sanglants: naissance du fait divers* (Paris: Fayard, 1993), 103–10; original publication in Paris: Philippe du Pré, 1604. All translations of this text in this essay are my own.

8. *Supplice d'un frère et sœur*, 109.

9. Sara McDougall, in her article "The Making of Marriage in Medieval France," *Journal of Family History* 38 (2013): 103–21, asserts that there was "a clear pattern of behavior in which violations of incest prohibitions were broadly ignored" (114). Incest

prohibitions were quite broad until 1215 but not generally enforced; even when they were narrowed considerably, there was a great deal of room for maneuver (115). This is also the way in which the affair is presented by the contemporary accounts, and in one of the few books on the subject: Michel Carmona's *Une affaire d'inceste: Julien et Marguerite de Ravalet* (Paris: Fayard, 1987), so it seems that the medieval practices carried over well into the early modern period.

10. Maureen Quilligan, *Incest and Agency in Elizabeth's England* (Philadelphia: University of Pennsylvania Press, 2005), 10–11.

11. Ibid., 12

12. Ibid., 16.

13. Ibid., 23.

14. Ibid., 24.

15. Mitchell B. Merback, "Pain and Spectacle: Rituals of Punishment in Late Medieval Europe," in *The Thief, the Cross, and the Wheel: Pain and the Spectacle of Punishment in Medieval and Renaissance Europe* (Chicago: University of Chicago Press, 1998), 126–57.

16. Paul Friedland, *Seeing Justice Done: The Age of Spectacular Capital Punishment in France* (Oxford: Oxford University Press, 2012), particularly the section titled "Spectators and Spectacle," 119–91.

17. Merback, "Pain and Spectacle," 127.

18. Paul Friedland, "From Ritual to Spectacle: The Rise of the Penal Voyeur in Early Modern France," in *Seeing Justice Done*, by Friedland, 136 and 139.

19. Ibid., 136.

20. Rosset, *Les histoires mémorables et tragiques de ce temps* (1619), 209.

21. Kris Vassilev, "Théâtralité et narration: Le bonheur dans le crime de Barbey d'Aurevilly," *Cahiers de Narratologie* [online], 14 (2008): 3. All translations of this text in this essay are my own.

22. Ibid., 2.

23. Astrée Ruciak, "Autour de François de Rosset: La dimension monstrueuse dans les *Histoires tragiques*," *Réforme, Humanisme, Renaissance* 84 (2017): 73. All translations of this text in this essay are my own. This passage echoes the belief expressed in a number of treatises on monsters (monstrous bodies in particular), that Africa was the zone where monsters where created. See, for example, Jean Riolan, *Discours sur les hermaphrodits: Où il est demonstré contre l'opinion commune, qu'il n'y a point de vrays hermaphrodits* (Paris: Pierre Ramier, 1614), 1 (sig. A): "On dit que l'Africque produit tousjours quelque monstre nouveau." See also Rosset, *Les histoires mémorables et tragiques de ce temps* (1619), 207.

24. Rosset, *Les histoires mémorables et tragiques de ce temps* (1619), 207–8.

25. Ibid., 208.

26. Ibid., 208–9.

27. Ibid., 209–10.

28. Ibid., 213.

29. Claire Esnault, "Les scènes de supplice dans les *Histoires mémorables et tragiques* de François de Rosset," *Réforme, Humanisme, Renaissance* 73 (2011): 133. All translations of this text in this essay are my own.

30. Ibid., 133.
31. Rosset, *Les histoires mémorables et tragiques de ce temps (1619)*, 219.
32. Ibid., 219–20.
33. Ibid., 220.
34. Barbey d'Aurevilly, *Œuvres romanesques complètes*, 377. It should be remembered that the Napoleonic Code abolished laws against incest, although the legal response throughout the nineteenth century was more complex than this, with some protections in place for minors abused by those in authority over them (see Fabienne Giuliani, "Monsters in the Village? Incest in Nineteenth-Century France," *Journal of Social History* 42 [2009]: 919–32; see, in particular, 919–20). For a comprehensive history of incest in early modern France, see Elisabeth Clavarie and Pierre Lamaison, *L'Impossible marriage: Violence et parenté en Gévaudan, XVIIe, XVIIIe, et XIXe siècles* (Paris: Hachette, 1982).
35. Barbey d'Aurevilly, *Œuvres romanesques complètes*, 372. References to this author are to his *Œuvres romanesques complètes* unless otherwise noted. All translations of this text in this essay are my own.
36. Vassilev, "Théâtralité et narration," 3.
37. Ibid., 5.
38. Barbey d'Aurevilly, *Œuvres romanesques complètes*, 374.
39. Ibid., 368.
40. Ibid., 370.
41. Ibid., 371.
42. Ibid.
43. Ibid., 372.
44. Ibid., 373.
45. Ibid.
46. Ibid., 374.
47. Ibid., 375.
48. For an excellent reading of the poetics of these passages in particular, see Joyce O. Lowrie, "Barbey d'Aurevilly's *Une page d'histoire*: A Poetics of Incest," *Romanic Review* 90 (1990): 379–95.
49. Barbey d'Aurevilly, *Œuvres romanesques complètes*, 375–76.
50. Ibid., 378.
51. Armand Colin writes about Barbey's preference for ruins in his article "Restaurer, réparer: Barbey d'Aurevilly," *Littérature* 147 (2007): 54–68; the discussion of "Une page d'histoire" takes place on 67–68.
52. "Le bonheur dans le crime," *Les diaboliques*, in *Œuvres romanesques complètes*, vol. 2, 81–128.

# Solution and Dissolution
## Zayas's Darkening Threads

"The Dark Thread" examined in this volume recalls a terrifying genealogy of somber strands: from Crete, where Ariadne hands Theseus a thread by which he might perhaps survive and find his way out of the labyrinth, to the thread spun and severed by the three Fates who determine one's moment of death, or the sinister anointed thread of Celestina, when she conjures the Devil so that she can work her diabolical charms. (Today we are still captivated by threads—for example, email threads, because they, too, can command an awesome power.)

Though separated by more than eighty years, the short stories of Marguerite de Navarre's *Héptameron* (1558) and María de Zayas's *Novelas amorosas y ejemplares* (Amorous and exemplary tales) of 1637 and her *Desengaños amorosos* (Amorous disenchantments), published in 1647, share notable features—both formal and interpretive. It is important to differentiate the enterprises of each author and her response to the cultural climate in which she wrote, but I would like to indicate at this point that Zayas was an avid reader of Navarre and the models that inspired her to write. Like her predecessor, Zayas was steeped in the narratives of Boccaccio and Bandello, among others, in addition to sharing her identity as a noblewoman writing at a time when, for both authors, female authorship and publication were still daring ventures—especially given the salacious nature of their domestic narratives that claim to be incriminatingly true stories.

Whether we are dealing with what Thomas Pavel calls the "casuistic," psychologically focused *novella* based on deceptive reasoning and the perversion of morality or the "Augustinian" *novella* that dwells on the passions of the self-blinded lover—human nature and epistemology are the intense focus of both women writers.[1] I will focus most of my analysis on Zayas's appropriation of the *Héptameron*'s celebrated tales 32 and 43, but I would first like to offer a bit of information on Zayas's context before moving to my observations on her rethinking of these two tales that she conflates in her *Tarde llega el desengaño* (*Too Late Undeceived*), the fourth of her *Disenchantments*.

During her lifetime (1590–1661), Zayas was—by far—the most successful female author in Spain. Even more striking is the fact that her book sales were surpassed only by those of Cervantes, Quevedo, and Alemán.[2] Given the paucity of women writers in seventeenth-century Spain and also the undisputed brilliance of these three male authors, her publication record is truly exceptional. Outside of Spain she was published and translated widely—as well as having her masterfully woven stories misattributed to Cervantes, Scarron, and others. Paradoxically, however, though she was such a literary celebrity, virtually nothing is known about her life because of her own "dark thread"—that is her cohabitation for a time with the well-known playwright Ana Caro in Madrid.[3]

A writer of novellas, poetry, and theater, Zayas was, in fact, famous long before her twenty stories were published. Lope de Vega referred to her as "la inmortal María de Zayas" (the immortal María de Zayas), and Castillo Solórzano and others identified her as the "Sibyl of Madrid."[4] This repeated identification as "sibyl" makes sense given that her stories disclose the decay of the Spanish empire. In the prologues, epilogues and incidental remarks of her narrator, as well as commentaries of her inscribed storytellers and auditors, Zayas acquires a decidedly sibylline persona. While often laconic, she is consumed with a desire to expose abuses regarding issues of nationhood and empire, gender, class and race relations by corrupt practitioners—primarily the men who do not measure up to society's hallowed principles of virtue, honor, and related civic and family values.

Though many writers turn to the domestic scene in their theatrical as well as novelistic writing, Zayas is universally recognized for the excessiveness of her predation and gore in the victimization of virtually all the innocent women we encounter in her prose. She chooses this lurid form in keeping with the tabloid craze that gripped the reading public of her day. As Henry Ettinghausen observes, tabloids—*relatos de sucesos y avisos*—were "the most widely consumed form of reading in sixteenth- and seventeenth-century

Spain."⁵ Etymologically, the term "tabloid" was invented by a British pharmaceutical company in 1887, referring to "a small, flat, or compressed piece of a solid substance (especially a medical or chemical one), a tablet." Also, "compressed: concentrated, especially in order to be easily assimilated; sensationalistic; of or resembling tabloid journalism."⁶

Zayas's narratives have rightly been described as "linear" and "brief." This is the transparent style of tabloid, but paradoxically, she also consistently exploits the complex style of the *estilo culto*.⁷ Her work is filled with thematic incongruities as well, for example, her incongruous placement of verses dedicated to the flea (*la pulga*), immediately after the gruesome events narrated in *La fuerza del amor* (*The Power of Love*).

Zayas is known for her sadistic portrayals, narratives dealing with rape, torture, mutilation, and murder of the goriest kind. In fact, her stories are frequently more extreme in their violence than the prose of her male contemporaries. The excess registered by Zayas's violent prose has often scandalized nineteenth- and twentieth-century critics of her *Novelas*, the twenty stories which, by their relentless sadism verge on the pornographic, with case after case of victimized females. This predatory nature of sexual relations as depicted by Zayas, characterized by male predation and female victimization, has been a fruitful area of study in recent years. Outspoken authorial remarks as well as those of her inscribed narrators and auditors offer pointed indictments of official discourses and practices ranging from the theory and practice of matrimony to personal and familial honor, to state policies regarding race, religion, and class.

Yet, more than one message is at issue in Zayas's novellas. As Paul Smith explains of human nature in general and of the expression of subjectivity in particular—irrespective of historical period, "a person is not simply determined and dominated by the ideological pressures of any overarching discourse or ideology, but is also the agent of a certain discernment."⁸ No one is more aware of the staggering potential of human complexity and agency than Zayas, who understands and is committed to representing the diversity of human response. Angela Carter—a twentieth-century kindred spirit—expresses this idea in the female register by saying: "The notion of a universality of human experience is a confidence trick and the notion of a universality of a female experience is a clever confidence trick."⁹ Zayas, like Carter, appreciates the need to recast the (traditional, reductionist hence impoverishing) literary representations of relations between the sexes so as to represent more accurately both male and female fantasy and facilitation. Each of these women sees the representation of sex and violence as a valuable pedagogical tool.

Aware of this potential for literary violence as a means of social rethinking, Zayas exploits what Carter calls "moral pornography"—that is, a form of pornographic discourse that aims at promoting not sexual exploitation but its opposite—a critique of relations between the sexes operative in seventeenth-century Spanish society that has the potential to change the reader's perception of the word and of its officially sanctioned myths and abuses.

We tend to view "morality" and "pornography" as antithetical terms. Yet Carter advances a provocative pairing of these terms and the mentalities they represent that merits our consideration. By way of defining pornography, Carter writes that "pornography, like marriage and the fictions of romantic love, assists the process of false universalizing."[10] Simply stated, the "universalizing" tendency of pornography consists in its reductionist view of female (and also male) sexuality, whereby woman functions almost exclusively as, in Carter's words, "the fringed hole," and man as "the probe" that awaits her. The stunningly reductionist representation of subjectivity at issue in pornographic writing is clear; the positing of archetypal abstractions that have little to do with our daily lives, even in the sexual domain. As Carter explains: "We do not go to bed in simple pairs; even if we choose not to refer to them, we still drag there with us the cultural impediments of our social class, our parents' lives, our bank balances, our sexual and emotional expectations, our whole biographies."[11] Pornography can be harnessed for constructive purposes—recast into a positive social discourse, by offering an exposé that takes the form of an explicitly negative example. Zayas understood its ability to expose and critique the normative state of relations between the sexes. Indeed, she presents herself as a "moral pornographer"—an authorial stance which has, for many years, confounded readers.

Speaking of some of the more lurid and graphically repulsive details she writes into her text, the eminent twentieth-century German literary historian Ludwig Pfandl judged Zayas's work to be without redeeming value: "Can there be anything more gross and obscene, more non-aesthetic and repulsive, than a woman who writes lascivious, dirty, sadistic, and morally corrupt stories?"[12] Otis Green, in his monumental *Spain and the Western Tradition*, also registered disapproval of her tales for their inclusion of pornographic detail.[13] Likewise, it is no accident that the nineteenth-century novelist Juan Valera includes in one of his novels, *El comendador Mendoza*, a spinster who locks herself in her bedroom in order to savor the forbiddingly exciting stories written by Zayas—that no respectable lady would ever consider reading.

Beyond this prudish response registered by a few male critics, Zayas's graphic violence has elicited radically different interpretations: that she writes tales celebrating the *status quo* of Christian marriage and the need for decorous behavior,[14] that she writes cautionary tales designed to terrify women readers—especially wives who will judge their own domestic environments to be desirable by comparison with the gruesomely terrifying conditions endured by Zayas's females (that they will "thank their lucky stars"),[15] or that she writes to denounce the gender abuses of the so-called honor code.[16] And while each of these views is inscribed in her text, she engages in such representation of violence perhaps to an equal degree as a way of selling books—by cashing in on the "tabloid craze" that gripped the Spanish readers of her day. She is a supremely baroque thinker—committed to polysemy rather than the projection of one given ideological script.

A brief enumeration of the subjects contained within the pages of Zayas's text reveal their clearly sensationalist intent: torture, rape, dismemberment, murder, male as well as female cross-dressing, lesbian desire as well as male homosexuality, not to mention controversial treatments of race, ethnicity, and nationalism. In addition to victimized females (usually chaste wives), we find also—and this tends not to be highlighted in Zayas criticism—less frequently, but clearly visible, libidinous females who abuse their lovers or husbands and occasionally other women as well, in thoroughly reprehensible ways.

Zayas's violent, often lurid tales feed the craving for tabloid literature that characterized her reading public. She is often cited for her gendered perspective, whereby her stories obsessively detail abuses of the patriarchal structure. One wonders, however, who was buying and reading her? Given the overwhelmingly male literacy rate in Spain, if she was bent on exposing state-sanctioned cruelty, male heads of household would surely not purchase her texts or let them circulate among the women in their domestic sphere. Not to mention—as several critics have—that the sheer mass of violence done to women as represented in Golden Age literature does not conform to fact: it is grossly exaggerated.

Representation of this violence points to transference or sublimation of some kind—it represents something other than what it appears to represent. It figures the fear, both the politically sanctioned variety (the *auto-da-fe* mentality) and its subversive opposite—the emergence of the fragmented subject that interrogates its role amid and against the discourses of the state. The very identity of "Spanishness" in terms of race, class, and gender, along with the complexities they represent individually and collectively, were undeniably at stake.[17]

Like the tabloid press, Zayas plays on the fear and fascination at issue as the modern subject struggles to define itself in relation to the official, totalizing discourses of the state. The passion for this journalism emerges as a result of the increased interest in historical immediacy, or a semblance thereof, rather than the historically nonimmediate. Nonetheless, much of the material presented as historically accurate is patently false, most concerned with upholding sensationalism. (Eyewitness attestations of a 380-year-old Bengali man, the Turkish boy born with three eyes and three horns, etc., are indicative of these accounts.) And Boaistuau's *Histoires prodigieuses* (1561) are cut from the same cloth.

And even if a tabloid offers an explicitly moralizing message, it often serves (as so many of the *novelas* of the period do) as a smokescreen designed to endow the narrative with a veneer of propriety. It is a form of sublimation of the historically real, empirically experienced societal chaos of seventeenth-century Spanish life onto people and events found in print. It offers a measure of solace or contentment to the reader who considers him or herself fortunate not to have suffered similar catastrophes. Yet it also offers pleasure—a pleasurable escape that results from the voyeurism of forbidden, private, and compromising situations—a dimension of which Zayas was acutely aware.

Like the interpretive polysemy we see in the tabloid, Zayas is polysemous in her representations of social, political, racial, sexual, and gender categories, and the issue of white-black relations is a prime example of her nuanced appreciation of human subjectivity and its manifold complexities. Slavery is, of course, always a fascinating and lamentable phenomenon, one which Zayas addresses in conflicting ways. Many of her stories begin with an enumeration of the slaves—white and black (as well as the occasional eunuch)—in the service of a given household. She does not comment explicitly on this *status quo* phenomenon, yet she does, in the case of two of her stories, interrogate interracial relations provocatively. Amid the existence of white and black slaves owned by various masters, we find depicted in *El prevenido engañado* (*Forewarned but Not Forearmed*) (1:4) the widow who fends off a suitor, invoking as the reason for her behavior the obligatory year of celibacy to which she adheres in deference to the memory of her dead husband. What we learn from her suitor's surveillance, however, is the real reason for her reluctance to comply with his advances, namely, that she is shamelessly involved with her slave, a black man. Far from being the bereaved widow, she is the cause of the slave's death, which occurs as a result of her monstrous sexual appetite.

The scene is striking both in terms of gender and class since it figures women as being potentially as libidinous and predatory as men. Yet, given the relentlessness of her excess, the widow seems even more sinister. The fact that her partner is sick adds to the repugnance of this impression. That the tables are turned—with the woman sexually abusing a man rather than the normative male predator—offers a comment on the abuse of women, as well as a meditation on class difference; usually it is the male head of household who takes advantage of a powerless female servant.

The shock value of this black-white liaison also reflects the obsession with blood purity that had been official policy in Spain with respect to Jews and then Muslims. Here the white woman seems demonic by comparison with her reluctant, God-fearing black partner whose dying words implore his mistress to marry legitimately: "Qué me quieres señora? ¡Déjame ya, por Dios! ¿ Qué es esto, que aun estando yo acabando la vida me persigues? No basta que tu viciosa condición me tiene como estoy, sino que quieres que cuando ya estoy en el fin de mi vida, acuda a cumplir tus viciosos apetitos. Cásate, señora, cásate, y déxame ya a mí, que no te quiero ver, ni comer lo que me das; morir quiero, pues ya no estoy para otra cosa."[18] (What do you want of me, madam? Leave me alone, for the love of God! How can you pursue me even as I lay dying? Isn't it enough that your lasciviousness has brought me to this end? Even now you want me to satisfy your vicious appetites when I am breathing my last? Get yourself a husband, madam, marry, and leave me in peace. I never want to see you again! I won't touch the food you bring me; I want only to die, that's all I'm good for now.)[19] He is presented as morally superior. And the implications for both colonizer and colonized in the New World venture are as clear as the implications for Spanish racial intolerance at home. Zayas's message is hard to miss.

A different instance of racial anxiety surfaces in her *Tarde llega el desengaño* (*Too Late Undeceived*), a narrative modeled on Marguerite de Navarre's *Héptameron* tales 32 and 43. In the first of the well-known French tales, a wife commits adultery, as a result of which she is punished by her husband. To signal her ignominy, her husband shaves her head as well as hanging the deceased lover's skeleton in the defiled bedroom, to which she is confined. The husband intends this as perpetual punishment until a visitor convinces him that the lady's sincere contrition should suffice to reinstate her as his wife. She is reintegrated into the husband's life, their marriage is restored, they produce heirs, and live out their lives harmoniously. For her part, Zayas offers her readers a lurid remake of this move from conjugal estrangement to reconciliation. The visitor—here named don Martín—whose ship is blown off course and lands him on Grand Canary Island. Soon after his arrival, a man named Jaime offers to lodge Martín as he recovers from the harrowing voyage. The guest is unprepared, however, for the grim spectacle that lies in store.

As they are being seated for dinner, Jaime opens a small locked door from which a beautiful but very pale woman named Elena emerges, carrying a skull that serves as her drinking cup. This skull recalls Marguerite's repentant adulteress from tale 32, but with the notable difference that Elena is not adulterous. At this point, another woman enters the room; she is black and described as demonic in appearance: "Si no era el demonio . . . debía ser su retrato" (185) (If she wasn't the devil, she was his very likeness" [146]). The description of this woman's ugliness is contrasted with her beautiful dress and splendid jewels. We learn that she had formerly been a slave (along with four white slaves) in Jaime's employ—until she told him that Elena was committing adultery with her cousin, whom Jaime had taken in and treated like a son.

The black woman's words are, however, mendacious; she lies simply to get revenge against Elena's cousin, on whom she herself had designs, though he ignores her. Believing her story, Jaime elevates her to Elena's former status, giving her all of his wife's exquisite jewels and gowns, even feeding her from his plate, while Elena hunts under the table for the bones and scraps that are not worthy of the dogs:

> Se sentaron todos; la negra, a su lado, y don Martín y su camarada enfrente, tan admirados y divertidos en mirarla, que casi no se acordaban de comer, notando el caballero la suspensión, mas no porque dejase de regular y acariciar a su negra y endemoniada dama, dándole los mejores bocados de su plato, y la desdichada belleza que estaba debajo de la mesa, los huesos y mendrugos, que aun para los perros no eran buenos, que como tan necesitada de sustento, los roía como si fuera uno de ellos. (186)

(They all seated themselves, the gentleman beside the negress and don Martín and his companions across the table from them. The two guests were so amazed and distracted by the sight of her that they could hardly eat. Their host noted their amazement but that didn't make him desist from his continuous and affectionate attentions to his diabolical black lady. He picked out the tastiest morsels from his plate for her while he gave crusts and bones not fit even for a dog to the ill-fated beauty beneath the table. Ravenously she gnawed at them as if she were a dog. [147])

And it is at this point that Jaime explains the hideous spectacle. While he had been in Flanders, he received a message from a lady who wanted to meet him while keeping her identity secret. Jaime is blindfolded and led to her house, and, though the blindfold is removed, it is so dark during their tryst that he cannot see her face. They meet in this way for more than a month, and after each meeting he is given jewels and money in exchange for the sexual favors, like a male prostitute. In similar fashion, the sadistic treatment of Elena by her husband and his replacement of her by the black woman must have been equally scandalous.

Because Jaime is determined to learn the identity of his partner, he uses a bloody sponge to leave a trail to the lady's house. (This recalls—in a gorier key—the chalk on the back of Jambique's dress in *Héptameron* 43, by which her identity is revealed.) The lady—named Lucrecia—sends six henchmen to kill him, but he somehow survives being shot and stabbed. It is at that point that he meets and marries Elena (a Lucrecia look-alike). Suddenly, the black woman becomes mortally ill, confessing Elena's innocence and her own perfidy as she expires. Jaime stabs her and runs to beg Elena's forgiveness, but it is too late. She is dead, he goes mad, and Martín marries his beloved cousin, convinced of the need to disbelieve wicked servants. The narrator of this tale—Filis—concludes by pointing out the consummate cruelty of men. The horrific suffering inflicted by Jaime on his innocent wife is certainly despicable and unwarranted, but Filis's categorical condemnation of men fails to convince since none of this would have happened if the lustful Lucrecia had not seduced Jaime. Even more nefarious and destructive is, of course, the black woman's vicious lie—the immediate cause of Elena's martyrdom.

In addition to her function as a study in female evil, Zayas extends this meditation on villainy and lust in woman by bestowing the name Lucrecia (a byword for uxorial chastity and self-sacrifice) upon a character of tremendous—and tremendously transgressive—sexual appetites. And while not writing approvingly of her character, Zayas clearly enjoys registering for her reader the great potential that exists in female fantasy and facilitation. It is a bold and racy exposé. Elena is, similarly, the opposite of her classical namesake, Helen of Troy, the devastating beauty who was at the same time horribly divisive and deceitful. This Elena is instead a paragon of chastity and passive suffering.

By the juxtaposition of these two women and by the inversion of their legendary associations, Zayas underscores the error of typecasting. She also signals the impoverishing gesture involved in assigning one ethical abstraction to a given character, designating one exclusive significance to each narrative as traditional *exempla* do.

If we want to identify male cruelty toward women as the lesson, then what of the two female villains who set Elena's suffering in motion? On the positive side, the tale convinces Martín more than ever to beware the words of deceitful servants, and Jaime's terminal insanity caused by remorse also mitigates the message that Filis advances. It is excess—here in both senses: excess of lust, which leads to the sequence of horrific events that culminates in an excess or surplus of meaning. Thus, it is no surprise that Zayas chooses the name "Lysis" for the book's master of ceremonies, the Greek *contranym* "Lysis" (λύσις)—meaning both solution and dissolution.

## Notes

1. Thomas Pavel, "The Novel in Search of Itself," in *The Novel: Forms and Themes*, ed. Franco Moretti (Princeton, N.J.: Princeton University Press, 2007), 2:3–31.

2. See Agustín de Amezúa, ed. *Novelas amorosas y ejemplares de doña María de Zayas* (Madrid: Aldus, 1948), xxxi.

3. Castillo Solórzano refers to this close friendship in *La garduña de Sevilla*: "Acompáñala en Madrid doña Ana Caro de Mallén, dama de nuestra Sevilla," ed. Federico Ruiz Morcuende (Madrid: Espasa-Calpe, 1957), 67. Of this, M. Serrano Sanz writes, "Tuvo estrecha amistad con doña María de Zayas, y aun parece vivió en su compañía" (She was a close friend of doña María de Zayas, and it even seems that she lived with her). Cited from *Apuntes para una biblioteca de escritoras españolas* (Madrid, 1903–5), 1:177–79.

4. "¡Oh! Dulces Hipocrémides hermosas,/las espinas pangegeas/aprisa desnudad, y de las rosas/tejed ricas guirnaldas y trofeos/a la inmortal doña María de Zayas,/que sin pasar a Lesbos ni a las playas/ vasto mar Egeo/que hoy llora el negro velo de Teseo/ a Safo gozará Millenea" (Oh, sweet, beautiful Hipocrémides, quickly remove the Pangaion thorns and weave lovely garlands and trophies to the immortal doña María de Zayas who, without visiting Lesbos or the beaches of the vast Aegean Sea that now laments Theseus' black sail, will enjoy the Mytilean

Sappho), in Lope de Vega, *Laurel de Apolo: Colección de obras sueltas, assí en prosa como en verso de Frey Lope Félix de Vega Carpio* (Madrid: Antonio de Sancha, 1776), 165.

5. For the importance of claiming historical veracity, see Henry Ettinghausen, "The Illustrated Spanish News: Text and Image in the Seventeenth-Century Press," in *Art and Literature in Spain: 1600–1800. Studies in Honor of Nigel Glendinning,* ed. Charles Davis and Paul Julian Smith (London: Tamesis, 1993), 117–33. On the sensationalist tabloid literature of the day, see Henry Ettinghausen, "Sexo y violencia: Noticias sensacionalistas en la prensa española del siglo XVII," *Edad de Oro* 12 (1993): 95–107; his *Noticias del siglo XVII: Relaciones españolas de sucesos naturales y sobrenaturales* (Barcelona: Puvill, 1992); and Agustín Redondo, "Les 'relaciones de sucesos' dans l'Espagne du Siècle d'Or: Un moyen priviligié de transmission culturelle," *Cahiers de l'UFR d'Etudes Ibériques et Latino-Americaines* 7 (1989): 55–67. See also Robin Ann Rice, "Irrational Baroque Thought: Violence, Lovesickness and the Supernatural in *Tales of Disillusion* (1647) by María de Zayas," *Studia Metodologiczne* 35 (2015): 49–62.

6. *Oxford English Dictionary Online.*

7. See Paul Julian Smith, "Writing Women in Golden Age Spain: Saint Teresa and María de Zayas," *Modern Language Notes* 102 (1987): 238.

8. Paul Smith, *Discerning the Subject* (Minneapolis: University of Minnesota Press, 1988), xxxv.

9. Angela Carter writes about victimized females and sensationalist violence against them in relation to the Marquis de Sade, yet in a way that illuminates a reading of Zayas. See her *The Sadeian Woman and the Ideology of Pornography* (New York: Pantheon, 1979), 23. Her rewriting of classic fairy tales from a feminist perspective that takes into account the diversity of female agency is also relevant in connection with Zayas's enterprise (see *The Bloody Chamber* [New York: Penguin, 1992]).

10. Carter, *The Sadeian Woman and the Ideology of Pornography,* 12.

11. Ibid., 9.

12. Ludwig Pfandl, *Historia de la literature nacional Española en la Edad de Oro,* trans. Rubió Balaguer (Barcelona: Sucesores de Juan Gili, 1933), 370.

13. Green refers to a number of her stories as "pornographic." See his *España y la tradición occidental,* trans. C. Sánchez Gil (Madrid: Gredos, 1969), 4:164. For an insightful recent book on Zayas, see Eavan O'Brian, *Women in the Prose of María de Zayas* (Woodbridge, Suffolk: Tamesis, 2015).

14. Marcia Welles, "María de Zayas y Sotomayor and Her Novela Cortesana: A Re-evaluation," *Bulletin of Hispanic Studies* 55 (1978): 301–10.

15. Alessandra Melloni, *Il sistema narrative di María de Zayas* (Turin: Quaderni Ibero-Americani, 1976).

16. María de Zayas, *The Enchantments of Love: Amorous and Exemplary Novels,* trans. H. Patsy Boyer (Berkeley: University of California Press, 1990); María

de Zayas, *The Disenchantments of Love*, trans. H. Patsy Boyer (Albany: State University of New York Press, 1997). All English citations in this essay refer to these translations.

17. For a useful discussion of "Spanishness" in the Golden Age, see George Mariscal, *Contradictory Subjects: Quevedo, Cervantes, and Seventeenth-Century Spanish Culture* (Ithaca: Cornell University Press, 1991).

18. All citations from Zayas's Spanish refer to the *Novelas amorosas y ejemplares o 'Decamerón' español*, ed. Eduardo Rincón (Madrid: Alianza, 1980); and Alicia Yllera, ed., *Parte segunda del Sarao y entretenimiento honesto (Desengaños amorosos)* (Madrid: Cátedra, 1983).

19. Zayas, *The Disenchantments of Love*, trans. Boyer, 127–28.

MARÍA TAUSIET

# Evil Mothers
## From Devouring Witches to Deadly Ghosts

Since time immemorial, both the figure of the mother and, in particular, the inherent power of motherhood have sparked ambivalent emotional reactions, ranging from adoration to deep-rooted fear.[1] In antiquity, the conflicting elements of motherhood became fused in female deities who combined loving aspects such as nurture, protection, generosity, and love, with harmful features such as interference, dominance, manipulation, and possessiveness.[2] From India, Egypt, and Mesopotamia to Greece and Rome, quintessential femininity was embodied by a series of divinities who represented the breast of Mother Earth, responsible for both life and death. The idea of the Great Mother was shaped by the images of goddesses such as Kali (India), Hathor (Egypt), Ishtar (Mesopotamia), Hecate, Cybele, and Artemis (Asia Minor and the Greco-Roman world), to name but a few. Notably, while each had her own individual attributes, all combined both the positive and negative features of motherhood.[3]

### From Mother Earth to Medea

The idea that any act of creation inevitably results in another of destruction was expressed in various myths about the deathly jaws of the subterranean world: Mother Earth, fertile but avaricious, always ended up devouring her own offspring and growing fat on their corpses. Taking this image a step further, terrifying mothers who were renowned for feeding on little children—

the Greek Lamia, Roman striges, and monstrous ogresses of fairy tales, for example—constitute an archetypal figure present in many cultures.[4] These savage, half-animal monsters undoubtedly contributed elements to the classical myth of the witch in Europe, but the character who was most influential in establishing the archetype, thanks to her humanity and her close association with magic, was Medea.[5]

Originally a powerful goddess in the Greek pantheon, like her aunt Circe, Medea was turned into a simple sorceress in the Euripides tragedy first staged in Athens in 431 BC. She is the first-known woman in classical drama capable of killing her own offspring in cold blood and sound mind, but, more significantly, before she commits her terrible crime, Medea declares that because she brought her children into the world, she must also be the one to take their lives—a statement that recalls her primordial status as goddess-mother.[6]

The myth of the child-killing woman remained much the same throughout the Middle Ages, but in the late 1400s it began to merge with reality as numerous flesh-and-blood women were brought before the courts and accused of witchcraft. According to the treatises that began to be disseminated across Europe after the invention of the printing press (and that were to play such a key role in stoking the flames of the so-called "witch craze" of the late sixteenth and early seventeenth centuries), one of the crimes in which these innately evil women systematically indulged was the murder of newborn babies.[7]

As noted by Lyndal Roper, "Maternal hostility and fears about evil mothers could not easily be expressed directly in a society where Mary was revered by both Catholics and Protestants and where the image of the suffering Madonna was ubiquitous."[8] Indeed, unlike the female deities of antiquity, inhabited by both good and evil, the Christian mother, represented by the Virgin Mary, was idealized as the object of unconditional devotion. In fairy tales, the mother is often replaced by a stepmother, who keeps the former's memory alive.[9] In Marina Warner's words: "Mothers had to disappear in order for the ideal to survive and allow Mother to flourish as a symbol of the eternal feminine, the motherland, and the family itself as the highest social *desideratum*."[10] The taboo of the evil mother was disguised, therefore, in the figure of the wicked stepmother but also continued to be concealed within the monstrous ogresses and cruel witches capable of devouring their own children.[11]

The idea that women in general might be potential child-killers was definitively laid out in the well-known treatise published in Germany in 1486 and entitled *Malleus maleficarum*: "The hammer of witches, a weapon with which to pound witches and their heresies." According to the Dominican friars who wrote this influential manual that led to so many victims being burned at the stake, "since the demons carry out their practices through women and not through men, that infamous insatiable murderer [the Devil] contrives to adopt women rather than men as his partners."[12] In these circumstances, they claimed, women would see infanticide as their fourth option, if they had already failed to prevent intercourse, hinder conception, or bring about abortion.

A fifth and final choice, in the worst of cases, was also apparently available to witches. To quote the treatise's authors: "Where they don't cause a miscarriage, they eat up the baby or offer him to a demon."[13] And as if they had not made their point emphatically enough already, they then go on to underline the fact that, "contrary to the inclination of human nature and in fact in violation of the condition of all beasts, with the exception of the species of wolves, some sorceresses devour and consume babies."[14] Thus they turned the European witch into a flesh-eating monster—a metaphor for evil comparable to the demonized image of the cannibalistic indigenous peoples of the newly conquered Americas.[15]

The mythologizing of infanticide, as attributed to witches, speaks volumes, of course, about a deeply rooted cultural fear: that women might be capable of threatening not only human life but also the practice of patrilineality. How real a fear was this? What was the true extent of infanticide in early modern Europe? Given that it is by its very nature a highly clandestine crime, it is impossible to assess its real extent and impact. Although there were undoubtedly cases of deliberate child-killing by women who found themselves in desperate circumstances, most scholars believe it was a very rare phenomenon.[16] What we do know is that throughout the Middle Ages and early modern period, it was fairly common for children to be given up for adoption or simply abandoned at orphanages or monastic institutions.[17] Nevertheless, an obsession with the idea of the child-murdering mother persisted in both the oral tradition and written literature.[18]

Perhaps the most powerful literary example of this subliminal identification of witchcraft with murderous motherhood is to be found in *Macbeth* (1606). Here, the protagonist's alter ego is projected onto his wife: it is no coincidence that throughout the play "Lady Macbeth" is never named as such, making her the only leading female character in Shakespeare not to be referred to by name.[19] As an expression of Macbeth's split personality or, perhaps, the symbiosis of husband and wife, it is revealing that, just as Macbeth becomes a serial killer, Lady Macbeth is essentially presented as an inhuman mother.[20] She, of course, persuades her husband to commit his first murder, appealing first to his love, and then to his manhood. In order finally to convince him, however, she employs the most shocking and terrifying of arguments (albeit one that leaves Macbeth himself indifferent), declaring that despite having experienced a mother's love for her newborn child, she would have brutally murdered that child had she promised to do such a thing (as Macbeth has promised to kill Duncan): "I have given suck, and know how tender 'tis to love the babe that milks me: I would, while it was smiling in my face, have plucked the nipple from his boneless gums, and dashed the brains out, had I so sworn as you have done to this."[21] More than one scholar has made the connection between Lady Macbeth and the play's three witches.[22] Both she and the weird sisters openly express the protagonist's ambition and seem to be characterized by a disquieting mix of femininity and masculinity (the witches are bearded, and Lady Macbeth calls on the spirits to "unsex" her). Be this as it may, the Lady's infanticidal fantasy—which, had she actually carried it out, would have represented an assault on the social and political order—is reduced to a simple threat, and the masculine power base is ultimately reinforced.[23]

Generally speaking, the image of the mother as a potential child-killing monster was linked with that of the lustful and insatiable woman who would secretly do away with the illicit fruit of her womb in order to conceal her shameful behavior.[24] Very different from the stereotype of the nymphomaniac or man-eater (expressed in such colorful myths as that of the *vagina dentata*, or "toothed vagina"),[25] the single mothers we know of from documentary evidence who, in exceptional circumstances, did kill their own newborn babies, were almost always poor, many of them domestic servants.[26] Contemporary concerns about this state of affairs are reflected not only in the literature of the day,[27] but also in the legislation of various European countries in the sixteenth and seventeenth centuries,[28] notably a statute passed by the English Parliament in 1624 ("An Act to prevent the Destroying and Murthering of Bastard Children").[29] This law, which remained in force until the early nineteenth century, along with other similar acts passed elsewhere in Europe, was unjustly used to convict many women of infanticide even in the absence of decisive proof, namely the victim's body.[30]

To understand the obsession with infanticide throughout history, it is worth recalling that since at least late antiquity, accusations of child-killing had been used as a weapon against the prestige of political-religious enemies (the Christians in the Roman Empire, for example, or, once Christianity had established itself, sects such as the Gnostics or Montanists).[31] A common way of slandering followers of a different ideology was to spread the word that they indulged in orgies, and that the children conceived as a result were murdered. In the late Middle Ages, accusations of the ritual killing of young children, whatever their origins, were leveled against many religious minorities, to the extent that infanticide came to be seen as a distinguishing characteristic of heresy. From the twelfth century onward in particular, all kinds of "undesirables," including the Albigensians, the Waldensians, the Templars, and, very significantly, the Jews, were accused of torturing and murdering children as part of their rites and ceremonies.[32]

These "blood libels" occurred throughout Europe (Norwich, Lincoln, Cambrai, Trento, Toledo, Zaragoza, etc.), and they reveal the horror provoked by the very idea of infanticide, as well as its immense symbolic power to represent the most abhorrent behavior imaginable. Well into the sixteenth century, during the French wars of religion, certain Catholic propagandists, including some leading theologians at the University of Paris, accused Protestant groups of participating in scandalous orgies and of slaughtering children.[33] As Luc Racaut notes: "In the early modern period, infanticide was not exclusively associated with women and unwanted pregnancies. The killing of a new-born child was also regarded as a collective ritual, perpetrated by heterodox groups under the cover of darkness."[34]

## From Mothers to Witches

With this background in mind, it becomes easier to understand how the two basic models of femininity, as seen from a misogynist perspective (firstly, the evil woman—fundamentally lascivious—and secondly, the evil mother—in her most extreme incarnation, a murderess), began in the late 1400s to merge and create the archetype of the witch. According to theologians, witches had also to be classed as heretics (since they were believed to have renounced God and given themselves to the Devil), and hence could be pursued not only by the civil justice system but by the ecclesiastical courts as well. From today's perspective, one of the most striking aspects of most records of witchcraft trials, whether secular or religious, is that despite their unquestionable status as historical documents, they are every bit as inventive as many works of fiction, so rich are they from start to finish in weird and wonderful details and rhetorical flourishes.[35] To take just one example, some of the charges of child murder brought against real sixteenth- and seventeenth-century women—many of whom were ultimately sentenced to death as witches—include detailed infanticidal fantasies that surpass that of Lady Macbeth in sheer horror and brutality.[36]

One typical case is that of an inquisitorial trial brought in 1534 against an elderly woman from a little village in Huesca (northern Spain), who confessed under torture to a series of bloodcurdling and implausible crimes and was eventually burned at the stake.[37] Dominga Ferrer admitted that she had had intercourse with the Devil (whose virile member measured approximately "a palm and four fingers") and that, together with a friend of hers, also a witch, she had spent many a night killing babies in her local neighborhood. According to her confession, the Devil used to open the doors of the houses in which these children were sleeping, and the two women would murder them without their parents' realizing:

> She was called by Roiz Castellón ... who asked her to go and see his son who was sick. And she went to see him.... And that very Sunday came ... Gracia la Nadala ... who asked her if she wanted to go with her and they both went to the house of the said Roiz Castellón. And the devil opened the door. And they entered and went to the room where the said Roiz and his wife were sleeping. And they took the said child ... and took him to the kitchen. And the said Gracia la Nadala picked up embers from the fire and put the said child there ... to roast the small belly of the said child.[38]

A considerable number of the charges laid against "infanticidal witches" from various judicial sources have survived.[39] The most significant body of evidence, however, given its wealth of colorful details, the high number of people involved, and its importance in the wider history of witchcraft, is without doubt that relating to the Zugarramurdi witch trial.[40]

Investigations carried out by the Spanish Inquisition from 1608 onward into the crimes of witchcraft allegedly committed by certain residents of a number of Pyrenean villages close to the French border in Navarre (Zugarramurdi, Urdax, Vera, Lesaca, etc.) resulted in the notorious *auto-da-fé* held in Logroño on 7 and 8 November 1610. This began with an endless procession of clerics, behind whom came the fifty-three penitents accused of heresy (including the men and women charged with witchcraft). One by one the sentences were read aloud, and finally, on the evening of the second day, those found guilty of witchcraft who were still alive (some had died in prison; others had gone to the stake the previous day) abjured and swore their fidelity to the Catholic Church. Such was the impact of this episode of collective witchcraft (which involved two thousand defendants and a further five thousand suspects) that only two months later, in January 1611, a report of the trial proceedings was published, in duplicate, detailing all that had taken place in a purification ritual that seemed to anticipate the Final Judgment.[41]

Two aspects of this narrative are particularly relevant here: firstly, it includes one of the most exhaustive descriptions of the mythical witches' Sabbath; and secondly, of the crimes attributed to the participants in these demonic gatherings, infanticide is one of the most notable. According to the report, the male and female witches who had made a pact with the Devil, especially the women, used to take revenge on their adult enemies by poisoning them with certain powders. With children, however, their method was far more expeditious: "They suck the small children on the anus and vagina. Pressing hard with their hands and sucking strongly they draw and suck their blood. And with pins and needles they wound them in the temples and on the top of the head, and also in the spine and other parts and limbs of the body. And they suck their blood throughout them, whereas the devil says to them: Suck and swallow, since this is good for you! And after that the children die, or remain ill for long. And sometimes the witches kill them pressing them with their hands and biting their throat until they asphyxiate the children."[42]

Taking its tale of inconceivable horror one step further, the report details how the men and women would dig up corpses, tear them apart, and divide them into three shares ("one they boil, one they roast, the other they leave raw").[43] Then, at a nightmarish form of banquet,[44] on a table laid with black and dirty cloths, together with the Devil and a company of costumed toads, they feasted on the flesh of the dead ("that of the men is better and tastier than that of the women"), "the parents declaring that they have eaten their children, and the children their parents."[45]

The monstrous vision of the evil mother as represented *in extremis* in these child-eating witches was parodied in late eighteenth-century/early nineteenth-century Enlightenment Spain by two great figures: the dramatist Leandro Fernández de Moratín and the artist Francisco de Goya y Lucientes. Close friends until their dying day, the two men were insightful critics of contemporary society, both going into self-imposed exile in France after the restoration of the absolutist monarchy in Spain.[46] In his efforts to denounce Spanish obscurantism, as symbolized by tribunal of the Inquisition, on the two-hundredth anniversary of the Zugarramurdi trial Moratín published (under a pseudonym) a new edition of the Logroño *auto-da-fé* report, accompanied by a prologue and sixty ironic footnotes poking fun at the supposed witches' sabbath.[47] His aim was to show, with significant black humor, what damage the tribunal had done to Spanish history, with a view to shattering its prestige and bringing about its eventual abolition.[48] Moratín's satirical publication and the grotesque scenes of witchcraft created by Goya undoubtedly both drew inspiration from the same source. The motif of infanticide and child-eating witches recurs in several of the latter's works, including several of the etchings in his *Caprichos* series (1799). Some of these make direct reference to the implausible accusations levelled against the witches of Zugarramurdi—for example Capricho No. 45, in which three grotesque figures are depicted with a basket full of dead children, and the artist's caption reads, "There's plenty to suck."[49]

It has been claimed that the spirit of the Gothic novel is only really to be found in Spain in the works of Goya.[50] As a man who championed both reason and the power of the imagination, and who took delight in portraying the world of the irrational, the melancholy, and the monstrous, attracted by the darkest aspects of human nature, he was ahead of his time in combining the ideals of the Enlightenment and of Romanticism.[51] He was certainly an exceptional figure in Spain's artistic scene, his work displaying the antisuperstitious and rebellious nature of the earliest Gothic narrative (which had originated in England, with a nationalist component, as opposed to the continental world and Catholicism represented, above all, by Italy and Spain). By contrast, with their focus on upholding Catholic ideals, Spanish adaptations of Gothic novels transformed these characteristically transgressive stories into simple morality tales, using their most lurid elements as a tool with which to indoctrinate readers.[52]

A typical example of this practice is Agustín Pérez Zaragoza's edition of an anthology of both moralizing and humorous horror stories by the mysterious French writer J. R. P. Cuisin (1777–1845).[53] In the Spanish version, each tale is preceded by a somewhat sermonizing introduction that undercuts the parodic slant of the original.[54] Even more significantly, however, Pérez Zaragoza omitted three stories that he considered particularly scandalous.[55] In one of them, a beautiful young woman from a good family is made pregnant by her seducer and, so as not to lose her reputation, gives birth in secret and buries the child in the garden of the family home. When a servant discovers the body, she decides to commit suicide. But the story does not finish there—just when memories of the event are beginning to fade, rumors start to spread about certain extraordinary happenings: every year a bloodstained lily grows on the site of the child's grave, and the inconsolable ghost of the young mother continues to haunt her former home.[56]

The transformation of the myth of the evil mother from *devouring witch* to *deadly ghost* occurred in Europe during the Enlightenment and early Romantic era. As Gábor Klaniczay's studies have shown, while witchcraft trials were gradually diminishing in number, the world of the spirits (the latter being thought of as demons or the souls of the dead) was beginning to take on increasing importance.[57] If in countries such as Spain, France, and Italy the former obsession with witches was being replaced by a preoccupation with demonic possession (although the two phenomena would continue to be interrelated), in central and eastern Europe, the decline in witchcraft coincided with the rise in vampirism.[58]

Stories of both demonic possession and vampirism show that a more impersonal and abstract concept of magic was being developed. Whereas people had previously believed their misfortunes were caused by the ill will of certain flesh-and-blood individuals—human scapegoats who could be persecuted—the doctrine of demonic possession shifted responsibility to the devil or devils who were taking control of innocent beings on a daily basis. On the other hand, the belief in vampires, apparitions, ghosts, souls in torment, and so on, was used to attribute evil to specific dead people, thereby exonerating the victims of their attacks.[59]

This switch of focus from witches to spirits and ghosts was reflected in the spheres of religion, philosophy, science and, above all, literature. In many early Romantic stories, the evil mother, traditionally incarnate in the shape of a bloodthirsty goddess, devouring witch, or young child-killer, adopted a guise that was considerably more ambiguous and subtle, though no less threatening: that of the dominant mother who might not physically eliminate her children but nonetheless exerted a debilitating influence over them—her daughters in particular. This overwhelming maternal power often persisted even after death, resulting in the identification of daughters with their mothers or, worse still, in the former simply fading away, their life force—whether we call this energy or autonomy—draining from them, as if the mother's vampire-like spirit were continuing to suck their blood from beyond the grave.[60]

## Notes

1. "Mothers! The very word always strikes me like a blow! What power does it possess, that I cannot bear to hear it said?" (Johann Wolfgang von Goethe, *Faust* II, 1 [1832; Munich: Verlag C. H. Beck, 2007], 193). "Mothers, would that you were not ignorant of the fact that you are usually to blame when a man becomes evil" (Juan Luis Vives, *Instrucciones de la mujer cristiana*, trans. Juan Justiniano [1523; Madrid: Signo, 1936], II, XI.9, 144). This essay is part of the Spanish National Research Council (CSIC) research project *Images and Phantoms of Iberian Science, 16th-18th Centuries* (HAR2014–52517-P).

2. See C. G. Jung, *The Archetypes and the Collective Unconscious* (Princeton, N.J.: Princeton University Press, 1968), 85ff.

3. See Wolfgang Lederer, *The Fear of Women* (New York: Grune & Stratton, 1968).

4. See Erich Neumann, *The Great Mother: An Analysis of the Archetype* (Princeton, N.J.: Princeton University Press), 1955.

5. See María del Pilar Puig Mares, *Madres en la literatura española: Eros, honor y muerte* (Caracas: Universidad de Venezuela, 2004), 201–12.

6. Euripides, *Medea*, lines 1063 and 1240. See Alicia Morales Ortiz, "La maternidad y las madres en la tragedia griega," in *La madre en la Antigüedad: literatura, sociedad y religion*, ed. Esteban Calderón Dorda and Alicia Morales Ortiz (Madrid: Signifier, 2007), 141.

7. See Stuart Clark, *Thinking with Demons: The Idea of Witchcraft in Early Modern Europe* (Oxford: Oxford University Press, 1997); and Walter Stephens, *Demon Lovers: Witchcraft, Sex, and the Crisis of Belief* (Chicago: University of Chicago Press, 2002).

8. Lyndal Roper, "Witchcraft and Fantasy in Early Modern Germany," in *Witchcraft in Early Modern Europe: Studies in Culture and Belief*, ed. Jonathan Barry, Marianne Hester and Gareth Roberts (Cambridge: Cambridge University Press, 1996), 234.

9. See Bruno Bettelheim, *The Uses of Enchantment: The Meaning and Importance of Fairy Tales* (Harmondsworth: Penguin, 1978), 68–69.

10. Marina Warner, *The Absent Mother, or Women against Women in the Old Wives' Tale* (Hilversum: Verlorem, 1991), 30.

11. Female ogres or ogresses originally appeared in the fairy tales of Neapolitan writer Giambattista Basile (1575–1632). The term was first used in French by Charles Perrault in his *Sleeping Beauty*, based on one of Basile's tales and included in his *Histoires ou contes du temps passé* (1697).

12. Christopher S. Mackay, ed., *The Hammer of Witches: A Complete Translation of the "Malleus Maleficarum"* (Cambridge: Cambridge University Press, 2009), 211.

13. Ibid.

14. Ibid.

15. Allison P. Coudert, "The Ultimate Crime: Cannibalism in Early Modern Minds and Imaginations," in *Crime and Punishment in the Middle Ages and Early Modern Age*, ed. Albrecht Classen and Connie Scarborough (Berlin: Walter de Gruyter, 2012), 521–43.

16. See Keith Wrightson, "Infanticide in European History," *Criminal Justice History* 3 (1982): 1–20; Linda Pollock, *Forgotten Children: Parent-Child Relations from 1500 to 1900* (Cambridge: Cambridge University Press, 1983); Stephen G. Post, "History, Infanticide, and Imperiled Newborns," *Hastings Center Report* 18, no. 4 [1988]: 14–17); and Mark Jackson, ed., *Infanticide: Historical Perspectives on Child Murder and Concealment, 1550–2000* (Burlington, VT: Ashgate, 2002).

17. See Richard C. Trexler, "Infanticide in Florence: New Sources and First Results," in *Power and Dependence in Renaissance Florence: The Women of Renaissance Florence* (New York: Medieval and Renaissance Texts and Studies, 1993), 35–53.

18. See Susan Staub, "Early Modern Medea: Representation of Child Murder in the Street Literature of Seventeenth-Century England," in *Maternal Measures: Figuring Caregiving in the Early Modern Period*, ed. Naomi J. Miller and Naomi Yavneh (Burlington, VT: Ashgate, 2000), 333–47; and Susan Staub, *Nature's Cruel Stepdames: Murderous Women in the Street Literature of Seventeenth Century England* (Pittsburgh: Duquesne University Press, 2005).

19. See William Shakespeare, *Macbeth*, ed. Sandra Clark and Pamela Mason (London: Bloomsbury Arden Shakespeare, 2015), 153.

20. Stephanie Chamberlain, "Fantasizing Infanticide: Lady Macbeth and the Murdering Mother in Early Modern England," *College Literature* 32, no. 3 (2005): 72–91.

21. Shakespeare, *Macbeth*, 1.7.54–58.

22. See Peter Stallybrass, "Macbeth and Witchcraft, "in *Focus on Macbeth*, ed. John Russell Brown (London: Routledge, 1982), 191–92; and Dympna Callaghan, "Wicked Women in Macbeth: A Study of Power, Ideology, and the Production of Motherhood," in *Reconsidering the Renaissance*, ed. Mario A. Di Cesare (Binghamton: New York: Medieval and Renaissance Texts and Studies, 1992), 355–69.

23. "The play that begins by unleashing the terrible threat of destructive maternal power ... ends by consolidating male power." See Janet Adelman, *Suffocating Mothers: Fantasies of Maternal Origin in Shakespeare's Plays* (London: Routledge, 1992), 122. Another example of the profound fear of negative aspects of motherhood is represented by the Queen of Night in Mozart's *The Magic Flute* (1791). Here, the heroine Pamina's possessive, wrathful and vengeful mother, the very personification of evil, is defeated by Sarastro, a priest of the sun, who symbolizes light, goodness and also patrilineal succession, since he succeeds in abolishing the ancient rite of male sacrifice.

24. J. R. Dickinson and J. A. Sharpe, "Infanticide in Early Modern England: The Court of Great Sessions at Chester, 1650–1800," in *Infanticide*, ed. Jackson, 35–51.

25. See François Delpech, "Le vagin denté: Variantes ibériques," in *Des Monstres*, ed. Carmen Val Julián and Maryse Vich Campos (Paris: Cahiers de Fontenay, 1994), 11–31.

26. Johanna Geyer-Kordesch, "Infanticide and the Erotic Plot: A Feminist Reading of Eighteenth-Century Crime," in *Infanticide*, ed. Jackson, 93–127.

27. This includes folk ballads about murdering mothers who are then faced with the ghosts of their children, who warn them that in the afterlife they will either have to undergo various expiatory ordeals, or go straight to hell. See David Atkinson, "History, Symbol and Meaning in 'The Cruel Mother,'" *Folk Musical Journal* 6, no. 3 (1992): 359–80.

28. Such legislation was passed in the Holy Roman Empire in 1532, and in France in 1556. However, no law in the Spanish code expressly concerned the murder of an infant. See Peter C. Hoffer and N. E. H. Hull, *Murdering Mothers: Infanticide in England and New England, 1558–1803* (New York: New York University Press, 1984), 13; and Nazanin Sullivan, "What Is Public and Notorious: The Rhetoric of Reputation in Sixteenth-Century Castilian Infanticide Trials" (paper presented at the Sixteenth Century Society Conference, New Orleans, October 2014).

29. Jackson, ed., *Infanticide*, 4; Jackson, *New-Born Child Murder: Women, Illegitimacy and the Courts in Eighteenth-Century England* (Manchester: Manchester University Press, 1996).

30. Mark Jackson, "Suspicious Infant Deaths: The Statute of 1624 and Medical Evidence at Coroners' Inquests," in *Legal Medicine in History*, ed. M. Clark and C. Crawford (Cambridge: Cambridge University Press, 1994), 64–86.

31. Norman Cohn, *Europe's Inner Demons: The Demonization of Christians in Medieval Christendom* (London: Pimlico, 1993).

32. M-M. Fragonard, "La détermination des frontières symboliques: Nommer et

définir les groupes hérétiques," in *Les frontières religieuses en Europe du XVe au XVIIe siècle*, ed. R. Sauzet (Paris: J. Vrin, 1992), 37–49.

33. Luc Racaut, "Accusations of Infanticide on the Eve of the French Wars of Religion," in *Infanticide*, ed. Jackson, 18–34.

34. Ibid., 34.

35. See Natalie Zemon Davis, *Fiction in the Archives: Pardon Tales and Their Tellers in Sixteenth-Century France* (Cambridge: Polity, 1988); and María Tausiet, "Por el sieso y la natura: Una lectura literaria de los procesos por brujería," *Edad de Oro* 27 (2008): 339–64.

36. See David Harley, "Historians as Demonologists: The Myth of the Midwife-Witch," *Social History of Medicine* 3 (1990): 1–26.

37. See the trial against Dominga Ferrer, la Coja. Pozán de Vero (Huesca), 1534, Archivo Histórico Provincial de Zaragoza (AHPZ), C. 31–2.

38. See María Tausiet, "Witchcraft as Metaphor: Infanticide and Its Translations in Aragón in the Sixteenth and Seventeenth Centuries," in *Languages of Witchcraft: Narrative, Ideology and Meaning in Early Modern Culture*, ed. Stuart Clark (London: Macmillan, 2001), 181; and María Tausiet, *Ponzoña en los ojos: Brujería y superstición en Aragón en el siglo xvi* (Madrid: Turner, 2004), 226–32.

39. See Sarah Christine Shippy Copeland, "Constructions of Infanticide in Early Modern England: Female Deviance during Demographic Crisis" (master's thesis, Ohio State University, 2008).

40. See Julio Caro Baroja, *Las brujas y su mundo* (Madrid: Revista de Occidente, 1961); Gustav Henningsen, *The Witches' Advocate: Basque Witchcraft and the Spanish Inquisition* (Reno: University of Nevada Press, 1980); Gustav Henningsen, ed., *The Salazar Documents. Inquisitor Alonso de Salazar and Others on the Basque Witch Persecution* (Leiden: Brill, 2004); and Jesús Mª Usúnariz, ed., *Akelarre: la caza de brujas en el Pirineo (siglos XIII-XIX): Homenaje al profesor Gustav Henningsen*, RIEV, Cuadernos 9 (2012).

41. See Manuel Fernández Nieto, *Proceso a la brujería: En torno al Auto de Fe de los brujos de Zugarramurdi. Logroño, 1610* (Madrid: Tecnos, 1989).

42. Ibid., 66.

43. Ibid., 68.

44. See Gerardo Fernández Juárez, "Comer en el aquelarre: Entre lo sublime y lo repugnante: Una perspectiva trasatlántica," *Revista de Dialectología y Tradiciones Populares* 69, no. 1 (2014): 95–112.

45. See Fernández Nieto, *Proceso a la brujería*, 69.

46. In 1824 Goya fled to France to escape Fernando VII's persecution of the liberals. He took refuge in Moratín's home in Bordeaux. On April 16, 1828, the artist died, at the age of eighty-two. Moratín survived him only by two months, dying at the age of sixty-eight.

47. See *Auto de fe celebrado en la ciudad de Logroño en los días 7 y 8 de noviembre de 1610. Segunda edición, ilustrada con notas por el Bachiller Ginés de Posadilla, natural de Yébenes, in 8º* (Madrid: Imprenta Real, 1811).

48. By the time Moratín published his text, the Inquisition's power was already virtually inexistent, as the organization was abolished first by Napoleon in 1808 and then,

officially, by the Cortes de Cádiz in 1813. It was reestablished by Fernando VII between 1814 and 1820, however, and was only definitively abolished in 1834, after his death.

49. According to the *auto* report, all the witches "carried with them a basket with a handle" (see Carmelo Lisón Tolosana, *Las brujas en la historia de España* [Madrid: Temas de Hoy, 1992], 243–68).

50. See Miriam López Santos, *La novela gótica en España (1788–1833)* (Pontevedra: Academia del Hispanismo, 2010), 105–6.

51. See Edith Helman, *Trasmundo de Goya* (Madrid: Revista de Occidente, 1964); and *Los caprichos de Goya* (Madrid: Alianza, 1971).

52. See López Santos, *La novela gótica en España (1788–1833)*, 111–49.

53. J. R. P. Cuisin, *Les ombres sanglantes: Galerie funèbre de prodiges, evénements merveilleux, apparitions nocturnes, songes épouvantables, délits mystérieux, phénomènes terribles, forfaits historiques, cadavres mobiles, têtes ensanglantées et animées, vengeances atroces et combinaisons du crime puisés dans des sources réelles. Recueil propre à causer les fortes émotions de la terreur* (Paris: Veuve Lepetit, 1820).

54. See Agustín Pérez Zaragoza, *Galería fúnebre de espectros y sombras ensangrentadas [. . .]* , 12 vols. (Madrid: D. J. Palacios, 1831).

55. The three in question were the third, fifth, and tenth "Ombres," dealing respectively with incest, infanticide, and the sex life of a nun. All three were included in another, less well-known Spanish edition (see Basilio S. Castellanos and Julián Anento, *La poderosa Thémis o los remordimientos de los malvados*, vol. 4 [Madrid: Ramón Verges, 1831]).

56. See "El infanticidio," in Castellanos and Anento, *La poderosa Thémis o los remordimientos de los malvados*, vol. 4, 52–68. Unlike Goethe's Marguerite, lover and victim of Faust, who achieves redemption, the protagonist of this story is doomed to wander abroad like a ghost or soul in torment.

57. See Gábor Klaniczay and Éva Pócs, eds., *Demons, Spirits, Witches*, 3 vols. (Budapest: Central European University Press, 2005–8).

58. On the interrelation of the interest in witches and demonic possession, see Brian P. Levack, *The Devil Within: Possession and Exorcism in the Christian West* (New Haven: Yale University Press, 2013), 191–214; and María Tausiet, *Los posesos de Tosos (1812–1814): Brujería y justicia popular en tiempos de revolución* (Zaragoza: Instituto Aragonés de Antropología, 2002). The myth of vampirism was a synthesis of traits from earlier beliefs in figures such as revenants, pressing spirits, bloodsucking witches, werewolves, etc. (see Gábor Klaniczay, "The Decline of Witches and the Rise of Vampires," *Ethnologia Europea* 17 [1987]: 165–80).

59. See James B. Twitchell, *The Living Dead. A Study of the Vampire in Romantic Literature* (Durham, N.C.: Duke University Press, 1981), and Michael J. Dennison, *Vampirism. Literary Tropes of Decadence and Entropy* (New York: Peter Lang, 2001).

60. As yet, there has been relatively little research into the theme of female vampires (and specifically vampire mothers). See, however, Pilar Pedraza, "La madre vampira," *Asparkia* 10 (1999): 43–52; and María Tausiet, "Madres espectrales: *Vampyr* (Carl Theodor Dreyer, 1932) y sus antecedentes literarios," in *Brujas de cine*, ed. María Jesús Zamora (Madrid: Abada, 2016), 91–117.

MICHAEL MEERE

## On Specters and Skulls
### Rosamund and Alboin in Seventeenth-Century French Tragedy

The eighth-century Benedictine monk Paul the Deacon tells the story of the Lombard king Alboin who, in 567, defeated the Gepid king Cunimond, made a drinking cup out of his skull, and forced Rosamund, the dead king's daughter, to marry him.[1] Five years later, in 572, during a banquet at Verona, an inebriated Alboin had the skull cup sent to Rosamund to drink "merrily with her father."[2] The queen was deeply anguished upon hearing this order and immediately began to devise a plan with Alboin's foster brother, named Helmechis, to avenge the death of her father by having Alboin murdered. Helmechis persuaded Rosamund to admit Peredeo, another courtier, to the plot. Because Peredeo refused to assassinate the king, Rosamund switched places in bed one night with her dressing-maid who was also Peredeo's mistress; as a result, he had intercourse with the queen without realizing it was she. Once the queen revealed her identity, she gave Peredeo an ultimatum: he could either assent to murder the king or be accused of rape, which would result in his own death. Peredeo chose regicide to save his own life. One afternoon while the king was napping, Rosamund bound the king's sword to the head of the bed and she let Helmechis and Peredeo into the room.[3] Alboin awoke and reached for his sword, in vain, and, as Paul the Deacon writes, "this most warlike and very brave man being helpless against his enemy, was slain as if he were one of no account, and he who was most famous in war through the overthrow of so many enemies, perished by the scheme of one little woman." Upon Alboin's death, Helmechis attempted to usurp the kingdom; failing to do so, however, he and Rosamund fled to Ravenna, where the Byzantine Longinus was prefect. Once Rosamund and Helmechis arrived there, Longinus began to urge Rosamund to kill Helmechis so that she could marry Longinus. She acquiesced, and, while Helmechis was in his bath, Rosamund offered him a cup of poison that she claimed was for his health. When Helmechis felt the effects of poison, he forced Rosamund to drink the rest of the cup's contents by drawing his sword upon her, and in Paul the Deacon's words, "these most wicked murderers [Rosamund and Helmechis] perished at one moment by the judgment of God Almighty."[4]

The Rosamund and Alboin story—one that revolves around family violence and revenge plots—provided exquisite raw material for tragic tales and tragedies;[5] indeed, this story proliferated throughout Europe from the sixteenth to the late nineteenth centuries.[6] Matteo Bandello wrote a version of it in his *Novelle* (1554), which François de Belleforest translated and expanded into French in 1570.[7] Giovanni Rucellai's *Rosmunda* is the earliest extant tragedy written in Italian,[8] while William D'Avenant's first tragedy was a reworking of the story.[9] German, Dutch, Neo-Latin, and Swedish dramatic adaptations also exist.[10]

In seventeenth-century France, four playwrights adapted the Rosamund and Alboin story for the stage: Nicolas Chrestien des Croix (?–ca. 1620); Claude Billard (1550–1618/23); an anonymous Normand poet; and Balthasar Baro (1596–1650).[11] Chrestien and Billard are believed to have been rival court poets, writing in the first decades of the seventeenth century.[12] Baro—a contemporary of Pierre Corneille (1606–1684), Pierre Du Ryer (1605–1658), and Jean de Rotrou (1609–1650)—was a renowned playwright and a *homme de lettres* of repute.[13] Next to nothing, on the other hand, is known about the identity of the anonymous playwright.[14] While some scholars have analyzed these plays discretely, only Lancaster E. Dabney and Elliott Forsyth have compared Chrestien's and Billard's versions, and no scholar has conducted a comparative study of all four plays.[15] And yet, such a study would offer insights into the variety of dramatic practices and the ways in which they coexisted, conflicted, and/or changed during the first half of the seventeenth century. For the purposes of this essay, I have chosen to home in on two macabre (if not proto-Gothic) components of these plays—the specter and the skull—to suggest that the supernatural in the earlier plays, and its relative absence in the later ones, greatly determines the ways in which the playwrights make use of the Rosamund and Alboin story for their respective audiences. In particular, the presence or absence of the specter and the skull—as dramaturgical devices—helps explain the rather drastic changes in the queen's character from Chrestien's *Alboüin* and Billard's *Alboin* to the anonymous *Rosimonde* and Baro's *Rosemonde*. Hence, I will investigate the relationship between the supernatural and the natural and argue that as the seventeenth century progressed, the direct intervention of the supernatural that was so common in humanist and post-Renaissance tragedy regressed and made way for more secular conflicts between humans on the temporal plane. By using the dramatic adaptations of this story as case studies, I contend that this shift complicates Rosamund's capacity to take action, notably with regard to revenge and regicide.

## Specters

Chrestien's and Billard's tragedies both open with the appearance of a ghost, whereas *Rosimonde* and Baro's *Rosemonde* suppress this character.[16] Chrestien's ghost is Comonde, Rosemonde's father (Cunimond), who, after pronouncing a monologue, enters into dialogue with the fury of revenge, Tysiphone. Billard begins his tragedy with a monologue by the ghost Totyle, king of the Goths.[17] There is no physical description of the ghosts when they appear onstage, but Chrestien's Rosemonde describes the shade of her father, who unceasingly presents himself before her eyes. He is "pale and disfigured," with "large chunks of his brain falling down his handsome face and large drops of blood flowing from his wounds" (Palle, et defiguré, [...] de son Chef la ceruelle / Tomboit à gros morceaux dessus sa face belle. / De ses plaies le sang à gros boüillons couloit).[18] The physical appearance of such ghosts would perhaps strike fear into the audience, but this is not the sole purpose of these supernatural figures.[19]

Indeed, in sixteenth- and early seventeenth-century tragedies, the ghost and pagan deities are commonplace and act as expository characters who inform the spectators/readers of the plot that is about to unfold.[20] Some critics have derided the prophetic ghost for "tell[ing] too much,"[21] but this would be to misunderstand the notion of suspense in these plays. As Terence Cave has argued, suspense operates on a horizontal, or linear level, whereas allegory is structured vertically.[22] In other words, humanist tragedies still very much operated in an allegorical mode, with a definite *telos* in mind apparent right from the start, and in which a superior fate, or something supernatural, controlled or determined the outcome of the story. Thus, suspense for humanist poets was produced in new inventions or digressions rather than in the uncertainty of the ending,[23] so outlining the plot of the play would not take away from the pleasure of watching or reading how the poet treated the subject.[24]

During the 1620s and 1630s, however, allegory lost its foothold on tragedy, and suspense became based on more secular contingencies, accidents.²⁵ This trend coexisted with the rise in popularity of tragicomedy, in which playwrights exploited themes of unexpected events such as shipwrecks and the like, or mistaken identities, disguise, and cross-dressing. Indeed, the earlier plays evoke the inconstancy of fortune, a commonplace idea in humanist tragedy, but they counter the power of chance by presenting God as the safeguard of moral uprightness by punishing the wicked who betray the king. Chrestien's subtitle "la vengeance" (revenge) gestures toward not only Rosemonde's revenge against Alboüin but also God's divine counter-revenge against all those who betrayed the king.²⁶

Returning to the dramatic function of the supernatural ghost, it not only incites fear and announces the events that are about to unfold but also, in the case of Chrestien's and Billard's plays, at least, has a third function: it can affect the living characters and their behavior. First of all, like in many revenge plays such as Shakespeare's *Hamlet* and *Macbeth*, the ghost recalls the past and calls for retribution. This function is particularly evident in Chrestien's play, as Comonde invokes the fury Tysiphone, the fury who avenges and punishes crimes of murder such as parricide, and Tysiphone agrees to avenge Comonde's murder.²⁷ Moreover, Comonde and Tysiphone engage in a long dialogue that foresees Rosemonde's vengeance, degeneracy, and ultimate demise.²⁸ In Billard's tragedy, though the Erinyes are absent from the stage, the ghost Totyle invokes them in a vehement, epizeuxistic plea to carry out the necessary outcome of the play: "Sus, Eumémides, sus, sus, sus, que l'on attise / Les feus de ma vengeance" (Attack, Erinyes, attack, attack, attack, may my fires of revenge be kindled).²⁹

Besides recalling the past and crying for revenge, the ghost can also contaminate a living character's spirit with its own. In effect, in Billard's tragedy, the ghost of Totyle expresses this very desire, to infect Rosemonde:

> Ie veus, ie veus suiuy des fieres Euménides,
> Lui soufler dans le sein les pointes homicides,
> La consumer d'amour, la perdre de transport:
> Que d'vn desir vangeur elle auance la mort
> A son sot de mary, pour iouir insensee,
> D'vn Adonis errant au fond de sa pensee.³⁰

> (I want, I want, followed by the proud Furies, to blow into her breast hard homicidal thoughts, to consume her with love, to lose her completely with a desire to take revenge that will quicken the death of her

foolish husband, to take mad pleasure with an Adonis erring in the depths of her mind.)

Rosemonde's adulterous desire for Elméchide (Helmichis) is subsequently beyond her own control. Indeed, from the moment Rosemonde steps onstage, she hopelessly suffers from her burning and destructive love for Elméchide despite herself.[31] Totyle has successfully corrupted Rosemonde, and, by taking away her own will, paradoxically, the ghost has given her more power to affect the other characters around her. After all, Rosemonde is an enslaved wife, a station that she repeats throughout the play (in all of the adaptations), yet she is able to change the course of history thanks to the powers that the specter has proffered her.

Even though ghosts cease to speak and thus physically exit the stage after the expository acts in Chrestien's and Billard's tragedies, the specters do not disappear from the play altogether in that they reemerge in the words of the characters. In Chrestien's *Alboüin*, for example, Rosemonde is haunted by her father's spirit even before she is forced to drink out of his skull.[32] Rosemonde tells her governess Polycrite that she dreamt of her father, who incited her to avenge his death, and "sans cesse ie voy des yeux de mon esprit / Mon Pere qu'Alboüin cruellement meurtrit" (ceaselessly I see with my mind's eyes my father whom Alboin cruelly murdered).[33] Polycrite attempts to quell Rosemonde's fears by arguing against the veracity of dreams—a commonplace debate in Renaissance tragedy—and the two women end the scene by deciding to make a sacrifice so that God may remove such ghastly images (ces Nocturnes Images).[34] This sacrifice, however, will not change the unfolding of the events as Rosemonde, upon seeing her father's spirit, has already begun to lose a hold on her own sanity, and the specter has begun to blur "the boundary between appearance and reality just as much as the boundary between life and death."[35] Drinking out of her father's skull, however, as we will see in the next section, will be the nail in the coffin for Rosemonde's sanity, and it will send her on a path of (self-)destruction.

In Baro's *Rosemonde*, no ghost speaks onstage, and none are listed as characters embodied by actors, but once the queen learns that her father is in fact dead and has drunk from his skull, she, too, sees his spirit in a waking hallucination (as in Belleforest's narrative version), and he orders her to kill Albouyn, according to his and the Fates' law. Speaking to her confidant Axiane, Rosemonde exclaims:

Mon pere n'est donc plus ; ô cruauté du sort!
O coup rude à souffrir! Cunimond est donc mort!

Ah! je n'en doute plus, je voy, je voy son ombre,
Qui *pour quelques moments* sort du Royaume sombre,
Afin de me prescrire et me faire une loy
De ce que les destins ont desiré de moy.
Vangeons-nous, Axiane, armons-nous de bonne heure,
Il faut perdre Albouyn, les Dieux veulent qu'il meure.[36]

(My father no longer lives. O cruel fate! Such a harsh blow to endure! Cunimond is thus dead! Oh! I no longer doubt it, I see, I see his shade, which has *for a few moments* left the dark kingdom, in order to summon me and to enforce a law that fate has destined for me. Let us avenge ourselves, Axiane, let us arm ourselves in good time. Albouyn must perish; the gods want him dead.)

Despite the manifestation of Cunimond's ghost in Rosemonde's mind, and contrary to Chrestien's adaptation, Baro's play minimizes the role and importance of the specter, for it appears only for a fleeting moment (pour quelques moments) rather than unceasingly (sans cesse). Instead, in Baro's adaptation, Rosemonde quickly moves on to more terrestrial and concrete concerns of preparing for Albouyn's murder by summoning Ermige (Helmichis).[37] Rosemonde does invoke the specters again in the following act, just before Albouyn is killed, but the ghosts' identities remain unknown, and Rosemonde refuses to allow them to have any hold over her. In fact, she claims that her betrayal is more frightful than the supposed phantoms that haunt her, again only for a brief moment. Rosemonde:

Cessez craintes, soupçons, fuyez ces vaines images,
Qui pouvez estonner les plus braves courages,
Ne me tourmentez plus. Mais quels spectres hideux!
Axiane les suit; ah! destins ce sont eux
Qui portent [...]
. . . . . . . . . . . . . .
Un masque moins affreux que n'est ma perfidie.[38]

(Cease, fears and suspicions; go away, empty images, which can scare the bravest hearts. Torment me no longer. But what hideous specters! Axiane is following them. Ah, fate! They [the specters] wear [...] a mask that is less horrid than my treachery.)

The oscillation between Rosemonde's determination to kill Albouyn and her reluctance to do so thus hinges on the tension between the supernatural and the natural worlds. If Rosemonde follows the macabre supernatural order, Albouyn dies; if she follows the natural order, Albouyn lives. At the same time, however, Rosemonde is not in complete control of the situation. The rival lovers, Ermige and Paradee, are determined to avenge Albouyn's affront against both Rosemonde (by making her drink out of her father's skull) and themselves (taking Rosemonde as his own wife and thus depriving them of her). In the general economy of the plot, therefore, the ghosts lose their supernatural power over Rosemonde as the play briskly returns to the physical world of Albouyn's assassination in the hands of Ermige and Paradee. This oscillation does not exist in Chrestien's and Billard's tragedies, notably because in their plays the realm of the dead and the supernatural have utter control over the lives of the living.

As for the anonymous *Rosimonde*, the only time a ghost is mentioned is after the violent battle scene between Helmichis's and Alboin's men in which the victor,[39] Alboin's *favori* Philadon, surprised by his unlikely defeat of three other armed men, believes that he is dreaming or under a spell. Helmichis arrives and confronts Philadon about the cadavers that litter the stage, but Philadon is delirious and thinks that Helmichis is a magician who has just put them to sleep. Helmichis, confused, asks Philadon: "Est-tu encor vivant? ou bien si c'est un ombre, / Je te croyois desja dans ce royaume sombre" (Are you still alive? Or if this is a ghost, I believed you already to be in that dark kingdom) (3.5, 46). When Philadon remains incapable of answering any question whatever, Helmichis realizes that Philadon has defeated his companions, and he kills Philadon in return (3.5, 47). The figure of the ghost is thus ironized in *Rosimonde*, for there is never any ghost at all, and all of the action remains on the temporal, physical plane, whereas the spiritual, metaphysical is utterly evacuated from the play.

## Cunimond's Skull

The quintessential moment in the archetypal Rosamund story is the banquet during which Alboin presents his wife with the skull of her dead father, Cunimond, as a drinking cup. This affront ignites her ire and enflames her desire for revenge. The plays exploit this scene to varying degrees, and I will examine each play in turn, in ascending order of importance. The anonymous *Rosimonde* seems to place the skull-cup scene deliberately in the background of the action. While the specter does not appear in *Rosimonde*, the skull also has less significance than in other adaptations of the story. Rosimonde mentions the skull only once, when Helmichis reprimands her for accepting Alboin as her husband. She retorts:

> Cette coupe jadis qui causa mon tourment,
> Redouble encor un coup icy mon sentiment!
> Helas je n'ose plus entrer dedans la couche,
> De ce monstre inhumain, le baiser bouche à bouche
> Que je meure plustost; Helmichis venge-moy,
> Accepte s'il te plaist les offres de ma foy.⁴⁰

> (This cup that formerly caused my torment intensifies yet again this feeling! Alas! I no longer dare enter into the bed of that inhuman monster. I'd rather die than kiss him mouth to mouth. Helmichis, avenge me. Please accept the offer of my love.)

Hence it is not the drinking out of her father's skull that incites Rosimonde to plot against Alboin, as in the other versions; rather, it is a thing of the past that only serves as a reminder of her status as a poor captive who has been taken away from her native land because of war (une pauvre captive / Que la guerre esloigna de sa natale rive).⁴¹ The revenge plot derives, in fact, from Helmichis, not Rosimonde, desiring to punish Alboin's affront in taking Rosimonde as his wife.⁴²

Billard makes more substantial use of the skull by having Rosemonde invoke the supernatural—her dead father, Megara, Alecto, and others—after having drunk from it.⁴³ She exclaims, in effect, that Alboin has, by forcing her to drink out of the skull, interrupted the peace that one owes to the dead, to her paternal ashes, to the manes who err in eternal darkness ("[Alboin] ma contraint, forcee [. . .] à boire dans le tais / De mon pere meurtry, interrompre la paix / Que nous devons aus morts, aus cendres paternelles, / Aux Dieux Manes errans sous les nuits eternelles").⁴⁴ However, Rosemonde detests Alboin from the start of the play, so it is no surprise that being forced to drink out her father's skull spurs her to avenge her father's death and to bring ruin upon the entire Lombard kingdom, no matter the cost.⁴⁵

Baro's *Rosemonde* also refers to the skull-cup incident as a deciding factor in the queen's determination to plot against Albouyn, but Baro has invented a more convoluted plot in which the skull figures. In a monologue, awaiting Ermige's arrival from his tent, Rosemonde laments:

O tragique repas! ô funeste moment!
Cette fatale couppe a donc mes mains soüillees,
Un vin meslé de sang mes levres a moüillees,
Et celuy dont je suis le sepulcre animé
Nourrit par sa substance un corps qu'il a formé.[46]

(O tragic meal! O abominable moment! This fatal cup has thus soiled my hands, my lips have been wet with a wine mixed with blood, and he, from whom I am a living tomb, nourished a body that he formed by his substance.)

There appears to be a profane imitation of the sacrament of transubstantiation at play in the scene, in which Rosemonde is transformed by drinking the wine mixed with her father's blood, out of his own skull. Although Rosemonde's monologue is rather brief here, the skull incident is mentioned again in the play, as a memory that ignites Rosemonde's fury against Albouyn and helps her to justify the regicide as she oscillates between killing and sparing Albouyn:

Toutefois ce cruel [. . .] M'a fait mesler mon sang à celuy de mon pere.
Ah! de cette action l'horrible souvenir
Me porte à des fureurs qu'on ne peut retenir.

(However this cruel man made me mix my blood with my father's. Oh! The memory of this horrible action incites a rage in me that one cannot hold back.)[47]

It is Chrestien's *Alboüin*, though, that makes the most complex use of the skull. When the tragedy opens, Rosemonde is a docile and content wife and queen, yet her character undergoes a complete reversal after she drinks out of the skull. Rosemonde's abrupt change may show Chrestien's attempt to appeal to rudimentary psychology.[48] However, the skull, a synecdoche for the father, his valor, and his violence, has a truly transformative effect on the queen by unleashing memories of trauma, triggering Rosemonde's revenge and, as a result, lead her to commit an unstoppable chain of violence. It is as if she were possessed, contaminated, by her father's ghost, who becomes a walking dead with nothing to lose. Rosemonde expresses this sentiment when speaking with Polycrite. As she drank from her father's skull, says Rosemonde, her "heart shrunk with grief" and her "complexion changed many times" ("Tout aussi tost le cœur me serra de douleur, / Et mon teint rechangea plusieurs fois de couleur"); henceforth, she pursues the grave because of her mournful sorrow, and only death will be able to stop her murderous ambitions ("Il n'y a que la mort qui puisse terminer, / Le bourreau qui mon cœur est venu dominer").[49] Life and death collapse, and Rosemonde has become a shell of her past self.[50] Through the skull, her father's specter has taken over her body and mind, making her "take on a troubling, new identity, thereby becoming [her]self a specter in the broad sense."[51] Yet she acquires power and is pushed to avenge her father's death without fear of the consequences. According to the internal logic of the play, Rosemonde's decision to take action stems from supernatural forces: her father and Tysiphone, who seem to be transmitted through the skull, a relic-object that has reified the ghost of her father and given her the strength to take revenge on her father's murderer.

### Rosamund: From Villain to Ambiguous Heroine

The presence and absence of the supernatural in these plays, represented by the specter and reified by Cunimond's skull, even if they can be read as simple allegories of Rosamund's psychology, can help explain her character and the degrees to which the plays condemn the queen's actions. Chrestien's play, like Belleforest's tragic tale, focuses on a denunciation of dangerous femininity and passionate revenge, while Billard's tragedy censures Rosemonde's adultery and isolates this sin as the cause of Alboin's ruin. Chrestien's and Billard's Rosemonde participates in a network of symbolic women, like Medea, who represent the worst moral attributes of femininity that one finds in the tragic tales and tragedies of the sixteenth and seventeenth centuries: lasciviousness, greed, cruelty, absence of scruples, trickery, venality, and so forth.[52] Billard indirectly evokes Medea when Rosemonde declares that she will go to the most solitary places to invoke the demons and ghosts, monsters and titans, to avenge her father.[53] Belleforest, however, likens her not to Medea but to Deianira and Delilah,[54] whereas Chrestien's Rosemonde compares herself to other strong historical and mythological women who would not allow themselves to be subjugated by men: Thaïs, Tomyris, Camma, Eryxo, and Berenice.[55] Chrestien's and Billard's Rosemonde is an unequivocally evil villain who spirals out of (man's) control, committing adultery and murder, and who can be stopped only by being killed.

*Rosimonde* and Baro's play, however, are more indirect and ambiguous in promoting their ethical stances vis-à-vis the queen and her actions. In particular, these two versions reduce the queen's power and thus give her less influence in the unfolding of the action. In *Rosimonde* and Baro's *Rosemonde*, the queen is not yet married to Alboin/Albouyn but promised to Helmichis/Ermige, and, in both, Alboin/Albouyn chooses to take her away from his men to marry her by force himself. These events do not appear in the historical record: this invention provides the characters with a more collective motive to kill the king rather than ascribing it to any sort of contamination by supernatural spirits or to the skull-cup incident. These tragedies thus place the queen and Helmichis/Ermige in a more pathetic position and intensify the king's selfishness and cruelty.

In *Rosimonde*, moreover, while the queen does not waver to wish Alboin's death, it is Helmichis who takes charge once he learns of Alboin's actions, while the queen adopts a more passive role.[56] The queen also shows weakness when Longin insists that she kill her husband,[57] and she pronounces *stances* in which she oscillates between saving and murdering her second husband.[58] These changes in Rosimonde's character result in a more conflicted and sympathetic figure who has shifted from a bloodthirsty, irascible, even possessed madwoman to a wronged queen who struggles with her conscience to avenge her father's death, to punish the tyrannical king, and to kill Helmichis despite herself.

Whereas Rosimonde adopts a more passive role in the anonymous playwright's version of the story, Baro's Rosemonde is a strong queen who is significantly, and paradoxically, more undecided and reluctant to kill the king.[59] Once she finds out that Albouyn has sent his henchman Argiran to kill her, Baro's Rosemonde vacillates between her desire to kill Albouyn and reproaching herself for having such blasphemous thoughts.[60] After Ermige and Paradee announce that they will kill Albouyn, Rosemonde regrets her decision,[61] and, when the men return to announce the king's murder, Rosemonde bemoans his death.[62]

Baro's ending, furthermore, is the most unexpected and ambiguous of the four versions. In short, Paradee declares his love to Rosemonde, but she rejects him, so he promises to get revenge by poisoning Ermige.[63] Ermige greatly regrets and has gone mad for having committed the crime of regicide;[64] in turn, Rosemonde asks a doctor named Alcame for a cure.[65] She does not know, however, that the potion is in reality the poison that Paradee has prepared. Ermige is about to commit suicide when Rosemonde arrives with the potion.[66] Upon realizing that she has been tricked and that Ermige has died by drinking her supposed medicine, Rosemonde then drinks the rest of the poison, of her own accord, to perish with her beloved.[67] Baro diverges significantly from the traditional narrative of a double murder to end the play with a pathetic love suicide.

In turn, Rosemonde's fierce character is attenuated, which allows the audience to pity the lovers rather than fear their wrath. Baro's play does underscore the treachery of Rosemonde's and Ermige's act of regicide by providing moral, divine, and ideological arguments,[68] but the queen's confidant Axiane also declares that she will bury Rosemonde and Ermige together, and, to end the play, hopes that she may imitate Rosemonde's courage, presumably by committing suicide herself.[69] Baro thus provides an ambiguous ending to the play: despite the general ethical message of the play that condemns Rosemonde's sacrilegious revenge against the king, the last lines of the tragedy nonetheless praise Rosemonde's fortitude and self-sacrifice, and thus depict her as a troubled heroine who merits the audience's compassion and awe.

The Rosamund and Alboin story offered seventeenth-century French playwrights a tragic tale that they were able to exploit in many different ways. All four adaptations accuse Rosamund and her henchmen of taking revenge into their own hands for a personal affront against a (sacred) king, even if he behaved tyrannically. However, each play has its own particular angle to address the problem. On one hand, Chrestien's and Billard's plays explicitly engage with the relationship between the natural and the supernatural, by implementing the specter and the skull cup as dramaturgical devices, to promote moralizing and overtly didactic messages. On the other, *Rosimonde* and Baro's tragedy cater to their audiences' pleasure and entertainment by creating plots that do not pit the human characters against the supernatural but show them struggling with their own psyches and other human characters.

In this essay, then, I have taken into account the pervasive circulation of this story, its signs, and images to explore how, like the Gothic, it can help us understand various modes of destructive violence, social repressions, and disturbing sexual energies.[70] In effect, to explain Rosamund's character and her capacity to take action, I have paid particular attention to the importance of the supernatural in the earlier plays, which, in the fictional world of the theater, influences the behavior of the living with the help of supernatural beings and Cunimond's skull. These elements are very prevalent in Chrestien's and Billard's plays, but diminished, if not completely absent in *Rosimonde* and Baro's *Rosemonde*. By no means do I intend to suggest, however, that the metaphysical interplay between the dead and the living disappeared in seventeenth-century letters and thought; rather, it was displaced out of tragedy and into other genres, such as the machine play, opera, and later into the Gothic. To be sure, the posthumously published essay "On the Supernatural in Poetry" (1826) by the Gothic novelist Ann Radcliffe (1764–1823),[71] which reignited seventeenth-century debates regarding terror and horror through the lens of the Burkean sublime,[72] would interrogate and put in the foreground, yet again, the power of the dead over the living.[73]

## Notes

1. The Gepids were a Germanic tribe related to the Goths, located in northeast Italy. The Lombards originated in southern Scandinavia. The following, abridged synopsis comes from Paul the Deacon's *History of the Lombards*, one of the earliest and most influential accounts of the events: Paul the Deacon, *Historia Langobardorum (History of the Lombards)*, rev. ed., ed. Edward Peters, trans. William Dudley Foulke (1907; Philadelphia: University of Pennsylvania Press, 2003), 1.27.49–52; 2.28.81–2.30.86.

2. Ibid., 2.28.81.

3. There is some confusion in Paul the Deacon as to who murdered the king, though most contemporary sources agree that both Helmechis and Peredeo killed Alboin (Paul the Deacon, *History of the Lombards*, 2.28.82–83n1).

4. Ibid., 2.29.85. After their deaths, Peredeo was sent to Constantinople, where the emperor Justin ordered his eyes to be torn out (2.30.86). The author does not, however, recount Peredeo's death; rather, he praises him for killing two of the emperor's men despite his blindness.

5. In his recent book, John D. Lyons urges us to move away from the Idealist view of the tragic and "to conceive tragedy as a combination of personal roles and events, something closer to an 'actantial' conception of the tragic." In other words, "What is tragic is the representation or perception of a certain configuration of incidents (whether fictive or real) that lead to severe bodily harm, death, and, usually, the resultant need to dispose of one or more cadavers. Much that is called tragic does not take place in a struggle between heroes on the battlefield but rather, as Aristotle notes in pointing toward the source of the best subjects of tragedies, *within a certain number of families*" (*Tragedy and the Return of the Dead* [Evanston, Ill.: Northwestern University Press, 2018], 6–7, emphasis added). This conception of the tragic is central to many of the essays in the current volume, as Lyons points out in the introduction.

6. The bibliography that follows (in notes 7–11) is not exhaustive. A more thorough search must be conducted to find all of the versions of this story. Nonetheless, this preliminary list of texts amply shows the richness of the story and its popularity throughout Europe since the Middle Ages. Moreover, while the dramatic adaptations of Mariamne and Herod, for example, have benefited from a comprehensive study, no such study exists that examines and compares the Rosamund and Alboin plays. This would make for a very worthwhile project. See Maurice J. Valency, *The Tragedies of Herod and Mariamne* (New York: Columbia University Press, 1940).

7. Matteo Bandello, *La terza parte de le novelle* (1554), ed. Delmo Maestri (Alessandria: Edizioni dell'Orso, 1996), 18th Tale, 92–97; François de Belleforest, *Le quatriesme tome des histoires tragiques, partie extraites des œuvres italiennes du Bandel, et partie de*

*l'invention de l'autheur françois* (1570) (Turin: J. Farine, 1571), 73rd Tale, 547–98. This story is also found in Sebastian Münster's *Cosmographia* (1544), translated by Belleforest: *La cosmographie universelle de tout le monde* 1.2 (Paris: Michel Sonnius and Nicolas Chesneau, 1575), 599–600, 1738–39. In English, we find this story, a translation of Bandello, in George Tuberville, *Tragicall Tales* (London: Abel Jeffs, 1587), 5th Tale, 142–58. Numerous other prose versions existed before Bandello's *Novelle*, notably Boccaccio, *De casibus virorum illustrium* (ca. 1355–74), trans. Laurent de Premierfait, *Des cas des ruynes des nobles hommes et femmes* (ca. 1490), 8.17; and Niccolò Machiavelli, *Florentine Histories* (1532), trans. Laura F. Banfield and Harvey C. Mansfield Jr. (Princeton, N.J.: Princeton University Press, 1990), 1.8.17–19.

8. Giovanni di Bernardo Rucellai, *Rosmunda* (performed ca. 1515/16, printed 1525), in *Le opere*, ed. Guido Mazzoni (Bologna: Nicola Zanichelli Editore, 1887), 41–106. Antonio Cavallerino also adapted the story in the sixteenth century: *Rosimondo regina, tragedia* (1582?). In the seventeenth century, Angelita Scaramuccia wrote an adaption of the story titled *La Regina Rosmonda* (Pietro Salvioni: Macerata, 1619); in the eighteenth century, Vittorio Alfieri wrote a fictional account of Rosamund after Alboin's murder in *Rosmunda, tragedia* (performed in 1779, printed in 1780), which served as the base text for several nineteenth-century (musical) versions, such as Giovanni Battista Canovai, *Rosmunda, tragedia lirica* (Florence: Fioretti, 1868); and Cassiano Zaccagnini, *Rosmunda, melodramma tragico in due atti* (Florence: G. Galletti, 1840). In the twentieth century, Sem Benelli wrote *Rosmunda, tragedia* (1911); and Carlo Campogalliani made a film: *Rosmunda e Alboino* (*Sword of the Conqueror*), 1961.

9. William D'Avenant, *The Tragedy of Albouine, King of the Lombards* (London: Felix Kingston, 1629). In the nineteenth century, the story as a dramatic text resurged in England. For example, Henry Bellyse Baildon, *Rosamund, a Tragic Drama* (London: Longmans, Green, 1875); and Algernon Charles Swinburne, *Rosamund, Queen of the Lombards* (London: Chatto and Windus, 1899).

10. In German: Rudolph Otto Consentius, *Alboin, Trauerspiel in Drei Akten* (Stuttgart, 1842); Wilhelm Fellechner and (music by) Richard Metzdorff, *Rosamunde und der Untergang des Gepidenreiches: Große Oper in 5 Akten* (1873); Friedrich Wilhelm Schuster, *Alboin und Rosimond, Trauerspiel in fünf Aufzügen* (1884). In Dutch: Jacob Stryus, *Albonus en Rosimonda treur-spel,* (1631). In Latin: Jacobus Zevocotius, *Rosimunda, tragoedia* (1621). In Swedish: Urban Hjärne, *Rosimunda, tragedi* (1665). The Lombards' Scandinavian origins might explain Hjärne's interest in this story.

11. Nicolas Chrestien des Croix, *Rosemonde, ou la vengeance, tragédie* (Rouen: Théodore Reinsart, 1603), revised with a new title, *Alboüin, ou la vengeance, tragédie* (Rouen: Théodore Reinsart, 1608); Claude Billard, *Alboin, tragédie*, in *Tragédies françoises* (Paris: D. Langlois, 1610), 137r–162v; Anonymous, *Rosimonde, ou le parricide puny, tragédie* (Rouen: Louys Oursel, 1640); Balthasar Baro, *Rosemonde, tragédie de Monsieur Baro* (Paris: Antoine de Sommaville, 1651). Among the French playwrights who adapted the story, only Chrestien de Croix names his sources: Paul the Deacon, Machiavelli, and Munster (perhaps via Belleforest). Unless there are remarkable variations, I will use Chrestien's 1608 *Alboüin* rather than the original *Rosemonde* from

1603. For the remainder of the article, I spell the characters' names in accordance with the different dramatic adaptations. I was able to read Chrestien's and Billard's plays online, whereas Baro's and the anonymous poet's plays were not accessible electronically. In turn, I consulted Baro's play at Harvard's Houghton Library while attending the Mellon School for Theater and Performance Research in June 2016, and *Rosimonde* at the Bibliothèque de l'Arsenal.

12. Lancaster E. Dabney, *Claude Billard, Minor French Dramatist of the Early Seventeenth Century* (Baltimore: Johns Hopkins University Press, 193), 110. Sybile Chevallier-Micki has uncovered that Chrestien was known as a *maître-ès-arts* and was also a priest in Champ-Cervon (today Le Grippon, since January 2016). "Tragédies et théâtre rouennais (1566–1640): Scénographies de la cruauté" (Ph.D. diss., Univ. Paris-Ouest Nanterre La Défense, 2013), 582–83, https://bdr.u-paris10.fr/theses/internet/2013PA100019.pdf.

13. Baro's oeuvre has recently piqued the interest of researchers; Bénédicte Louvat is directing a project to edit his theatrical texts. Thus far, one volume has appeared, and it includes *Le Cléosandre* (1624), *Saint Eustache martyr* (1649), and *Cariste* (1651), in *Théâtre complet*, vol. 1 (Paris: Classiques Garnier, 2015).

14. Roméo Arbour attributes the play either to Guérin de Bouscal or Jacques Crosnier, called Du Perche. *L'ère baroque en France: Répertoire chronologique des éditions de textes littéraires, Troisième partie, 1629–1643* (Geneva: Librairie Droz, 1980), 511. Others give Du Perche the first name Nicolas. The attribution to Du Perche appears to have originated in Louis-César de la Vallière et al., *Bibliothèque du théâtre françois depuis son origine*, vol. 3 (Dresden: Michel Groell, 1768), 15. Paul Lacroix reiterated this attribution in the *Bibliothèque dramatique de Monsieur Soleinne*, vol. 1 (Paris: Administration de l'Alliance des Arts, 1843), 263. Henry Carrington Lancaster contests Lacroix's attribution but does not propose an author (*A History of French Dramatic Literature in the Seventeenth Century*, pt. 2: *The Period of Corneille [1635–1651]*, vol. 1 [Baltimore: Johns Hopkins University Press, 1932], 194n11). The play is dedicated to Messire P. F. Sieur Marquis de C. T. Baron de la B., whose identity is also unknown. To add to the mystery of this text, according to Arbour, the bookseller (*libraire*) Louis Oursel sold only three other texts in the seventeenth century: two English-language grammars (*Alphabet anglois: Contenant la prononciation des lettres avec les declinaisons et conjugaison*; *Grammere angloise pour facilement et promptement apprendre la langue Angloise*) and an edition of François de Rosset's *Histoires tragiques*. All three appeared in 1639 (*L'ère baroque*, 434–35, 450–51, 469). According to Alain Riffaud, Robert Féron was the printer of the play (*Répertoire du théâtre français imprimé entre 1630 et 1660* [Geneva: Droz, 2009], 120).

15. Dabney, *Claude Billard*, 115–18; Forsyth to a lesser extent, in *La tragédie française de Jodelle à Corneille (1553–1640): Le thème de la vengeance. Edition revue et augmentée* (Paris: Honoré Champion, 1994), 334–35. Dabney also devotes an entire chapter to Billard's *Alboin* (*Claude Billard*, 68–76). In his analysis of Chrestien's play, Forsyth describes it as a *pièce macabre* that places too much importance on violent scenes and moralizing discourses, while he criticizes Billard's tragedy for being a singularly flat

work (*La tragédie française*, 267–82, 334). Enrica Zanin, inspired by Forsyth's analyses, has compared the adaptations of Rucellai, Chrestien, Billard, Scaramuccia, and Cavallerino from the vantage of what she labels the "pedagogy of revenge" (pédagogie de la vengeance) (*Fins tragiques: Poétique et éthique du dénouement dans la tragédie de la première modernité [Italie, France, Espagne, Allemagne]* [Geneva: Librairie Droz, 2014], 362–68). In Thomas L. Zamparelli's chapter on *Alboin*, Zamparelli compares the tragedy with Billard's *Saül* and *Panthée* to contest conventional criteria against which Billard's theater has been negatively critiqued, such as the "baroque" and the three unities, and ultimately argues that these plays "require a new type of reading or viewing" (*The Theater of Claude Billard: A Study in Post-Renaissance Esthetics* [New Orleans: Tulane Studies in Romance Languages and Literatures, 1978], 75). Chevallier-Micki bookends her doctoral dissertation on stage design in Rouen with *Rosimonde*. She suggests that the play "establishes a delightful mixing of genres. The reversals of the heroine's passions are as numerous as the onstage deaths, the clumsy changes in register create a great energetic force, and the profuse stage directions participate in the economy of the short and quick play, unfortunately without interest other than the elevated rhythm" (établit un réjouissant mélange des genres. Les revirements des passions de l'héroïne sont aussi nombreux que les morts sur scène, les changements de registre, maladroits, projettent un fort dynamisme, et les nombreuses indications de jeu participent à l'économie de la pièce, courte, rapide et, malheureusement, sans autre intérêt que ce rythme soutenu) ("Tragédies et théâtre rouennais," 276). Lancaster provides an even harsher value judgment of the play: "The play is carelessly written. . . . [The playwright] had no regard for rules of unity, propriety, preparation, or versification. A number of unnecessary characters are introduced. There are three distinct plots that follow one after another. What unity there is lies in the character of the heroine, but she is too superficially portrayed to redeem the tragedy. In short the work is obviously the composition of a provincial, only partly in touch with the dramatic movement of his day" (*History of French Dramatic Literature*, 2.1.195). Given these descriptions, one might be reminded of decadent English tragedies of the 1630s and 1640s. On one hand, in fact, it is possible that the playwright may have been aware of contemporaneous English theater; D'Avenant did have his version of the story printed in 1629, after all. On the other, the so-called "tragedy" *Rosimonde* could be read as a parody, for the playwright seems to be aware of other famous plays of its time, notably *Le Cid* (1636) and *Horace* (1640) by the Rouennais Pierre Corneille (1606–1684), and it turns well-known tragic situations into ridiculous farces. The title of the play itself, which replaces the silent "e" in Rosemonde with a pronounced "i," to Rosimonde, very well may indicate such parodical potential. Finally, neither Lancaster in *History of French Dramatic Literature* nor Zanin in *Fins tragiques* include Baro's play, but Lise Michel has studied it with regard to the representation, politics, and ethics of regicide in French tragedy alongside other plays, with a passing mention of the anonymous *Rosimonde*: "Régicide et dramaturgie dans la tragédie française, de *La mort de César* de Scudéry (1636) à la *Rosemonde* de Baro (1650)" (*Littératures classiques* 67, no. 3 [2008]: 115–29).

16. No modern editions of these plays currently exist. For Chrestien's and Billard's

plays, I will cite act and page number(s); for *Rosimonde* and Baro's play, I will cite act, scene, and page number(s).

17. Dabney disparages the choice of Totyle as he does not have a direct link to the Rosamund story (*Claude Billard*, 73), yet Paul the Deacon opens the second book, which recounts Alboin's assassination, with Totila and the defeat of the Goths at the hands of the Italian Narses and the Longobard Alboin (*History of the Lombards*, 2.1.53–54). Moreover, it is possible that Billard avoided putting a desire for revenge into the mouth of Rosamund's dead father, as her vengeance will cause her own demise. It is rather cruel that a father would put his revenge above his own daughter's life, a sentiment that Chrestien's Comonde expresses once he realizes this grim outcome: "Mais ie plains Rosemonde, helas! las! ie la plains! / Innocente soufrir des tourmens inhumains! / Ma geniture helas!" (But I pity Rosamund, alas! Alas! I pity her! Innocent woman to suffer inhuman tourments! My daughter, alas!) (1.8).

18. Chrestien, *Rosemonde*, 3.42.

19. Jacques Scherer writes that playwrights sometimes brought ghosts onstage to incite terror ("font quelquefois venir en scène l'ombre de ces morts pour produire la terreur"), but he does not propose other purposes of the ghost in the unfolding of the action (Jacques Scherer, *La dramaturgie classique en France* [Paris: Nizet, 1954], 169). On the staging of ghosts as illusions (*songes*), see Jacques Morel, *Agréables mensonges: Essais sur le théâtre français du XVIIè siècle* (Paris: Klincksieck, 1991), 35–37. On the various functions of the ghost, both in theory and in practice in Italy and France at this time, see François Lecercle, "L'automate et le fauteur de troubles: Les usages de l'ombre dans la tragédie de la Renaissance," in *Dramaturgies de l'ombre*, ed. François Lecercle and Françoise Lavocat (Rennes: Presses universitaires de Rennes, 2005), 31–67.

20. See Olivier Millet, "Faire parler les morts: L'ombre protatique comme prosopopée dans les tragédies françaises de la Renaissance," in *Dramaturgies de l'ombre*, ed. Lecercle and Lavocat, 85–100.

21. Dabney, *Claude Billard*, 73.

22. Terence Cave, *Pré-histoires: Textes troublés au seuil de la modernité* (Geneva: Droz, 1999), 139–41.

23. Ibid., 130–32.

24. One might also think of this dynamic in terms of "atmosphere" as opposed to "character," as Timothy Reiss has suggested. In Reiss's view, playwrights of Chrestien's and Billard's generation prioritized an atmosphere in which characters are placed, whereas the next generation of dramatic poets highlighted the characters' actions as crucial to the development of the plot. Fate and destiny do not disappear as the seventeenth century progresses; however, it is no longer expressed by external, supernatural characters (i.e., ghosts and gods) but put into the mouths of the living characters themselves: the "overshadowing atmosphere disappears, to be replaced by the spectator's anxiety" (Timothy J. Reiss, *Toward Dramatic Illusion: Theatrical Technique and Meaning from Hardy to Horace* [New Haven: Yale University Press, 1971], 33–54,

44). Reiss compares and contrasts Alexandre Hardy's *Mariamne*, which opens with the ghost of Aristobule, with Tristan l'Hermite's *La Mariane*, which has Hérode awaken from a dream in which the ghost appears to him before the tragedy begins, yet similar remarks can be made about the presence and absence of ghosts in the contemporaneous adaptations of the Rosamund story.

25. For more on the topic of chance, see John D. Lyons, *The Phantom of Chance: From Fortune to Randomness in Seventeenth-Century French Literature* (Edinburgh: Edinburgh University Press, 2011).

26. Forsyth, *La tragédie française*, 278–79. Similarly, the subtitle of *Rosimonde*, "ou le parricide puny" (or the punished parricide), can refer both to the punishment of Alboin for having murdered his father-in-law as well as to that of Helmichis and Rosimonde for having slayed the sovereign, although, significantly, the notion of divine or supernatural vengeance does not appear in *Rosimonde*.

27. Chrestien, *Alboüin*, 1. 2; 4.

28. Ibid., 1.4–8.

29. Billard, *Alboin*, 1.140r.

30. Ibid., 1.139v–40r.

31. Ibid., 2.143v–44v.

32. Belleforest adds this detail after she has been presented with her father's skull: "Ce estoit sans cesse qu'elle auoit deuant les yeux Gomond Roy Gepide son pere massacré" (She ceaselessly had her slaughtered father before her eyes, the Gepid king Cunimond) (*Quatriesme tome*, 561). This particularity does not exist in Paul the Deacon's account.

33. Chrestien, *Alboüin*, 3.43.

34. Ibid., 3.45.

35. Lyons, *Tragedy and the Return of the Dead*, 153.

36. Baro, *Rosemonde*, 3.4.5, emphasis added.

37. Ibid., 3.4.46.

38. Ibid., 4.2.65.

39. Anonymous, *Rosimonde*, 3.4.40–45. This battle scene between the six men might very well be a parody of the famous one between the Horace and the Curiace brothers as Corneille represents it in *Horace*, a tragedy that was first performed in March 1640 but read in various *salons* before the public performance. *Rosimonde* was also printed in 1640, though it is unknown in which month.

40. Ibid., 2.4.31.

41. Ibid., 2.1.19.

42. In *Rosimonde*, as in Baro's *Rosemonde*, Rosamund is betrothed to Helmichis but is forced, and greatly distressed, to marry her father's murderer, Alboin, echoing Chimène's famous dilemma in Corneille's *Le Cid*.

43. Billard, *Alboin*, 5.156v–57v.

44. Ibid., 5.156v.

45. Hannibal, a nobleman, expresses this concern just after Rosemonde's final monologue (Billard, *Alboin*, 5.159v).

46. Baro, *Rosemonde*, 3.4, 46–47.
47. Ibid., 4.2.64.
48. Forsyth, *La tragédie française*, 281.
49. Chrestien, *Alboüin*, 4.56–58.
50. Rosemonde as a "living dead" might lead one to think of the *devotus*, which Giorgio Agamben has analyzed alongside the figure of *homo sacer*, in *Homo Sacer: Sovereign Power and Bare Life*, trans. Daniel Heller-Roazen (Stanford: Stanford University Press, 1998), 59–64.
51. Lyons, *Tragedy and the Return of the Dead*, 162.
52. On Medea, see *Théâtre de la cruauté et récits sanglants*, ed. Christian Biet et al. (Paris: Robert Laffont, 2006), 452–58.
53. "I'iray par l'Vnivers, aus lieux plus solitaires / Inuoquer les Demons, les ombres mortuaires, / Les monstres, les Tytans [...] Pour me vanger." (I will go through the Universe, to the most solitary places / To call upon the Demons, the shadows of the dead, / The monsters, the Titans [...] to get my revenge.] (Billard, *Alboin*, 5.157r–v).
54. Belleforest, *Quatriesme tome*, 581.
55. Chrestien, *Alboüin*, 4.55.
56. Anonymous, *Rosimonde*, 3.4.29–31.
57. Ibid., 5.1.66–67.
58. Ibid., 4.5.63–65.
59. I have shown that Billard's Rosemonde is a relentlessly treacherous and reprehensible spouse and Chrestien's Rosemonde only very briefly expresses some hesitation in pursuing revenge (Chrestien, *Alboüin*, 4.55).
60. Baro, *Rosemonde*, 4.2.63–65.
61. Ibid., 4.3.67–68.
62. Ibid., 4.4.69–72.
63. Ibid., 4.5.73–74.
64. Baro presents Ermige as a faithful subject of Albouyn who only avenges Rosemonde lest she end her own life (3.5.53–55).
65. The doctor is named as Nicanor in the list of actors.
66. Baro, *Rosemonde*, 5.5.84.
67. Ibid., 5.5–6.86–93.
68. Michel, "Régicide et dramaturgie," 128.
69. Axiane: "Je veux de Rosemonde imiter le courage, / Et d'eternelles pleurs moüillant ces tristes lieux / Tout ce que j'ay de sang sortira par mes yeux." (I will imitate Rosemonde's courage, / And bathing these sad places with eternal tears / All my blood will flow from my eyes.) (Baro, *Rosemonde*, 5, 93).
70. Fred Botting, "Preface: The Gothic," in *The Gothic*, ed. Botting (Woodbridge: D. S. Brewer, 2001), 5–6.
71. Ann Radcliffe, "On the Supernatural in Poetry," *New Monthly Magazine* (1826): 145–52. It would be apropos to mention that Radcliffe uses examples from Shakespeare rather than from Gothic novels.
72. According to Radcliffe, the indeterminacy of horrible events, terror, leads to

the sublime, whereas the accumulation of unambiguous horrific atrocities "nearly annihilate" the reader's and/or spectator's responsive capacity. This line of reasoning continued into the twentieth century, especially since the late 1960s and 1970s, when Robert Hume and Robert Platzner debated the issue. For Hume, as for Radcliffe, there were two kinds of Gothic: the Terror-Gothic and the Horror-Gothic (Robert Hume, "Gothic versus Romantic: A Revaluation of the Gothic Novel," *PMLA* 84 [1969]: 282–90; Robert L. Platzner, "'Gothic versus Romantic': A Rejoinder," *PMLA* 86 [1971]: 266–74). Terror-Gothic was represented by Horace Walpole (1717–1797) and Radcliffe, whereas William Thomas Beckford (1760–1844), Matthew Gregory Lewis (1775–1818), Charles Robert Maturin (1782–1824), and Mary Shelley (1797–1851) deploy the Horror-Gothic. Terror-Gothic holds the reader's attention through suspense or dread, but Horror-Gothic attacks frontally with events that shock or disturb. The former elaborates possibilities that never materialize; the latter heaps a succession of horrors upon the reader or spectator.

73. Scholars of French dramatic theory of sixteenth- and seventeenth-century tragedy will be familiar with similar debates. On one hand, horrific spectacles in the first few decades of the seventeenth century included violent acts such as torture, rape, mutilation, cannibalism, murder, and so forth, directly put onstage for the spectators to see. On the other, as John D. Lyons has argued, at least in the case of *La poëtique* (1639) by Hippolyte-Jules Pilet de La Mesnarière (1610–63), terror in seventeenth-century French tragedy involves some kind of mediation of these horrific acts, most usually through language, to put these events in the past tense, away from the spectators' eyes and into their imaginations (John D. Lyons, *Kingdom of Disorder: The Theory of Tragedy in Classical France* [West Lafayette, IN: Purdue University Press, 1999], 55–68). Fabien Cavaillé has recently revisited the debates surrounding the question of violence in poetic treatises in France and Italy in the sixteenth and seventeenth centuries (*Alexandre Hardy et le théâtre de ville français au début du XVIIè siècle* [Paris: Classiques Garnier, 2016]), especially the first part, titled "Ensanglanter la scène? Une controverse sur la force pathétique du spectacle violent en Italie et en France (XVIè-XVIIè siècle)," 35–130.

CAROLINE WARMAN

## "Autre fait arrivé au château de Nicklspurg, en Moravie"
### Diderot and the Horrid Case Study

The "dark thread" hypothesis seems to be made for application to Diderot's work, and vice versa. Its first swathe of propositions—that violence within the family in both high and low culture is the fundamental motor of tragedy, that as an art form tragedy becomes etiolated when cut off from its lurid underpinning, and that the *histoires tragiques* exemplify this fruitful cross-pollination—all resonate in interesting ways with his *Entretiens sur "Le fils naturel"* (Discussions about *The Natural Son*), which lobbies for the establishment of the *drame bourgeois*, that is, a form of drama that connects directly to recognizable family dilemmas, neither mocking its lowborn characters as comedy does nor presenting a God-like elite in the way of neoclassical tragedy. Furthermore, we also find important confirmation within Diderot's work of the dark thread's rejection of the (received and largely anglophone) view that the Gothic is specific to the late eighteenth century and a response to its particular historical moment, given that the Gothic's potent mix of lurid violence, bizarre families, and the frightful unknown had been strongly present in culture at least since the proliferation of the *histoires tragiques* in the sixteenth century. In the case of Diderot, it is his novel *La religieuse*, or *The Nun*, which can be drawn on to demonstrate that what is normally associated with the Gothic in fact preexisted its emergence. This is probably more convincing than the existing account of the Gothic, which does indeed often mention *The Nun* but does so with reference to the precursor model. Thus it is supposed to have heralded the Gothic novel with its themes of forced imprisonment, cruelty, and sexual frustration, not to mention its gloriously beautiful young female victim. Yet the "heralding" motif can also be reassigned in temporal terms away from "being in advance of and in some way causing the rise of" (which would have been hard, given that it wasn't published until 1796) to "already being there," thereby again confirming John Lyons's intuition of the "dark thread." Finally, the aspects of "copia" and "varietas" that Hervé Campangne identifies as being an important aspect of the fifth volume of Belleforest's *Histoires tragiques*, with their accompanying "parcours encyclopédique," as Campangne puts it, also have important resonance for Diderot the *encyclopédiste*.[1] So it is clear that Diderot's work and this "dark thread" hypothesis are mutually illuminating.

However, this essay will look at a much less obviously promising text of his—one of his last, least well-known and also least-appreciated works, the *Eléments de physiologie* (Elements of physiology), which he was still working on until soon before his death in 1784. It is a descriptive analysis of the human body and its brain functions, presented uniquely as phenomena of matter and therefore without soul.

The *Eléments de physiologie* starts with element and organism, then places humans within a universe of matter, thereafter focusing in on the human body, always looking at its component parts in the context of the properties and behavior of matter. It works through questions of perception and sensation as widely shared by all animals including humans and then considers questions of language, memory and imagination, the elements of human self-consciousness, and awareness of time and decline. It urgently asks a series of relaying questions, each one of which leads to the next: What is an organized being? Organized to do what? In what way? How can an organized being become a human? What is sensation? What is movement? What is memory, and what is madness? What is love, what is hunger, what is health?

The model of nature it works with is of connected cause and effect over time, from simple to complex. The same explicatory model is used to structure the book as a whole. Particular interest is shown in the shifts from one class of beings to the next, and a similar writerly interest is shown in transitions from one topic to the next. The style and treatment of any particular topic is tightly logical, in that it proceeds by "if this, then this" steps, but it is also exploratory, and therefore not always predictable. Diderot often uses syllogisms to force us to compare things we would never think of comparing, for example, love and hunger.[2] Diderot the materialist wishes to get his reader to understand and face the depth of continuity between human and all other living beings, and his relativizing comparisons are often astonishing (comparing the speed of flow in rivers and blood, for example), while the case studies and exemplifications can be bizarre (a comparison between fingers and pincers) or grotesque (the love affairs of the genitally malformed). Partly this is in order to get the reader's attention, to make him or her inhabit an unhabitual perspective, and to experience the pages being read via the imagination. Partly it is simply to describe this depth of continuity and break down preconceived barriers between humans (endowed with mind, and thus special), and the rest of nature. It is a fundamentally atheist text, and not, therefore, one would have thought, the most obvious arena for the dark thread hypothesis to play out, particularly if we associate the dark thread with the irrational, and Diderot's *Eléments de physiologie*, this sort of materialist textbook, with the famed rationalism of the Enlightenment. And yet, it is surprisingly framed and even shot through with elements of the dark thread in its various aspects. It contains the inexplicable, monstrous, and supernatural, and also family tragedy. Let us start with the monstrous.

> L'univers ne semble quelquefois qu'un assemblage d'êtres monstrueux.
> Qu'est qu'un monstre? Un être, dont la durée est incompatible avec l'ordre subsistant.
> Mais l'ordre général change sans cesse.[3]
>
> (Sometimes the universe seems to be nothing other than an assemblage of monstrous beings.
> What is a monster? A being whose continuance is incompatible with the subsisting order.
> But the general order changes ceaselessly.)

So we know of course that "monster" in the early modern period was a capacious term and did not mean some outsize hairy thing with big teeth, although it could also mean that.[4] It is the term that designates deformity of some sort, something that diverges from the natural. But it is clear that for Diderot, it is not a diversion; it is not *unnatural* or *contre* nature.[5] It *is* nature, and nature emphatically includes humans: "Il n'y a pas sur toute la surface de la terre un seul homme parfaitement constitué, parfaitement sain. L'espèce humaine n'est qu'un amas d'individus plus ou moins contrefaits, plus ou moins malades." (There is no single man on the whole surface of the earth who is perfectly formed, perfectly healthy. The human species is nothing other than a mass of individuals who are more or less deformed, more or less ill.)[6] This particular extract comes from the conclusion, but the book as a whole opens with a similar sort of statement, and there are many other such.⁷ There is only ever infinite variation on malady and monstrosity. The rational, the abstract, the universalizing generalisation seem to have little place here. So much for the stereotype of the rationalizing Enlightenment.

The next passage seems to take all these aspects and twist them even further. It comes from Diderot's *Pensées sur l'interprétation de la nature* (*Thoughts on the Interpretation of Nature*), published in 1753, and it is Pensée 40: "Les grandes abstractions ne comportent qu'une *lueur sombre*. L'acte de la généralisation tend à *dépouiller* les concepts de tout ce qu'ils ont de *sensible*. A mesure que cet acte s'avance, les *spectres corporels s'évanouissent*; les notions se retirent peu à peu de *l'imagination* vers l'entendement; et les idées deviennent purement *intellectuelles*." (Big abstractions only shed a somber glimmer. The act of generalizing tends to strip concepts of everything that is living and feeling about them. As this process continues, bodily ghosts disappear; notions withdraw bit by bit from the imagination and move toward the understanding; ideas become purely intellectual.)⁸ So, big abstractions only shed a somber glimmer. Generalizations tend to strip concepts of their living feeling aspects. As this act of generalizing—notice that it is an act—advances, the bodily specters (or corporeal ghosts or the specters of the body) faint away; notions withdraw bit by bit from the imagination toward the understanding, and ideas become purely intellectual.

The vocabulary is that of sensibility, with a clearly Gothic tinge—the somber glimmer, the bodily specters, the fainting. Is Diderot appropriating this vocabulary simply to spice up his writing or perhaps just to ironize the Gothic melodrama innate to the imagery—and even his own topic—in this book with its *intellectual ideas*? I don't think so. It is too potently paradoxical to be nothing more than a stylistic flourish, too much of an inversion of what we might expect, and (we might add) is therefore typical of Diderot. Here it is the material body that is spectral, and vanishes, rather than the more obviously immaterial or ethereal world of intellectual abstraction. And by inverting what might seem to be the more obvious associations, Diderot forces us to see that it is absurd for the body to be the ghost that vanishes, when *obviously* it is real; according to the logic of this inversion, therefore, ideas that are purely intellectual are *not* real.

This reading would suggest that Diderot is using the dark thread vocabulary derisively, to undermine the immaterial in all forms. Beyond that, I would suggest that Diderot is *also* playing with the *inexplicability* of the body (drawn out by analogy with ghosts) and also with the way ghosts *disrupt* the notion of rational regularity, or abstraction: the body—again by analogy—disrupts "rational" expectations. And at the same time, the supernatural or spectral has been realigned with the real, which is in turn colored by the spectral's unignorable, disruptive, anxiety-inducing unknowability, and presumably—in the context of the Eléments de physiologie—also deformity. From this point of view, the individual stories—all the actual bodies and their particular conformations and lived difficulties—are the real and also the disruptive, the disturbing, the ill, the monstrous; and without the imagination they cannot be comprehended.

So, if for Diderot the materialist, abstractions are impossible, then every point must be exemplified, personalized, incorporated, embodied. And this is often done by means of a striking tale of tragedy, as we will not be surprised to hear given Diderot's statements about illness,[9] and the most striking of them don't come singly but in multiples, sticking out of the text like pins, or rather, seeing as they're in footnotes, *underpinning* it. The two longest footnotes in the book by far are just such. In the manuscript version, the footnote handwriting is just as big as it is in the main body of the text. The illustration shows how they displace the supposedly "main body" of the text. And in looking at images of the manuscript it is interesting to consider printing conventions according to which a footnote is printed smaller than the main text, and whether we ought to revisit our assumptions about the relative importance or hierarchy between the different parts of the text.

The footnote is in part 2 of the *Elements de physiologie*, which describes the elements and parts of the human body, in the long chapter on reproduction and how it occurs.[10] (Diderot presents five different theories.) This footnote gives examples of the statement in the main body of the text about it being possible to get pregnant even when—as the writer carefully puts it—the woman is infibulated, that is, without any apparent sex organ. The first case relates how the lover of a young woman with this particular problem is not put off but simply requires her to "indulge him in a different way," as the text coyly says, and she is happy to oblige. Her stomach starts to swell and she calls a doctor, who pronounces her pregnant. She has no difficulty proving to him that this is impossible, and yet her stomach and bosom continue to swell, and she calls him a second time. He swears she's pregnant, but the young woman and her lover pay no attention. After nine months she has terrible pains, and after horrendous tearing a baby is born "by the same route he was conceived." Diderot finishes by saying he does not know whether the mother and child died or not but that her particular "formation" is in no way uncommon. He then supplies his scholarly source.[11]

The second instance starts with the title quotation, that is, "another true

Ruisch a trouvé la semence de l'homme et de la femme dans la matrice d'une femme qui venait d'être tuée par un matelot avec lequel elle avait pris querelle immediatement après en avoir été connue. Mais Harvey a disséqué des biches sans nombre immediatement après l'approche du cerf, et n'a jamais trouvé de liqueur seminale dans leur matrice. Il n'y a vû d'abord qu'un point animé autour duquel se sont successivement arrangés les divers membres qui composent l'animal.

Dans la matrice de la lapine on n'y voit rien les cinq ou six premiers jours. Le 7.e on apperçoit un embrion, puis

Sobat s'etait plaint plusieurs fois de sentir remuer quelque chose dans son ventre, et particulierement trente heures avant sa mort; mais on avait attribué ce simptome aux eaux, que l'on supposait. Il ne restait aucun doute sur la maniere dont cet homme pouvait avoir engendré, mais pour s'en rendre encore plus certain, on s'empara de son compagnon de lit, on le mit aux fers, et par des menaces reiterées on lui fit avouer ce que l'on soupçonnait violemment (gazette des deux ponts année 1775. n.º 72)

Diderot, *Eléments de physiologie*, BnF, Manuscrits, NAF 13762, ff.98r story that took place in the castle of Nicklsburg in Moravia"—a good German setting for a Gothic story. It involves a twenty-two-year-old soldier whose stomach started swelling and who complained of nausea. He was treated for dropsy, which had no effect. His stomach kept growing, but he felt fine, and it had no impact on his ability to carry out his duties, with which he kept on very cheerfully. Then, on 3 February 1773, he suddenly had acute pains in his lumbar region. First he was treated with sedatives, which didn't work; then they gave him a lumbar puncture, which also didn't work. They tried bleeding him. Nothing worked, and the pains just grew worse and worse. He started going into convulsions. After ninety-seven hours of suffering, he died. This was all so surprising and baffling that an autopsy was performed, and imagine everyone's surprise—interjects the source narrator—when they discovered a sort of cyst or sac in the soldier's abdomen in which they found a perfectly formed—although dead—baby boy. This sack was of course a uterus, which communicated with the rectum by means of a very narrow tube that was smaller even than the ink feeder in a fountain pen. Otherwise, the soldier was "perfectly" male both internally and externally. The unnamed and unpersonalized observers then remember that the soldier had complained he felt something moving inside him about thirty hours before he died. The story ends balefully: "they" are in no doubt about how this all happened, but just for the avoidance of doubt, they seize the soldier's bedfellow, clap him in irons, and repeatedly "threaten him" until he finally admits what "they" had "violently suspected." And there, with a cursory reference to the source, the footnote ends.[12]

Of course, the history of medicine and of law is full of bizarre "cases" that sometimes leap off the page in a way that brings to their subjects to life—as many have noticed, not least Natalie Zemon Davis in her work on Martin Guerre and on the pardon cases in *Fiction in the Archives*.[13] This aspect is not a sideline for the *histoires tragiques* topic but on the contrary is central, a very rich and deep meeting of high and low cultures, where the educated writer—a literate observer, whether lawyer or doctor—commits to writing the events and words of those being observed, generally in accordance with certain forms of professional code. These sorts of "cases" are obviously problematic and revealing in equal measure, but when a writer such as Diderot adopts and re-uses them, they begin to resonate in an entirely new way. His framing of these two tales and the way in which he brings them together give them great prominence, even just in terms of space on the page.

Lightly sketched as they are, both stories are full of human detail and character—the lovers in the first story who eagerly find a way round the woman's irregular physical formation and who repeatedly ignore the doctor's prognosis; in the second, the cheerful character of the soldier who willingly gets on with his duties, and the intimacy of the hidden relationship. The economy of the telling and the narrative trajectory increase, I would argue, the impact of the shadows around the story—that which is not known, or not said. The not knowing whether the mother and child died in the first increases both the reader's sense of the observer's callousness while also returning attention to the human outcome—certainly shocking and probably tragic for those involved. The shape of the Moravian story is not dissimilar, in that the relation of the everyday duties and interactions end in baffled suffering and tragedy. In this case, however, it seems more intensely tragic: the soldier suffers for ninety-seven hours, he does die, and so does the child, while his "bedfellow," or rather his *lover*, not only loses him but is imprisoned because of their relationship, the violence of the suspicion being a transposition, we assume, of the way in which he is treated. Diderot's retelling and reframing sharply juxtaposes the precise and sceptical empiricism of the doctor anatomist with a complex human situation in time—the emphasis is not only on the person with the malformed body but on the human relationships he or she has, and on the consequences of the bodily malformation on those relationships. The distance of the recording eye in combination with the intensity, strangeness, and tragedy of the human events make for a powerful mix—lurid, bizarre, and borderline inexplicable, they constitute what looks to me very much like *des histoires tragiques*.

The effect that the presence of these and other such narratives have on the *Eléments de physiologie* as a whole is to make sure we don't get lost in abstractions about matter and its movement. They tell us what it feels like to be a piece of matter, or a piece of malformed matter, with love and tragedy. Not special, not heroic, yet still intense, still worthy of attention and compassion. They are part of Diderot's answer to the philosophical question about what happens to identity, individuality, and the all-round unique specialness and perfection of the human being when viewed as nothing more or less than the temporary happenstance of material organization. The notions of identity or selfhood with their theological and hierarchical dimensions may all fall away when humans are viewed as a certain species of animal, and what is left may well be both fragile and impermanent,[14] but perception and experience—what it feels like to be alive—are no less complex or intense. Or, in these cases, tragic. That for me is the resonance of these tales. They do join together high and low culture; they involve ordinary people in horrid and extreme situations that are nonetheless recognizable, and that are tragic.

We claimed earlier that the *Eléments de physiologie* are surprisingly framed and even shot through with elements of the dark thread in its various aspects, on the one hand, the inexplicable, monstrous, or supernatural; and on the other, family tragedy. But the supernatural was the least present element—and the passage that mentions ghosts was from the *Pensées sur l'interprétation de la nature*, not from the *Eléments de physiologie*. However, a fully fledged ghost theme does emerge at the end of the *Eléments de physiologie*, in a rather surprising way for the materialist proof that it is. In the conclusion, certainty about what is real and what is not, all based on material embodiments of one sort of another, suddenly disappears to make way for a sort of spectral idealism of great poetic intensity: "Qu'aperçois-je? Des formes; et quoi encore? Des formes; j'ignore la chose. Nous nous promenons entre des ombres, ombres nous-mêmes, pour les autres et pour nous. Si je regarde l'arc-en-ciel tracé sur la nue, je le vois; pour celui qui regarde sous un autre angle, il n'y a rien." (What do I see? Forms: and what else? Forms; things are unknown to me. We walk between shadows, shadows ourselves, to others and to ourselves. If I look at the rainbow traced across the skies, I see it; someone else looking from another angle sees nothing there.)[15] This then develops into a fully fledged ghost story: "Une fantaisie assez commune aux vivants, c'est de se supposer morts, d'être debout à côté de leurs cadavres et de suivre le convoi. C'est un nageur qui regarde son vêtement étendu sur le rivage. Homme qu'on ne craint plus, qu'avez-vous alors entendu?" (A fantasy that is quite common among the living is to imagine oneself dead, standing next to one's own corpse and following the funeral convoy. It's the same as a swimmer looking at his clothes laid out on the bank. Man we no longer fear, what did you hear then?)[16]

Again, this is multilayered. This vision of following one's own funeral procession may be a fantasy, but it gathers its own fictional impetus. The interjected depiction of a swimmer looking back at this clothes laid out on the shore adds another dimension, giving more imaginative investment to the scenario, which is now overlaid with a second narrative line.[17] And then Diderot apostrophizes the dead man directly—so it is no longer a scenario of a living man imagining himself dead but of a living man talking to a dead man, a dead man whom we no longer fear, because he's dead, although at the moment of asking this peremptory question, the dead man's experience of listening to people talking about him is already in the past.[18] So his being dead exists in time. The *Eléments de physiologie* ends just a few lines later, after a reference to stoicism, and with a recommendation not to fear death. So this ghostly scenario occupies a prominent place, as prominent if not more so than the big swelling of the footnote we looked at before. What could it possibly mean that Diderot ends his materialist treatise of the human body and mind on this note?

It is probably not because Diderot means to undermine his materialist position or move toward scepticism or idealism. It feels more accurate to say that what Diderot is doing after all his conscientious, precise, and lengthy explanation of the body and how it works (or more often, how it doesn't work) is making sure that the ultimate emphasis is not on knowledge transmission or on the author himself as a vehicle of knowledge, but rather, on the unknown—what do we know really?—and also on the human experience of not knowing, which is to fear and to imagine. And this, I think, is the role of the dark thread in the *Eléments de physiologie*, which is to maintain the strong imaginative presence of the unknown within the text, and that's why it frames it and is shot through with it, surprising though that is, given that this is a treatise on physiology.

## Notes

Chapter title: "Another true story that took place in the castle of Nicklsburg in Moravia," in Diderot, *Eléments de physiologie*, ed. Paolo Quintili (Paris: Champion, 2004), 250, authorial footnote. All translations are by the author unless otherwise specified.

I thank the Society for Seventeenth-Century French Studies for awarding me an Amy Wygant Research Bursary in July 2016 to conduct research for this article in Paris.

1. François de Belleforest, *Le cinquiesme tome des histoires tragiques*, ed. Hervé Campangne (Geneva: Droz, 2013), xiii.

2. For instance: "L'amour est plus difficile à expliquer que la faim: car le fruit n'éprouve pas le désir d'être mangé" (Love is harder to explain than hunger, because the piece of fruit feels no desire to be eaten) (Diderot, *Eléments de physiologie*, Paris: Champion, 2004, ed. P. Quintili, 328).

3. Ibid., 265.

4. See, for example, Wes Williams, *Monsters and Their Meanings in Early Modern Culture: Mighty Magic* (Oxford: Oxford University Press, 2011); and Charles T. Wolfe, ed., *Monsters and Philosophy*, Texts in Philosophy 3 (London: College Publications, 2005).

5. On Diderot and monsters, see Andrew Curran, *Sublime Disorder: Physical Monstrosity in Diderot's Universe*, SVEC, 2001, 01 (Oxford: Voltaire Foundation, 2001); and Emita Brady Hill, *The Role of "le Monstre" in Diderot's Thought*, Studies on Voltaire and the Eighteenth Century 97 (Banbury, Oxfordshire: Voltaire Foundation, 1972). Wolfe (*Monsters and Philosophy*) also discusses Diderot.

6. Diderot, *Eléments de physiologie*, 359. See also the pre-Tolstoyan "Il n'est qu'une manière de se porter bien; il y en a une infinité de se porter mal" (There is only one way of being well; there are infinite ways of being ill), 347.

7. As these beginning and ending paragraphs show, there is no perfect or "normal" type: it is worth considering in the context of this "dark thread" hypothesis that, in this period, "normal" means "perpendicular," and there is no word that exactly renders

this modern concept (see C. Warman, "From Pre-normal to Abnormal: The Emergence of a Concept in Late Eighteenth-Century France," *Psychology and Sexuality* 1, no. 3 [2010]: 200–213; and Peter Cryle and Elizabeth Stephens, *Normality: A Critical Genealogy* [Chicago: Chicago University Press, 2017] for an in-depth study of the development and establishment of the concept of "normality").

8. Denis Diderot, *Œuvres philosophiques*, ed. Michel Delon and Barbara De Negroni (Paris: Gallimard Pléiade, 2010), 313, my emphases.

9. As quoted above, note 6.

10. Diderot, *Eléments de physiologie*, 249–51.

11. He writes, "Je tiens ce fait de Monsr Louis, secrétaire de l'académie de chirurgie" (It was Mr Louis, Secretary of the Academy of Surgery, who told me this). Antoine Louis (1723–1792), whom Diderot implies had related it directly to him, was a friend of his and a contributor to the *Encyclopédie*. He had published on this topic *An imperforata mulier possit concipere?* (1755) (see *Eléments de physiologie*, ed. Jean Mayer, in *Œuvres complètes de Diderot* [Paris: Hermann, 1987], vol. 17, 429n269; and Diderot, *Eléments de physiologie*, ed. Paolo Quintili, 250n86).

12. *Gazette des Deux-Ponts* (1775), no. 22. At the beginning of the anecdote, he had also referenced "Mr Nuch, chirurgien-major des troupes de la garnison de ce château" ("Mr Nuch, surgeon-major of the troops garrisoned in this castle) as having certified it (see Diderot, *Eléments de physiologie*, ed. Mayer, 430n270; and Diderot, *Eléments de physiologie*, ed. Paolo Quintili, 250n87). Motoichi Terada's new edition corrects the source reference and reprints it entire (*Eléments de physiologie*, Paris: Editions Materiologiques, 2019, 247 and 433–435.)

13. Natalie Zemon Davis, *Fiction in the Archives: Pardon Tales and Their Tellers in Sixteenth-Century France* (Cambridge: Polity, 1987).

14. This is D'Alembert's realisation in his great monologue in *Le rêve de d'Alembert*: "Et vous parlez d'individus, pauvres philosophes! laissez là vos individus." (And then you talk of individuals, you poor philosophers! Stop talking about your individuals.) See *Rêve de d'Alembert*, ed. Colas Duflo (Paris: GF Flammarion, 2002), 104, and, for the translation, *Rameau's Nephew and D'Alembert's Dream*, trans. Leonard Tancock (London: Penguin, 1966), 181.

15. Diderot, *Eléments de physiologie*, 360.

16. Ibid., 361.

17. This scenario reworks the topos of Pyrrhonist scepticism about the relativity of perception, viz., for a person standing on the shore, a ship appears in motion, whereas for a person standing on the ship, it's the shoreline that seems to move. This and other topoi about sensory perception and deception were ubiquitous in early modern discussions of scepticism and would have been well-known to Diderot. The original discussion they refer to is Sextus Empiricus, *Against the Logicians* 414 (*Adversos mathematicos* or *Hypotyposes*). With thanks to Tim Chesters for this elucidation and reference.

18. Neil Kenny's *Death and Tenses: Posthumous Presence in Early Modern France* (Oxford: Oxford University Press, 2015) provides a brilliant analysis of the tenses that are used to refer to and talk about the dead (although this particular passage does not feature).

GUY SPIELMANN

## At the Dark Edge of Enlightenment
### Early Modern Vampires

There may be no better example of a dark thread in the Western tradition than that which has been spun around vampires. First, because it remains vivid in the early twenty-first century, through the current vogue of vampire fiction in literature, film, and TV series, yet it goes back to the earliest stages of civilization: there are references to vampire-like creatures, real or imagined, in virtually every recorded human culture, going back thousands of years. It is also a complex thread, composed of several motley strands: if nowadays vampires appear to be the stuff of fantasy, they have been, at times, at the core of intense scientific, theological, and legal debates. Finally, since the 1960s, vampirism in all its forms has emerged as an object of scholarly inquiry, which has both strengthened the thread and diversified its composition.

The newest developments of vampirology, however, have not (yet) reversed a tendency that has prevented it from becoming a completely legitimate science: the illusion that vampires and vampirism form a single, coherent whole, and the often unconscious overemphasis placed on a "classical" period stretching from the publication of John William Polidori's novella, *The Vampyre*, in 1821, to the release by Universal Studios of the screen version of *Dracula* in 1931, with a concomitant neglect of the "archaic" period, which occupies roughly one hundred years between the middle of the seventeenth century and the middle of the eighteenth.

In its widest extent, vampirology must therefore examine medical reports, journalistic accounts, treatises by religious authorities, in addition to myriad forms of artistic representation: poems, novels, plays, films, television series, as well as less mainstream forms like adult role-play, cosplay, and video gaming. At first glance, this thread seems to unfold linearly and rather neatly: medical reports, newspaper articles, and theological tracts relating to vampirism, which abounded in the early modern period, then disappeared as fiction took over, around 1820. The thread was never completely ruptured, however, since fictional treatments were hardly based on imagination but informed by "factual" accounts of earlier times. A crucial moment in the determination of "the vampire" as we now know it came in the late Victorian period, in the British Isles, with the publication of *Carmilla* by Joseph Sheridan Le Fanu (1874) and *Dracula* by Bram Stoker (1897), but the construction of vampirism as a distinct and prominent mental object in the Western psyche really goes back to the mid-1600s.

Yet a careful perusal of the vampirology output since the beginning of the twentieth century—from Dudley Wright's 1914 *Vampires and Vampirism*, and the hugely influential *The Vampire: His Kith and Kin* by Montague Summers (1928)[1]—shows a paradoxical attitude: while the same early texts in Latin and German are always studiously referenced, one gets the uneasy impression that the author (especially Summers, who usually writes in English) may actually not have read any of them. There has obviously been an overreliance on a late French compendium, first published in 1746, when the great early modern wave of alleged vampiric activity was already on the wane. Other, no less important texts seem to have been almost completely ignored by scholars, either because they were never translated into English or French, or because their relevance is not immediately manifest.

As a result, although a standard (but incomplete) corpus of reports and treatises seems familiar to all those even only casually interested in the topic—they are routinely mentioned even in television documentaries targeted at a general audience—their content has been filtered and, more often than not, altered by translation, fragmentation, and erroneous quotation. Moreover, those who have bothered to consult original texts do not always possess the indispensable background knowledge about the period to interpret them correctly. From a methodological perspective, vampirology, inherently suspicious as a serious discipline, still stands on shaky ground, but we have the means—and, I will argue, good reason—to impart it with academic rigor and credibility.

In actuality, very few individuals who came in direct contact with alleged vampiric activity could produce a cogent report, and these experiences all took place in remote areas of eastern Europe, in circumstances unfamiliar to the observers. It should be emphasized that the people directly involved did not have a voice in the constitution of this discourse—illiterate peasants who most probably did not master the language of the church (Latin) and state officials (German) conducting investigations and writing up reports. We shall never know the exact form or content of this oral tradition, especially since those who eventually gave it written form did not follow any sort of ethnographic protocol in gathering the information from local populations; besides, they pursued an agenda (religious, political, military, medical) that radically biased their framing of the phenomenon.

Vampirology, then, essentially involves discourse analysis and textual hermeneutics of a peculiar kind: the point is not so much to determine "the truth" behind the reports as to reconstruct the process through which vampirism developed as a belief system on the basis of a very limited number of direct observations, later amplified into a vast discursive network spanning all major intellectual centers in Europe. Once we have obtained a reasonably complete picture of this network (a task complicated by the sheer amount of textual material in four languages), we may try to assess its significance: what can we learn about Europe in the Age of Enlightenment from the fact that some people literally believed in the existence of vampires and that some others were compelled to argue at considerable length over not just the reality of vampirism but the meaning of beliefs and practices around it?

An additional complication is that the texts we need to study have accrued a very different status over the years. Some are still little known, like *Magia posthuma* (Magic by the dead) by von Schertz (1704), which has been dutifully referenced by each and every latter-day vampirologist, even though almost no one has in fact seen it—its very existence remained doubtful for three centuries, until several copies were finally located. It turns out that the overwhelming majority of references originate in a single work by someone with no prima facie experience: Dom Calmet, a cleric from Lorraine, theretofore known for his biblical exegesis, who published in 1746 a comprehensive *Dissertation sur les apparitions des anges, des démons et des esprits. Et sur les revenans et vampires* (Considerations on apparitions of angels, demons and spirits. And on the returning dead and vampires) as a means to provide an authorized point of view on the controversy over vampires, which at that point had been raging throughout Europe for twenty years.[2]

This treatise was hardly the only one of its kind, and it did not even reflect official church doctrine: when Pope Benedict XIV issued a ruling on how to treat vampires in 1752,[3] he looked for advice not to Calmet but to

Archbishop Giuseppe Davanzati,[4] who had penned his own *Dissertazione sopra i vampiri* (Considerations on vampires) in 1739.[5] Be that as it may, the *Dissertation* was inordinately successful: immediately translated in English and German, it soon became the go-to title about early modern vampirism, and finally achieved global fame in 1772, when Voltaire gave it a scathing, sarcastic review.[6] By then, however, not only had accounts of vampiric activity ceased for over three decades, but debates on their veracity had reached a *terminus ad quem* with the promulgation by Empress Maria Theresa of two decrees: one in 1755 affirming that vampirism was a superstition,[7] followed by another in 1766 prohibiting the rituals usually carried out to deal with all forms of witchcraft and *magia posthuma*,[8] including the unearthing, staking, and decapitation of suspected vampires.

At this point, it seems indispensable to go back to the original reports, with a particular concern for time, place, the context in which they appeared, their purpose, and the means through which they were disseminated.

Scattered accounts of vampiroid cases that can be found throughout Europe, from ancient times to the Renaissance, are of no relevance because none had a wide or lasting impact: they failed to trigger mass hysteria, to inspire scholarly curiosity, or provoke a notable reaction by state or religious authorities. They remain entirely circumscribed within the chronicles in which they were consigned.

For most specialists, early modern acknowledgment of an undead problem originates in two sources: (1) a 1689 memoir in German by Johann Valvasor, *Die Ehre des Herzogthums Krain* (The glory of the Duchy of Carnolia), a multivolume survey of Carniola (*Krain*), in Istria (present-day Croatia and Slovenia);[9] and (2) two articles in the French periodical *Mercure galant* of 1693 and 1694, discussing the "Stryges de Russie." We must immediately recognize the uneven status of these sources: Valvasor's self-published *The Glory of Carnolia* was and has remained an extremely obscure work in the context of European thought and culture of the late seventeenth century, whereas the *Mercure* was read extensively by Western elites. Moreover, Valvasor reports two incidents of alleged vampirism—notably that of a man called Giure Grando in 1672—as if they were no more remarkable than any other *curiosa* he sees fit to mention; and while today's vampirologists often acknowledge Grando as the "first modern vampire," his case did not arouse much interest at the time, or when *The Glory of Carnolia* was issued. Once the vampire mania of the 1730s was in full swing, Valvasor's account was too old and not compelling enough to deserve much attention.

Conversely, the first significant account that should have appeared on the radar screen of vampirology has gone largely unnoticed;[10] it consists of little more than a paragraph desultorily inserted in a 1659 letter recounting political and military events in the Baltic region by Pierre Desnoyers,[11] secretary to the queen of Poland, and otherwise known for his activities in occultist circles. This letter enjoyed very limited readership, as Denoyers's correspondence was not collected and published until two centuries later, but it remerged in 1693, the year Desnoyers died, in a slightly different version printed in the May issue of the *Mercure Galant*, under the title "Article fort extraordinaire" (A most extraordinary piece). The author of the text remained unidentified (not altogether rare in the *Mercure*), and, in spite of obvious similarities, there is no definitive evidence that the second version is attributable to Desnoyers himself, other than a much longer letter "in the form of a thesis" by one Marigner, which ran in the same gazette seven month later, referring to the earlier piece as having been sent by Desnoyers.[12]

In the second part of his "thesis," Marigner reiterates his predecessor's story almost verbatim, adding a lengthy discussion of the precise nature and causes of vampirism. As a preamble, he cites various strange accounts from the Bible and ancient authors, noting that "All these diverse tales and such, are not altogether without basis, and there were facts that inspired these kinds of stories."[13] Marigner's own interpretation relies on what he terms "physics," but it is a physics heavily tinged with Paracelsian spiritualism, which, after nearly eighty pages of extremely convoluted explanations, yields no other conclusion than "the resurrection of bodies is miraculous, and can only be effected by the Almighty, who will lead our soul and our body to being ultimately reunited, either in reward or in eternal pennance."[14] The problem, as he analyzes it, is that, under the influence of a "grossly humid" climate, the Russians are "given to carnal and sensual passions" and act upon the dictates of their imagination rather than of their "intellective" capacities,[15] which leads them to entertain superstitious beliefs.

In a final twist, Marigner nevertheless concedes that there must be something supernatural about the *stryges*, although they clearly do not fall under the rubric of demonic possession, and he remarks that neither the ministrations of the church nor the application of medical remedies have been able to suppress a "vexation" that can only be stopped by unorthodox folk rituals.[16] After this troubling admission, Marigner closes his thesis on the acknowledgment that since "the secrets of divine justice and mercy are unknown to man," he eagerly and completely submits to church doctrine, leaving a better explanation for "superior minds" to determine.[17]

After Valvasor's 1689 chapter on Kringa, the 1693 and 1694 letters in the

*Mercure* are generally considered as the earliest explicit reports of vampiric activity; certainly they were the most intensely mediatized, given the *Mercure*'s readership. Yet those willing to pore through the some 110 pages of this "letter" were no doubt puzzled to no end by contradictions in the author's reasoning and unsettled by the admission that vampirism reports were quite reliable but that neither religion nor science offered a conclusive explanation. As for the Roman Catholic dogma that Marigner claims to observe scrupulously, it had at the time no specific provisions for dealing with vampires.

In addition, a useful, complementary perspective could be drawn from another, earlier (1657) account from a Jesuit "relation" by a French missionary stationed in Greece, Fr. François Richard, who describes the beliefs and rituals associated with the *vroucolacas* (βρυκόλακας) on the island of Santorini. Again, though this text was cited in other works of the early eighteenth century (notably Tournefort's),[18] it has not always been referenced by latter-day vampirologists; perhaps the location and context made it seem irrelevant, although an attentive reading leaves no uncertainty as to the nature of the phenomenon. The term "vampire" itself would not appear for another two decades, but all of these creatures—Valvasor's *strigun*, Desnoyers's *upierz*, Marigner's *stryges*, and Richard's *vroucolacas*—differ only in name, as well as in certain minute details of their behavior and the measures taken to combat them. In every way that matters, they definitely belong to the vampiric infestation that was to reach its peak a few decades later.

In order to appreciate the value of this early vampire literature, it is therefore crucial to assess it in light of the ulterior, better-known texts that we can subdivide in two categories:[19]

1. Firsthand reports by military physicians who were sent to by the Austrian authorities to investigate cases of alleged vampirism in two Serbian villages, Kisolova in 1725 (the Peter Plogojowitz case),[20] and Medvegya in 1732 (the Arnond Paole case);[21]

2. Analytical and speculative commentaries by lay or religious scholars who attempted to make sense of the Serbian events based on the aforementioned reports, without any direct involvement, and which often echoed earlier treatises on related topics such as Roh's 1679 *De masticatione mortuorum* (On the chewing by the dead),[22] Ranft's 1725 *De masticatione mortuorum in tumulis* (On the chewing by the dead in their tombs),[23] the anonymous *Acten-mäßige und Umständliche Relation von denen Vampiren oder Menschen-Saugern* (Actual and cir-

cumstantial relation on so-called vampires, or suckers of humans) of 1732,[24] Zopf's 1733 *Dissertatio de vampyris serviensibus* (Considerations on Serbian vampires),[25] or Harenberg's 1733 *Vernünftige und Christliche Gedancken über die Vampirs* (Sensible and Christian thoughts on the vampires),[26] to name just a few.

The first question is one of place: What do the sites of reported vampiric activity have in common? The answer is somewhat complicated by geographical spread and uncertain toponymy, in which "Hungary" (Ungarn, in German) tends to designate any and all lands east of Austria. While the 1725 and 1732 events occurred in the same area in the fledgling kingdom of Serbia, bordering a province of the Habsburg empire then known as the Banat of Temeswar (Temeschwaren Banat), the 1672 case of Giure Grando had taken place in Carniola (Krain), several hundred miles to the east; Desnoyers's 1659 letter was written in Danzig (Gdansk), a port on the Baltic sea, and refers to a disease allegedly common in the Ukraine, more than a thousand miles to the north. As for the incidents involving *vroukolakas* recounted by Father Richard, the locale shifts to the Aegean Sea, much farther south.

The 1725–32 outbreaks were situated in the heart of a particularly contested region, at times known as the Militärgrenze, a buffer zone temporarily seized from the Turks in 1718,[27] but, as it turns out, *all* of these vampire-infested lands shared a history of violent conflict and, most tellingly, of occupation or control by the Ottoman Turks. It should appear as no coincidence that vampire-related crises were concentrated in what Peter Bräunlein has called "the frightening borderlands of Enlightenment,"[28] regions that, between 1683 and 1778, existed under variable names, with ever-shifting borders, and under different political and religious regimes. Their isolated, often remote rural or insular location undoubtedly played a significant part as well; later commentators like Davanzati and Voltaire noted that no vampire activity was ever recorded in a large city, suggesting that it was nothing but a superstition of backward country bumpkins, a conclusion also reached in 1755 by Empress Maria Theresa's physician, Gerhard van Swieten, who was commissioned to submit a definitive opinion on the matter.[29]

Desnoyers's qualification of vampirism as a strange and unexplainable "malady" in his original 1659 letter changed forty years later into the nefarious activity of reanimated corpses that suck the blood of the living, possibly under the influence of a demon, but the initial framing of the phenomenon as a medical issue by Austrian authorities anticipates the eventual parallel between vampiric infestation and the plague, which in the early eighteenth century was introduced into western Europe from Ottoman territories. When imperial decrees on the matter were eventually published, it was in the *Codex sanitario-medicinalis Hungariae*, a collection of texts relative to public health issues, many of them epidemics designated as *pestis*, that is, "plague"—then a vague category including all kinds of communicable diseases that the science of the day was unable to explain or treat, an additional source of anguish. The vampire phobia of the 1720s and 1730s reflected a diffuse but persistent dread of control loss: at the margins of civilized Europe, events were taking place for which reason was unable to account, just as the very existence of certain states was threatened by the constant military pressure from Turkish armies. Vampires came as a perfect metaphor of invasion by an impure Other—a fact that did not escape Bram Stoker, whose Count Dracula leaves his Transylvanian hinterland to take over London. In his 1922 film version of the novel, *Nosferatu*, F. W. Murnau outdid Stoker in returning to the original trope by setting the action in a Baltic city, "Wisborg" (Wismar), which is overrun by a plague epidemic brought to Germany by Count Orlock and thousands of rats.[30] At that point, though, the vampire's eastern European origins were no longer evocative of a Turkish menace but rather of a perceived threat from Jewish mass emigration to the West; a thinly veiled metaphor, given Orlock's appearance as both a rat and a then typical caricature of a Jew.[31]

Early reports also illustrate the fact that vampires were not always primarily identified as blood suckers but rather as revenants in corporeal form who harassed the living (usually relatives) in a number of ways, yet seldom ever physically harmed them. In some instances, when coffins were dug up and opened, the dead were found swimming in blood, chewing their shroud (hence the *masticatione mortuorum* of Ranft and Rohr's treatises) and their own limbs—a ghastly sight no doubt, but one that does not amount to incontrovertible evidence of predatory activity on the living. What does transpire from all reports is that corpses were not normally decomposing and gave various signs of life: they looked plump, with rosy cheeks, their hair and nails had kept growing, and they cried out when they were staked. Rituals performed to put them to final rest are also quite comparable from one instance to another; by and large, they emulated those customarily employed for witches, since a leading explanation for vampirism (at least by the common folk) made it a form of black magic, *magia posthuma*, and it has been observed that one phenomenon rose to prominence just as the other was fading.[32]

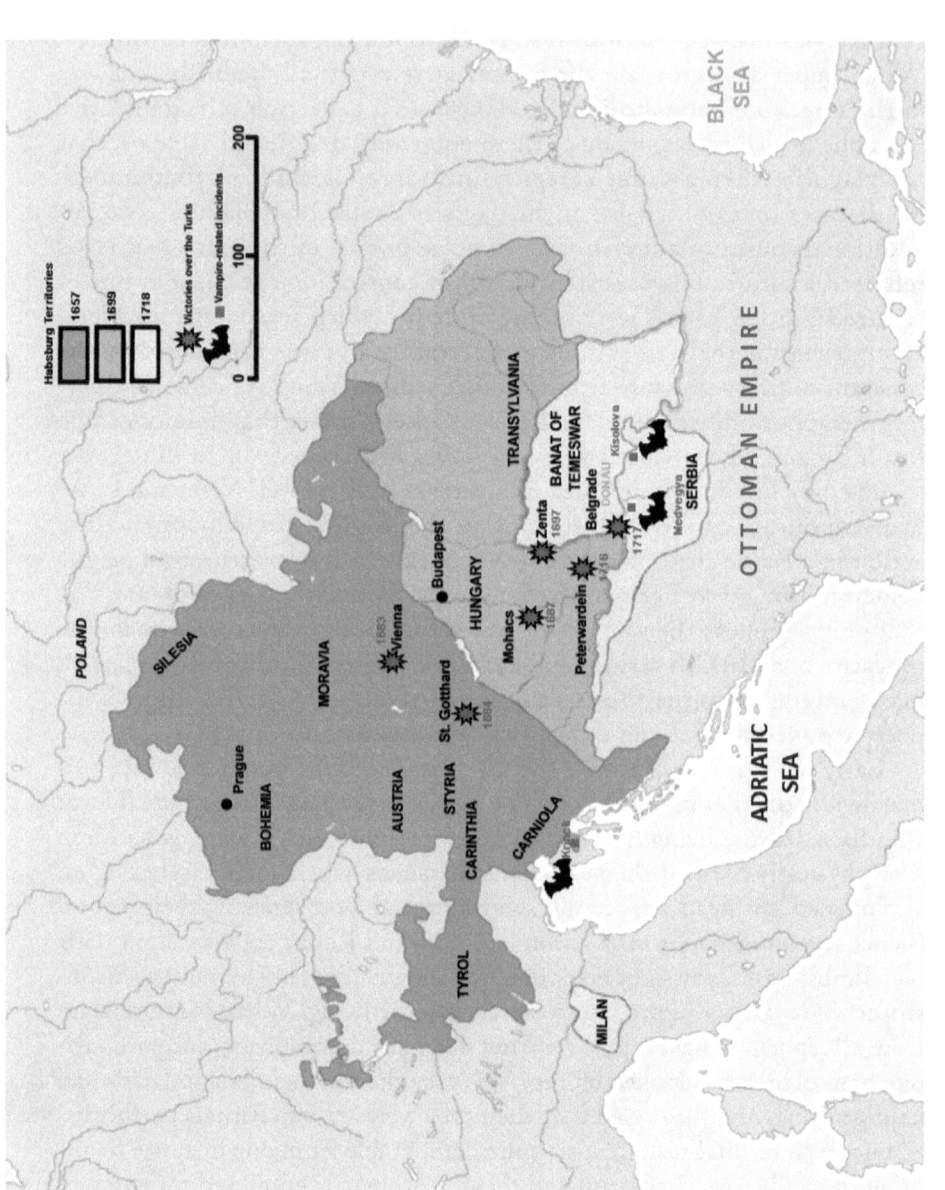

Vampire incidents.

Demonstrably, most of the authors of vampire-related texts had not directly witnessed the events they discuss and analyze. This important detail is underlined by the rhetorical formulas through which they both distance themselves from firsthand accounts that, for a rational, educated man, stretch belief, yet affirm their veracity—they originate from "eminently trustworthy" people. Until the 1725 medical report on the Plogojowitz case, only two individuals wrote about something they had actually seen, and both of them deal with the Greek *vroucolacas*: the aforementioned Father Richard and, a half century later, Pitton de Tournefort, a scientist whom Louis XIV sent to survey the flora and (in an unusual combination) customs of the Near East. Despite their dissimilar points of view, the priest and the botanist reached the same conclusion: the Greeks' belief in the undead was a perversion of Christianity, induced by schismatic Orthodox dogma and their proximity, and at times subjugation, to the Ottomans. Tournefort the scientist appears even more disappointed than his predecessor after failing to convince the people of Mykonos that the man they had taken out of the grave was in fact quite dead; he evokes with unmitigated disgust the stench from the rotting corpse. Tournefort realizes that his rational arguments carry no more weight than those of Father Richard, whom, ironically, the Greeks cite to him as an authority in support of their conviction that the *vroucolacas* are real. He finally reckons that "in light of this, how can we not admit that today's Greeks are not Great Greeks, and that ignorance and superstition reign supreme among them?"[33] For all intents and purposes, these Greeks are undistinguishable from the Serbians whose complaints of vampire infestation would garner European-wide attention two decades later.

A perusal of early modern sources proves that the dark thread of vampirism is far more complex and less homogeneous than one might imagine from its representation in secondary literature, and eventually in fiction. Reports on alleged cases had existed since the dawn of civilization, but they did not coalesce into a single coherent discursive whole until the mid-seventeenth century, and it took another hundred years to develop a stable, permanent model of what a vampire was, what it did, and how to fight it. This was not achieved through a multiplication of vampiric incidents, however; in fact, after the much-publicized Plogojowitz and Paole cases of 1725–32, we find fewer and fewer reports, while pamphlets, treatises, theses, and other speculative texts multiply vertiginously. Austrian laws declaring vampires to be a fallacy and forbidding the exhumation and mutilation of corpses hardly quelled the flow of discourse on the topic: in 1772, Voltaire criticized Calmet and mentioned Tournefort's 1717 memoir as if both were still very much pertinent, whereas Davanzati's nephew saw fit to publish the *Dissertazione sopre i vampiri* in 1774, thirty-five years after the manuscript's completion. Calmet's *Dissertation* was reprinted multiple times and translated in various languages throughout the eighteenth century; the standard English edition, retitled *The Phantom World*, was issued as late as 1850.

Actual, visceral fear of the undead, of course, always remained limited to uneducated people in remote areas of eastern Europe, but for decades, intellectual elites found vampirism irresistible as a topic for speculation, because the precise, factual reports filed by military physicians made it impossible to summarily dismiss it as a figment of the imagination of superstitious Danubian peasants. The Austrian authorities had little choice but to respond to reports of vampiric activity, in order to maintain peace and order in the outer reaches of the empire; but in doing so, and by going along with rituals that the locals performed on suspected vampires, they only gave credence to the very beliefs they would have liked to suppress. Like the legendary vampire itself, the dark discursive thread of vampirism, once unleashed onto the world, could only be temporarily cut off; it could never be completely destroyed.

## Notes

1. Dudley Wright, *Vampires and Vampirism* (London: W. Rider; Philadelphia: David McKay, 1914); Montague Summers, *The Vampire: His Kith and Kin* (London: Kegan Paul, Trench & Trubner, 1928).

2. Augustin Calmet, *Dissertation sur les apparitions des anges, des démons et des esprits et sur les revenans et vampires de Hongrie, de Bohême, de Moravie et de Silésie* (Paris: De Bure, l'aîné, 1746); *Dissertations upon the Apparitions of Angels, Demons, and Ghosts, and Concerning the Vampires of Hungary, Bohemia, Moravia, and Silesia* (London: Cooper, 1759).

3. Benedetto XIV [Prospero Lorenzo Lambertini], *De servorum dei beatificatione et de beatorum canonizatione* (On the beatification and canonization of saints, 1734–38), in *Benedicti XIV Pont. Opt. Max opera Omnia in tomos XVII distributa* (Prato: Typographia Aldina, 1839–47), vol. 4, bk. 1, chap. 21, §4, 244–45. On this work, see Riccardo Saccenti, "Il de servorum Dei beatificatione et Beatorum canonizatione di Prospero Lambertini, papa Benedetto XIV: Materiali per una ricerca," in *Le fatiche di Benedetto XIV: Origine ed evoluzione dei trattati di Prospero Lambertini (1675–1758)*, ed. Maria Teresa Fattori (Rome: Edizioni di Storia e Letteratura, 2011), 121–52.

4. Davanzati was a personal friend of Lambertini before the latter's accession to

the papacy in 1740; his particularly progressive views have earned him the nickname "Enlightenment pope" (see Rebecca Messbarger, Christopher M. S. Johns, and Philip Gavitt, eds., *Benedict XIV and the Enlightenment: Art, Science, and Spirituality* [Toronto: University of Toronto Press, 2016]).

5. Giuseppe Antonio Davanzati, *Dissertazione sopra i vampiri* [. . .] (1739; Naples: Fratelli Raimondi, 1774). The text initially circulated in manuscript form (see Francesco Paolo de Ceglia, "The Archbishop's Vampires: Giuseppe Davanzati's Dissertation and the Reaction of 'Scientific' Italian Catholicism to the "Moravian Events," *Archives internationales d'histoire des sciences* 61 [2011]: 487–510).

6. Voltaire [François-Marie Arouet], "Vampires," in *Questions sur L'Encyclopedie, distribuées en forme de dictionnaire* [*Dictionnaire philosophique*], pt. 9, 2nd ed. (London: n.p., [1771–] 1772), 129–32; *A Philosophical Dictionary, from the French of Voltaire*, ed. J. G. Gurton (London: John and Henry Hunt, 1824), vol. 6, 304–8.

7. "Resolutio caesaro-regia: Eliminatio superstitionis *de Vampyris*, 17 Martii 1755," in *Codex sanitario-medicinalis Hungariae*, ed. Francis-Xavier Linzbauer, no. 568 (Buda: Typis Caesareo-Regiae Scientarum Universitatis, 1852–56), 716–25.

8. "Lex caesaro-regia ad exstirpendam superstitionem ac rationalem judicationem criminalem Magia Sortilegii. 5 Novbr. 1766," in *Codex sanitario-medicinalis*, no. 575, 776–96.

9. Johann Weichard, Freiherr von Valvasor, "Krink," in *Die Ehre des Herzogthums Krain*, vol. 9 (Laybach [Ljubljana], 1689), 317–19.

10. To my knowledge, it is only mentioned by Koen Vermeir in "Vampires as Creatures of the Imagination," in *Diseases of the Imagination and Imaginary Disease in the Early Modern Period* (Amsterdam: Brepols, 2012), 341–73, a translation of "Vampirisme, corps mastiquants et force de l'imagination: Analyse des premiers traités sur les vampires (1659–1755)," published in the French journal *Camenae*, no. 8 (December 2010), and, to a lesser extent, by Jaume Albiol and Jordi Ardanuy in an article in Catalan, "Les referències al terme 'upierz' en els textos de Gabriel Rzączynski i de Pierre Des Noyers," *Upir: Revista de Folklore* 38 (December 2013): 90–96. Even a thorough survey like Klaus Hamberger's *Mortuus non mordet: Kommentierte Dokumente zum Vampirismus 1689–1791* (Vienna: Turia und Kant, 1992) does not take into account Desnoyers's 1659 letter.

11. Pierre Des Noyers, "Lettre CCXXXV ] [à Ismaël Bouillaud] de Dantzig (13 décembre 1659)," in *Lettres de Pierre Des Noyers, Secretaire de La Reine: de Pologne Marie-Louise de Gonzague [ . . . ] pour servir à l'histoire de Pologne et de Suède de 1655 à 1659* (Berlin: B. Behr [E. Bock], 1859), 560–62.

12. Mr de Marigner, "Sur les stryges de Russie," *Mercure Galant* (February 1694): 13–119. See Marigner, "Sur les stryges de Russie," 14: "Voyez la relation entière qui nous en a été envoyée de Pologne, par défunt notre amy Monsieur Desnoyers" (See the complete account which was sent to us from Poland by our late friend Monsieur Desnoyers). The first part of this piece was the "Lettre en forme de Dissertation de Mr Marigner Sr du Plessis, Ruel et Billoüard, Avocat au Parlement de Paris, adresée à Mie Charles de Volaud de Matheron, Seigneur d'Aubenas, de Salignac et d'Entrepierre, Gentithomme

de Provence, sur les Créatures des Elemens, et autres sujets invisibles, corporels ou spirituels, sur les Stryges de Russie / et sur la Physique occulte de la baguette," *Mercure Galant* (January 1694): 58–166.

13. Marigner, "Sur les stryges de Russie," 27: "Toutes ces diverses fables & autres, ne sont pas tout à fait sans fondement, & il y a eu des realitez qui ont servi de sujet à ces sortes de discours."

14. Ibid., 101–2: "C'est pourquoi la ressurection de son corps est miraculeuse & un effet de la Toute-puissance, par laquelle il conduit nostre ame & notre corps dans leur réunion, à une récompense, ou à une peine éternelle."

15. Ibid., 107–9, passim.

16. Ibid., 117–18: "Cette vexation commune & ordinaire dans la Russie, & non ailleurs, n'est point une maladie naturelle, & il y a quelque chose de surnaturel qui y est meslé. Ce n'est point aussi une possession ou obsession du Démon, puisque les vexez n'ont point fait de pacte avec luy. Et ce qui m'y confirme encore plus, c'est que les remèdes spirituels de l'Eglise, ny tous les remèdes ordinaires que la Médecine a inventez, & que l'on a pratiquez, n'ont jamais réussi sur ce fait." (This vexation, common and ordinary in Russia, and not elsewhere, is not a natural malady, and there is something supernatural in it. It is neither a possession nor an obsession by the Demon, because the vexed have not made a pact with him. And what confirms my opinion still more is that neither the spiritual remedies of the Church nor the ordinary ones that Medicine has devised and that have been used, have ever been efficacious in such cases.) *Vexation* is attested in the *OED* with a similar meaning: "The action of troubling or harassing by aggression or interference."

17. Ibid., 118–19.

18. Joseph Pitton de Tournefort, "État présent de l'Église grecque," in *Relation d'un voyage du Levant fait par ordre du Roi: Contenant l'histoire ancienne & moderne de plusieurs isles de l'Archipel, de Constantinople, des Côtes de la Mer Noire, de l'Armenie, de la Georgie, des frontières de Perse & de l'Asie Mineure [. . .]* (Paris: Imprimerie Royale, 1717), vol. 1, Lettre III, 131–36. Davanzati, Calmet, and Voltaire all mention it.

19. Such cut-and-dried distinction did not obtain at the times: the text of the 1755 decree "Eliminatio superstitionis *de Vampyris*," for instance, places the *Visum and Repertum* on the same standing as Calmet's *Dissertation* and, more surprisingly, a passage on vampires in Boyer d'Argens's 1737 *Lettres juives* (*The Jewish Spy*).

20. Kameralprovisor Frombald, *Copia eines Schreibens aus dem Gradisker District in Ungarn, Wienerisches Diarium*, 21. Juli 1725 (Vienna: Kayserliche Hof-Buchdruckerey 1725), 11–12. This report includes the first-known occurence of the term "Vampyri," notably transcribed in roman script while the rest of the text is printed in blackletter (gothic) typeface.

21. Johannes Flückinger, et al., *Visum et repertum, über die so genannten Vampirs, oder Blut-Aussauger, so zu Medvegia in Servien, an der Türckischen Granitz, den 7. Januarii 1732 geschehen. Nebst einem Anhange von dem Kauen und Schmatzen der Todten in Gräbern* (Nuremberg: Johann Adam Schmidt, 1732).

22. Phillipp Rohr, *Dissertatio historico-philosophica de masticatione mortuorum*,

*qvam Dei & superiorum indultu* [...] *& respondens Benjamin Fritzschius* (Lipsiae [Leipzig]: Michaelus Vogtius [Mickael Vogt], 1679).

23. Michael Ranft, *De masticatione mortuorum in tumulis* (Leipzig: 1725); *M. Michael Ranfts, Dicaoni zu Nebra, Tractat von dem Kauen und Schmatzen der Todten in Gräbern, Worin die wahre Beschaffenheit derer Hungarischen Vampyrs und Blut-Sauger gezeigt, Auch alle von dieser Materie bißher zum Vorschein gekommene Schrifften recensiret werden* (Leipzig: Teubners Buchladen, 1734).

24. W. S. G. E., *Acten-mäßige und Umständliche Relation von denen Vampiren oder Menschen-Saugern, Welche sich in diesem und vorigen Jahren, im Königreich Servien herfürgethan* (Leipzig: Martini, 1732).

25. Johann Heinrich Zopf (1691–1774), *Dissertatio de vampyris serviensibus quam supremi numinis auspicio praeside M. Joanne Henr. Zopfio gymnasii assindiensis directore, publice defendet, responens Christianus Fridericus van Dalen, Emmericensis* (Duisburg: Johannis Sas, 1733).

26. Johann Christoph Harenberg, *Vernünftige und Christliche Gedancken Uber die Vampirs, Oder Bluhtsaugende Todten, So unter den Türcken und auf den Gräntzen des Servien-Landes den lebenden Menschen und Viehe das Bluht aussaugen sollen, Begleitet mit allerley theologischen, philosophischen und historischen aus dem Reiche der Geister hergeholten Anmerckungen Und entworfen* (Wolffenbüttel, 1733).

27. Ratified a year after the victorious siege of Belgrade by Prince Eugen of Savoy, the Treaty of Passarowitz (1718) gave Austria control of the Banat and northern Serbia, but areas south of the Danube returned under Ottoman dominion in 1739, after their victory over Habsburgian armies at Grocka.

28. Peter J. Bräunlein, "The Frightening Borderlands of Enlightenment: The Vampire Problem," *Studies in History and Philosophy of Biological and Biomedical Sciences* 43, no. 3 (2012): 710–19. A version in German has also been published as "Furchterregende Randzonen der Aufklärung: Skandalon Vampirismus," *Zeitschrift für Anomalistik* 15 (2015): 55–87.

29. *Vampyrismus von Herrn Baron Gerhard van Swieten verfasset, aus dem Französischen ins Deutsche übersetzet und als ein Anhang der Abhandlung des Daseyns der Gespenster beigerücket* (Augsburg, 1768).

30. Friedrich W. Murnau, *Nosferatu, eine Symphonie des Grauens*, script by Henrik Galeen (Germany: Joffa-Atelier/Prana Films, 1922).

31. See, in particular, the hand-drawn image of a rat-like Orlock on the poster by Albin Grau (1884–1971), who was also the film's art director and set and costume designer.

32. See Gabor Klaniczay, "The Decline of Witches and the Rise of Vampires under the Eighteenth-Century Habsburg Monarchy," in *The Uses of the Supernatural* (Princeton, N.J.: Princeton University Press, 1990), 169–237; reprinted in *The Witchcraft Reader*, ed. Darren Oldridge (London: Psychology Press, 2002), 387–98.

33. Tournefort, "État présent de l'Église grecque," 136: "Après cela ne faut il pas avouer que les Grecs d'aujourd hui ne sont pas grands Grecs & qu'il n y a chez eux qu'ignorance & superstition."

PHILIPPE ROGER

# Darkness at Noon
## Sade's Way to Terror

Starting to work on this essay, I did what I suppose all of us do these days, if only to delay the confrontation with the blank page: I googled "Sade" and "gothique" (together, *gothique* in French). I was slightly surprised, but in no way disappointed, to be directed to a site called "Forum gothique," run by the "Communauté gothique" (Gothic Community) and to an exchange that had taken place five years earlier between an outsider, Camilla, and regulars on this site.

Camilla—a perfect name for a Gothic novel, which seems to be her real name—a student in comparative literature preparing for a master's in a French university, was asking for help: "I may be wrong," Camilla said, "but I get the feeling that Sade's texts have been a major influence on the culture which is central to your Forum. So, should some of you be ready to offer their views on that, I would be very grateful."[1] Right or wrong, this student in distress got a fresh rebuke from "Miss Candide" (site alias; reference to Voltaire uncertain): "What about that? Do we, Goths, look like lousy sado-masochists using their own excrements to pen nice little obscenities on the walls after raping a nun with a crucifix?"[2] Poor Camilla's query once discarded, regulars on the site went back to more serious business than writing a master's thesis in comparative literature. Miss Candide, turning away from Camilla, engaged in a less than academic discussion with "Mamzelle Bulle" and finally declined Mamzelle Bulle's explicit advances by saying: "Sorry. Sade traumatized my sexuality forever."

Judging from this short incursion on the Gothic web, it did not look as if Sade was *persona grata* among all French Goths. There was, however, more than a little unfairness in the treatment inflicted on earnest Camilla, since the same site, in 2008, had indeed posted a long biographical piece on Sade (entirely drawn from Wikipedia) that had elicited applause and thanks from the same "Gothic community," followed by numerous exchanges pro and con. Naive as it was, Camilla's query was not outlandish, whereas Mademoiselle Candide's violent outburst suggested denial.

The apparently whimsical treatment of my own query by Google raised other questions. What about the reliability of the global operator that had led me directly to this less than imperishable exchange between Camilla and Miss Candide? How seriously could one take the digital Oracle, when the first item to pop up after typing "Sade" and *"gothique"* happened to be a weird chat session between contemporary French Goths? Giving more thought to the matter, though, I got the uncanny feeling that Google, in the best oracular tradition, had indeed given an oblique and allegorical answer to the question implied by my "random search." While Camilla's innocent *faux pas* obviously bore testimony to the frequent association being made, today, between Sade and the Gothic—far beyond the scholarly definitions of the "Gothic" as a literary genre[3]—Mademoiselle Candide's strongly worded rebuff looked like a mirror image of the reluctance, among most French Sadians, to associate the name of Sade with anything "Gothic." If the modern oracle had not provided a detailed, documented answer, it had certainly offered (just like its predecessors in Delphi or Cumae) a useful *caveat* concerning the contentious relationship between Sade and le *gothique*.

Let's now turn away from the Gothic community, and to the academic community. Evidence of a recent or renewed scholarly interest, in France, in both the Gothic literary tradition and a Gothic Sade, can be found in the growing number of publications on or around those topics over the past two decades.[4]

In spite of being praised by poets and writers, most notably the surrealists—or perhaps precisely for that reason—Gothic novels long remained on the outskirts of the French academic village. During the 1960s and 1970s, being generally regarded as ideologically conservative, they benefited only marginally from the more open attitude in academic circles toward noncanonical genres and texts, although they did gain some visibility in connection with the flurry of studies on utopian and fantastic writings.[5] It seems significant, however, that Maurice Lévy's comprehensive study *Le roman "gothique" anglais: 1764–1824*—his *thèse d'État* discreetly published in 1968 by a university press with limited circulation—only gained full visibility in 1995, when reprinted in a paperback edition by a major publishing company based in Paris.[6]

Twenty years later, the trend has not lost its momentum, with recognizable effects on Sadian studies. A subtle clue to the rapprochement between Sade and the Gothic in French academia was given in 2014, with a new paperback edition of collected short fictions by Sade. Those texts had remained unpublished in Sade's lifetime. A first edition had been published in 1926 by Maurice Heine under the title *Historiettes, contes et fabliaux*—a title that reflected the heterogeneous nature of these *contes*, short stories, and "anecdotes" ranging from the tragic (in the sense of the *histoires tragiques*) to the facetious or the lewd. Subsequent editors—Gilbert Lély, Jean-Jacques Pauvert, and Annie Le Brun—adopted the same title. Breaking with this well-established tradition, the 2014 French editor, Michel Delon, substituted his own title: *Contes étranges*—"Strange tales"—to *Historiettes, contes et fabliaux*. The change hinted at a spectacular shift in perspective: whereas the former title referred to genres and forms associated with the past, from the Middle Ages to the seventeenth century, the new one pointed in the opposite direction, toward Romanticism and, more widely, nineteenth- and twentieth-century literature,[7] while linking Sade to fantastic[8] and "dark" fiction. This drastic redirection of the critical gaze presented the editor with difficulties of which he, as an expert Sadian, must have been aware. In his preface, Delon underlined that the tales in the volume "stay away from absolute darkness" (la noirceur absolue) and that most of them, in fact, have a nontragic, conciliatory ending.[9] Why, then, *Contes étranges* rather than *Historiettes, contes et fabliaux*? The best answer to that question might be suggested by the cover illustration of the paperback, a 1942 painting by surrealist artist Dorothea Tanning, entitled *Voltage*. Through this pictorial reference, an unambiguous tribute was being paid to the artistic and intellectual movement responsible for both Sade's apotheosis *and* his association with the Gothic: the surrealist movement. Delon's *Contes étranges* edition can thus be seen as an intriguing attempt to reconcile two traditionally conflicting approaches: the anti-academic surrealist reading exalting a Gothic-fantastic-utopian-revolutionary Sade as a precursor of the most radical modernity, on the one hand, and, on the other hand, an academic, historicized reading of Sade's works emphasizing his immersion in the literary culture of his generation through a close scrutiny of his sources, borrowings, rewritings—and plagiarisms.

It is hardly necessary to recall the important part played by the surrealists, André Breton in particular, in the promotion of a Gothic Sade. Coming in the wake of Apollinaire's rehabilitation of Sade as a writer in the early years of the twentieth century, the surrealists were instrumental in changing the perception of his œuvre, by closely associating him with the *"roman noir"* and the "*fantastique.*" Breton did not hesitate to establish a parallel between Sade's and Charles Maturin's worlds, despite the fact that there is little in common between *Juliette* and Maturin's *Melmoth the Wanderer.* Whatever the gap between the two writers' mental universes and sets of values, they do share, according to Breton, a "dazzling" *noirceur* (darkness), and on that sole basis, he felt authorized to brush aside their many differences to pronounce Charles R. Maturin and the Marquis de Sade brothers in darkness. Maturin, Breton wrote in "Situation de Melmoth" (a mock-Sartrian title), had being granted "the gift of the deepest 'blacks,' those which also allow for securing the most dazzling accumulation of lights."[10] While in Breton's eyes, other Gothic novels, including Radcliffe's, paled in comparison with Sade's *Justine*, a book "incomparably darker" (*plus noir*) than *The Romance of the Forest* and "altogether of a completely different darkness,"[11] Maturin was granted admission, along with Sade, in the VIP section of the Surrealist Hall of Dark Fame.

No less important for the surrealists, however, was Matthew Lewis. Both Breton and Eluard praised his writings and made *The Monk* mandatory reading among their friends and followers, here again associating the name of the Gothic novelist with Sade's. (In that particular case, the possibility of a direct link was not unsubstantiated, as we will see in a moment.) Even more committed to both Sade and Lewis was Antonin Artaud. A fervent reader of Sade, Artaud had selected Sade's "Eugénie de Franval," a mischievous short story of incest and crime, to become part of the repertoire in his "Theater of cruelty."[12] An admirer of the Gothic novel, Artaud published in 1931 his own version of *The Monk*—"narrated by Antonin Artaud," as the full title goes.[13] Less a translation than a rewriting, Artaud's *Le moine* can be regarded as accomplishing practically (in a work of art) the dream shared by the surrealists and Artaud, of a fusion between Sade and the Gothic. In his *Moine*, Artaud did not only "inherit Lewis and the Gothic under Sade's shadow" but was directly "influenced by Sade in his own rewriting of Lewis's novel," as John Phillips has observed.[14] Indeed, without Sade on his mind, would Artaud have so easily detected in Lewis's novel what he then called the "truly *philosophical* smell of death"?[15]

At the core of the surrealist interpretation of Sade and the Gothic as being strongly connected lies the oxymoronic metaphor of a luminescent blackness—and not much beyond that. On virtually all grounds (narrative, thematic, religious, political), abyssal differences can easily be detected between Sade and even those closest to him among Gothic novelists. However, such was (and remains) the prestige of his surrealist warrants that the ghost of a Gothic Sade never ceased to haunt the Sadian critical tradition. Far from fading away with the disappearance of Breton, Artaud, and the first surrealist generation, the notion of a linkage between Sade and the Gothic would soon be reinforced by the works of Annie Le Brun. After meeting with Breton in 1963, Annie Le Brun became the talented heir to the surrealist vision of a Gothic Sade—a vision that she helped to rejuvenate by her works on Sadian castles and other spaces of transgression. Her first interest, chronologically speaking, had been for the Gothic novelists and their "castles of subversion."[16] Her subsequent association with Sade's pugnacious publisher Jean-Jacques Pauvert (1926–2014) encouraged her to move toward Sade's castles and revisit the relationship between Sade and the Gothic novelists in a new perspective, emphasizing in their respective plots a similar treatment of space as well as a fascination for places of confinement. A nonacademic and, at times, vocally anti-academic independent writer, Annie Le Brun has thus kept very much alive a reading of Sade that makes him not so much the fellow traveler of Melmoth the Wanderer, as in Breton's time, but a soul mate of the Gothic novelists, sharing with them a taste for elaborate, heavily coded, gloomy architecture, as well as a keen sense of the theatrical nature of sexual fantasy. Downplaying the religious and supernatural components in the Gothic novel, while giving front stage to spatiality and theatricality, Annie Le Brun was able to make the case for a Gothic Sade more convincing than it had ever been in surrealist writings from the 1920s to the 1940s.

Despite such prestigious and talented advocates, Sade's Gothic affiliation has most often been met, in France, with skepticism or outward hostility. Major commentators, from Bataille to Blanchot, not to mention Barthes, ignored the Gothic thread in Sade. Even Gilbert Lély, Sade's biographer and the editor of the *Complete Works*, although a surrealist poet himself, never made much of Sade's Gothic filiation. Contradictions were pointed out: between Sade's unflinching rationalism and the Gothic taste for the supernatural; between Sade's militant atheism and a literature with a visible Christian (Anglican) background or agenda; between Sade's revolutionary or progressive political stands and the conservative subtext that many readers, unimpressed by Breton's analysis, perceived in Gothic novels.

Skepticism and suspicion did not stop there: in the eyes of many French critics, the problem was not only that Sade was being misread; it was also that the Gothic genre was undefinable and, some were quick to add, thoroughly *un-French*.

Rivalry between France and England over the novel as a genre had run high throughout the eighteenth century; it took a new turn, however, during its last decade, when the Gothic fad hit continental Europe. Sade's own works provided evidence of this competitive spirit being rekindled by the Gothic tsunami. His 1800 *Idée sur les romans* explicitly challenged the English (Gothic) novelists, designated by Sade as "those conceited rivals" (ces fiers rivaux). In that short text, which served as a preface to his volume *Les crimes de l'amour*, Sade called French writers to arms, or to their pens, urging them to bring forth new works that would testify to the fact that "we [the French] also are creators."[17]

We will come back to *Idée sur les romans*, but it is worth emphasizing right now the intertwining, around the "Gothic question," of national (or nationalist), as well as literary and political issues—the major political issue at stake being the connection (or lack of) between the pervasive character of the Gothic fashion and the impact of the French Revolution on European sensibility. More than a century after Sade's challenge to the "fiers rivaux" beyond the Channel, Maurice Heine, a pioneer of Sadian studies in the 1920s and the first editor of *The 120 Days of Sodom*, would revive the quarrel and give it a new twist. Heine, who also belonged to the surrealist intellectual and political milieu, was perfectly willing to recognize "Gothic" elements in Sade's œuvre, but he adamantly denied any British "influence" on the marquis. Criticizing Miss Alice Killen's 1915 academic dissertation on the influence of English Gothic literature in France, he blamed her for ignoring Sade altogether (although it is only fair to say that she could hardly have done otherwise at the Sorbonne in 1915!), and asserted Sade's rights in terms of both anteriority and originality.[18] It is now generally admitted that Walpole's *Castle of Otranto* remained without much echo for at least a generation. As for Ann Radcliffe, whose first book translated into French appeared in 1797, she could not have influenced Sade's first works, written in the Bastille, such as *Aline et Valcour*, *The 120 Days of Sodom*, or *The Infortunes of Virtue*, the first draft of *Justine*. The most interesting part of Heine's argument, however, bore on *The Monk*. Heine tried to demonstrate, rather convincingly, that Sade was more likely to have influenced Matthew Lewis (who had come to Paris in 1791 and could have bought and read *Justine*) than Lewis Sade. Whatever the bias of this devoted Sadian scholar, his chronology was correct,[19] and the points he made in his groundbreaking article "Le marquis de Sade et le roman noir," published in 1933 by the *Nouvelle Revue Française*,[20] are still worth being kept in mind for a sound appreciation of Sade's relationship to the Gothic novel.

It would be a mistake, however, to reduce the French-English rift over the Gothic to petty chauvinistic quarrels. The French hostility or malaise vis-à-vis Gothic novels reflected cultural differences that ran much deeper and made the French suspicious of or puzzled at the very notion of "Gothic." This reluctance (of which Sade himself offers a perfect example) has been a key factor in the long-lasting French resistance to the notion of a Gothic Sade supported by Breton and his affiliates. Sade's forced enlistment under the Gothic banner appeared all the more unjustifiable for the fact that the word *"gothique"* written on this banner did not convey, in France, any clear or distinct idea. In that respect, it seems quite telling that Maurice Lévy, author of the already mentioned authoritative *Le roman "gothique" anglais*, should have placed the first adjective of his title in quotation marks—a clear indication that "roman gothique" was a dubious neologism for French academics in 1968.

Only in the past three decades or so was the adjective *gothique* definitely naturalized in French to refer to the Gothic novel. However, it can still raise French tempers when applied to Sade, as illustrated by Alain Rey's reaction to another recent edition of Sade's short stories. When Margaret Crosland chose to publish her translations of Sade's tales under the title *The Gothic Tales of the Marquis de Sade*,[21] the reputed lexicographer and critic responded in anger. "*The Gothic Tales of the Marquis de Sade* apparently makes for a good-selling book title," Rey noted sarcastically. He found quite unfortunate, however, that this particular translator should have felt at liberty to impose upon Sade's writings a word made meaningless by decades of "Anglo-Saxon" misuse. By stretching the signification of "Gothic" to refer to "any tale of terror with supranatural traits," Rey explained, Anglo-Saxon critics had paved the way for the ludicrous extension of the "Gothic label" to all sorts of trashy contemporary productions, from American *pulp fictions* to comic books depicting sorcerers, and more generally to "all those horrifying stories that Anglo-Saxons are so fond of."[22] Beyond the irritating, catchy title, what infuriated the French lexicographer was a sloppy "Anglo-Saxon" use of the word "Gothic," which he deemed irrelevant, at best, or ill-intentioned, at worst.[23] Any discussion of Sade's supposed Gothicism should thus take into account, on the one hand, the semantic rift over the term, and, on the other hand, an underlying sense of literary competition between France and England. Mixed together, the two ingredients have shaped a quarrel as old as the Gothic fashion itself.

We have already alluded to the semantic discrepancies in the terminology between the English and French languages. From Sade's time to Maurice Heine's, the Gothic novel went in France by many other names—except *gothique*. There is probably more than one reason for that, starting with the bad reputation of everything associated with the Middle Ages in eighteenth-century France. Before the French Revolution, *gothique*, as an adjective, had been used by art critics and *amateurs* to dismiss the artistic productions of the "dark ages" as primitive and tasteless. From architecture and art, the word *gothique* had swiftly migrated, with the same negative connotation, to all possible spheres of human activity. In Sade's generation, "Gothic taste" and bad taste were synonyms. During the French Revolution, the adjective came to be routinely used to disqualify institutions, habits, behaviors associated with the Ancien Régime: being branded *"gothique"* was like being given the kiss of political death. Not only did Sade invest the word *gothique* with the same negative connotations that prevailed among his contemporaries; he also chose "Ostrogoths"[24] as one of his favorite terms of abuse—long before Captain Haddock, Tintin's friend in Hergé's comic books.[25]

We owe to François-Xavier Pagès de Vixouse (1745–1802), a prolific author active during the revolutionary period under the pen name of François Pagès, the first metalinguistic remarks made in France on the Gothic as a literary genre: "This genre is called the *black manner*, the *English manner*,"[26] Pagès wrote in a book published in Year VII (1799). Pagès's observations come as a confirmation that the French, at the time (and for a long time) ignored the English term *Gothic* and created their own descriptive vocabulary by borrowing the word *manner* from the vocabulary of painting: whatever it was, the Gothic novel was a *manière*. From the nineteenth century on to the last few decades of the twentieth century, *roman noir* and *genre noir* have been the two terms most frequently used, until the very recent naturalization in French of *roman gothique*. In the 1820s, while the Gothic vogue was beginning to recede in Great Britain, French *literati* were still busy coining denominations for it. In 1823, Charles Nodier, a famous writer and critic, suggested calling it "the frenetic school" (*l'école frénétique*).[27] The phrase did not really catch on, but it is revealing of the French perception of the English Gothic novels as excessive and pathological; Antonin Artaud might well have it in mind one century later when he wrote of the "frenetic appeal" he was hearing in *The Monk*.[28] Last but not least, someone we will meet again soon, Michel Foucault, deliberately avoided the English notion of the Gothic, consistently referring to *romans de terreur* (terror novels), an unusual phrase in French, to delineate a wide corpus ranging from Radcliffe to contemporary fiction.

What about Sade himself? In his *Idée sur les romans*, Gothic novels remain unnamed. Sade refers to them only as "the new novels." He describes them as belonging to a new "genre" that deserves critical attention.[29] His stand about those "new novels," however, has often been misread or oversimplified on two key issues: the intrinsic value of the new genre and its link with the historical situation.

It is no surprise that supporters of a Gothic-leaning Sade have read the paragraphs devoted to English Gothic novels in *Idée* as proof of Sade's admiration for, and adhesion to, the new genre. A close look at the text suggests otherwise. While Sade is ready to admit that those novels are "not without merit," his approbation is immediately qualified. Not all Gothic novels deserve praise; as for the genre itself, it faces a fatal, structural dilemma. Sade's first move consists of establishing a clear hierarchy among English novelists in favor of Lewis and his *Monk*, which he deems "superior on all grounds to the bizarre impetus of Radcliffe's brilliant imagination."[30] But whatever Matthew Lewis's talent, he is no less trapped than Ann Radcliffe in what Sade sees as an inherent contradiction. The Gothic novel, Sade explains, must either "développer le sortilège" (by which Sade means: unfold or explain the magical elements in the plot), or never "raise the curtain" (i.e., leave the inexplicable events unexplained). Choosing the first option and providing the reader with rational explanations, "one ceases to captivate." Choosing to keep the mysteries mysterious, on the other hand, "one falls into the utmost implausibility" (invraisemblance). This is the "reef," Sade concludes, of a genre that he sees as intrinsically flawed.

As for the possible linkage between the Gothic and the Revolutionary events in France and Europe, an often-quoted sentence in *Idée* does suggest a direct causal link: the new genre, Sade writes, is "becoming the necessary fruit of the convulsions felt in Europe."[31] However, this elliptic statement should be read with caution. Nowhere does Sade, in *Idée*, support or suggest the notion that the "new novels" could have been "inspired" by the revolutionary events. Not only are revolutionary events or situations conspicuously absent from the plots of Gothic novelists, even in the late 1790s—an absence that could not go unnoticed by contemporary readers—but the idea of the English Gothic novel having its roots in the French Revolution is chronologically flawed. Sade is perfectly aware of the fact that the genre preceded the French Revolution, and he would under no circumstances jeopardize the credibility of his ambitious historical and philosophical survey of the novel through the ages, by committing a factual error of that magnitude. The "fruit" metaphor in Sade's sentence must then be interpreted in a different way. Sade is not arguing that the revolutionary "convulsions" in Europe *produced* the "roman noir"—obviously, this had not been the case. He is trying to account for the (delayed) success of the Gothic novel in France and in continental Europe by suggesting that the extraordinary experiences introduced in everyday life by revolutionary violence and political turmoil have made audiences receptive to a genre best characterized by the deliberate staging of *excesses*. In short, Sade is analyzing the Revolution as a favorable context for the reception, not as the mold of the genre. Gothic novels, according to Sade, had benefited from the gloomy circumstances, which called for new fictional forms. It had become "necessary" for novelists to answer the public demand for more intense, dramatic, somber stories, which could resonate with the pervasive sense of danger and monstrosity felt by many—especially among the educated readers—in the 1790s.

Was the Gothic novel the sole possible answer to that demand? Absolutely not. While spelling out those reasons for the success of the Gothic novelists, Sade is promoting another way to terror—his own. To better challenge the *fiers rivaux* from England, French novelists should not shy away from cultivating other forms of fictional horrors—and this is exactly what Sade has in mind to do in his *Crimes of Love*, the volume of collected stories to which *Idée sur les romans* serves as an introduction. Sade is therefore quite personally interested in emphasizing the qualitative leap in emotions that has occurred as a consequence of the Revolution and the European wars. As proven by the surprising success of the "black manner," old novels have become obsolete overnight, because of the actual violence of real life. Gothic novels, however, are the symptom, not the solution.

Sade, in effect, swiftly moves to underline the shortcomings of the Gothic novel. While capitalizing on the violent realities of the time, the Gothic novel has taken a wrong, mystifying, escapist path. Far from translating into fiction the dreadful *infortunes* experienced in their flesh and minds by so many people in times of political chaos, Gothic novelists took the easier road of exaggerated, extravagant supernatural narratives: "to secure the readers' interest," Sade sarcastically observes, "it had become necessary to call Hell for help";[32] it had become necessary, he continues, "to go and find in the country of chimaeras what everybody could know by simply digging out the History of Man in this age of Iron"—or, indeed, in any other age, since history itself, in Sade's eyes, is an endless return of the worst. By relying on the supernatural to strike stronger blows, the new novelists, whatever their "merits," are driving the novel into an impasse. To energize the novel and electrify readers living in violent times, one must take another path. One must "fouiller l'histoire de l'homme"—dig up the history of humanity—by focusing on the ages of historical turmoil. Sade's hypothetical conclusion should thus be read as utterly ironic: "If within that genre [the black novel] a work appears good enough to reach the target without breaking itself on either reef [Sade is referring to the above-mentioned dilemma of the Gothic novel], far from blaming it for its ways and means, we will then praise it as a model." But this is precisely what the Gothic novelists will never be able to achieve. Other paths should therefore be taken, more "real" and no less somber, indeed all the darker for the crude light shed on historical "reality"—a task to which Sade himself would devote the later part of his life, writing the gloomiest possible "historical" novels.

Sade's interest in the Gothic wave that hit France in the mid-1790s[33] is nevertheless undeniable.[34] As a struggling and sometimes "famished" writer, how could he remain indifferent to a genre that had become a commercial success? Challenging the English fashion in 1800 with *Les crimes de l'amour*, Sade was in fact fighting the second round in a game in which he had lost the first: on the stage, as a playwright.

There are many reasons for Sade's theatrical failures, ranging from his lack of diplomacy in his dealings with actors to his inability (or unwillingness) to erase from his plays uncanny and morally alarming elements. Not to mention bad luck. When at long last he was given a chance to present *Oxtiern* on a Parisian stage, the first night coincided with the revolutionary takeover of Parisian theaters by militant *sans-culottes*; according to witnesses, the play was interrupted before anyone in the audience could hear a line. But the most important reason could lie in the changes in public taste observed by Sade himself as early as 1790.

In a letter written in May 1790, Sade complained: "By the way, we have now Trappist monks on the French stage. After being treated to cardinals in *Charles IX*,[35] nuns in the comedy entitled *The Convent*,[36] we are now being given *Le comte de Comminges*, a drama by Monsieur d'Arnaud.[37] The action takes place in the monastery of the Trappist Order. There are no other actors than monks, no other decoration than a graveyard and a few crosses. People are fighting to get in [on y étouffe]. So much have we become English. . . . What am I saying? Anthropophagi! . . . Cannibals!"[38]

Sade detected something distinctly un-French in that gloomy, dark, and bloody vogue of *"drames à l'anglaise"* (English-style dramas) that had *preceded* both the Reign of Terror and the vogue of the "Gothic novel" in the late 1790s. His comment also suggests a question: If those works did not reflect revolutionary violence, could they possibly have created an atmosphere favorable to dark deeds and bloody excesses? Another letter, written the same month, suggests as much. Speaking of the violent episodes taking place in southern France in that same spring of 1790, Sade wrote: "Valence, Montauban, Marseille are theaters of horrors where cannibals, every single day, perform [exécutent] English-style dramas which make your hair stand on end."[39] The viral force of English-style horrors is suspected of triggering real-life horrors or, more accurately, reactivating an inveterate taste for blood.

We must keep in mind Sade's sarcastic attitude toward the "English" invasion of both the novel and the stage when trying to interpret the occasional "Gothic" motifs in Sade's novels. Maurice Heine and others have documented such characters or episodes, which stand conspicuously apart in Sadian fiction, such as the episode of the "hermit of the Apennines," a wicked giant living in a secluded castle in the middle of a lake.[40] The description, loaded with Gothic stereotypes, reads as an amused wink to the French reader.

Another interesting passage is the narration of Justine's escape from the convent of Sainte-Marie-des-Bois. In the pitch-dark courtyard, Justine finds herself stumbling on uneven soil and unidentified debris. Stooping to satisfy her curiosity, she realizes that she is holding a skull in her hands, but her repulsion does not prevent her from wondering whose skull it is she is holding. Could it be the skull "of my dear Omphale?" Could it be the skull of "poor Octavie, who was so beautiful, so sweet, so kind?"[41] I find it difficult to take this monologue at face value.

Still another example of a humorous play on Gothic commonplaces can be found in the description of the sinister torture vault in the same 1791 novel: "Imagine, Madam, a round-shaped vault, 25 feet in diameter, with black carpeted walls decorated only by the most lugubrious objects, such as skeletons of all kinds of sizes and bones disposed in the shape of the cross of Saint Andrew—*des ossements en sautoir*." Introducing in the macabre depiction a phrase normally used for royal orders and other signs of distinction, Sade turns these bones into sheer *décorations*, in both senses of the word. The comical intention is beyond any doubt. Maurice Lévy, however, has suggested another interesting layer of interpretation: those bones, he writes, belong "to a baroque, and all things considered, conventional, sensibility."[42] "Conventional" may sound a bit strange in that context; the term, however, is quite acceptable if referring to a rhetorical code borrowed from the baroque and playfully appropriated by Sade. Sadian bones are more signs than things—hence their comical effect. Skulls and bones in *Justine* are not pre-Lovecraftian Things roaming in the Night; they have nothing to do either with the decomposed, putrid Lewisian corpses. In that sense, it can be said that their function is indeed to establish a convention: a rhetorical protocol of horror that goes directly against the suggestion of horror itself. Sade's exploitation of a codified repertory of signs—like introducing larches in landscapes to signify gloom, or promising metaphorical "cypresses" to victims before killing them—turns Death itself into a clear emblem, not a dark, spectral, unshaped presence.

Such examples suggest the intertwining, in Sade's writings, of proximity with, and ironical distance from, the Gothic topoi—an attitude that seems confirmed by a curious note in the draft of *Idée sur les romans*. This note had been introduced by Sade in his manuscript at the end of the passage on Radcliffe and Lewis. For reasons unknown to us, this planned footnote praising a French Gothic novel by Bellin de la Liborlière did not find its way into the published book. However, Sade retained it in his literary portfolio.

Bellin de la Liborlière, an aristocrat and an *émigré* who had been permitted to come back to France after the 1798 amnesty, was the author of one of the first successful French "dark novels," *Célestine ou les époux sans l'être* (Célestine or the unmarried spouses) (Hamburg, 1798). But less than a year later, he also published a very funny spoof entitled *La nuit anglaise*,[43] which Maurice Lévy regards as the best French satire of Gothic novels and their readers. It seems revealing that the only French dark novelist Sade ever praised happens to have been the most brilliant parodist of the genre.

Sade's unpublished footnote is an interesting elaboration on the theme, previously mentioned, of the dilemma proper to the Gothic novel. While praising *Célestine* as "an ingenious novel" (un roman ingénieux), Sade rephrases his opposition to Gothic mysteries being explained. He half-jokingly declares that he would rather be allowed to "believe in ghosts, if he is to be amused by ghosts," adding: "Is it so necessary to say everything . . . especially when one allows himself to do everything!"[44]

Gothic novelists take so many liberties with plausibility that trying to restore plausibility at the last page of their extravagant tales is simply ludicrous. The unequivocal critique of Radcliffian "final explanations" comes with a subtle perfume of persiflage and private joke, with the phrase "tout dire," a direct allusion to Sade's own philosophy to "say everything," whatever the cost.

Sade's peculiar combination of humor (well identified by Breton) and referential irony keeps him miles away from the Gothic novelists at the very moment when he would seem closest to them. His alleged proximity with the Gothic genre, its themes and atmosphere, is undeniable, but entirely parodic in its nature: it is one of the many languages "borrowed" or "stolen" (as Barthes would say) by Sade. The gap remains abyssal between his novels and theirs, and deeper than any of the feudal moats surrounding their castles.

Sade is an atheist; Gothic novelists have religious backgrounds and, in most cases, religious agendas. The only ghost, in Sade's eyes, is God—whom he likes to call an "execrated ghost."[45]

Sade does not believe in the supernatural; Gothic novels revel in it.

Sadian Eros is characterized by the immediate and complete fulfillment of desire (if you belong to the right cohort), whereas Gothic novels stage a sexuality barred by obstacles—*The Monk* being a perfect example, according to Artaud, of such "barriers."[46] Sadian characters aim at "apathy" to maximize *jouissance*; Gothic characters are "frantic."

To put it bluntly, would we even be debating Sade's relationship to the Gothic if it were not for one single narrative element: the Castle (and its twin architectural structure: the Convent)? As suggested by Annie Le Brun's own intellectual itinerary,[47] the castle might well be the only way to bridge Sadian and Gothic universes. Since Horace Walpole's *The Castle of Otranto*, architectural fantasy has been at the core of the dark genre, and most specialists of the Gothic have pointed at stereotyped architectural decors, along with the supernatural, as the two distinctive features allowing us to sort out Gothic novels from sentimental or fantastic novels.

There are indeed many castles in Sade's life: the family castle at La Coste, in the Apt Valley—a place of dazzling luminosity rather than dazzling darkness; the two dungeons of Vincennes and the Bastille, where Sade spent a dozen years. By comparison, castles do not seem to play as prominent a role in his œuvre—with the notable exception, of course, of the imaginary castle of Silling, hidden at the top of a horrendous mountain in the heart of the Black Forest, which is to shelter the orgies of the libertines in *120 Days of Sodom*. Silling is central to all interpretations of Sade as a Gothic author. We must then focus on it, even though we will not have time for a complete visit.

In the prologue to *120 Days of Sodom*, Sade describes in great detail the many obstacles (natural and otherwise) that make Silling inaccessible to unwanted visitors. Difficult path, impenetrable forest, gated hamlet with armed scoundrels, abrupt mountain, abyssal gap, broken bridge, moat, walls and walls again: going to Silling is no easy ride. However, once on top, then inside, the reader witnesses a complete change of scenery. In sharp contrast with the terrifying mountains, he is now greeted in a welcoming *"plaine,"* or *"petite plaine"*—the word is repeated four times on a single page.[48] Upon entering the castle itself, the contrast becomes even more striking. Not only do the awesome, hostile, ragged peaks disappear from sight, but a luxurious, state-of-the-art interior materializes as promptly as if operated by expert stagehands in one of those *pièces à machines* that delighted French operatic audiences of the time. Culture substitutes for nature as one walks into the dwelling, unexpectedly endowed with all the refinements of urban or suburban houses of pleasure. "Prettiness" and comfort are the distinctive traits of the less than Gothic locale: "From the gallery [forming the last protecting wall], one entered a very pretty dining lounge [un très joli salon à manger], furnished with cabinets equipped with *tours* connecting them directly to the kitchens, so you could be served hot meals rapidly and without being waited on by any servant."[49] Then follows a minute description of the interior of the castle, in perfect contrast with the exterior.[50]

This first glimpse *inside* Silling is quite revealing. The spooky fortress is a place of luxury, characterized by its *joliesse*[51] and modernity. The emphasis put on the *tour* (turn) sent a clear message to contemporary readers. Originally a revolving mechanism at the entrance of hospices and churches allowing parents to abandon their children anonymously, the *tour* had become, in the eighteenth century, an architectural device typical of the *petites maisons*, those houses of pleasure built on the outskirts of Paris for discreet sexual encounters or *"parties de débauche."* Once *inside* Silling, the contemporary reader found himself (or herself) on familiar libertine ground.

From this topographical and architectural preamble placed by Sade on the threshold of his most (in fact, only) "claustral" novel, two conclusions can be drawn. First, the site of the castle is chosen for its remoteness more than for its frightening aspects. Its isolation is characteristic of all utopias, here turned into dystopia. Moreover, the ominous surroundings are deterrents only for potential intruders; they are not meant to terrorize the future victims (whose impressions leave the libertines quite unmoved) or the reader. Once *inside* the castle, as we will see in a moment, all this pseudo-Gothic gloom vanishes: indoors, all is order and beauty, luxury, sensual delight. Most of all, it is calm and quietness the libertines want. As Sade puts it in a jocular way: "Et là que de tranquillité!" Silling may look like a Gothic castle. It is really an enclosed, protected "garden of delights" located in a "small plain": a *locus amœnus* in disguise.

Second, the Sadian castle is a double structure, a Russian doll. The rough, "gothic" outside hides a modern hedonistic locale. Silling is well-heated, well-lit, well-furnished with all kinds of amenities and gastronomical treats. In that respect, the place often described as the archetypal Sadian castle, while occasionally playing on "dark" stereotypes, belongs to a well-established French tradition of libertine novels or short stories associating sexual pleasures with luxurious and refined private spaces: the castle and its enchanting gardens overlooking the Seine in Vivant Denon's *Point de lendemain*; the little house of pleasure in Bastide's *La petite maison*; and last but not least, the secret garden of delights located under the formidable Bastille in Robert-Martin Lesuire's astonishing novel entitled *Charmansage*.

*Charmansage*, published in 1792, begins before the Revolution and ends shortly after Bastille Day. It tells the incredible adventures of an attractive, honest, and patriotic young man who, in spite of his name (*Charmingwise*), keeps running into trouble and getting imprisoned, most often for obscure reasons. Spinning the full yarn of his bizarre adventures is quite impossible as well as unnecessary. Suffice it to say that being imprisoned in the Bastille, that most horrible of all dungeons, and trying to escape through the well in the courtyard, Charmansage encounters, instead of Gothic skeletons and English ghosts, a secret harem of charming young women. They are the illegitimate daughters of every single important historical figure of the finishing century, from the Duke of Richelieu, a notorious *libertin*, to Voltaire. Needless to say, Charmansage, the first man ever to enter this secret garden under the Bastille, is welcomed with intense curiosity, which soon turns into enthusiastic hospitality.

Is Lesuire's novel a parody of Gothic novels? It is hard to say. Gothic novels, in 1792, had not quite yet made their way to Parisian bookstores, even though, according to Sade, English gloom had already invaded the stage. Whatever the case, *Charmansage* reveals a propensity, among French novelists, to take dungeons lightly—even the most frightful of all, the Bastille, the "Hell of the living," as the Abbé de Buquoy had called it in 1719. Sade, as we will now see, gives many signs of sharing the same ironical attitude toward the gloomy *clichés*.

Needless to say, Sade's œuvre is not always playful. Horrors are committed. Terror often seems to prevail. But terror of what? And which horrors? Answering those questions should help us identify the shade of dark particular to Sade, and distinguish it from the "black manner" that the French critic Pagès, in 1799, deemed characteristic of the English Gothic novel. Paraphrasing Oscar Wilde's famous saying about the Americans and the British being separated by a common language, we could say that the Gothic and Sadian "manners" are separated by a common lexicon, with a key word: *horror(s)*, the revolving door between the two universes. Opposing *horrors* to *horror*, Sade engineers a semantic *tour* allowing for the two separate worlds to communicate while maintaining their statutory isolation.

As "felt," as experienced, *horror* applies to the victims. "Everything spreads a tenebrious horror upon me," Justine says.[52] *Horror* is subjective in the full etymological sense of the term: it is what the victim is subjected to—while *horrors* (in the plural) always have the objectivity of the performed action. Justine, as a "victim," often expresses her pains, sorrows, anxieties, in a seemingly Gothic vein; her narrative, however, is permanently contaminated from the inside by another language, the language of horrors (in the plural), which is the language of domination. Here is a good example of such a discursive contamination: "The shadows of the night began to spread upon the forest that kind of religious horror which at the same time breeds fear in timid souls and criminal schemes [le projet du crime] in ferocious hearts."[53] The pseudo-Gothic "religious horror" experienced and expressed by Justine in her narrative is contradicted, in the last part of the same sentence, by another voice—unmistakably the author's—offering the reader another choice: planning and executing horrors rather than living "timidly" in horror. Putting a phrase such as *le projet du crime* in Justine's mouth, Sade makes his virtuous *infortunée* testify to the permanent duality between horror and horrors, giving the last word to the latter.

For the libertine, horror is not something you feel, but something you do. It is a project, the execution of which must intervene without delay, and be immediately followed, after completion, by another "criminal project." Victims are penetrated by horror; libertines perpetrate horrors. Those horrors, committed as soon as conceived, are not only different in nature but clearly antagonistic to the horror experienced by the victims. While more complete and elaborated definitions of Sadian libertinage have since been proposed by critics and philosophers, it should be underlined that Sadian libertines most frequently content themselves with this pragmatic self-definition: *"Faire des horreurs."* Deliberately "doing horrors" and never living through the subjective experience of horror is what sets the libertines apart from nonlibertines, while at the same time warranting the paradoxical and contentious harmony—the *concordia discors*—between *libertinage* and real (not fictional) life.

For *horrors* are not only what the Sadian libertine wants to do, and does do: *horrors* are what goes on everywhere, in every land, at all historical periods. While horror (in the singular) is "chimerical," horrors are *the* real. "What!" Eugénie exclaims in the *boudoir*, "Were there really places in the world where such horrors have been condoned?"[54] Her question, of course, is purely rhetorical, allowing Dolmancé to confirm that, yes indeed, all horrors have been, somewhere, some place, committed, excused, condoned or even praised. Not only in secluded castles: in Parisian boudoirs as well, in charming country houses, in Italian picturesque villages. Not only in the Black Forest but on top of volcanoes and on Mediterranean beaches, in the heart of Africa as well as in snow-clad Russia.

In Sade's novels, outdoor horrors are no less exciting than horrors committed inside in damp vaults: in fact, Juliette and many of her companions seem to enjoy their wildest experiments on Mount Vesuvius or the central square in Naples. More importantly, however, horrors in full light are the rule, *not* horrors in the dark. Jean Fabre, a pioneer of Sadian studies at a time when Sade was not yet welcome at the Sorbonne, once wrote: "This black Doctor [Sade] never vowed himself to the Dark."[55] I don't know about Sade being a Doctor—even in theology—but no one can disagree with Fabre when he reminds us of Sade's hostility to darkness and his lack of interest for creatures crawling in the dark. Not even Annie Le Brun, the most brilliant advocate of a Gothic Sade! "Even though all the elements of the *roman noir* can be found [in Silling] in a more concentrated form than anywhere else," Le Brun wrote in 1987, "Sade is announcing, without any ambiguity, his intention to show for the first time in full light [en pleine clarté] what makes our tenebrous heart beat."

She concludes on this (self-addressed?) question: "One could even ask oneself whether Sade, taking advantage of the labyrinthine courtyards inside Silling and its luxurious furnishings, did not take us out and away from the black universe, to throw us into the crude light of horror."[56] Sade does want to "throw us into the crude light of horror"—or better, perhaps, "horrors." We can agree on that with Annie Le Brun. Horrors in full light, darkness at noon, is what makes Sade's œuvre so exceptional and unbearable. That is also the reason why the Gothic could only be, for him, a laughingstock when on stage, and when in novel form, a good material for parody.

Speaking of Sade in *Words and Things*, Michel Foucault famously defined the libertine as "he who, while yielding to all the fantasies of desire and to each of its furies, can, but also must, illumine their slightest movement with a lucid and deliberately elucidated representation."[57] Much less known than this page in *Words and Things* is a 1977 interview in which Foucault comments on the obsession of darkness in Sade's times: "A fear haunted the second half of the 18th century: a fear of dark space, of the obscure screen blocking the complete visibility of things, people, truths."[58] Bentham's *Panopticon*, which Foucault had edited, was part of an effort to "dissolve all black chambers where political arbitrary was being fomented." Which brings Foucault to mention the *romans de terreur* and specifically Radcliffe, whose "imaginary spaces" are, in his words, "the 'counter-image' of the transparencies and visibilities that one tried to establish" in that age. Coming back to Bentham's *Panopticon*, Foucault thus concluded: "The panopticon is kind of utilizing the 'castle' shape (a dungeon surrounded by walls) to paradoxically create a space of detailed visibility."[59]

"Detailed visibility" is exactly what the libertine is in search of, and Sadian castles, much more than new castles of Otranto, are the Sadian version of the *Panopticon* as described by Foucault. This is made quite explicit in one particular episode of *La nouvelle Justine ou les malheurs de la vertu*. In this passage, Justine, narrating her misfortunes to her sister Juliette, endeavors to describe an underground torture vault, where prominently and incongruously sits a "vast canapé." For more than half a century, the *canapé* or sofa had been a required piece of furniture in French libertine narratives, even giving its title to one of the most popular of them, *Le canapé couleur de feu*, a story written by Louis-Charles Fougeret de Montbron and published (anonymously) for the first time in 1741. The particular canapé described by Justine is not of the color of fire, though; it is "black." However, while distinguishing itself by this somber color from the usual boudoir paraphernalia, Sade's canapé also distinguishes itself from Gothic props by its function, which is to serve as an erotic *Panopticon*: "the extremity of that vault," Justine makes clear for her sister and the other listeners, was occupied by a large black canapé, from where "all the atrocities of this place revealed themselves to the gaze" (se développaient aux regards toutes les atrocités de ce lieu).[60]

The postrevolutionary writer, the genuine "new novelist" to whom Sade was appealing in *Idées sur les romans*, must dare sit on this black settee from where he will see and register the "unscrolling" of all horrors and human atrocities. Such is Sade's way to Terror—a terror that has little to do with dark mysteries and goblin tales, grounded as it is in Sade's anthropological and historical pessimism. In that sense, we should not be surprised that Sade, in his final years in the asylum at Charenton, while secretly writing what probably would have been an aggravated version of *120 Days of Sodom*, was working on gloomy and bloody historical novels.[61] Doing so, Sade was not only trying to fool his jail keepers or placate his censors. Relocating Evil in Man, not the Devil, and in History, not Fantasy, he was treading his own path toward a "new novel" defined against the Gothic novel, and reweaving the thread of the old *histoires tragiques* to expose history itself as a tragedy.

## Notes

1. http://www.forum-gothique.com/sade-culture-gothique-t13739.html; posted May 15, 2011. All translations are mine unless otherwise noted.
2. Ibid.
3. Witness also to that lasting link is the acronym S.A.D.E. (for "Sanctus amenus dominus erecta") given to a Gothic music association by its founder, Mr. Labesse. "Sanctus amenus dominus erecta," which does not make much sense in Latin, should be understood, according to Mr. Labesse, as, "Give us a saint and the master will rise"—which does not make more sense to me, but then, I am an outsider, just like poor Camilla.
4. See, for instance, Elisabeth Durot-Boucé, *Le lierre et la Chauve-souris: Réveils gothiques* (Paris: Presses Sorbonne Nouvelle, 2004); and *Imaginaires gothiques: Aux sources du roman noir français*, ed. Catriona Seth (Paris: Desjonquères, 2010).
5. Until the 1960s, utopias and so-called utopic writers, especially those active during the nineteenth century, stirred more interest among historians of ideas, social historians, and political scientists than among scholars of literature. This century-old trend—which can be traced back to Marx's polemics against "utopian socialists"—was reversed in the 1960s and 1970s with philosophers like René Schérer and literary critics like Barthes emphasizing the textual dimension of utopia, with Fourier becoming the prime focus of attention. Tzvetan Todorov's *Introduction à la littérature fantastique* (Paris: Seuil, 1970) helped legitimize a scholarly approach to the "littérature fantastique," which had been traditionally kept at arm's length by French academia; academic and pedagogical books appeared in its wake, like Irène Bessière's *Le récit fantastique: La poétique de l'incertain* (Paris: Larousse Université, 1974).
6. M. Lévy, *Le roman "gothique" anglais: 1764–1824*, Publications de la Faculté des Lettres et Sciences humaines de Toulouse, 1968; new ed. (Paris: Armand Colin, 1995).

7. Hawthorne's *Weird Tales* have been translated into French as *Contes étranges*.

8. "Two of the tales," Delon explains, "deserve attention inasmuch as they reveal a Sade wandering in the direction of the *fantastique*, at a time when this vein is blooming" ("Éditer Sade: *Les contes étranges*," *La Revue italienne d'études françaises*, May 2015; http://rief.revues.org/1054).

9. The French word used by Delon is "accommodements" (Sade, *Contes étranges* [Paris: Gallimard, Folio-Classique, 2014], 24).

10. "Le don des 'noirs' à jamais les plus profonds qui sont aussi ceux qui permettent les plus éblouissantes réserves de lumière" (A. Breton, "Situation de Melmoth," in *Melmoth. L'homme errant*, trans. J. Marc-Chardourne, [Paris: Pauvert, 1965], xx).

11. Ibid., xiii.

12. See Franco Tonelli, "From Cruelty to Theatre: Antonin Artaud and the Marquis de Sade," *Comparative Drama* 3, no. 2 (Summer 1969): 79–86.

13. M. G. Lewis, *Le moine raconté par Antonin Artaud* (Paris: Denoël & Steele, 1931).

14. See the convincing argument made by John Phillips in "Circles of Influence: Lewis, Sade, Artaud," *Comparative Critical Studies* 9, no. 1 (Edinburgh: Edinburgh University Press, 2012): 69, 62.

15. M. G. Lewis, *Le moine raconté par Antonin Artaud* (Paris: Gallimard; Folio, 1966), 11 ("philosophique" is underlined by Artaud).

16. See Annie Le Brun, *Les châteaux de la subversion* (Paris: Jean-Jacques Pauvert et Garnier-Frères, 1982). In 2010, Gallimard (Collection Tel) republished in a single volume her 1982 book on the Gothic and her subsequent essay on Sade entitled *Soudain, un bloc d'abîme* (1986), an editorial decision that spectacularly emphasized the association between Sade and the Gothic tradition.

17. D. A. F. Sade, *Idée sur les romans*, in *Œuvres complètes* (Paris: Cercle du Livre Précieux, 1966), 10:22.

18. See M. Heine, "Le marquis de Sade et le roman noir," *Nouvelle Revue Française* 239 (August 1933); expanded version (Paris: N.R.F., 1933 [hors commerce]); reprinted in M. Heine, *Le Marquis de Sade*, ed. and preface Gilbert Lély (Paris: Gallimard, NRF, 1950).

19. There has been some debate about the chronology of Lewis's presence in Paris. His first biographer, Mrs. Baron-Wilson, published an important letter sent by Lewis from Paris with the date 7 September 1792, while admitting that Lewis's letters "are deficient in dates" (*The Life and Correpondence of G. M. Lewis* [London: Henry Colburn, 1839], 51). Maurice Heine probably relied on that rather unreliable source. (John Berryman, who wrote the preface for the 1952 Grove Press edition of *The Monk*, uncharitably called Mrs. Baron-Wilson's book "adulterated" and "child-like" [17]). Lewis could have been in Paris in 1791 rather than 1792, according to Maurice Lévy, a correction that does not harm Heine's argument, since *La nouvelle Justine* had appeared in 1791. We do know for sure that Lewis wrote most of *The Monk* in The Hague during the summer of 1794.

20. Maurice Heine, "Le marquis de Sade et le roman noir," in *Le Marquis de Sade*, 211–31.

21. *The Gothic Tales of the Marquis de Sade*, trans. Margaret Crosland (London: Peter

Owen, 2011): "A collection of de Sade's stories utilizing gothic conventions and questioning sexual and societal mores" (cover).

22. A. Rey, entry "Gothiques," in *Dictionnaire amoureux du diable* (Paris: Plon, 2013), 424. Rey does not stand alone in his denunciation of the pervasive use of the "gothic tag" by Anglo-Saxon scholars. Maurice Lévy, in his authoritative 1968 work, while not going as far as excluding *Melmoth the Wanderer* from the Gothic genre (as Rey does), has also criticized what he perceived as a sloppy use of the term *gothic* in American academia (see, for instance, *Le roman "gothique" anglais. 1764–1824*, 389n1). Written in the wake of Lévy's study, with many references to Rey's works, Élizabeth Durot-Boucé's *Spectres des lumières: Du frissonnement au frisson: Mutations gothiques du XVIIIe au XXIe siècle* (Paris: Publibook, 2008) discerns an "americanization" of the Gothic genre itself as soon as it "crossed the Atlantic," while English and continental Gothic novelists kept an ironic distance to the genre ("Lewis is a little boy having fun"), "what is particular to American Gothic is the fact that it expresses a deep anxiety related to historical crimes and the perversity of human desires casting their shadow on what some would like to see as the luminescent American Republic" (40).

23. Sade has been used by "English critics and publishers" to "establish a link" between Gothic narratives and the French Revolution, Rey suggests in the same entry of his *Dictionnaire amoureux du diable* (423). Whatever the merit of his argument, Rey does not bolster it by suggesting that Sade's pronouncement on the Gothic genre, having been "the necessary product of the revolutionary blow resonating in all Europe," has been "attributed" to Sade ("On attribue à Sade ce jugement"), as if it had been fabricated by perfide Albion's mischievous critics. Although not accurate, the (presumably retranslated) quotation can easily be traced to Sade's *Idée sur les romans*, which will be discussed later in this piece.

24. The term *Ostrogoths* in Sade's texts refers to a combination of stupidity, backwardness, and bigotry. Neoconservative moralizing literary critics are debunked as "ces ostrogoths" in a note written at Charenton ("Notes littéraires," in *Œuvres complètes*, 15:17); see also Sade's tirades against the "stupid Ostrogoths who had me put in jail" because of *Justine* ("Note relative à ma détention," ibid., 15:27). Most revealing is Sade's use of "Ostrogoths" as a synonym of "Welches" (a Voltairian term of abuse for backward Frenchmen hostile to the ideas of the Enlightenment) in a polemical note he inserted in his historical novel *Isabelle de Bavière* (ibid., 497n64).

25. "Ostrogoth(s)" is among the 213 insults and curses used by Haddock in *Tintin's Adventures*. For a complete list of Haddock's curses in English translation, see www.tintinologist.org/guides/lists/curses.html.

26. François Pagès, *Amour, haine et vengeance, ou histoire de deux illustres maisons d'Angleterre* (Paris: An VII), 1:v–vi; qtd. in Lévy, *Le roman "gothique" anglais*, 477.

27. Lévy, *Le roman "gothique" anglais*, 383.

28. Ibid., 365.

29. "Let us agree on the fact that this genre, whatever what is being said about it, is not without merits" (Sade, *Idée sur les romans*, in *Œuvres complètes*, 15:15).

30. Ibid.

31. Ibid.

32. Ibid.

33. Ann Radcliffe had three novels translated into French in the year 1797 alone and a fourth one in 1798: *Les châteaux d'Athlin et de Dunbaye; Julia, ou les souterrains du château de Mazzini* (French title for *A Sicilian Romance*); *L'Italien ou le confessional des pénitents noirs;* and *Les mystères d'Udolphe*.

34. Rearrested and placed in administrative confinement in 1800, Sade includes Radcliffe in a list of his "desired" books, mentioning Radcliffe's "*Œuvres,* 11 volumes," and more specifically, *Le Château d'Udolphe, La forêt* (published in 1794), *L'Italien,* and *Julien* (probably for *Julia*).

35. Marie-Joseph Chénier's tragedy *Charles IX, ou la Saint-Barthélémy,* later retitled *Charles IX, ou l'école des rois,* premiered at the Comédie-Française on 4 November 1789. The success and scandal were enormous.

36. It is difficult to decide which play Sade had in mind. Between 1789 and 1799, no fewer than twenty-six claustral plays were performed in Paris, several of them prior to Sade's 1790 remarks. However, very few can qualify as "comedies." Carmontelle's *Le couvent des religieuses,* written for the "théâtre de société" in 1789, when Sade was still imprisoned, should probably be ruled out. Sade could be referring to Pierre Laujon's *Le couvent, ou les fruits du caractère et de l'éducation,* which premiered on 16 April 1790 at the Théâtre de la Nation, a few weeks before Sade wrote his letter. Sade was at the time courting the ex-Comédiens-Français of the Théâtre de la Nation to have his own plays accepted and performed on their stage.

37. The third example given by Sade of the gloomy Anglomania prevailing on the Parisian stage refers to an old play successfully revived. Baculard d'Arnaud's *Les amants malheureux, ou le comte de Comminge,* inspired by the *Mémoires du comte de Comminge* (1735), by Claudine Guérin de Tencin, had premiered in 1764. Baculard d'Arnaud was well known to Sade (if not much appreciated by him) as a *protégé* and frequent guest of Sade's father.

38. D. A. F. Sade, Lettre à Gaufridy [end of May 1790], in *Œuvres complètes,* 12:479–80.

39. D. A. F. Sade, Lettre à Reinaud, 22 May 1790, in *Œuvres complètes,* 12:475. The southern French cities devastated by civil strife are "des théâtres d'horreurs," emulating the horrifying English dramas staged in Paris.

40. The episode is narrated in part 3 of the *Histoire de Juliette,* in *Œuvres* (Paris: Gallimard, Bibliothèque de la Pléiade, 1998), 3:699ff. The giant's appearance, Juliette comments, was frightening enough to "make us believe for a minute that we were speaking to the Prince of Darkness." But of course the Russian-born giant Minski is just another very real *libertin,* not a supernatural fiend.

41. "Ce crâne est peut-être celui de ma chère Omphale, ou celui de cette malheureuse Octavie, si belle, si douce, si bonne" (Sade, *Justine ou les malheurs de la vertu,* ed. M. Delon, in *Œuvres* [Paris: Gallimard, Bibliothèque de la Pléiade, 1990], 2:283).

42. Lévy, *Le Roman "gothique" anglais: 1764–1824,* 353.

43. See Lévy's enthuiastic description of the novel (ibid., 491). While underlining similitudes between Bellin's preface to the second edition of his book and Sade's *Idée sur les romans,* Lévy is inclined to deem them coincidental. Contacts between Sade and Bellin, however, cannot be ruled out.

44. D. A. F. Sade, *Notes littéraires*, in *Œuvres complètes*, 15:24–25.

45. On the same page, the "exécrable fantôme" is invited to "go back into the darkness you were born from" (*Notes littéraires*, in *Œuvres complètes*, 15:19).

46. Most of Artaud's "Avertissement," placed as an introduction to his translation (or "narration") of *The Monk*, is devoted to describe the various "barrières" erected by Lewis's "sadistic" imagination against the sexual urge of his own creature, Ambrosio.

47. Annie Le Brun emphasized, in a 1986 interview, that she was immersed in Gothic castles when she started working on Sade: "I started writing on Sade when I was working on the *roman noir* and the castles in those books" (A. Le Brun, *Sade, Allers et détours* [Paris: Plon, 1989], 19).

48. D. A. F. Sade, *Les 120 Journées de Sodome*, in *Œuvres complètes*, 13:45.

49. Ibid., 13:46.

50. From what we know of La Coste in the 1770s and what one could guess wandering in the ruins of the castle before its absurd "reconstruction" in the 1970s—at the time, elegant mouldings and cornices could still be observed on what remained of the interior walls—the same contrast could be found in Sade's family castle between a "feudal" exterior appearance and a "pretty," comfortable if not luxurious, interior (including a space for theatrical performances). What Silling and La Coste have in common is not their supposed "gothic" architecture but, rather, their dual structure. Many medieval castles at the time sheltered interiors refurbished in the more refined and confortable style of the eighteenth century. La Coste was certainly "feudal" but not damp, dark, misty . . . or haunted.

51. Alain Robbe-Grillet, "Sade et le joli," in "Sade," special issue of *Revue Obliques*, no. 12–13 (1977): 59.

52. Sade, *Justine*, ed. Delon, 2:173.

53. Ibid., 2:172.

54. "Quoi! ces horreurs ont pu s'excuser quelque part?" (Sade, *La philosophie dans le boudoir*, in *Œuvres complètes*, 3:402).

55. J. Fabre, préface to Sade's *Les crimes de l'amour*, in *Œuvres complètes*, 10:xii: "Ce noir Docteur ne se vouait pas aux ténèbres."

56. A. Le Brun, "Un précipice au milieu du salon," in *Sade, aller et détours* (Paris: Plon, 1989), 69.

57. M. Foucault, *The Order of Things* (London: Routledge Classics, 2002), 228.

58. M. Foucault, "L'œil du pouvoir" (1977), *Dits et écrits* (Paris: Quarto-Gallimard, 2011), 2:196.

59. Ibid.

60. Sade, *Justine*, ed. Delon, 2:1016.

61. Sade's historical novels have long been underestimated and understudied. Chantal Thomas was among the first Sadian scholars to show their importance ("Isabelle de Bavière, dernière héroïne de Sade," in *Sade, écrire la crise*, ed. M. Camus and Ph. Roger [Paris: Belfond, 1983]). Two dissertations have been recently devoted to them: Chiara Gambacorti's "Sade: Une esthétique de la duplicité: Autour des romans historiques sadiens" (Paris: Classiques Garnier, 2014); and Michèle Vallentini's "Sade dans l'histoire: Du temps de la fiction à la fiction du temps" (Paris: Classiques Garnier, 2017).

ALISON BOOTH

# Anachronism, Heterotopia, and Gender in Anglophone Gothic

The willful errors of Gothic flout history and geography, decorum and plausibility. The *faits divers* or *histoires prodigieuses* that feed into Gothic novels are not to be believed, even when the ominous sounds are explained by wind in the shutters. Anglophone Gothic outrages taste and taboos as well as the dictates of class, gender, and religion. While critics have long recognized the gender politics in such topoi as the imperiled heroine in the haunted castle, I extend this approach to highlight the dimensions of blatant artifice in the immersive worlds of the Gothic genre, specifically anachronisms and heterotopias. Gothic's settings, historically improper, invite more emphasis on space than is characteristic in narrative studies, which tend to privilege time as the axis of a verbal medium. A view of time-space in certain Gothic fictions can offer perspectives on the class and gender politics of the genre beyond a single historical context. My examples are two highly staged prose works: Horace Walpole's *The Castle of Otranto*, the first publication to be dubbed "Gothic" in English, in its second edition, 1765; and Robert Louis Stevenson's *Strange Case of Dr Jekyll and Mr Hyde* [sic], published in 1886.[1] Different as these works are in relation to what might be called the birth and decadence of Anglophone Gothic, it is telling that Walpole invokes theater and Stevenson anticipates cinema. These frequently imitated texts rework conventions in extravagantly connected or obstructed spaces, out-scale doubles of male overreachers, and detours from Protestant, heterosexual domesticity.

Other examples in intervening decades might well support my exploration of anachronistic heterotopias—I briefly consider *Frankenstein* of 1818—and I do not claim a special affinity or influence between Walpole and Stevenson. I intend my spatial inspection of the Gothic anachronistic heterotopias in Walpole's and Stevenson's fiction to take us behind the scenes to see the way Gothic effects have been produced, and to suggest some of the cultural work performed by these entertainments.

The two novellas ring changes on the age-old device of the double, itself symptomatic of a collapse of generations and bodily boundaries in a perverse time-space. The divergent plots of *Otranto* and *Jekyll and Hyde*, as in romance generally, depend upon warped genetics, as when families eliminate or replace the mother, circumventing lawful marriage or licensed procreation. More interestingly, these classics present an edifice as a body, a portal as an orifice, and they play in distinctive ways with illegitimate access to compartments. These thoroughly interpreted texts each afford a somewhat different focus on settings that elide and stymie functions: the castle or private home has a subterranean passage or back stair leading to other institutions—church, laboratory, office. Proper spaces such as castles or policed streets or the comfortable upper-class sanctum skew into sexual violence and murder. Gothic fiction in its Anglophone heyday up to 1820 often imperils a heroine with rape; at the fin de siècle, those night streets might harbor Jack the Ripper,[2] but of course a male night walker might go either way.

## Revising a Spatial History of Gothic

The evolution of literature known as Gothic is beyond the scope of the Sadleir-Black and Lévy collections in the University of Virginia Library and of the diverse assembly of essays in this volume. But an understanding of the spatio-temporal displacements that create such indelible effects in *Otranto* and *Jekyll and Hyde* can gain from a review of the heterogeneous development of the traditions in Europe and Britain. Critical accounts of these Gothic traditions can be contradictory, in part because the genre mixes geohistorical travesties. Where does Gothic come from, and where do we stand toward it? As we stand toward a heterotopia in the Foucauldian sense: a dis/location where an observer is not, where one confronts Other time-places. Fred Botting adopts Michel Foucault's concept of heterotopias as sites of "counteraction" to the reader's location: *other* to the present subject: "The main features of Gothic fiction . . . are heterotopias: the wild landscapes, the ruined castles and abbeys, the dark, dank labyrinths, the marvelous, supernatural events, distant times and customs."[3] This spatial vocabulary compiles a distorted dictionary that writers in the Gothic mode consult.

Several irreconcilable narratives of Gothic's development attempt to derive or define the terms of its dialect of other time-spaces. Gothic as a term has its origins in an insult analogous to "barbaric." It presupposes an imagined history that displaces the legendary Goths (invaders of Rome) into a Catholic menace from France or Italy. Any attempt to map the perceived ethnic menace in Anglophone Gothic would show that North-South invasion has flipped to South-North. Yet in architecture and other associations, Gothic can be associated with a northern and indigenous Catholic past.[4] The British Reformation generated an othering of Catholicism, while the same era fostered phobias not only of superstition but also of extremes of learning; Enlightenment, too, could be seen as an invasion from the Continent. The point is not that there is one historical etiology or animus for the horror and terror of Gothic, but a buffet of temptations. Indeed, I consider deliberate faking of origins as the deepest common ground of Gothic. Michael Gamer suggests that English writers legitimated a fad for German horror materials half-smothered in documents.[5] Angela Wright similarly traces a mid-eighteenth-century Franco-British exchange of irresistible yet repellant narratives.[6] But at the point of the Gothic craze in Britain, 1790–1820, something besides salacious tales of violence, papacy, and natural philosophy might also be imported across the Channel: political Terror. Studies of British Gothic often tag it as reaction to the French Revolution, understating the French and German antecedents and the ambivalence toward both Catholicism and science. Gothic novelists were sometimes referred to as Terrorists, their aim being to rouse the reader, and perhaps to change the subject from current events.

Many have noted this complex adaptability of Gothic conventions—aided by translation and adaptation—to evoke psychological, aesthetic, and political disturbances across many geographical dimensions as imperialism worked its transformations. In Victorian versions, the menace may come from the Empire, from internal corruption of various kinds, or from "natural" rather than supernatural sensation—bigamy, imposture, madness—within the country house or suburban home. Instead of the haunted house and imperiled heroine, the fiction may imagine a homosocial group of professional men working vigilante-style against police and bourgeois convention, in secret rooms and anonymous streets. As the professions and science gain authority, the Gothic Other morphs from medieval occult arts to the new magic of science, replacing the monk with the mad scientist—a synopsis of the shift from Walpole to Stevenson, perhaps.

While the historical map of Anglophone Gothic has never been fixed or logically oriented, that has been altogether a fine source of frissons, not least of creepy spaces. The settings and structures of hetero-chronotopes, we might say, range widely in Anglophone Gothic. Gothic fiction especially underlines spatial interpretation, as in Franco Moretti's mapping: "where it happens" seems preternaturally significant, with a kind of agency that competes with characters and events.[7] Critical explorations of Gothic have favored psychoanalytic keys perhaps more than historical because of the significance of space. In Gothic texts, description seems to take on a life of its own in uncanny locations and abject encounters. Freud's concept of the uncanny famously turns on a reversal of language for the familiar house, the *unheimlich*. The uncanny, according to Freud, may arise from the return of the repressed; from the monstrous showing of something alive that should be dead, inanimate, and hidden; from the unfamiliar in the home—ingredients we would see in *Otranto* and *Jekyll and Hyde* as in many other Gothic fictions. Julia Kristeva's concept of abjection has similarly aided interpretation of Gothic affect. As Robert Miles puts it, "the abject occupies a border zone between desire and the super-ego," partaking "of both 'enjoyment' and disgust"; the liminality of abjection can emerge from the breakdown of religious or national orders, conditions underlying Gothic.[8] Foucauldian heterotopias, potentially uncanny or rousing abjection, range beyond Botting's list of wild landscapes and castles to include museums or prisons, sites of discipline and nation-building; composites of diverse times and purposes, transgressions of the blueprints of property or bodily boundaries.

Although space has been relatively neglected within narrative studies, some theorists have affirmed spatial reading to uncover haunted histories of colonialism and gender and racial exploitation. From some angles, the thematics of space expose the structure of power more explicitly than do the thematics of time. For example, Susan Stanford Friedman, in "Spatial Poetics and Arundhati Roy's *The God of Small Things*," reviews a small tradition of theorizing space in narrative to counter the "hegemony of temporal modes of thought."[9] Friedman's reading of permitted or prohibited spaces helpfully links Foucault's concept of heterotopia to Bakhtin's term *chronotope*, or time-space, referring to the signifying settings in various genres. Each chronotope invokes the kinds of narrative taking place there. The chronotope of the castle seems to predetermine the action of imprisonment, siege, invasion, usurpation, and of course, the romance of chivalry and its corollaries, forced marriage and adultery, in the dramas of dynastic power. Just think laboratory or Victorian street, and you can conjure existents and events in a mental storyworld. As the narrative of ancestry, illicit sexuality, and violence in *The God of Small Things* suggests, chronotope can be fate.

Trajectories through haunted spaces are inherent to Gothic, the haunting often a symbolic aftermath of history. The heterotopias of Gothic also entail anachronisms, worked through in hauntings from the past and doublings of character and action. Narratives entail movement in space and passage of time, inscribing irreversible loss of presence. Julian Wolfreys views this as an inherent haunting: "all stories are, more or less, ghost stories," as traces of unresolved memories reside.[10] A Gothic journey can dead-end, or can lead to an inspection of repositories of the uncanny. Or Gothic may throw characters hither and yon on maps or through tunnels and caves. The nervous action is simultaneously an anxious temporal crossing of narrative levels, analepsis or prolepsis, flashback or forecast; hidden identities, long-lost fathers, devilish doubles, and all sorts of primitive avatars surface in catastrophic ways. The metalepses or recursions of levels and zones of time and space in Gothic generate the scenarios of the chase and the detective prowl. Readers and critics join in: as if the dream logic of supernatural events and magical settings creates the gaps that provoke interpretation, audiences and experts become as fixated on clues as any of the detector-witnesses in a story by Poe or Machen or Conan Doyle.

In the heterotopic and anachronistic settings and amid the pressures of captivity, escape, and discovery, Gothic texts work up our bodily sensations. Gothic wants to *get* you in the body, the tool for experiencing space—wants to raise your pulse and your hair, or forestall an overwhelming urge to flee. The house, I have noted, is a reliable Gothic topos: a space that surely gets at bodies where they live. Gaston Bachelard elaborates on the figuration of the house as a body, a structure of memory aligned with the family romance, which we might term the psychoanalytic layout.[11] While an edifice creates an order or hierarchy, its inhabitants are displaced and dislodged by other times and places; in Gothic, the mad, the antique, or vengeful can inhabit any compartment of the building. There are always too many doors to monitor. Gothic has made a business of perhaps age-old tricks of storytelling, not just in the motifs of captivity, assault, escape, illicit gazing but also in sensory deprivation or overload. Darkness is a friend to Gothic, depriving the sense of sight, while hearing is overstimulated. Helpless as a protagonist may be, the reader collaborates with the threatening agency, turning words on a page into an experience of story-world space.

### Overreaching and Over-reading in Walpole and Stevenson

A complex literary history intervenes between the pioneering, monk-and-castle English Gothic of Walpole and the modernist, urban, dystopian allegory of Stevenson. I can illustrate some of this development with a glance at *Frankenstein*, another work that unites realist settings and characterization with supernatural provocations of gender trouble. *Frankenstein* in a sense adds the elements of anachronistic science, contemporary cities, and travel to Walpole's archaic caves and crusades. Victor Frankenstein studies alchemy in Enlightenment Europe and anticipates Dr. Jekyll's futuristic self-cloning. Mary Shelley's novel for the most part eschews the haunted house, but as in all three texts, the mother is moribund or absent, servants are caught in the crossfire, and the plots are set in motion by violence against a child. Prince Manfred, Frankenstein, and Dr. Jekyll/Mr. Hyde are comparable male overreachers, usurpers of patriarchal power. Their antagonists are supernatural bodies out of proportion: the giant parts of Alfonso's statue that bring down the castle; the Monster made at giant scale from dead body parts; and the short, crude avatar of Jekyll's evil, Mr. Hyde. These doubles collapse the generations of heteronormative procreation. Like *Frankenstein*, *Otranto* and *Jekyll and Hyde* ostensibly begin in dreams and culminate in tragedy; they invite maps or floorplans and dramatization of a complex chase. The obsessive family romance in *Otranto* multiplies interchangeable princesses, whereas *Jekyll and Hyde* occludes women. In both Walpole's and Stevenson's compressed tales, the plot is resolved by revealed identity: the peasant Theodore is Jerome's son and the true heir; the vile protégé Hyde is Dr. Jekyll's alter ego.

As in so many Gothic fictions, documents or competing testimonies subdivide the texts, undermining the authentication that they seem to serve. The explorer Walton is writing letters or a journal redacting layers of testimony. Was the text of *Otranto* found in the library of a northern Catholic family and translated from Italian by the fictitious William Marshal? Stevenson's counterpart for Walton and Marshal is the professional observer Utterson, who is confounded by Dr. Jekyll's handwriting on a check or a will that names the alter ego as heir. Documentary details and frame narratives seem to claim the truth of the places and events that defy the known physical world. Curiously, biographical anecdotes associate these works with dream visions and challenges to invent a timely novelty in fiction.

While indebted to contemporary fiction, *Otranto* also feels like a play, consisting largely of external action and spectacular events and dialogue rather than reported thought. Walpole's engagement with drama and the growing taste for Shakespeare has been well established. Walpole's preface to the second edition specifically invokes Shakespeare to defy neoclassical unities (imposed on England by French critics) and to justify the mixture of comic "low" characters in the novella's tragic action. Stevenson dispenses with comedy in scenes more novelistic than theatrical; instead, he predicts the potential of moving pictures, as if his novella were a screenplay for its own future adaptations. The observing character, Utterson, is subject to bad dreams after hearing about one of Hyde's violent acts: "the great field of lamps of a nocturnal city" inexorably produces "a scroll of lighted pictures" in the mind's eye. This cinematic image leads Utterson to imagine what might be an enactment of *Frankenstein*: a rich man's bedroom is invaded, "the curtains of the bed plucked apart," and the sleeper forced to obey the Shelleyan Monster in "its bidding" "at that dead hour."[12] The existential dread and disgust seem closer to home in the more modern works.

Having sketched common grounds for comparison, let me turn to more detail of action and setting in *The Castle of Otranto*, followed by its more recent counterpart, *Dr. Jekyll and Mr. Hyde*. Walpole's ostensibly original work of course has mixed European antecedents. Francophone *histoires tragique*, migrating from Italian sources, strike a chord with any reader familiar with Walpole's proto-Romantic bloodbath of usurpation and genetic collapse. Walpole, according to Wright, would have been suspected as Francophile, hence effeminate and unpatriotic, after the Seven Years' War; the Shakespearean claims in the second preface to *Otranto* reconfirm his Englishness.[13] In the first preface, in contrast, the author had devised a mongrel, remote derivation: Marshal vouches for an authentic document because it was written in an age that believed in such supernatural events. This editorial persona also invites a Romantic interest in the originals of literary settings: "Though the machinery is invention, and the names of the actors imaginary, I cannot but believe . . . the story is founded on truth. The scene is undoubtedly laid in some real castle. The author seems frequently, without design, to describe particular parts. . . . Curious persons, who have leisure to employ in such researches, may possibly discover in the Italian writers the foundation on which our author has built."[14] This flatters the reader who might emulate polyglot antiquarians and confirm the *foundation*, physical and epistemological, of the tale. And indeed, contemporaries and critics catch the reference: Otranto corresponds with the layout of a bachelor gentleman's residence a few hours from London by coach (in Twickenham): Strawberry Hill. Of course, Walpole had concocted this house as a series of knowing allusions to historic architecture, launching the neo-Gothic revival. Miles notes "Walpole's triple masquerade as the Catholic gentleman who pretends to be a Counter-Reformational priest who in turn forges a twelfth-century text," uniting "ancient romance and modern novel."[15] It is as if the queer politician-author leads a double life somewhat in the manner of the physician in Stevenson's novella, getting away with it in his own hybrid retreat.

Gothic fakery permits self-induced horror and delight, while the chronotope of castle or old country estate allows a middle-class reader to playact feudalism. An introduction to a 1901 edition of *Otranto* illustrates the class-crossing pleasure of heterotopic anachronism as it praises Walpole for reviving romance. Before Walpole, "the huge volumes which were once the pastime of nobles and princes ... shrank into abridgements, [and] were banished to the kitchen and nursery, or, at best, to the hall-window of the old-fashioned country manor-house."⁴⁶ Instead, with Walpole, the 1901 editor imagines a fantasy resembling Catherine Morland's in Jane Austen's parody *Northanger Abbey*: a young reader who spends a "solitary night" in one of the rare, unremodeled ancient mansions, verbosely overreacting to "gigantic ... figures dimly visible in the defaced tapestry, the remote clang of the distant doors which divide him from living society, the deep darkness which involves the high and fretted roof of the apartment, the dimly-seen pictures of ancient knights, renowned for their valour, and perhaps for their crimes, the varied and indistinct sounds ... and, to crown all, the feeling that carries us back to ages of feudal power and papal superstition, ... [exciting a] sensation of supernatural awe, if not of terror."⁴⁷ In the feudal world that Walpole reimagines centuries hence, from the comfortable layout of his remodeled country house, the usurping prince no sooner sees his only son crushed by a giant helmet (portent of Alfonso, the "real owner" of the castle) than he tries to take his son's place by possessing the son's fiancée, Isabella; like Henry VIII, he would divorce his wife to beget an heir. The anachronistic castle becomes the tyrant's agent, yet the captive object of desire can learn to circumvent its plot against her. I illustrate with a passage of passages, as the focalizing heroine, Isabella, flees Prince Manfred, her would-be rapist. The text runs on as the architectural layout interrupts. Any corridor or bedchamber is liable to be a scene of sexual violence, whereas a church or altar is a sacred zone. Isabella,

> whose resolution had given way to terror ... continued her flight to the bottom of the principal staircase. There she stopped, not knowing whither to direct her steps. ... The gates of the castle she knew were locked, and guards placed in the court. Should she, as her heart prompted her, go and prepare Hippolita [Manfred's wife] for the cruel destiny that awaited her, she did not doubt but Manfred would seek her there, and that his violence would incite him to double the injury he meditated [rape], without leaving room for them to avoid the impetuosity of his passions. Delay might give him time to reflect ... if she could, for that night at least, avoid his odious purpose. Yet where conceal herself! How avoid the pursuit he would infallibly make throughout the castle! As these thoughts passed rapidly through her mind, she recollected a subterraneous passage, which led from the vaults of the

castle to the church of saint Nicholas. Could she reach the altar before she was overtaken, she knew even Manfred's violence would not dare to profane the sacredness of the place; and she determined, if no other means of deliverance offered, to shut herself up for ever among the holy virgins, whose convent was contiguous to the cathedral. In this resolution, she seized a lamp, that burned at the foot of the stair-case, and hurried towards the secret passage.

The lower part of the castle was hollowed into several intricate cloisters; and it was not easy for one under so much anxiety to find the door that opened into the cavern. An awful silence reigned throughout those subterraneous regions, except now and then some blasts of wind that shook the doors she had passed, and which grating on the rusty hinges were re-echoed through that long labyrinth of darkness.[18]

The virgin reasons that her assailant's nocturnal arousal is temporary, and that he is omnipotent only within the space he rules. An adrenaline-fueled recollection of a tunnel that links the zones of church and state is a characteristic combination of eerie dream logic and obvious stage business. Notice the intricate nether parts explored in a panicked defense of chastity, amid the necessary sensory deprivation of darkness combined with the stimulus of sound. Isabella's escape, aided by a lurking hero who happens to be hiding in that same warren of cloisters, became a topos of Gothic, parodied by Austen: of course Isabella's lamp is blown out, and the clanging escape hatch alerts the pursuers.

A mysterious knight and his cavaliers arrive to put the wrong to right, but in effect it is the women and servants, with the priest and the disguised scion of the true house, who undermine exchange between men. Women may be pawns in marriage, or long to retire to the convent next door, but they see action and have plenty to say, and subvert the tyrant's plans. The various "ladies" or princesses are constantly mistaken for each other in the Castle; they may be allies or rivals. In short order, too short for tragedy perhaps, Manfred murders his own daughter at the supposed sanctuary of the altar (mistaking her for Isabella) and must abdicate (he survives, a penitent). As in the Victorian novella, an overreacher believes he can be a law unto himself in his home. Outsized, armored limbs protrude along the gallery, and a statue assumes the form of a giant that destroys the edifice: the house as both castle and family.

*Jekyll and Hyde* seems to occupy realist, contemporary London rather than generic medieval Italy, and the mystery centers on a peculiar house on a much smaller scale: instead of finding ourselves in a castle cursed to implode when its rightful owner has outgrown it, we are gradually admitted into a wandering city residence with an inner room that must be broken into as two bodies shrink into one corpse. This novella does not follow the layout of the author's home, but the circle of cosmopolitan professional gentlemen in the story seems contemporary and contiguous with Stevenson's literary circle. Whereas Walpole, son of a prime minister, may have also seemed too foreign, Stevenson was an uprooted Scotsman. Here the doubt about the heteronormative emerges from the narrative more than the biographical context. The unnamed desires that Jekyll wishes to repress and indulge, the suggestion of blackmail, and other signals have encouraged a queer reading of *Jekyll and Hyde* as an allegory of the homosexual closet related to *The Picture of Dorian Gray*. In the world of Stevenson's novella, there is no possibility of confusing ladies for each other. London is somehow devoid of named women, or any women above the servant class, and there is far more description of setting and much less dialogue than in *Otranto*. Marriage is moot in a cohort of bachelors. A doctor develops a drug that allows him to transform into an embodiment of his own willful desires. In due course, this licentious persona takes over its creator's life. Their relation is metaphorically both a family dyad and a container and thing contained: "Hyde was indifferent to Jekyll, or remembered him as the mountain bandit remembers the cavern in which he conceals himself from pursuit. Jekyll had more than a father's interest; Hyde had more than a son's indifference."[19] One night, a maidservant looking down through a window to the street witnesses Hyde's impulsive murder of a mild, elderly Member of Parliament, Sir Danvers Carew, perhaps for an unheard innuendo or no provocation at all. The crime becomes a furore in the newspapers, "notable" for the "high position of the victim," but not of course of the witness.[20] More pervasively, anyone who comes near Hyde feels an instinctual revulsion from his aura of habitual criminality. This city-wide scandal and shared abjection is quite out of keeping with the tone of sentiment and honor and the sublime that pervades the inhabitants of a castle in Walpole's neo-Shakespearean tale. In Stevenson, the only occupants of homes are the single gentlemen and servants, who are well informed about the layout of the buildings and the privileges of visiting gentlemen, and come in handy for scenes of panic and exposure, without a hint of the comic contretemps that pass the time in *Otranto*.

*Jekyll and Hyde* happens to begin with an anecdote of a crushed child (not a frail, princely heir smashed by a giant helmet), but the tone of incident is naturalistic, barely removed from the time and place of a reader of newspapers. Before the reported scene of violence, the novella has begun comfortably enough with an establishing shot of a neighborhood. The passage, very different from

Isabella's nighttime escape above, similarly interjects opportune, interconnecting entries and exits, contrasting spaces, and agency in inanimate structures. Two gentlemen go on their habitual Sunday stroll, happening upon

> a by-street in a busy quarter of London. . . . The inhabitants were all doing well, . . . emulously hoping to do better still, and laying out the surplus of their gains in coquetry; so that the shop fronts stood along that thoroughfare with an air of invitation, like rows of smiling saleswomen. Even on Sunday, when it veiled its more florid charms . . . , the street shone out in contrast . . . like a fire in a forest; and with its freshly painted shutters, well polished brasses, and general cleanliness and gaiety of note, instantly caught and pleased the eye of the passenger.
>
> Two doors from one corner, on the left hand going east, the line was broken by the entry of a court; and just at that point, a certain sinister block of building thrust forward its gable on the street. It was two storeys high; showed no window, nothing but a door on the lower storey and a blind forehead of discoloured wall on the upper; and bore in every feature, the marks of prolonged and sordid negligence. The door, which was equipped with neither bell nor knocker, was blistered and distained. Tramps slouched into the recess and struck matches on the panels; children kept shop upon the steps; the schoolboy had tried his knife on the mouldings; and for close on a generation, no one had appeared to drive away these random visitors or to repair their ravages.[21]

Close on a generation has allowed ravages. Such description, characteristic of fiction writers at least from Dickens onward, personifies the built environment as Romantic conceits personify nature; the writer thinks up the equivalent of a subterraneous passage. We are in the real city, but recast as a story-world of expectation to be fulfilled. The seemly street betokens a feminine nation of shopkeepers. The one sinister building is like one of the degenerating "down-going men" with whom the tolerant lawyer, Utterson, is said to be willing to consort (but Hyde will be too far down even for him).[22] The blind forehead mindlessly thrusts and prolongs its contradiction to the decorous, feminine commerce around it. This proves to be a rear entrance, promiscuously used by strangers, with all the obscenity that might connote.

Here, an approach to this sordid doorway prompts Richard Enfield, Utterson's cousin, to narrate the first witnessed crime of the still-unknown Mr. Hyde, when the heinous "Juggernaut" or "Satan" trampled a working-class girl. When the horrified crowd apprehends him, Hyde leads them to this door to get a check to pay for his heedlessly relished violence. Jekyll himself, not unlike a reader of Stevenson's lurid tale, willingly pays for uninhibited horror. The money, like the text that is beginning to betray fictionality in the abnormal events related between gentlemen, must be a forgery. But a genuine check comes out of "Black Mail House."[23] Jekyll can still bank on his wealthy identity, however duplicitous it is.

As in *Otranto*, there is a palpable analogy between overwrought architecture and illegitimate embodiment; a monster has usurped an establishment. Here, it is less a history play than visceral science fiction; instead of medievalist fantasy, the disintegration of domestic spaces and body parts seems contemporary. Thus Stevenson plays less with anachronism (though traces of a previous tenant haunt that place) and more with the abjection of heterotopia. The house certainly "looks like Queer Street,"[24] as we see in passages describing what is exposed to the crime-solving team, Utterson and the manservant Poole. The assault on the doctor's interior cabinet seems both animal and sexual, yet the interior is a picture of genteel comfort in spite of its uncanny monster (echoing the early scene of the charming street with the obscene door).

> Poole swung the axe over his shoulder; the blow shook the building.... A dismal screech, as of mere animal terror, rang from the cabinet. Up went the axe again ... four times the blow fell; ... it was not until the fifth, that ... the door fell inwards on the carpet.... There lay the cabinet before their eyes in the quiet lamp-light, a good fire glowing and chattering on the hearth, the kettle singing its thin strain, a drawer or two open, papers neatly set forth on the business table, and ... the things laid out for tea: the quietest room, you would have said, and, but for the glazed presses full of chemicals, the most common-place that night in London. Right in the midst there lay the body of a man sorely contorted and still twitching.[25]

The "besiegers" must investigate, as if to raise a series of suppressed thoughts.

Jekyll has hoped to solve the problem of human civilization in his own room, a satellite of contemporary domesticity, disregarding the whole house. This domicile looks like a gentleman's townhouse in front and in back is a kind of medical institution in disuse, not unlike the ruined brewery that houses Miss Havisham in *Great Expectations*. The intestinal connections and inward sightlines seem gratuitously asymmetrical as if built over time by changing intentions. Mostly the property is occupied by the

> theatre, which filled almost the whole ground story and was lighted from above, and by the cabinet, which formed an upper story at one end and looked upon the court. A corridor joined the theatre to the door on the bystreet; and with this the cabinet communicated separately by a second flight of stairs. There were besides a few dark closets and a spacious cellar.... Each closet needed but a glance, for all were empty, and all, by the dust that fell from their doors, had stood long unopened. The cellar, indeed, was filled with crazy lumber, mostly dating from the times of the surgeon who was Jekyll's predecessor; but even as they opened the door they were advertised of the uselessness of further search, by the fall of a perfect mat of cobweb which had for years sealed up the entrance.[26]

The serial penetration of dead rooms seems to open pages of episodes with no story. A surgical theater would have seen postmortem demonstrations, not soliloquys of the guilt-ridden Macbeths or Manfred of Otranto. The Gothic escape of the heroine through a subterranean passage to a medieval church has been too long disused to serve in this narrative. The modern usurper cares nothing for his dynasty but lodges the object of his desire within his own mortal body, neglecting even the public service of his profession, let alone the incestuous heterosexual reproduction that Manfred intends.

Much more could be added about distorted chronotopes in these two works and in the complex traditions they share. I have depicted some of the repertoire of collapsed historical and generational time and overdetermined social settings that Walpole and Stevenson draw upon for their influential Gothic novellas. Clearly, writers are not limited to castles, laboratories, or metamorphic doubles to stir up the effects of Gothic. A spatial approach to this historically saturated genre cannot be a static geometry, as it adapts to the many political, aesthetic, and psychoanalytic promptings of each era. Such a focus can learn to read description closely, somewhat against the grain of the egregious passions and actions that make these tales unforgettable and frequently adapted, as in Utterson's night vision of a scene from *Frankenstein*. The haunted spaces of Gothic: like Catherine Morland or the reader in the 1901 preface to *Otranto*, a reader uses an old, multipurpose, inscrutably animated house to spark alarming interpretations, colluding in the effect and conspiring to break through forbidden doors. The perverse story-world of Gothic is our *cauchemar*. Remember, too, that scurrying around opening and closing doors and hearing voices and stumbling over body parts is also the stuff of farce.

# Notes

1. Horace Walpole, *The Castle of Otranto: A Gothic Story*, ed. W. S. Lewis (Oxford: Oxford University Press, 1998); Robert Louis Stevenson, *Strange Case of Dr Jekyll and Mr Hyde*, 3rd ed., ed. Martin A. Danahay (Peterborough, Ontario, Canada: Broadview, 2015). Citations of these works will refer to these editions by short title.
2. Martin Danahay, introduction to *Jekyll and Hyde*, 11–26. A dramatization of *Jekyll and Hyde* closed down in response to the Jack the Ripper terror (16–17).
3. Fred Botting, "In Gothic Darkly: Heterotopia, History, Culture," *A Companion to the Gothic*, ed. David Punter (Oxford: Blackwell, 2001), 3–14. Botting cites p. 24 of Michel Foucault, "Of Other Spaces," *Diacritics* 16, no. 1 (1986): 22–27; ibid., 9. Like "gothic," the term "heterotopia" can be stretched toward meaninglessness.
4. On the complex national and religious contexts, see Robert Miles, "Abjection, Nationalism and the Gothic," in *Essays and Studies 2001: The Gothic*, ed. Fred Botting (Cambridge: Brewer, 2001), 47–70.
5. Michael Gamer, "Gothic Fictions and Romantic Writing in Britain," in *The Cambridge Companion to Gothic Fiction*, ed. Jerrold E. Hogle, 85–104 (Cambridge: Cambridge University Press, 2002).
6. Angela Wright, *Britain, France, and the Gothic, 1764–1820: The Import of Terror* (Cambridge: Cambridge University Press, 2013); regarding Walpole, 16–32.
7. Franco Moretti, *Atlas of the European Novel 1800–1900* (London: Verso, 1999), 70.
8. Miles, "Abjection," in *Essays and Studies*, ed. Botting, 50–51.
9. Susan Stanford Friedman, "Spatial Poetics and Arundhati Roy's *The God of Small Things*," in *A Companion to Narrative Theory*, ed. James Phelan and Peter Rabinowitz, 192–205 (Oxford: Blackwell, 2007).
10. Julian Wolfreys, *Victorian Hauntings: Spectrality, Gothic, the Uncanny and Literature* (New York: Palgrave, 2002), 3.
11. Gaston Bachelard, *The Poetics of Space* (Boston: Beacon, 1984).
12. Stevenson, *Jekyll and Hyde*, 40–41.
13. Wright, *Britain, France, and the Gothic*, 23. It has been easy to read Walpole as gay (17).
14. Walpole, *Otranto*, 7–8.
15. Miles, "Abjection," in *Essays and Studies*, ed. Botting, 59.
16. Anonymous, introduction to *The Castle of Otranto*, by Walpole (London: Cassell, 1901), iv.
17. Ibid., xviii–ix.
18. Walpole, *Otranto*, 26–27.
19. Stevenson, *Jekyll and Hyde*, 83.
20. Ibid., 47.
21. Ibid., 34.
22. Ibid., 33.
23. Ibid., 35–36.
24. Ibid., 36.
25. Ibid., 81.
26. Ibid., 82–83.

JENNIFER TSIEN

# Inassimilable
## Gothic Francophobia in "The 'Haunted House' in Royal Street"

It is a popularly held belief that Louisiana is, as Charles L. Crow has remarked, "especially suited to Gothic narrative.... Its historic cultural center, New Orleans, has some claim to be the capital of American Gothic."[1] As reasons for this special status, Crow mentions the state's long and violent history, its inhabitants' tendency to dwell on the past, and the voodoo tradition brought over by Haitian exiles in the early 1800s. Yet another reason why this region is associated with horror can be found in its perceived foreignness within the United States. Because of this setting, writers and filmmakers can claim to expose to the rest of America the sinister doings of a different culture with, perhaps, a different moral code. George Washington Cable was one of the earliest writers to put New Orleans on display as a horror capital. He transformed the local legend of the Delphine Lalaurie, notorious slave-torturer, into a short story published in 1888 and entitled "The 'Haunted House' in Royal Street."[2] In the story, evil emanates not only from the villainess but from the Creole culture that he depicts as complicit in her crimes.

The content itself is not original to Cable: it had allegedly circulated as a rumor for years when Harriet Martineau wrote it down for what was probably the first time. Martineau was a British journalist and antislavery activist who chronicled her visit to America in her 1838 memoir *Retrospect of Western Travel*. When she arrives in New Orleans, she hears of a recent scandal that consists of the following facts: A Creole lady named Madame Lalaurie lived in a house on the corner of Royal Street and Hospital Street (now Governor Nicholls Street) in the French Quarter. She and her family enjoyed the lifestyle of the high bourgeoisie, receiving illustrious guests and entertaining lavishly. One day, there was a fire in the kitchen, and, when people entered the building to help, they discovered hidden rooms in which Mme Lalaurie had kept slaves in chains, slaves whom she had obviously tortured and mutilated. When the news of this discovery spread, it caused a riot outside the house. Madame Lalaurie brazenly escaped in her carriage. After her escape, the frustrated crowd destroyed her house and furnishings to express their outrage. Meanwhile, the villainess eventually reached France and continued to live unpunished.

George Washington Cable took Martineau's report and used it as the basis for his short story. He even takes whole sentences from Martineau's text and folds them into his own. His agenda, like hers, is to expose the abuses of slavery to advance racial justice. Whereas Martineau's account is straightforward and clearly nonfictional, Cable plays on the borderline between fact and fiction—as we can see in the use of quotation marks in the title—and he also adds a sophisticated literary framework and a great deal of rhetorical ornamentation. His narrative is divided into six sections: In the first, the narrator apostrophizes the reader, who is presumably a tourist, and proceeds to lead this person through the abandoned house on Royal Street. The second, third, and fourth sections, the core of the text, go back in time to narrate the incidents that I summarized above. Finally, the fifth and sixth parts fast-forward to the years approaching the narrator's era and together serve as a long epilogue in which Cable tells us the fate of the house after the departure of Madame Lalaurie. Notably, he recounts how the building was used as a school for girls of all races and how a group of white supremacists, the White League, entered the school and forcibly segregated it.

In general terms, the foreign population depicted in the "Haunted House" is Creole, but at times Cable focuses more specifically on the French part of this mixed identity. The Creole identity was claimed by the descendants of French and Spanish settlers in Louisiana, in deliberate opposition to Anglo-Americans, who began arriving in the late eighteenth century.[3] This context allows Cable to import the age-old rivalry between France and England to Louisiana and to exploit the stereotypes about the French that the British have held for centuries. We may assume from her name that Mme Lalaurie is simply of French descent, but the narrator at some point admits that her maiden name was McCarty, "a genuine Spanish-Creole name, although of Irish origins, of course."[4] What these mixed origins have in common is the Catholic religion, which was viewed with great suspicion by the English and American Protestants. In this sense, Cable continues the tradition, studied by Victor Sage, of British Gothic literature that demonizes Latin, Catholic cultures. As Sage argues, English and Irish Gothic novels were written as cautionary tales in which Protestant characters suffer horrible fates when they come into contact with Catholicism.[5] The religious rivalry explains the presence of evil monks, ruined convents, and relics of the Inquisition in the works of Ann Radcliffe and others. In Cable's case, the rivalry is based not so much on theological differences as on a clash of cultures, one of which happens to be Latin, monarchical, and Catholic and the other, Anglo-Saxon, republican, and Protestant.

Cable's story features a number of typically Gothic tropes, notably a sinister-looking house; ghostly apparitions; and a family with shameful secrets. However, its setting in New Orleans after the Louisiana Purchase of 1803 adds a political dimension that is absent from, say, *Dracula* or *The Castle of Otranto*. In his story, Cable places the guilt not only on Mme Lalaurie but on the whole of Creole society that builds a wall of secrecy around her. The crimes committed are shown, on the one hand, as a bizarre anomaly and, on the other, as symptomatic of a foreign culture that represents a violent, irrational, and despotic past. This sinister Creole culture keeps itself closed off from the more progressive Anglo-American population, to which the narrator and reader presumably belong.

This pact of silence that surrounds Mme Lalaurie appears from the very beginning, in the description of the house itself. For example, the narrator who leads the reader on a tour of the now-empty house remarks: "You hear the walls and rooms saying those soft nothings to one another that they so often say when left to themselves."[6] In view of the Creole-American tensions, we can infer that these parts of the house that whisper to each other but not to visitors represent the Creoles who gossiped among themselves but kept ugly secrets from outsiders. The closed window shutters, "by the very intensity of their rusty silence," express a "hostile impenetrability."[7]

We see this same insularity later in the narrative frame, when a "distinguished foreign visitor" to New Orleans asks about the tortured slaves many years after the events: "The rest of the company sat aghast, while the hostess silenced him by the severe coldness with which she replied that 'she knew nothing about it.'"[8] The immediate reason for their refusal to speak is that

Mme Lalaurie's daughter is present, but the incident tells us about the policy of closing ranks against non-Creoles.

Within the core narrative, we learn that, even though Mme Lalaurie's own friends had been disturbed by the rumors that she was abusing her slaves, they dared not confront her. Some make an attempt to investigate, but they are disarmed by the rules of French politeness, as we see in several instances, of which I will cite two. In one case, a male friend defends Mme Lalaurie against accusations, "as he returned her courteous bow,"[9] by insinuating that the rumors about her are merely the products of American spite. In another case, an Anglo-American lawyer becomes suspicious enough to investigate. Unfortunately, instead of taking matters into his own hands, he sends his Creole clerk to confront the lady. His mission is to remind Mme Lalaurie of the French law that sets minimal standards for the treatment of slaves. The law alluded to is the Code noir, but it proves less potent than the codes of gallantry, since "the young law student on making his visit was captivated by the sweetness of the lady . . . and withdrew filled with indignation against anyone who could suspect her of the slightest unkindness to the humblest living thing."[10] Because the clerk and the law are both of French descent, they prove to be useless in the face of Mme Lalaurie's charm. The clerk's failure to uncover the villainess's secrets, I believe, is due to his stereotypically French indulgence toward women.

The formal deference of men toward women was part of French politeness, which many associated with the Ancien Régime monarchy and with the feminization of the whole society. People outside of France, as well as French Enlightenment thinkers and Revolutionaries, criticized courtly manners and the influence of women as responsible for weakening the state.[11] Even though this story takes place in the early nineteenth century, there are indications that the Creoles are living in the past, specifically in a pre-Revolutionary or monarchist world. For example, the narrator hints that King Louis-Philippe (reign 1830–1848) was a guest in Mme Lalaurie's home in 1798, during his exile.[12] Her alleged charm and social standing, which mask her perverse crimes, make her resemble Mme de Merteuil in *Dangerous Liaisons* or some of the Marquis de Sade's protagonists. In all of these cases, one can see that the inherent hypocrisy of politeness, as well as the protagonists' position in the social hierarchy, mark their brand of evil as possible.

Whether the Creoles who surround Mme Lalaurie are loyal to the pre-Revolutionary monarchs or to those of the Restoration, they confirm the fears that Americans had when Louisiana first joined the United States in 1803. The stereotypes played a role in actual debates that took place during the Louisiana Purchase. As historian Peter Kastor documents, politicians were reluctant to give Louisiana residents the full rights of American citizens because they considered them, in terms of mentalities, unready for democracy.[13]

In a larger sense, Cable depicts Creoles as living in the past and Anglo-Americans as living in the present or future, even as they exist side by side in the French Quarter of New Orleans. The mere possibility that Creole identity could be compatible with modernity is dismissed by the narrator in the first part of the story, when he addresses his visitor, "by all means see early whatever evidences [sic] of progress and aggrandizement her hospitable citizens wish to show you"; he then immediately undercuts this statement by telling his guest, "And yet I want the first morning walk that you [take] to be in the old French Quarter,"[14] succinctly alluding to both its past and its foreignness with the words *old* and *French*. Then he commands, "Go down Royal Street," evoking a street name that refers to a political system that is no longer in power, the "royal" Ancien Régime. Since he mentions that the house is situated on a corner with Hospital Street, he could well have called his story "The 'Haunted House' on Hospital Street."

The setting thus prepares us for the archaic characters and barbaric actions that the narrator will present to us. First of all, if the French Quarter hails back to the Ancien Régime, then the rioting crowd in front of Mme Lalaurie's house resembles the Revolutionary mob. The initial discovery of the chained and tortured slaves is reminiscent of the storming of the Bastille, when the protesters opened the gates of the ancient fortress in an attempt to free the prisoners who were allegedly held inside, and destroyed the building. In both cases, the thought of people being held captive drives crowds into a frenzy. In Cable's narrative, the mob "of all classes and colors"[15] is so blinded by rage that they even kill Mme Lalaurie's horses and black coachman. In these scenes, the focus is not on the rioters' sense of justice but on their irrationality: "The sudden southern nightfall descended, and torches danced in the streets and through the ruined house. The débris was gathered into hot bonfires. . . . The night wore on, but the mob persisted. They mounted and battered the roof; they defaced the inner walls. Morning found them still at their senseless mischief, and they were 'in the act of pulling down the walls when the sheriff and several citizens interfered and put an end to their work.'"[16] The all-out destruction implies that this emotional type of crowd dynamic is typical of the French character; therefore, they cannot provide an acceptable solution to the problem. At this stage, only American law, in the form of policemen, can reestablish order.

After her crimes are discovered, Mme Lalaurie flees to Paris. Even though she is a Creole, thus by definition born in the New World, we can imagine this voyage as a "return" in the sense that Louisiana's mother country is France, so going to the metropole is a return to origins. One could also say that the villainess travels back in time, if one presumes that political systems are on a progressive scale from despotism to democracy. Under this presumption, one could say that even though she inadvertently sparks a miniature French Revolution in her neighborhood, she refuses to take part in this violent transition to a modern political system. While the crowd enters the new order maintained by American lawyers, notaries, and policemen, she travels in the opposite direction. Significantly, she leaves the more developed parts of the city in her carriage and rushes along the Bayou Road through a dark tropical landscape until the road ends before she boards a ship to France. She goes from civilization to wilderness and from the New World to the Old, symbolically reversing the trajectory of her ancestors when they settled in Louisiana. This voyage back in time continues when the narrator adds that after Paris, she retreats to the countryside, which suggests an even further regression to a primeval France, and she is rumored to be killed in a most primitive way, by a boar during a hunting party.

In some ways, it is odd that Cable should associate the French with the Ancien Régime, because he disregards the major role that the French *philosophes* played in the Enlightenment and in the conception of the United States government. If Cable had been faithful to historical facts, he could have depicted the French as more progressive than the Anglo-Americans, since slavery was abolished in France earlier than in the United States. As Theresa Goddu demonstrates, a French writer such as John Crèvecœur can also use Gothic tropes to criticize Anglo-Americans' abuse of slaves.[17]

## The Problem of Assimilation

"The 'Haunted House' in Royal Street" can be read as a conflict of cultures within one city, but the story can also be read using the Freudian terms that scholars typically apply to Gothic novels. Both interpretations intersect in the concept of *assimilation*. On the one hand, assimilation applies to national identity in the aftermath of the Louisiana Purchase, when the original thirteen states of America tried to absorb the newly acquired population whose origins were predominantly French and Spanish. The conflicts arising from Louisiana residents' inability or refusal to conform to Anglo-American culture was a preoccupation apparent in much of George Washington Cable's writings.

The equation between foreignness and horror is evident in the very title of Cable's collection of stories that includes "The 'Haunted House' in Royal Street": *Strange True Stories of Louisiana*. If we examine the word "strange" of the title—a word that appears repeatedly in our story—we can see that its etymology leads us to the Latin root *extra*, which denotes "outside" or "of another country." Tellingly, Cable's stories are strange precisely because they are foreign, since the lifestyle and mentalities that they depict are unfamiliar to Anglo-American readers. We could also note one small detail in the very title of the short story that hits a discordantly alien note: the preposition "*in* Royal Street" suggests French grammatical usage rather than English ("*dans la rue*"), since Americans would tend to say "*on* Royal Street." From the very titles of the collection and of the individual story, then, Cable signals to readers that they are about to encounter something unfamiliar. There are thus elements of this story, from the main character to prepositions in the title, that cannot or will not become American.

To explain the other use of the word *assimilation*: Critics such as Julia Kristeva have described objects of fear, for example in literature of horror, as things that cannot be fully explained away or assimilated by the human mind. In terms of the plot of the story, Mme Lalaurie's actions are never explained in any satisfying way. Even though she is defeated in the end, in the sense that she loses her possessions and her place in society, the law does not exactly triumph, since it leaves her unpunished. This lack of resolution is, according to David Punter, typical for the Gothic text, in which the law, in the shape of policemen, investigators, and notaries, tries to fight against the irrational forces of evil, but even when these authority figures win, evil leaves something behind that cannot be explained. This lack of explanation is important in the legal sense, since justice is never truly attained, but also in the psychological sense. The power of horror lies, according to Julia Kristeva, in the inability of the mind to "assimilate" it: she tells us how frightening it is to have something present, close by, but impossible to assimilate—in French, *inassimilable*.

The presence of these Creoles within the shifting borders of the United States created the need for Anglo-Americans to somehow fit them into their worldview. George Washington Cable met their needs by giving them, through his fiction and essays, images of these people that they could accept. As Stephanie Foote explains, such "local color" narratives of various genres, consumed largely by readers from the original thirteen states, were intertwined with the political assimilation of new territories into the nation.[18] Gothic literature in particular provided an added element: the idea that the

American readers lived in a world of progress while the quaint new citizens that the country had acquired still lived in the past.

In regard to the past that haunts the present, Leslie Fiedler, in a classic interpretation of American Gothic literature, argued that ideals such as American progress, success, and optimism were built upon the intentional forgetting of the injustices perpetrated to build the nation.[19] What has been rejected by the narrative of American progress inevitably returns in fiction, for example, in the form of Edgar Allan Poe's living corpses or, we could add, Cable's half-dead slaves. Horror ensues when the suppressed past haunts modern Americans and reminds them of their guilt. In Cable's case, the past is found living simultaneously with the present, in the form of suspicious Creole neighbors.

Jennifer Greeson takes Fiedler's argument further and claims that much nineteenth-century American literature situates this guilt in the South, and in one chapter she specifically demonstrates how this applies to George Washington Cable's Louisiana. Analyzing his short story "Jean-ah Poquelin," Greeson notes that Cable depicts Creoles as sickly and regressive: "The 'Creole' locals of tropical America are not able to transform their own colonial way of life in order to participate in historical progress."[20] Instead, they stagnate in their ruined homes, so "it is only the U.S. takeover of Louisiana that advances the plot of the story, interrupting what would otherwise become a stagnant cycle."[21] The shameful past of the United States is therefore located not only among southerners but among this specific group of foreigners who dwell in the past. Obviously, this placement of France and the United States on a scale of progress does not correspond to historical reality but to the anti-French mentalities of nineteenth-century Americans.

Scholars of Gothic literature such as Fiedler have often relied on the Freudian concept of the uncanny or, in its original German, *das Unheimliche*. It is significant for this study that the etymology of the word *unheimlich*, as Freud points out, is related to the word *heimisch* (homelike); therefore the term can mean "un-homelike" or "the opposite of what is familiar."[22] The "haunted house" is certainly not a home. On one hand, it provides the opposite of comfort and security to some of its inhabitants, and on the other hand, the people living there suddenly find themselves, like the Creoles, living in alien territory.

The uncomfortable feeling of the *unheimlich* occurs, according to Freud, when we behold the "return of the repressed." In other words, when we think we have overcome a stage of development, yet something appears to remind us of our past: for example, a superstition we had abandoned. Freud claims that the most *unheimlich* thing—the ultimate past that people would rather not think about and that gives us the feeling of horror—is the mother's womb: they do not want to be reminded that "this *unheimlich* place . . . is the entrance to the former *Heim* [home] of all human beings . . . the place where each one of us lived once upon a time."[23] If there is an analogy to be made between a home and a female body, one could suppose that the hidden part of Mme Lalaurie's house is like a monstrous womb from which adult slaves emerge, which creates an uncanny spectacle for the bystanders. The fact that the slaves are so weak and "helpless"[24] that they must be carried evokes the image of grotesque newborn babies, even though they are in fact adults, and some are even very old. The narrator mentions that they are incapacitated from being forced to stay in one position for too long, much like fetuses who lie in cramped positions until birth.

The *unheimlich* image of the mother's body plays a role in Kristeva's idea of horror, which is what remains when one progresses from one stage of development to another. In a child's development, the Lacanian imposition of the name of the father would mark the transition from past to present. While early stages of childhood are formless and indistinct, the father brings language, law, and the ability for the child to become a fully formed discrete subject. Kristeva makes an analogy between the child's experience and the evolution of a whole society. She refers to matriarchal societies that are succeeded by patriarchal ones—from pagan to Judaic, for example. In such cases, the male rulers impose laws banning elements of the past, which are now seen with disgust and horror. Many of these laws involve the mother's body, such as the taboos about mother-son incest and those involving birth, breastfeeding, and menstruation: "Ritualization of defilement is accompanied by a strong concern for separating the sexes, and this means giving men rights over women. The latter, apparently put in the position of passive objects, are none the less felt to be wily powers, 'baleful schemers' from whom rightful beneficiaries must protect themselves."[25] This fear of women's scheming influence, in spite of their inferior institutional powers, is precisely the situation that was associated with Ancien Régime France. In Lacan's and Kristeva's theories, the past is female and progress is male, both in terms of a child's development and in a society's way of looking at its own evolution.

We can see how Kristeva's theory could be applied to the notorious house on Royal Street. In Kristeva's schema, the building itself would represent the inchoate state of existence before the law imposes itself and before things are named—that is, before the father's law makes its appearance. Appropriately, the house is run by women, first by Madame Lalaurie, to whom her daughters and slaves are subordinate; the narrator describes her husband as being of "lesser importance."[26] She owns the house herself, and she keeps "the management of her money affairs, real estate, and slaves mainly in her own hands."[27] She represents the "archaic mother" that Kristeva describes as threatening to the new patriarchal order.[28] In the subsequent part of Cable's story, the school is run by schoolmistresses who oversee only girls. We can see that the archaic French matriarchy inherent to the house, or the "survival of a matrilineal society" that Kristeva evokes,[29] is twice put to an end by the literal intrusion of male forces.

In the first case, men such as lawyers and policemen come to bring much-needed justice to a horrifying situation. Until then, Madame Lalaurie's crimes were not only unnamed because outsiders did not know exactly what was happening, but because polite friends censored themselves and words went missing. For example, before the discovery, one of Mme Lalaurie's friends says, "The truth is those jealous Americans—" and ends his statement with a blank.[30] In Kristeva's vision, they are living in a primitive matriarchal stage in which language has not yet been imposed. This prelinguistic stage appears in the form of typographical blanks, pointed silences, unnamed and unnamable fears, and the indistinct sounds emanating from the house. From an Anglo-American's point of view, the Creole's awkward grasp of English also suggests that they live in an infantile state, grappling with a newly introduced language. This idea presumes that the Anglo-Americans dismiss the specificity of French as a distinct other language.[31] The silences and inarticulate whispers of the house that had suggested Creole solidarity against outsiders could suggest an absence of language, typical for an archaic society.

Law is also nonfunctional at this point in the story, since in one occasion the law clerk is powerless and as if emasculated before Mme Lalaurie's charm. In another case, Mme Lalaurie's slaves are sold, but they are bought back by her relatives, who return them to her, exposing a kind of incestuous relationship among the ruling elites of the Old French Quarter. Once the law imposes itself on the house, language becomes possible: what were once uncertain rumors become legal depositions, notarial records, and newspaper articles. Previously, facts were hopelessly unstable: "They say that Louis Philippe, afterwards king of the French, once slept in one of its chambers. That would have been in 1798; but in 1798 they were not building such tall buildings as this in New Orleans—did not believe the soil would uphold them. . . . I should like to know if the rumor is true. Lafayette, too, they say, occupied the same room. Maybe so."[32] Even simple facts like names were shifting and uncertain: "Her surname had been first McCarty . . . then Lopez, or maybe first Lopez and then McCarty, and then Blanque."³³ The unnamed slaves never speak directly in the story, surely because they are either captive in the back rooms and on the verge of death, or functioning but living in fear of punishment. Only the cook, who took the initiative to set the fire that exposed everything, gives a deposition, but after the law has definitively ended Mme Lalaurie's regime.

In the last two sections of the story, when the White League intrudes into the school, the girls had lived in a state of racial nondifferentiation, which had been tolerated by the teachers. It is clear that the narrator sympathetically depicts the girls and the teachers as victims, while in this case, he shows those who bring differentiation as the villains. The men appear and force the girls to verbally declare to which race they belong, an unwelcome imposition of the masculine law. It is particularly significant that the girls have no last names, just dashes: Marie O—— or Coralie——, for example. They and their teachers resist, as far as they are able, the labeling by race.

In both cases of intrusion, the house that gives its name to the story represents the inchoate, matriarchal past. Just as embassies are legally considered foreign territory within the host country, the house on Royal Street exists in a different era than the rest of the city and the rest of the country, which have supposedly progressed politically. In Mme Lalaurie's case, Cable implies that that the house facilitates a perverse form of evil, while in the case of the school, it protects a benevolent Creole attitude of racial nondifferentiation. It is the Anglo-Americans who unjustly impose labels and laws. Specifically, they wish to bring a binary system of black and white that will replace the more permissive classifications of the Creole racial system.³⁴

Once the "law of the father" has been imposed in Louisiana and Mme Lalaurie's crimes have been exposed, the young nation of the United States can look upon her crimes with horror, as something that they have overcome. American readers can look with some satisfaction at an element that has been purged from society to make it more "civilized." Mme Lalaurie's contemporaries can tell themselves that they are more ethical slave owners, while the readers in Cable's time can feel relieved that the era of slavery is past. Cable suggests that both are hypocritical for denying that there is still pervasive injustice based on race.

Madame Lalaurie refuses to be assimilated into the American system of law but also into our cultural memory. The fact that we cannot explain her brand of evil makes her an example of a remnant of the past that cannot be "resolved," in the sense of a puzzle but also, like the repulsive milk skin that Kristeva mentions at the beginning of *Powers of Horror*, in the sense that it does not dissolve into the liquid. For this reason, the ghosts of this story keep returning, as in Freud's return of the repressed but also in the shape of Kristeva's concept of writing that holds up the abject past in order to "re-memorialize" it, to turn it into an object of disgusting yet desirable contemplation.

### Conclusion: Horror Tourism

For centuries, aesthetic philosophers had wondered at our ability to enjoy looking at a violent action in a play or a painting, while we would abhor it in real life. Gothic literature's popularity depended on this paradox of reception, and Cable's story is no exception. While our morality may disapprove of the torture of slaves—even regular slaveholders viewed this case with horror, according to Martineau—stories like these continue to fascinate us.

According to Thomas Ruys Smith, such feelings evoked by Cable certainly influenced tourists who sought out grotesque sights in New Orleans. Cable's narrator seems to welcome and anticipate the tourist's gaze. He remarks on the difficulty of getting access to the house, since the owners wish to keep away thrill-seekers. The narrator reports that the landlord turned away more than three hundred visitors one winter, but he enjoins us to imagine "the three thousand who would call if they knew its story."[35] Cable's writings themselves contributed to creating the New Orleans tourism industry. As Arlin Turner informs us, many travelers who visited New Orleans came with copies of Cable's story collection *Old Creole Days* in hand, hoping that the real city would correspond to his vision of it.[36] And the French Quarter tour still includes this story.

In the final step in the progression that Kristeva traces, the abject that has been left behind but continues to resurface becomes the object of a combination of horror and fascination. Literary language names the previously unnamable and stirs up a perverse desire. This is one way to interpret the almost ritualistic retelling of the Mme Lalaurie story in New Orleans to the present day, by locals to tourists, by authors, and most recently by the director Ryan Murphy. The house itself has become a spectacle to all those who are as horrified as they are titillated by the story.

### Notes

1. Charles L. Crow, *History of the Gothic: American Gothic* (Cardiff: University of Wales Press, 2009), 89.

2. George Washington Cable, "The 'Haunted House' in Royal Street," in *Strange True Stories of Louisiana* (1888; repr., Gretna, LA: Pelican, 2005), 192–232.

3. Several competing definitions of the term still create confusion to this day. One includes Louisianians of any race who claim French or Spanish blood, especially people of mixed white and black ancestry. Another definition of *Creole* applies strictly to mostly urban and upper-class white residents of French descent; it excludes blacks, as well as white Acadians/Cajuns, who were often lower-class farmers of French descent by way of Canada. For an in-depth study of this complex and little-understood word, see Arnold Hirsch and Joseph Logsdon, eds., *Creole New Orleans: Race and Americanization* (Baton Rouge: Louisiana State University Press, 1992).

4. Cable, "The 'Haunted House' in Royal Street," 200.

5. Victor Sage, *Horror Fiction in the Protestant Tradition* (London: Macmillan, 1988).

6. Cable, "The 'Haunted House' in Royal Street," 192–232.

7. Ibid., 193.

8. Ibid., 224–25.

9. Ibid., 202.

10. Ibid., 204.

11. Dena Goodman states that "French culture was characterized by a fear of the power of women, defined as 'influence.' No matter how men revised the laws regarding issues as seemingly diverse as marriage and monarchical succession, the specter of extralegal female 'influence' continued to haunt and threaten them." Rousseau in particular revolted against "an effeminate and false society" in which male thinkers had to please women in salons, in his *Letter to d'Alembert*. In his opinion, when French men "aimed solely to please women," "they became effeminate, womanish" (see Dena Goodman, *The Republic of Letters: A Cultural History of the French Enlightenment* [Ithaca, NY: Cornell University Press, 1994], 9–10, 55, 54).

12. Cable, "The 'Haunted House' in Royal Street," 193–94.

13. Peter Kastor, *The Nation's Crucible: The Louisiana Purchase and the Creation of America* (New Haven: Yale University Press, 2004).

14. Cable, "The 'Haunted House' in Royal Street," 192.

15. Ibid., 216.

16. Ibid.

17. Theresa Goddu, *Gothic America: Narrative, History, and Nation* (New York: Columbia University Press, 1997).

18. Stephanie Foote, *Regional Fictions: Culture and Identity in Nineteenth-Century American Literature* (Madison: University of Wisconsin Press, 2001).

19. Leslie Fiedler, "Charles Brockden Brown and the Invention of the American Gothic," *Love and Death in the American Novel* (New York: Criterion, 1960), 126–61.

20. Jennifer Greeson, *Our South: Geographic Fantasy and the Rise of National Literature* (Cambridge: Harvard University Press, 2010), 262.

21. Ibid., 263.

22. Sigmund Freud, "The 'Uncanny,'" in *Complete Works*, vol. 17 (London: Vintage, 2001), 220.

23. Ibid., 17:245.

24. Cable, "The 'Haunted House' in Royal Street," 210.

25. Julia Kristeva, *Powers of Horror: An Essay on Abjection*, trans. Leon S. Roudiez (New York: Columbia University Press, 1982), 70.

26. Cable, "The 'Haunted House' in Royal Street," 200.

27. Ibid.

28. Kristeva, *Powers of Horror*, 77.

29. Ibid., 70.

30. Cable, "The 'Haunted House' in Royal Street," 202.

31. Other writings by Cable do include speeches in French by the Creole characters, so we see that they master one language. However, he places great emphasis on their faulty English, for example in *Les Grandissimes*, which includes long quotations in phonetic dialect. Cable also became famous on the lecture circuit by imitating the Creole accent, to the hilarity of American audiences, as recounted in Arlin Turner, *George W. Cable: A Biography* (Baton Rouge: Louisiana State University Press, 1966).

32. Cable, "The 'Haunted House' in Royal Street," 193–94.

33. Ibid., 200.

34. This transition from the Creole classification of free whites, enslaved blacks, and free people of color (often mixed-race and in possession of special legal privileges) to the Anglo-American black/white dichotomy was the context behind the *Plessy v. Ferguson* decision by the U.S. Supreme Court. The case involved a mixed-race Creole in 1890s New Orleans.

35. Cable, "The 'Haunted House' in Royal Street," 195.

36. Arlin Turner, "George W. Cable's Beginning as a Reformer," *Journal of Southern History* 17, no. 2 (May 1951): 135–61.

JOCELYN MOORE

# Houses That Live and Die
## From Greek Tragedy to the Gothic

Greek tragedy provides a model for one of the most characteristic features of Gothic literature: the haunted house animated by supernatural forces. As the visual backdrop for the Attic theater, the façade of the house concealed danger. What happened there, out of sight of the audience, was often suicide, entrapment, and murder among kin. The capacity of the tragic house to contain and to reveal such horrors anticipates Sigmund Freud's suggestion that what makes the *unheimlich*—literally the "un-home-ly"—also "uncanny" is not the absence of the house, but its presence.[1]

While most Gothic authors do not point toward this tragic precedent, Edgar Allan Poe's title "The Fall of the House of Usher" (1839) seems to allude to the well-known fall of one of tragedy's leading families, the "House of Atreus," whose violence was so enormous as to attract a throng of spirits, Furies, that besieged the house and its members. Usher's house is traditionally understood in terms of its Gothic features,[2] some of which borrow indirectly from E. T. A. Hoffmann's *Das Majorat* (1817).[3] However, for a reader mindful of ancient tragedy, there are striking similarities that invite us to follow a "dark thread" back to Aeschylus's *Agamemnon* (458 BC) in the *Oresteia* trilogy.[4] Poe criticized the Gothic genre as he found it, for instance, in the popular sensationalizing stories published by *Blackwood's Edinburgh Magazine*;[5] in "The Fall of the House of Usher" he seems to propose a different, classically inspired Gothic.[6]

Absent from many Gothic house models available to Poe but common to Usher's and Agamemnon's haunted abodes is the house's anthropomorphic character and its identification with its inhabitants.[7] The house does not play a significant role in Seneca's *Agamemnon*, a literary precedent we might expect to have been influential for Poe since this Roman author was more prominent in early modernity and through the nineteenth century.[8] Aeschylus, on the other hand, develops the house as a character in its own right, personifying it with eyes and voice and breathing it alive with infesting Furies. Agamemnon's house becomes a symbol for the well-being of its individual inhabitants and collective household. Poe mirrors Aeschylus's metonymy of house and inhabitant to create a mansion in which the owner, Roderick Usher, merges completely with his mansion; eerie correspondences include the house's "vacant and eye-like windows" and Roderick's "large, liquid, and luminous eye" (231 and 234).[9] Alongside the parallel depictions of the house, several details connected to the house in Poe's story have distinctive parallels in *Agamemnon*: the female figures who embody the house's threat—Poe's Madeline and Aeschylus's Clytemnestra—and throngs of spirits infesting the house point toward the influence Aeschylus's play.[10]

If "Gothic" implies a text or object that can build fearful suspense, marking a moment in literary history in which gloomy, isolated mansions begin to fill the pages of narrative fiction, we can see that Greek tragedy anticipates this attention to a family's pollution and to the site of the interkin violence that tragedy often portrays. *Agamemnon*, a house-obsessed play, focuses attention on the physical house from its first lines when the watchman, describing himself crouched on top of the house like a dog (3), provocatively refers to the dark history that the house knows, which "the house itself, were it to take a voice, would speak most plainly" (οἶκος δ' αὐτός, εἰ φθογγὴν λάβοι, / σαφέστατ' ἂν λέξειεν [37–38]).[11] Cassandra, the Trojan princess and prophet, substantiates the watchman's claim with her lengthy description of the violence the house has seen, the murders that will soon take place there, and by conjuring an image of the angry spirits that currently inhabit the house: Furies (Erinyes). As she prepares to enter the house where she knows she will die, Cassandra frames the full horror of this space: "I address these gates here as the gates of Hades" (Ἅιδου πύλας δὲ τάσδ'ἐγὼ προσεννέπω [1291]).

*Agamemnon*'s plot progresses with an intensifying fear for the chorus and audience about what will happen inside the house.[12] Clytemnestra lures Agamemnon and Cassandra into the house, where Clytemnestra exerts tight control. The queen convinces Agamemnon to seal his fate and enter the house by trampling over precious textiles from the house's stores, an act that Agamemnon himself frames as "to-destroy-the-house" (Δωματοφθορεῖν [948]).[13] The theatrical backdrop of the house intensifies the impact of Clytemnestra's murders; it first blocks the chorus and audience from seeing the acts, building suspense and inviting the spectators to imagine the worst. It then thrusts the tableau with the horrible result into the theater: Clytemnestra standing over the corpses.[14] When the house has finished its blocking and revealing role, it implodes upon itself while Aeschylus's distressed chorus watches the house collapse to the ground (1530–34)—an event that confronts Poe's narrator also.

The façade of Usher's house frames Poe's short story: Poe's narrator, like Aeschylus's watchman and chorus, directs the audience's gaze upon the house from outside. In his opening sentence the narrator writes, "I found myself . . . within view of the melancholy house of Usher" (231). From this perspective where he catches his first glimpse he reflects on the setting, the tarn, and house and establishes its generally melancholic effect, returning to it throughout several paragraphs of reflection. The environment the narrator constructs from this fixed vantage point resembles a dramatic setting—a setting to which is easily referred—for his short story.[15] Unlike the Greek chorus, Poe's narrator can go inside Roderick's house, which develops depth and subdivisions: chambers, hallways, and the farthest recessed donjon where Madeline is entombed. Entrance into the house draws the narrator and audience closer to the dangerous space, escalating fear, and enables the narrator to pursue the causes of the house's, and its owner's, ailment.

Although the story's action moves to the house's interior, its edifice makes the first and final impression on the narrator and audience and has a palpable relevance to what happens in the story's main body: inside the house the narrator turns from the house's façade to the face of Roderick Usher[16] as he works to diagnose the source of the disease afflicting both. The correspondence of Roderick Usher's moribund nature and the sickliness of his house keeps the image of the house's exterior in the reader's mind even though it is not the backdrop of the story's central portion. As in *Agamemnon*, Poe introduces the domestic edifice as an icon to convey the idea that the house is an animate object, perhaps more specifically, an object animated by infesting organisms. Poe employs this foreboding effect, common in Gothic literature, to introduce the disease that infests house and inhabitants at once: the house's sickness corresponds almost completely to Roderick's sickliness. While he is in the house, the narrator watches Roderick's condition and frequently comments on his facial appearance. Usher's decline, as displayed in his face, marks the house's impending final collapse, which narrator and audience view from the exterior at the story's end.

In *Agamemnon*, an effect of the correspondence of house and inhabitant is that although Agamemnon appears robust, the audience knows that the king cannot be healthier than his house. It is the herald who first presents the tantalizing personification of the house upon which he is crouched. Rather than reveal Clytemnestra's adultery and murderous plot, he suggests that the audience imagine what the house could tell if it had a voice, implicitly fashioning anthropomorphic eyes and memory for the house, as well.[17] Later in the play Cassandra, as one scholar puts it, "gives the house, so to speak, the voice it has been craving,"[18] renewing the guard's personification. She refers to the house as "knowing of many kin-slaying evils" (πολλὰ συνίστορα / αὐτόφονα, κακὰ [1090–91]) and also "god-hating" (μισόθεον [1090]). When she envisions the violence that took place within the house, Cassandra refers to the house as a living being that "breathes blood-dripping murder" (φόνον δόμοι πνέουσιν αἱματοσταγῆ [1309]). The blood-red textiles that Clytemnestra rolls out for her husband to trample, it has even been suggested,[19] might give the impression of the house's tongue: a fearful visual image of the house as a living being.

Not only is Agamemnon's house a living being, it is constructed out of the family that inhabits it, especially Agamemnon. Clytemnestra calls her husband "a firm-footed pillar of the lofty roof" (ὑψηλῆς στέγης / στῦλον ποδήρη [897–98]). Shortly after, she describes Agamemnon as a piece of the physical landscape surrounding the house: a tree which shades the house cool in the summer heat (966–67). He is also the fire on the house's hearth, warming it in the winter (968–72). These images associate Agamemnon with a principal concern of Greek domestic architecture: heating and cooling in a fluctuating climate. After Agamemnon's death, Clytemnestra attempts to fill his position as household- and political leader and describes herself in terms of the house's "hearth" in a famous double entendre (1484–85).[20] The close sequence of the demise of the house and its owner accents their correspondence: the house collapses on itself following Agamemnon's death.

Poe's personification of Usher's house is even more central to the story than that in *Agamemnon*, so much so that Poe merges the house with Roderick's identity and exposes a nebulous set of infesting organisms that undermine Usher's mental stability together with the physical stability of his house. In his initial survey of the house, the narrator twice mentions "vacant and eye-like windows" (231) that suggest the narrators' description of Roderick's eyes (234 [twice], 235, 241, 242, and 244). In a similar manner, the "fine tangled webwork" of fungi growing on the house (233) anticipates Roderick's "web-like" hair with its "wild gossamer texture" (234). Personifications of the house are especially thick in the inset song, "The Haunted Palace," that Roderick sings (238–39). The palace, a double for Roderick's house, at first "reared its head," blushes, has doors of ruby and pearl that suggest a mouth, and boasts "yellow banners" that suggest hair for the house (238). It also has "luminous windows" (238) that evoke the repeated description of Roderick's eyes as luminous (234 and 241). At the end of the story, Madeline emerges from doors within the house that appear to the narrator as "ponderous and ebony jaws" (245).

The house and its inhabitants are codependent not only in Poe but in Aeschylus, where the physical house shows that Agamemnon's household is at stake. *Agamemnon* conveys the same concern as most Greek tragedies, in which the household was endangered[21] by violence between family members, either blood kin or spouses,[22] or by other forms of destruction to the family including war (*Trojan Women*), death of a critical member (*Alcestis, Ajax*), or family strife (*Andromache, Oedipus at Colonus*). The depiction of the physical house was not just a metaphor for the human members but defined, in part, the household. The Greek word *oikos* is the closest to "family" and signified not only family members but possessions and the house itself. *Genos* referred to the continuing generations of a family for which the physical house, handed down, is an obvious marker. The English phrase "House of Atreus" emphasizes a clan-like element of the family's patriline that is especially conducive to describing the "curse of Atreus" handed down over generations from Atreus or Tantalus before him. In Aeschylus's play, the physical house is an important image for the intergenerational dysfunction of the family's line as well as the crisis of its current household.

Poe may hint that he finds inspiration in Aeschylus for the correspondence of house and humans: the name he gives the house, "House of Usher," seems a conspicuous play on Aeschylus's title, and the narrator reflects on the oddity of this name early in the story. He ascribes it to an anomalous character of the Usher family that their ancestral house is not "Usher" but "House of Usher." The family is unusual because it had no "collateral offspring" and "the entire family lay in the direct line of descent" so that "this deficiency . . . of collateral issue, and the consequent undeviating transmission, from sire to son, of the patrimony with the name . . . had, at length, so identified the two as to merge the original title of the state in the quaint and equivocal appellation of the 'House of Usher'—an appellation which seemed to include, in the minds of the peasantry who used it, both the family and the family's mansion" (232). Poe emphasizes the degree of correspondence of house and inhabitants. The narrator's explanation of this assimilation exposes the family's precarious situation also, since he hints at dangerous inbreeding and emphasizes that the whole line now depends on Roderick and his twin sister, as Roderick says (236).

Literal animation of Roderick's house underlies the correspondence of house and owner. Early in the story the narrator alludes to Roderick's "shadowy superstition" that his house is "tenanted" by an unspecified force (235); only later does the narrator explain Roderick's theory of the "sentience of all vegetable things" (239). Roderick Usher believes that the fungi growing on the house, the decaying trees around it, and the tarn pooling in front, all of which were prominent in the narrator's initial description of the house's exterior, bring to life the personified structure, generating its fearsome power.

One of the mysterious animating forces is the tarn's "rank miasma," a noticeably Greek word that perhaps indicates Poe borrowing a signal dynamic from *Agamemnon*. *Miasma*, or pollution, is a force that threatens throughout the larger *Oresteia* trilogy: pollution from the family's pattern of interkin violence attracts demonic spirits, Furies, to the house and family members. In *Agamemnon* current sources of pollution for the house are Agamemnon's recent sacrifice of his daughter Iphigenia and Clytemnestra's murders of Agamemnon and Cassandra, combined with the latter's adultery with Aegisthus. The house is significant as a container for pollution, since, to the Greek mind, pollution adheres to physical things.[23] The Furies, whom Cassandra envisions as infesting the house (1468, 1481, 1500–1504, and 1508),[24] convey how pollution of the recurring murders inheres in the physical house: the house exerts an animate force as Cassandra perceives it, as it "breathes blood-dripping murder" (φόνον δόμοι πνέουσιν αἱματοσταγῆ [1309]). Multiplying references to blood in the play's second half lead to Clytemnestra murdering Agamemnon and Cassandra, which Clytemnestra frames as the rehearsal of earlier violence in the family (1497–1504).[25] Cassandra's vision of slaughter behind the house's façade also emphasizes the house's ability to hold pollution.[26]

Poe incorporates his own Aeschylean Furies-like figures in the spirits that inhabit the palace in the inset ballad "The Haunted Palace." This song has an additional connection to Greek tragedy in the way it mirrors the Greek chorus, first since it is a song included within prose, and second because the song uses the first-person plural voice, "we," alongside third-person narration.[27] Miriam Fernandez-Santiago comments that the song imitates the function of a chorus; the chorus reframes the themes of the play from a new generalizing perspective, introducing new images and reflecting some of the spectators' possible emotions.[28] The singer contemplates a palace's edifice, mirroring the image of the house's façade that opens and closes the story. In the ballad the house undergoes a tragic transformation over time, which its inhabiting spirits convey. At first, in the second line, the young house was "by good angels tenanted" (238). In the third and fourth stanzas, outsiders see "spirits" inside the palace "moving musically"; the singer also calls them a "troop of Echoes," resinging the words of their king. The friendly figures are replaced in the fifth stanza by new ones, "evil things, in robes of sorrow," who "assailed the monarch's high estate." Finally they inhabit the palace, dancing "to a discordant melody" and "like a rapid ghastly river / through the pale door, a hideous throng rush out forever, and laugh" (239).

Poe's good and bad spirits resemble Aeschylus's Furies since they not only inhabit the palace but torment its human inhabitants. Remarkably, both sets of spirits are envisioned as a group of singers.[29] Cassandra describes her vision of the Furies in the house as a "chorus" or "a group of singers" "that never leaves this house. They sing in unison, but not pleasantly, for their words speak of evil" (τὴν γὰρ στέγην τήνδ' οὔποτ' ἐκλείπει χορὸς / ξύμφθογγος, οὐκ εὔφωνος· οὐ γὰρ εὖ λέγει [1186–87]). She continues to call the Furies a "reveling-band" *komos*, that "remains in the house" (1189) and "attacking the house, sing a song of the initial ruin, *ate*" (ὑμνοῦσι δ' ὕμνον δώμασιν προσήμεναι / πρώταρχον ἄτην [1191–92]). This description is very close to Poe's inset song, whose band "assailed the monarch's high estate" and go on to dance "to a discordant melody" just as Cassandra's band sings "discordantly" (οὐκ εὔφωνος). While Agamemnon's Furies both literally infest Agamemnon's house and symbolize the polluting curse that plagues the family, Poe's spirits inhabit an elaborately constructed metaphor for the human mind.

In *Eumenides*, the final sequel to *Agamemnon* in the *Oresteia* trilogy, Furies act as the chorus, eventually transforming into friendly spirits—a transformation Poe reverses. Their problematic infestation of Agamemnon's house gives way to them occupying a new space, a site for cult worship at Athens. In both the *Oresteia* and "The Fall of the House of Usher," the daemons suggest that the family owns an inexorable fate. Aeschylus does not insist on a "curse" on the family of Atreus but includes Aegisthus's description of himself as accomplice to the Furies in bringing just vengeance on the family (1582–1611). The Furies do not drive the family to violence but punish the kindred murder; nonetheless, they mark recurring revenge-driven violence that turns into an unbreakable cycle. Poe similarly leaves the source of Roderick's and his house's disease a mystery. When the narrator arrives, it is evident that something already is impelling Roderick toward his eventual action of entombing his sister alive. The narrator's early emphasis on the family's unusual inbreeding, which places weight on the brother-sister pair, seems an explanation for Roderick's morbid disposition (232). In the inset song, it is the "evil things" that attack the palace (238), but in the rest of Poe's story the causality of the family's fate in relation to Roderick's character and actions is ambiguous and bidirectional. Poe's spirits and Aeschylus's Furies convey a tragic fate or destiny for the owner of each of the houses they inhabit.[30]

Cassandra's entry into Agamemnon's house is full of suspense but also fully conscious of the coming horror: the Trojan princess moves into the house wholly confident that she will die in that space. Roderick Usher is a Cassandra-like figure in that he is uniquely aware of the house's animation, whereas other characters and the audience cannot fully understand what he does until it is too late. Roderick and Cassandra perceive the mortal danger the houses hold for each of them.

Over the more than two hundred lines (1080–291) between when Cassandra descends from her chariot and her actual entrance through the *skēnē* door, Cassandra encounters gruesome visions as she gazes upon the house of Agamemnon. These shock the chorus as Cassandra delivers disturbing images of the house in lyric outbursts:[31] she sees Thyestes's children who were slaughtered, "these babies here, crying over their slaughter and their flesh, roasted and eaten up by their father!" (κλαιόμενα τάδε βρέφη σφαγὰς / ὀπτάς τε σάρκας πρὸς πατρὸς βεβρωμένας [1095–96]). When the chorus pushes her to clarify, Cassandra is able to relate more directly the truth of the house's history, Clytemnestra's current scheming (1100–104),[32] and to prophecy as well the future murder of Agamemnon and herself (1256–81).[33] Only now, Cassandra explains, does she avoid Apollo's curse that no one will ever heed her (1170–213). Cassandra's speech represents a noticeable development from the silence with which she faced Clytemnestra, who attributed it to an inability to speak Greek (1060–61) or madness (1064–67). Cassandra's prophetic expressions center around the horror of the house: as her clarity of communication builds, she also articulates the power in the house.

Like Cassandra, Roderick possesses intuitive knowledge of his house's workings. Soon after the narrator arrives to visit, Roderick prophecies his death: "I shall perish" (235), but the narrator first attributes it mainly to Roderick's internal psychology and hypochondria. When Madeline's body is in the vault, the narrator begins to pay more credence to Roderick's perception of the house. Thus he relates Roderick's theory that the "sentience of all vegetable things" (239) gives the house a living force. When the narrator becomes aware of "certain low and indefinite sounds ... at long intervals" (241) the story begins to reveal to the narrator and reader what Roderick and the house know is happening.

Poe prolongs the revelation by interspersing narration of "Ethelred and the Dragon" with the growing awareness of Poe's narrator. Sounds interrupt this story: a "cracking and ripping sound" (243) after Ethelred rips apart the hermit's cottage, then "low and apparently distant, but harsh, protracted and most unusual screaming or grating sound," and finally a "distinct, hollow, metallic, and clangourous, yet apparently muffled reverberation" (244). Although the narrator is incapable of interpreting the sounds emanating from unseen portions of the house, Roderick understands. He sits "undisturbed" and rigid and "a sickly smile quivered about his lips" (244); his posture shows he is not surprised by the sounds. Roderick finally discloses what he knows "in a low, hurried and gibberish murmur as if unconscious" (244). His expression evokes Cassandra's ecstatic position in Aeschylus. He accurately prophecies what has happened and will happen, but his delivery is broken up by repetition, laughter, and a preponderance of dashes that Poe inserts. Like the prophetess Cassandra's inspired trance, Roderick gives the impression that he is unconscious of his listener and spills out words without control.

The effect of the extended revelation of Roderick's knowledge, like Cassandra's, is to emphasize what is beyond the sight and understanding of both narrator and reader. The house itself hides these events. In *Agamemnon* the edifice of the house, the set building, hides the awful truth, for which chorus and audience must depend on Cassandra as they gaze at the façade and later hear the sounds of the murder (1343 and 1345). Poe brings the suspense to a climax with Roderick's final exclamation, emphasizing the house wall that has hidden Madeline deep within the house, until the present moment: "I tell you that she now stands without the door!" (245). The reader and narrator are left anticipating what will emerge from the house's inner doorway.

If this moment in Poe's story evokes a dramatic staging, the next expands upon it: Madeline emerges from the concealed part of the house in a scene that suggests a dramatic tableau: "The huge antique panels to which the speaker pointed, threw slowly back, upon the instant, ponderous and ebony jaws. It was the work of the rushing gust—but then without those doors there DID stand the lofty and enshrouded figure of the lady Madeline of Usher" (245). The focus on the doors themselves, their revealing function, and the appearance that they open of their own accord all suggest dramatic staging. Likewise, Madeline does not walk out through the doors but appears as though conveyed into the scene.[34]

The effect of the narration is similar to what Aeschylus's text suggests, where Clytemnestra appears outside the house, in a tableau, standing over the bodies of Cassandra and her husband.[35] In perhaps a nod to the murderess Clytemnestra, Poe describes Madeline's white clothes as stained with blood, offering no other explanation for this detail. In both scenes the house's hidden space unleashes female revenge upon a male family member in response to a fatal error on his part: Agamemnon sacrificed his and Clytemnestra's daughter, and Roderick has buried his sister alive.

The collapse of Usher's house provides a finale for this violence. As the narrator flees from the twins' piled corpses, he views the house fall:

> The radiance was that of the full, setting, and blood-red moon which now shone vividly through that once barely-discernible fissure, of which I have before spoken as extending from the roof of the building, in a zigzag direction, to the base. While I gazed, this fissure rapidly widened—there came a fierce breath of the whirlwind—the entire orb of the satellite burst at once upon my sight—my brain reeled as I saw the mighty walls rushing asunder—there was a long tumultuous shouting sound like the voice of a thousand waters—and the deep and dank tarn at my feet closed sullenly and silently over the fragments of the "House of Usher." (245)

Very near the end of *Agamemnon* the members of Aeschylus's chorus watch Agamemnon's house crash to the ground: "Bereft of the inventive thoughts of my mind, I do not know in what direction I should turn, with the house itself falling. I fear the house-destroying blow of the rainstorm, bloodstained" (1530–34). While it is unlikely that this was performed visually, a "thunder machine" (*bronteion*: an amphora full of stones) might have provided a sound effect while the chorus described this scene. Projected onto the house's façade through the chorus's words, the image of the house falling culminates its inhabitants' dysfunction and demise.[36]

The collapses of the houses conclude parallel trajectories of the house of Usher and Agamemnon's house. Reading their courses side by side reveals Poe using his Gothic haunted house to a similar effect as Agamemnon's house, sometimes with a dramatic flair. Poe exploits the house, both its exterior and interior walls, as device to block the reader's view. Madeline's effortless appearance coordinates seamlessly, as though choreographed, with the space of the house whose doors magically open as though choreographed.

This dramatic effect exploits the space of the house as a container for hiding horrible realities within—only to erupt them into the audience's view.[37]

While source criticism leaves us with some *aporia*, the resemblance of Poe's and Aeschylus's uses of the house suggests that Poe appreciated an overlap in the genres of Gothic and ancient tragedy and saw the potential of Agamemnon's house in particular as a container for the same uncanny within the Gothic haunted house.[38] Parallel house-collapses emphasize an idea that both Aeschylus and Poe appear intent to convey: that the physical house becomes a character its own right and corresponds to its human counterparts. For Aeschylus the house signified the well-being of both the household, a conspicuous concern on the Attic stage, and its members, who are collectively bound to the household's security. Poe seizes on this relationship and on the idea that the sickness of the house mutually influences and is influenced by its inhabitants' dysfunction. Endeavoring to build a more psychological horror, Poe magnifies the influence of the house on its residents by collapsing the boundaries of house and inhabitants. As a basis for parallel effects of horror in Poe and Aeschylus, each author's house pitches toward destruction and pulls its inhabitants, as though tangled in its very fabric, along to the same demise.

## Notes

I am most grateful to Gregory Hays and John Lyons for their valuable suggestions in writing this article.

1. Sigmund Freud in a 1919 essay "The Uncanny," in *The Uncanny* (2003), trans. David McLintock (New York: Penguin), 121–75, writes, "Heimlich thus becomes increasingly ambivalent, until it finally merges with its antonym unheimlich." Carol Dougherty, in her discussion of mobility in the tragic and Athenian household ("These *Metoikoi*": Living with Others, Living as Others in Aeschylus' *Oresteia*," *American Journal of Philology* 138, no. 1 [2017]: 579 and n. 4), relates Freud's collapse of *heimlich* and *unheimlich* here to Aeschylus's *Oresteia*.

2. On Poe in the Gothic tradition, see Benjamin Fisher, "Poe and the Gothic Tradition," in *The Cambridge Companion to E. A. Poe*, ed. Kevin J. Hayes (Cambridge: Cambridge University Press, 2002), 72–91. For example, Walpole's *Castle of Otranto* (1764) features paintings that walk and doors that open on their own, and in Charles Brockden Brown's early American Gothic story "Wieland" (1798), the family hears their house speak to them.

3. Poe likely experienced Hoffmann's story through R. P. Gillies's English translation (1826), and Walter Scott's summary in his critical essay "On the Supernatural of Fictitious Composition; and Particularly on the Works of Ernest Theodore Wil-

liam Hoffmann," *Foreign Quarterly Review* 1 (1827): 82–93. R. P. Gillies's full English translation, *German Stories, II* (Edinburgh: William Blackwood, 1826), may also have been available to Poe (see George B. Von der Lippe, "Beyond the House of Usher: The Figure of E. T. A. Hoffmann in the Works of Poe," *Modern Language Studies* 9 [1978–79]: 33–41). John Hardman's reception of Hoffmann in "The Robber's Tower," *Blackwood's Edinburgh Magazine* 146, no. 2 (1828): 874–84, suggests independent features in common with "Fall of the House of Usher," and Edward W. Pitcher argues for Hardman's influence on Poe, in "From Hoffmann's 'Das Majorat' to Poe's 'Usher' via 'The Robber's Tower': Poe's Borrowings Reconsidered," *American Transcendental Quarterly* 39 (1978): 231–35.

4. While scholars have suggested that Poe's title gestures toward the House of Atreus, they have not explored the dialogue between these two works. Darlene H. Unrue, "Edgar Allan Poe: The Romanticist as Classicist," *International Journal of the Classical Tradition* 1 (1995): 116, suggests that "the title . . . suggests a reference to the House of Atreus." Playwright Steve Berkoff explicitly related the two works by placing his versions of each side by side in his collection of plays, *EAST; Agamemnon; The Fall of the House of Usher* (London: John Calder, 1977).

5. Poe parodies the stories of Blackwood in "How to Write a Blackwood Article" and "A Predicament." Poe also bridled at the frequent description of his tales as "German," meaning German gothicism, as biographer Kenneth Silverman describes in *Edgar A. Poe: A Mournful and Never-ending Remembrance* (New York: HarperCollins, 1991), 153–54. Poe responds to such criticism in the preface to *Tales of the Grotesque and Arabesque* (1839): "If in many of my productions terror has been the thesis, I maintain that terror is not of Germany, but of the soul,—that I have deduced this terror only from its legitimate sources, and urged it only to its legitimate results."

6. For overview of classical allusions in Poe, see Unrue, "Edgar Allan Poe: The Romanticist as Classicist," 118n28; and Gregory Hays, "Ancient Classics," in *Edgar Allan Poe in Context*, ed. Kevin J. Hayes, 221–31 (Cambridge: Cambridge University Press, 2013). Unrue suggests the significance of classical authors and texts in shaping Poe's literary theory and worldview.

7. The mansion in Hoffmann's *Das Majorat*, as well as in Gillies's English translation, Scott's summary, and in Hardman's reception in "The Robber's Tower" (see note 3), does not feature the close identification of owner and house.

8. Inga-Stina Ewbank, "'Striking Too Short at Greeks': The Transmission of *Agamemnon* to the English Renaissance Stage," in *Agamemnon in Performance*, ed. Fiona Macintosh, Pantelis Michelakis, and Edith Hall (Oxford: Oxford University Press, 2005), 37–52. Another possible intermediate reception stands outside the scope of this essay: Seneca's *Thyestes* exploits the house in a parallel fashion to *Agamemnon*.

9. I refer to the page numbers of *The Complete Tales and Poems of Edgar Allan Poe* (New York: Random House, 1972).

10. That Poe knew Aeschylus's *Agamemnon* seems probable, but it is harder to ascertain the depth of acquaintance. Poe frequently refers to Greek tragedies in his

stories and reviews, which included reviews of a production of Sophocles's *Antigone*, several works of Columbia professor of classics Charles Anthon, and a translation of Euripides's plays. Unrue, in "Edgar Allan Poe: The Romanticist as Classicist," argues that classicism significantly influenced Poe's outlook on writing and his literary criticism (as expressed in "The Philosophy of Composition" and "The Poetic Principle"), even if it clashed with Poe's obvious Romantic and Gothic inspirations. Unrue suggests Poe's classicism is an underinvestigated influence but notes several scholars who have recognized classicizing, often rationalizing, aspects in Poe (ibid., 133). Hays, in "Ancient Classics," shows that Poe's classical references in his fiction are often superficial. On Poe's classical education, heavier on Latin than Greek, see Silverman, *Edgar A. Poe: A Mournful and Never-ending Remembrance*, 17–25, 29–30; and Hays, "Ancient Classics," 221–23. Since he was probably not a fluent Greek reader, his familiar references to Aeschylus may owe to Robert Potter's first English translation of Aeschylus (1777), in its fifth reprint by the time Poe wrote "House of Usher" (1839). Poe likely never watched the *Oresteia* on stage, since it was not performed in America until a performance at Harvard in 1906 (see Helene Foley, "The Millenium Project: *Agamemnon* in the United States," in *Agamemnon in Performance*, ed. Macintosh, Michelakis, and Hall, 308). But the significance of the house in this play is unmistakable in the play's text, even more so for a theater critic like Poe.

11. I use the Greek text and line numbering of Dennis L. Page, *Aeschyli septem quae supersunt tragoedias* (Oxford: Oxford University Press, 1972). All translations are my own.

12. Clytemnestra details the ominous path of fire-signals from Troy to Agamemnon's house, their final recipient (310–11).

13. John Jones, *On Aristotle and Greek Tragedy* (London: Chatto & Windus, 1962), 84–93, discusses the carpet scene as a waste of the household's resources, as does Oliver Taplin in *The Stagecraft of Aeschylus: The Dramatic Use of Exits and Entrances in Greek Tragedy* (Oxford: Oxford University Press, 1977), 313–14.

14. As Ruth Padel has discussed in "Making Space Speak," in *Nothing to Do with Dionysus?: Athenian Drama in Its Social Context*, ed. J. J. Winkler and Froma Zeitlin (Princeton, N.J.: Princeton University Press, 1990), 336–65, the house façade in the Greek theater marks movement between inside and outside as central to tragedy's meaning.

15. Miriam Fernandez-Santiago reflects on Poe's use of dramatic-type settings, which have been compared with contemporary landscape painting ("Poe's Play-full Narratives," *Edgar Allan Poe Review* 12, no. 2 [2011]: 86–87). She notes that the static quality of this setting that evokes dramatic space is characteristic for Poe, who often maintains the same perspective on characters within a scene and does not focus on their movement in and through an environment.

16. In Steve Berkoff's adaptation (*EAST; Agamemnon; The Fall of the House of Usher*), Usher takes the narrator's third-person description of the house into the first person, beginning, on page 89, "The house of Usher, my walls, are bleak walls, vacant eyelike windows."

17. Cf. Euripides's *Hippolytus*, 417–18, where Phaedra imagines the fear of adulterous women: "Do they not shudder at the dark, their, conspirator, and lest the chambers of the house should ever give out a voice?" (οὐδὲ σκότον φρίσσουσι τὸν ξυνεργάτην / τέραμνά τ' οἴκων μή ποτε φθογγὴν ἀφῇ).

18. Michael Ewans, "The Dramatic Structure of Agamemnon." *Ramus* 11, no. 1 (1982): 5.

19. Most recently argued by Rebecca McNamara, "The Ambiguous Home of Life and Death: The Symbolic Uses of the Skene and the Female in Aeschylus' Agamemnon," *Skene* 3, no. 1 (2017): 7–27.

20. The chorus of *Choephoroi*, 629, picks up on the same image when they state that a good woman's "hearth" should not be hot like Clytemnestra's.

21. Often as the domestic aftermath of—or response to—the heroic feats and epic wars of the epic genre, as has been argued, for instance, by Karen Bassi, in "Nostos, Domos, and the Architecture of the Ancient Stage," *South Atlantic Quarterly* 98, no. 3 (1999: 415–16.

22. Elizabeth Belfiore has calculated that significantly over half of extant and fragmentary tragedies centered on such violence in *Murder among Friends: Violation of "Philia" in Greek Tragedy* (New York: Oxford University Press, 2000).

23. See, for instance, W. Robert Connor, "The Razing of the House in Greek Society," *Transactions of the American Philological Association* 115 (1985): 91. A. F. Garvie, *Aeschylus: Choephoroi* (Oxford: Oxford University Press, 1986), 314, suggests other tragic passages describing polluted houses such as Aeschylus's *Eumenides* 63; Sophocles's *Electra*, 69, and *Oedipus Tyrannus*, 1228; and Euripides's *Iphigenia at Tauris*, 1216. On house purification, see Louis Moulinier, *Le pur et l'impur dans la pensée des Grecs d'Homère à Aristote* (Paris: C. Klincksieck, 1952), 92–93 and 233.

24. Connor, "The Razing of the House in Greek Society," 91nn 33 and 34, discusses the portrayal of their infestation.

25. Descriptions of blood dramatically increase in frequency at the end of *Agamemnon*: 698, 732–36, 1067, 1092, 1096, 1072, 1189, 1278, 1309, 1389–90, 1428, 1460, 1478, 1510, 1533–34, 1589, 1592, and 1656.

26. Cassandra's visions of bloodshed: 1090–92, 1096–97, 1186–87, 1217–22, 1291, and 1309.

27. Fernández-Santiago, "Poe's Play-full Narratives," 91n.

28. Fernández-Santiago, "Poe's Play-full Narratives," 90–91 and 99n47, notes that Poe "was familiar with Schlegel's interpretation of the function of the chorus in Ancient Greek tragedy."

29. The song explicitly marks the palace's correspondence to its owner the king, when it identifies the building as standing "In the monarch Thought's domain" (238), building on the story's conflation of Roderick and his house.

30. See Kent Ljungquist, "Uses of the Daemon in Selected Works of Edgar Allan Poe," *Interpretations* 12, no. 1 (1980): 31–39. Ljungquist shows that Poe daemons frequently transform between angelic and demonic states.

31. As Pat Easterling discusses in *"Agamemnon* for the Ancients," in *Agamemnon*

*in Performance*, ed. Macintosh, Michelakis, and Hall, 25–26, an ancient commentator describes that Cassandra's speech produced *ekplēxis*, consternation or terror.

32. She describes this in an even more gruesome vision, 1217–22, where the children, who look like dream-figures, carry their own entrails in their hands.

33. Cassandra says, "I will no longer teach from riddles" (φρενώσω δ' οὐκέτ' ἐξ αἰνιγμάτων, [1173]).

34. Fernández-Santiago, "Poe's Play-full Narratives," 86: "Characters in his [Poe's] tales do not typically move from one room to another. Instead what happens when such action is described is that they either enter or exit a particular setting."

35. The rolling *ekkuklēma* would have been a striking way to achieve the tableau in the Athenian theater.

36. For other house demolitions, see Jocelyn Moore, "When You Can't Go Home Again: The Destruction of the Oikos in Greek Tragedy" (Ph.D. diss., University of Virginia, 2017).

37. See note 30.

38. In scripting Poe's story, Steve Berkoff explains that he insists that "actors must be the house and its decaying fabric, must speak as stones and the memories of the house that are seared into its walls" (*EAST; Agamemnon; The Fall of the House of Usher*, 81).

# Selected Bibliography

Baldick, Chris. *The Oxford Book of Gothic Tales*. Oxford: Oxford University Press, 1992.
Bandello, Matteo. *Le novelle*. Bari, Italy: Laterza, 1910.
Barbey d'Aurevilly, Jules Amédée. *Œuvres romanesques complètes*. Edited by Jacques Petit. Paris: Gallimard, 1966.
Belleforest, François. *Le cinquiesme tome des histoires tragiques*. Edited by Hervé-Thomas Campangne. Geneva: Droz, 2013.
Biet, Christian, ed. *Théâtre de la cruauté et récits sanglants en France: XVIe–XVIIe siècle*. Paris: Laffont, 2006.
Billings, Joshua. *Genealogy of the Tragic: Greek Tragedy and German Philosophy*. Princeton, N.J.: Princeton University Press, 2014.
Boaistuau, Pierre. *Histoires tragiques*. Edited by Richard A. Carr. Société des textes français modernes. Paris: Champion, 1977.
Bondeson, Jan. *Buried Alive: The Terrifying History of Our Most Primal Fear*. New York: Norton, 2001.
Bourke, Joanna. *Fear: A Cultural History*. London: Virago, 2005.
Bowlby, Rachel. *Freudian Mythologies: Greek Tragedy and Modern Identities*. Oxford: Oxford University Press, 2007.
Boyle, Nicholas. "Goethe's Theory of Tragedy." *Modern Language Review* 105, no. 4 (October 2010): 1072–86.
Bozzetto, Roger. *Territoires des fantastiques: Des romans gothiques aux récits d'horreur moderne*. Aix-en-Provence: Publications de l'Université de Provence, 1998.
Bradley, A. C. *Shakespearean Tragedy*. 2nd ed. London: Macmillan, 1922.
Braund, Susanna. "Haunted by Horror: The Ghost of Seneca in Renaissance Drama." In *A Companion to the Neronian Age*, edited by Emma Buckley and Martin T. Dinter, 425–43. Chichester, West Sussex: Wiley-Blackwell, 2013.
Brooks, Cleanth. *Tragic Themes in Western Literature*. New Haven, Conn.: Yale University Press, 1955.
Brooks, Peter. *The Melodramatic Imagination: Balzac, Henry James, Melodrama, and the Mode of Excess*. New Haven, Conn.: Yale University Press, 1976.

Brownlee, Marina S. *The Cultural Labyrinth of Maria de Zayas*. Philadelphia: University of Pennsylvania Press, 2000.
Buckley, Matthew S. *Tragedy Walks the Streets: The French Revolution in the Making of Modern Drama*. Baltimore: Johns Hopkins University Press, 2006.
Burke, Edmund. *A Philosophical Enquiry into the Origin of Our Ideas of the Sublime and Beautiful*. Edited by Adam Phillips. Oxford: Oxford University Press, 1990.
Burks, Deborah G. *Horrid Spectacle: Violation in the Theater of Early Modern England*. Pittsburgh: Duquesne University Press, 2003.
Cable, George Washington. "The 'Haunted House' in Royal Street." In *Strange True Stories of Louisiana*, 192–232. 1888. Gretna, La.: Pelican, 2005.
Camus, Jean-Pierre. *Admirable Events: Selected out of Foure Bookes*. Translated by S. Du Verger. London: Thomas Harper for William Brooks, 1639.
———. *L'amphithéatre sanglant ou sont représentées plusieurs actions tragiques de nostre temps*. Paris: Cottereau, 1630.
———. *Les spectacles d'horreur, où se découvrent plusieurs tragiques effets de notre siècle*. Paris: Soubron, 1630.
Carr, Richard A. *Pierre Boaistuau's "Histoires Tragiques": A Study of Narrative Form and Tragic Vision*. Chapel Hill: Department of Romance Languages, University of North Carolina, 1979.
Chesters, Timothy. *Ghost Stories in Late Renaissance France: Walking by Night*. Oxford: Oxford University Press, 2011.
Clark, Stuart. *Thinking with Demons: The Idea of Witchcraft in Early Modern Europe*. Oxford: Oxford University Press, 1997.
Crow, Charles L. *History of the Gothic: American Gothic*. Cardiff: University of Wales Press, 2009.
Day, William Patrick. *In the Circles of Fear and Desire: A Study of Gothic Fantasy*. Chicago: University of Chicago Press, 1985.
Dennison, Michael J. *Vampirism. Literary Tropes of Decadence and Entropy*. New York: Peter Lang, 2001.
Downing, Lisa. *Desiring the Dead: Necrophilia and Nineteenth-Century French Literature*. Oxford: Legenda, 2003.
Eagleton, Terry. *Sweet Violence: The Idea of the Tragic*. Oxford: Blackwell, 2003.
Ellis, Kate Ferguson. *The Contested Castle: Gothic Novels and the Subversion of Domestic Ideology*. Urbana: University of Illinois Press, 1989.
Felski, Rita, ed. *Rethinking Tragedy*. Baltimore: Johns Hopkins University Press, 2008.
Fiedler, Leslie. "Charles Brockden Brown and the Invention of the American Gothic." In *Love and Death in the American Novel*, 126–61. New York: Criterion, 1960.
Freud, Sigmund. *The Uncanny*. Translated by David McLintock. New York: Penguin, 2003.
Goddu, Teresa A. *Gothic America: Narrative, History, and Nation*. New York: Columbia University Press, 1997.
Greenblatt, Stephen. *Hamlet in Purgatory*. Princeton, N.J.: Princeton University Press, 2001.

Haining, Peter, ed. *The Shilling Shockers: Stories of Terror from the Gothic Bluebooks.* London: Gollancz, 1978.
Hall, Edith. *Greek Tragedy: Suffering under the Sun.* Oxford: Oxford University Press, 2010.
Hammond, Paul. *The Strangeness of Tragedy.* New York: Oxford University Press, 2009.
Hayes, Kevin J., ed. *The Cambridge Companion to E. A. Poe.* Cambridge: Cambridge University Press, 2002.
Hegel, Georg Wilhelm Friedrich. *Phenomenology of Spirit.* Translated by Arnold V. Miller and J. N. Findlay. Oxford: Clarendon, 1977.
Hoffmann, Ernst Theodor Amadeus. "The Sand-Man." In *Weird Tales*, translated by J. T. Bealby, 1:168–215. New York: Scribner's, 1885.
Hogle, Jerrold E., ed. *The Cambridge Companion to Gothic Fiction.* Cambridge: Cambridge University Press, 2002.
Horner, Avril, and Sue Zlosnik, eds. *Le Gothic: Influences and Appropriations in Europe and America.* Basingstoke: Palgrave Macmillan, 2008.
Hoxby, Blair. *What Was Tragedy? Theory and the Early Modern Canon.* Oxford: Oxford University Press, 2015.
Hughes, William, David Punter, and Andrew Smith, eds. *The Encyclopedia of the Gothic.* Chichester, U.K.: Wiley-Blackwell, 2013.
Hume, Robert D. "Gothic versus Romantic: A Revaluation of the Gothic Novel." *PMLA* 84, no. 2 (March 1969): 282–90.
Javitch, Daniel. "The Assimilation of Aristotle's *Poetics* in Sixteenth-Century Italy," in *The Cambridge History of Literary Criticism*, vol. 3, edited by Glynn Norton, 53–65. Cambridge: Cambridge University Press, 1989.
Jobbé-Duval, E. *Les morts malfaisants, "larvae, lemures," d'après le droit & les croyances populaires des Romains.* Paris: Sirey, 1924.
Judet de La Combe, Pierre. *Les tragédies grecques sont-elles tragiques? Théâtre et théorie.* Montrouge, France: Bayard, 2010.
Kaufman, Pamela. "Burke, Freud, and the Gothic." *Studies in Burke and His Time* 13, no. 3 (1972): 2179–92.
Kerrigan, John. *Revenge Tragedy: Aeschylus to Armageddon.* Oxford: Clarendon, 1996.
Kristeva, Julia. *Powers of Horror: An Essay on Abjection.* Translated by Leon S. Roudiez. New York: Columbia University Press, 1982.
Lever, Maurice. *Canards sanglants: Naissance du fait divers.* Paris: Fayard, 1993.
Lévy, Maurice. *Le Roman "gothique" anglais: 1764–1824.* Toulouse: Publications de la Faculté des Lettres et Sciences humaines de Toulouse, 1968; new ed., Paris: Armand Colin, 1995.
Lewis, Matthew. *The Monk.* Edited by Howard Anderson. Introduction and notes by Emma McEvoy. Oxford: Oxford University Press, 2008.
Lyons, John D. *Kingdom of Disorder: The Theory of Tragedy in Classical France.* West Lafayette, Ind.: Purdue University Press, 1999.
———. *Tragedy and the Return of the Dead.* Evanston, Ill.: Northwestern University Press, 2018.

Malingre, Claude. *Histoires tragiques de nostre temps*. Rouen: Ferrand and Daré, 1641.
Maturin, Charles. *Melmoth the Wanderer*. Edited by Douglas Grant. Oxford: Oxford University Press, 2008.
Maupassant, Guy de. *L'inutile beauté*. Paris: Victor-Havard Éditeur, 1900.
Mazouer, Charles. "Ce que 'tragédie' et 'tragique' veulent dire dans les écrits théoriques du XVIe siècle." *Revue d'Histoire Littéraire de la France* 109, no. 1 (January 2009): 71–84.
McFarland, James. "The Death of Tragedy: Walter Benjamin's Interruption of Nietzsche's Theory of Tragedy." In *Tragedy and the Tragic in German Literature, Art, and Thought*, edited by Stephen D. Dowden and Thomas P. Quinn, 171–94. Rochester, N.Y.: Camden House, 2014.
Meere, Michael, ed. *French Renaissance and Baroque Drama: Text, Performance, Theory*. Newark: University of Delaware Press, 2015.
Moore, Jocelyn. "When You Can't Go Home Again: The Destruction of the *Oikos* in Greek Tragedy." Ph.D. diss., University of Virginia, 2017.
Morrison, Robert and Chris Baldick, eds. *The Vampyre and Other Tales of the Macabre*. Oxford: Oxford University Press, 2008.
Nodier, Charles. *Infernaliana*. Paris: Goetschy, 1822.
Norman, Larry F. *The Shock of the Ancient: Literature and History in Early Modern France*. Chicago: University of Chicago Press, 2011.
O'Malley, Patrick R. *Catholicism, Sexual Deviance, and Victorian Gothic Culture*. Cambridge: Cambridge University Press, 2006.
Poe, Edgar Allan. *Poetry and Tales*. Edited by Patrick F. Quinn. New York: Viking, 1984.
Punter, David, ed. *A Companion to the Gothic*. Blackwell Companions to Literature and Culture. Oxford: Blackwell, 2000.
———. *The Literature of Terror: A History of Gothic Fictions from 1765 to the Present Day*. London: Longman, 1980.
Radcliffe, Ann. *The Mysteries of Udolpho*. Edited by Bonamy Dobrée. Oxford: Oxford University Press, 2008.
———. "On the Supernatural in Poetry." Posthumously published. *New Monthly Magazine*, 2nd ser., no. 16 (1826): 145–52.
Rosset, François. *Les histoires mémorables et tragiques de ce temps*. Edited by Anne de Vaucher Gravili. Paris: Livre de Poche, 1994.
———. *Les histoires tragiques de nostre temps*. Geneva: Slatkine Reprints, 1980.
Sage, Victor. *Horror Fiction in the Protestant Tradition*. London: Macmillan, 1988.
Schiller, Friedrich. *Aesthetical and Philosophical Essays*. New York: Harvard Publishing, 1895.
———. *Sämtliche Werke*. Edited by Gerhard Fricke and Herbert G. Göpfert. 5 vols. Munich: Hanser, 1965–67.
Steiner, George. *The Death of Tragedy*. London: Faber and Faber, 1961.
Szondi, Peter. *An Essay on the Tragic*. Translated by Paul Fleming. Stanford, Calif.: Stanford University Press, 2002.

Todorov, Tzvetan. *The Fantastic: A Structural Approach to a Literary Genre*. Translated by Richard Howard. Cleveland: Press of Case Western Reserve University, 1973.

Twitchell, James B. *The Living Dead: A Study of the Vampire in Romantic Literature*. Durham, N.C.: Duke University Press, 1981.

Walpole, Horace. *The Castle of Otranto: A Gothic Story*. Edited by Nick Groom. 3rd ed. Oxford: Oxford University Press, 2014.

Weinberg, Bernard. "The Tradition of Aristotle's *Poetics*: I. Discovery and Exegesis." In *A History of Literary Criticism in the Italian Renaissance*, 349–423. Chicago: University of Chicago Press, 1961.

Williams, Wes. *Monsters and Their Meanings in Early Modern Culture: Mighty Magic*. Oxford: Oxford University Press, 2011.

Wolfreys, Julian. *Victorian Hauntings: Spectrality, Gothic, the Uncanny and Literature*. New York: Palgrave, 2002.

# Contributors

**Alison Booth**, Professor of English and Academic Director of the Scholar's Lab at the University of Virginia, specializes in feminist transatlantic Victorian studies, biographical narrative, and digital humanities. She directs Collective Biographies of Women, a database developed from the annotated bibliography of her book *How to Make It as a Woman: Collective Biographical History from Victoria to the Present* (2004). Booth's other books include *Greatness Engendered: George Eliot and Virginia Woolf* (1992) and *Homes and Haunts: Touring Writers' Shrines and Countries* (2016).

**Marina S. Brownlee** is the Robert Schirmer Professor of Spanish and Portuguese and Comparative Literature at Princeton University, where she specializes in medieval and early modern studies. Her books include *The Cultural Labyrinth of María de Zayas*; *The Severed Word: Ovid's "Heroides"and the "Novela Sentimental"*; *The Status of the Reading Subject in the "Libro de Buen Amor"*; *The Poetics of Literary Theory in Lope and Cervantes*; and the edited volume *Cervantes' "Persiles" and the Travails of Romance* (2019).

**Hervé-Thomas Campangne** is a Professor of French Literature and Culture at the University of Maryland, College Park. He is the editor of François de Belleforest's *Cinquiesme tome des histoires tragiques* (2013) as well as of Montfleury's tragicomedy *Trasible* (2013). He has published numerous articles on sixteenth- and seventeenth-century literature and culture that have appeared internationally in the *Revue d'Histoire Littéraire de la France*, *XVIIe siècle*, *Studi Francesi*, *Nouvelle Revue du XVIe siècle*, *Renaissance Quarterly*, the *French Review*, *Renaissance/Reformation*, and the *Sixteenth Century Journal*. He is currently preparing an edition of Belleforest's *Septiesme tome des histoires tragiques*, as well as a book on the history of France-USA relations.

## CONTRIBUTORS

**Timothy Chesters** is a University Senior Lecturer in sixteenth-century French literature at Clare College, Cambridge. He has published a book, *Ghost Stories in Late Renaissance France: Walking by Night* (2011), and several articles on the relationship between learned demonology and narrative in the French Renaissance. He has also published on connections between nineteenth-century writers and the literature of the French Renaissnance, with a particular emphasis on Flaubert. His latest project examines questions of social cognition (mind-reading, empathy, kinesic intelligence, inference-making) as worked through both in the modern cognitive sciences and in literary texts of the Renaissance and other periods.

**David LaGuardia** is a Professor of French and Comparative Literature at Dartmouth College. His books include *Intertextual Masculinity in French Renaissance Literature: Rabelais, Brantôme, and the Cent nouvelles nouvelles* (2008); *Trash Culture: Essays in Popular Criticism* (2008); and *The Iconography of Power: The French Nouvelle at the End of the Middle Ages* (1999). He coedited three volumes of essays, "Meaning and Its Objects," *Yale French Studies* 110 (Fall 2006); *Narrative Worlds: Essays on the French Nouvelle in 15th and 16th Century France* (2005); and *Memory and Community in 16th-Century France* (2015). He is currently working on a book about memory and memorial writing in Renaissance France.

**Kathleen Long** is a Professor of French in the Department of Romance Studies at Cornell University, and former director of Feminist, Gender, and Sexuality Studies. She is the author of two books, *Another Reality: Metamorphosis and the Imagination in the Poetry of Ovid, Petrarch, and Ronsard* and *Hermaphrodites in Renaissance Europe*, and editor of the volumes *High Anxiety: Masculinity in Crisis in Early Modern France*; *Religious Differences in France*; and *Gender and Scientific Discourse in Early Modern Europe*. She has written numerous articles on the work of Théodore Agrippa d'Aubigné, on gender in early modern Europe, and on monsters. She is preparing a translation into English of *The Island of Hermaphrodites* (*L'isle des hermaphrodites*), a book-length study of the works of Agrippa d'Aubigné, and another on the relationship between early modern discourses of monstrosity and modern discourses of disability.

**John D. Lyons** is Commonwealth Professor of French at the University of Virginia and Chevalier de la Légion d'Honneur. He was previously a professor of French and Italian at Dartmouth College. His books include *Tragedy* *and the Return of the Dead* (2018), *The Phantom of Chance* (2011), and *The Tragedy of Origins* (1996), as well as edited volumes, such as *Critical Tales: New Studies of the Heptameron and Early Modern Culture* (with Mary B. McKinley, 1994) and *The Oxford Handbook of the Baroque* (2019).

**Michael Meere** is an Assistant Professor of French and Medieval Studies at Wesleyan University. He is the editor of *French Renaissance and Baroque Drama: Text, Performance, Theory* (2015) and has published several articles on early modern theater, including "Theatres of Torture: Martyrs, Pagans and the Politics of Conversion in Early Seventeenth-Century France," in *Early Modern French Studies* (July 2015). He has also written the entry "French Renaissance Drama" for the *Oxford Bibliographies in Renaissance and Reformation* (2018). Alongside his scholarship on drama, he also directs French-language theater productions at Wesleyan.

**Jocelyn Moore** is a Postdoctoral Fellow at the St. Anselm Institute at the University of Virginia. She specializes in Greek tragedy, performance, and social history, especially of the family unit. She has presented and written on the household in numerous plays of Aeschylus, Sophocles, and Euripides. Her current projects include the reception of Aeschylus's *Agamemnon* in Seneca's *Thyestes* and a book on the destruction of the house and household in Greek tragedy.

**Philippe Roger**, Senior Research Fellow at the French National Center for Scientific Research, Professor at the École des Hautes Études en Sciences Sociales in Paris and the University of Virginia, is a specialist in eighteenth-century literature and culture. He has been writing regularly on Sade since his first book, *Sade: La philosophie dans le pressoir* (1976), and has coedited (with M. Camus) *Sade: Écrire la crise* (1983). More recently, he co-organized (with M. Rueff) the international colloquium "Les langues de Sade" at the University of Geneva (2015). His other publications include *The American Enemy. A History of French Anti-Americanism* (2005), which received the French-American Foundation and Gould Foundation Prize for best nonfiction book translated from the French). He has been the editor of *Critique*, founded by George Bataille in 1946, since 1996.

**Guy Spielmann** teaches French and performing arts at Georgetown University. His scholarly interests cover early modern European performing arts broadly conceived, with a particular focus on stagecraft and nonliterary genres (such as fairground theater and commedia dell'arte), as well as various forms of contemporary popular culture, notably film and comics. His books include *Le jeu de l'ordre et du chaos* (2002), on the relationships between comedy and sociopolitical order in the later part of Louis XIV's reign, and *Parades* (2006), on eighteenth-century farces performed on domestic stages. He is currently editing, at Classiques Garnier (Paris), the dramatic works of Charles Dufresny.

**María Tausiet** is an independent scholar who has worked as a researcher at the CSIC (Spanish National Research Council) in Madrid, and more recently has been invited as Scholar in Residence at the University of Virginia. Her research focuses on early modern and contemporary Spanish religious history. She has published books on witchcraft, religion, magic, demonic possession, and the history of emotions, as well as a number of articles about aspects of the Catholic Reformation. Her latest books are *El dedo robado: Reliquias imaginarias en la España Moderna* (The purloined finger: Imaginary relics in early modern Spain) (2013) and *Urban Magic in Early Modern Spain: Abracadabra Omnipotens* (2014). She is currently doing research on relics, ghosts, the notion of immortality and its depiction in scientific and fantastical representations of the afterlife.

**Jennifer Tsien**, Associate Professor of French at the University of Virginia, specializes in eighteenth-century literature. She is the author of *Voltaire and the Temple of Bad Taste* (2003) and *The Bad Taste of Others* (2012) and articles such as "Diderot's Battle against Books: Books as Objects during the Enlightenment and Revolution," in *Belphégor: Littérature populaire et culture médiatique* (2015). She is currently writing a book about the language of protest in colonial Louisiana.

**Caroline Warman** is an Associate Professor of French at the University of Oxford and a Fellow of Jesus College. She is the author of *Sade: From Materialism to Pornography* (2002) and has written widely on eighteenth- and nineteenth-century literature and intellectual history, including the chapter "Nature and Enlightenment" for John D. Lyons's *Cambridge Companion to French Literature* (2016). She has translated Isabelle de Charrière's *The Nobleman and Other Romances* (2012) and cotranslated (with Kate E. Tunstall) Denis Diderot's *Rameau's Nephew* (2014; 2nd ed., 2016). She led 102 students and tutors from Oxford University in the translation of *Tolerance: The Beacon of the Enlightenment* (2016). She is currently completing her book on Diderot's *Eléments de physiologie*.

# Index

Index does not include items from notes nor bibliography.

adultery, 36–37, 74, 84, 91, 94, 110–11, 133, 138, 200, 228, 230
Aeschylus, 1, 3, 16–17, 22, 24; *Agamemnon*, 225, 226–35; *Choephoroi*, 22; *Eumenides*, 231
Alboin and Rosamund story, 9, 129–31, 133, 135–47
America, Gothic in, 11, 12, 194, 211, 216, 218
Americas: travel to, 38; cannibals in, 118; race in, 212–22
ancestors, 23, 40, 94, 96–97, 200, 216, 229. *See also* family
Ancients and Moderns, Quarrel of, 15, 17, 27
apparition, 9, 23–24, 71, 76–77. *See also* ghost; specter
Ariosto, Ludovico, 89
Aristotle, 2–3, 5, 16, 18, 24–25, 37–38, 46, 54, 61, 92
Artaud, Antonin, 177, 181, 186; *Le Moine*, 177, 196
assimilation (cultural), 216–17, 221, 230
Austen, Jane, 204–5; *Northanger Abbey*, 204

Bandello, Matteo, 7, 10, 23, 25, 31, 36, 46, 48, 62, 104, 130
Barbey d'Aurevilly, J., 9, 82–89, 91, 93–101
Baro, Balthazar, *Rosemonde*, 130–31, 133–34, 136, 138–40
Barthes, Roland, 73, 178, 186
Bataille, Georges, 178
Belleforest, François de, 7–10, 25, 30–44, 46, 130, 133, 138, 146–47, 150, 158
Bellin de la Liborlière, 185–86; *Célestine ou les époux sans l'être*, 186

Bentham, Jeremy, 191
Billard, Claude, 130–33, 135–36, 138, 140
blood, shedding of, 22, 27, 58–59, 100, 120, 131, 166–67, 184, 228–30, 234; in Catholic eucharist, 61, 77–78; drinking of, 122, 128, 137, 166–67. *See also* family; murder; race
Boaistuau, Pierre, 7, 23, 25, 31–32, 36, 40, 43, 46–47, 61–62, 109
Boccaccio, Giovanni, 7, 53, 104
Bodin, Jean, 68
Bradley, A.C., 7, 19
Breton, André, 176–78, 180, 186
broadsheets, 8, 53. *See also* canard; pamphlets
brother, 3, 22, 24, 37–38, 57–58, 82–84, 86, 88–89, 91, 93–94, 96, 99–100, 129, 232. *See also* family
burial, 16–17, 22, 24, 26–27, 71–72, 84, 133, 167, 234; failure of, 24, 26, 169; place of, 123–24, 138, 169, 184. *See also* corpse
Burke, Edmund, 20–21

Cable, George Washington, 11, 211–13, 215–18, 220–22
Calmet, Dom, 162, 170
Camus, Albert, 12
Camus, Jean-Pierre, 23, 30, 33–35, 39; *Spectacles d'horreur*, 33–34
canard (literary genre), 34, 45–48, 51–53, 55, 57–58, 60–64, 72, 101. *See also* broadsheets; pamphlets
cannibalism, 27, 118, 148, 184

251

canon (literary), 5, 7, 12, 19–20
Cardano, Girolamo (Cardanus), 68–69
Catholics: as authors, 34, 76–77, 120, 129, 165; and demonology, 67; as foreigners in America, 213; as viewed by British Protestant writers of Gothic fiction, 10–11, 123, 178, 199, 213, 123, 199, 203; and Virgin Mary, 117; and witchcraft, 121
Carmontelle, Louis Carrogis, 195
Castiglione, Baldassare, 53, 63
*Castle of Otranto, see* Walpole, Horace
Cervantes Saavedra, Miguel de, 105, 115
Christianity, 5, 10, 70, 74, 108, 117, 166, 178; as component of *histoires tragiques*, 74, 77–78; and Idealist view of tragic, 5; and vampires, 166, 169. *See also* Catholics; monks; priests; Protestants
church, setting for plot, 198, 204–5, 209. *See also* convent
Cicero, 49
Clark, Stuart, 67
Collins, Wilkie, 25
colonialism, 110, 200, 218
convent (cloister), 184–85, 187–88, 195, 205
Corneille, Pierre, 6, 8–9, 19, 24–25, 130, 146–47; *le Cid*, 3; *Horace*, 9, 24; *Rodogune*, 3, 9, 19
corpse, 22–24, 26–27, 32, 71–72, 76, 116, 122, 157, 166–67, 169, 206, 218, 227, 234. *See also* burial
*Cortegiano, Il*, 53
*Cosmographie universelle* (Belleforest and Thevet), 31, 142
Creole, 11, 211–16, 218, 220. *See also* assimilation; foreignness

D'Alembert, Jean le Rond de, 159
daughter, 22, 24, 26, 32, 39, 71, 78, 84, 129, 205, 214, 230, 234. *See also* family
Davanzati, Giuseppe, 163, 166
D'Avenant, William, 130
de La Taille, Jean, 17, 38, 44
Defoe, Daniel, *Robinson Crusoe*, 38–39
deformity, 57, 151, 153. *See also* monster
Della Porta, Giambattista, 68

Delon, Michel, 176, 195–96
Delrio, Martin, 72
demonology, 67–72, 76
demons, 34, 45, 66–74, 76, 78, 104, 110–12, 118, 122–24, 138, 162, 164, 166, 230
Denon, Vivant, 188
Descartes, René, 67
Desnoyers, Pierre, 164–66, 171
devil, 74, 77–78, 87, 104, 111, 118, 120–22, 124, 128, 192. *See also* demons
Diderot, Denis, 12, 149–58; *Eléments de physiologie*, 150–51, 153–58; *Entretiens sur le fils naturel*, 149; *Pensées sur l'interprétation de la nature*, 152; *La Religieuse*, 149. *See also* monster
doppelgänger and double, 21, 23, 197–98
doubt, 49, 66–69, 75–76, 78, 90, 134, 155, 206
*Dracula. See* Stoker, Bram, vampires
Doyle, Conan, 201
Dreyer, Carl Theodor, 128
Du Ryer, Pierre, 130

Eluard, Paul, 177
emotions, 5, 16, 19–20, 38, 46, 53–55, 86, 98–99, 107, 116, 183, 215, 231. *See also* fear; pathos; pity
England: cultural rivalry with France, 11, 178–80, 183–84, 202–3, 212–13; and origin of Gothic narrative, 123, 178, 180–81
Enlightenment: American perceptions of, 214, 216; and belief in vampires, 165–67; and emergence of Gothic, 5–7, 10–11, 15, 30, 39, 122–23, 151–52, 199, 202
Ettinghausen, Henry, 105, 114
Euripides, 1, 3, 16–17, 25, 117; *Alcestis*, 229; *Andromache*, 229; *Trojan Women*, 229

Fabre, Jean, 190, 196
family, 3–4, 12, 16–17, 22, 26–27, 34, 49, 53, 57, 61, 91, 94, 96–98, 100–101, 105, 117, 123, 130, 149, 151, 157, 170, 187, 196, 201–2, 205–6, 212–13, 226, 228–32, 234–35. *See also* brother; daughter; incest; revenge
fantastic (literary genre), 8–9, 11, 32, 66–67, 72–73, 76–79, 175–76, 187

fate, 19, 26–27, 100, 104, 131, 134, 146, 200, 231–32
father, 3–4, 22, 24, 26, 37, 48, 50, 55–56, 78, 83–84, 88–92, 129, 131, 132–39, 145–47, 166, 169, 195, 206, 219, 221, 232. *See also* family; patriarchy
fear, 10–12, 18, 20, 26, 38, 49, 54, 76, 108–9, 116–18, 131–32, 138, 140, 148, 157–58, 167, 170, 189, 191, 203, 214, 217, 219–22, 226–27, 234. *See also* pathos; pity
feudal, 186, 196, 203–4. *See also* middle ages
Feutry, Aimé-Ambroise-Joseph, 30, 34–35, 37–40
Fiedler, Leslie, 218
film (cinema) as modern tragic form, 2, 23, 76, 142, 160–61, 167, 197, 203
Flaubert, Gustave, 67, 73; *Madame Bovary*, 67
folklore, 25, 71, 86, 126, 164
Ford, John, 1, 62
foreigners: as characters, 10, 23, 212–17; as sources of stories, 31; Creoles perceived as, 212–13, 217, 221
foreignness, 11, 39, 211, 215, 217
Foucault, Michel 181, 191, 198, 200
France: concept of tragedy in, 8–9, 16–17, 27; nineteenth-century fiction in, 65–66, 77–79, 82–101; reception of British Gothic in, 175–92; setting of tragic stories, 8, 10, 32, 34, 51–53, 73–76, 82–101; tragic tales written in, 35, 45, 47, 53, 60
Francophilia and francophobia, 203, 211–21
Freud, Sigmund, 7, 21, 26–27, 200, 218, 222, 225

gender, 9, 74, 76. 78, 82, 85–86, 90, 105, 108–10, 112, 118, 121–22, 138–39, 141, 197, 199–203, 205, 207, 209, 214, 219–21
*genos*. *See* family
ghost, 11, 14, 23–24, 32, 71–72, 123, 128, 131–35, 137–38, 145–46, 152, 157, 170, 177, 186, 201. *See also* apparition; specter
Gothic: as 18th–19th century cultural production, 2–3, 6, 10–12, 15–17, 19, 21, 23–27, 67, 75, 123, 130, 140, 149–50, 152, 155, 174–92, 197, 205, 213, 216–18, 225–27; 234–35; as continuation of pre-Idealist tragic tradition, 16–19; created by Walpole, 23–26; and French term *gothique*, 194; and Freudian uncanny, 21–22; praised by surrealists, 176–78; as product of Enlightenment, 11, 15–16; as reaction to positivism, 67; rejected by Sade, 181–92; in Spain, 123
Goths (historic nationality), 131, 141, 145, 199; confusion with "Goths" (lifestyle), 174–75
Goulart, Simon, 30, 33–34, 38–39
Goya, Francisco de, 122–23
grotesque, 8, 26, 122–23, 151, 219, 222
Gryphius, Andreas, 62
Guérin de Bouscal, Guyon, 143
guilt, 27, 34, 36, 94, 209, 213, 218. *See also* crime; revenge

Hardy, Alexandre, 1, 146, 148
Harenberg, Johann Christoph, 166
haunting, 11, 22, 133–34; and fantastic, 67; and history 94, 191, 200–202, 218–19; and reader response, 100. *See also* house; revenge
Hegel, Georg Wilhelm Friedrich, 5, 19–20, 27
Heine, Maurice, 176, 179–80, 184
heteronormative, 202, 206. *See also* sex
heterosexual, 197, 209. *See also* sex
heterotopia, 11, 14, 27, 198–201, 203, 205, 207–9. *See also* foreignness
*histoires tragiques* (literary genre), and similar narratives, 4, 8–10, 25, 30–40, 46, 51, 61, 67, 72–73, 82, 92, 149–50, 155–56, 176, 192. *See also* Boaistuau, Pierre; Malingre, Claude; Rosset, François de
Hitchcock, Alfred, 26. *See also* film
Hoffmann, E.T.A., 225
homosexuality, 74, 108, 206. *See also* sex
honor, family, 105–6, 108. *See also* revenge
horror, 6, 9–12, 16, 65, 71, 76, 84, 96, 120, 122–23, 140, 185, 189–91, 199, 203, 208, 211, 217–19, 221–22, 226, 232, 235; in *histoires tragiques*, 34, 38, 40, 48, 49, 54, 59, 61; horror tourism, 222; refusal of, by Schiller, 19, 27. *See also* emotions; fear; pathos; terror

## INDEX

hospitality and hosts, 3, 69, 111, 221, 189, 213, 215
house, tragic, 11–12, 59; "haunted," 123, 197, 199, 202, 208–9, 211–22, 225–35; imprisonment in, 112, 212; of pleasure, 188; as related to family, 16–17; 225–35; in tales of the fantastic, 65, 71, 75–76, 78–79; in Victorian fiction, 199–209. *See also* hospitality; uncanny
Hugo, Victor, 4

Idealism, 4–6, 16, 19–21, 157–58
incest, 16, 27, 45, 47, 74, 82–86, 91, 94, 97–99, 101, 128, 177, 209, 219–20. *See also* family; sex
infanticide, 16, 45, 47, 118–20, 122. *See also* murder
Iphigenia, 22, 230
Italy: setting of tragic stories, 10–11, 123, 129–41, 199, 205; source of tragic tales, 7, 25, 31, 51, 52, 60, 130, 202–3

Jack the Ripper, 198

kinship. *See* family
Kristeva, Julia, 200, 217, 219–22

Lacan, Jacques, 47, 62–63, 85, 219
de Lancre, Pierre, 72
du Laurens, André, 32
Lavater, Ludwig (or Loys), 68–69
Le Brun, Annie, 176, 178, 187, 190–91, 196
Le Fanu, Joseph Sheridan, *Carmilla*, 161
Le Loyer, Pierre, 69, 71–73, 75
Lesuire, Robert-Martin, *Charmansage*, 188–89
Lever, Maurice, 45, 62, 101
Lévy, Maurice, 175, 180, 185–86, 192–95, 198
Lewis, Matthew Gregory, 148, 185; *The Monk*, 177, 179, 182, 186, 193, 194, 196
Lope de Vega, 105
Louisiana, 211–18, 221
Louisiana Purchase, 213, 215–16

madness, 3, 16, 36, 139, 150, 199, 232

magic, 75, 77, 117, 124, 162, 167, 199
Malingre, Claude, 25
*Malleus maleficarum*, 117
Marguerite de Navarre, 7, 36, 43, 53, 77, 104; *Heptameron*, 36, 77
Maria Theresa (empress), 163, 166
Marie de France, 91
Marlowe, Christopher, 1
marvelous, 48, 70, 198; concept of, 8, 48, 61, 70–71, 100, 128, 198. *See also* prodigies; wonder
Mary (mother of Jesus), 117
Mary, Queen of Scots, 92
Maturin, Charles Robert, 148, 177; *Melmoth the Wanderer*, 177–78
Maupassant, Guy de, 65–67, 69–70, 79
Medea, 9, 60, 116–17, 138, 147
Medici, Catherine de', 94
melodrama, 35, 152
Middle Ages, 9–10, 57, 91, 117, 118, 120, 176, 180, 199, 205, 208–9
monks, 24, 177; and demonology, 117; as evil figures in narrative and drama, 184, 199, 201, 213
monster, 9, 37, 89, 118–19, 136, 151, 158, 183, 202–3, 208. *See also* deformity
Montaigne, Michel Eyquem de, 67–68, 70
mother, 3, 9, 22, 39, 50, 57–59, 71–72, 94, 116–20, 122–24, 153, 156, 198, 202, 216, 219–20. *See also* family
murder, 3, 9, 17, 22, 30–32, 47–48, 50, 59, 106, 108, 117–21, 129, 132, 134, 138–39, 198, 206, 225, 228, 230–34; decapitation as, 31, 35, 83, 163. *See also* infanticide; parricide; regicide
Murnau, F.W., *Nosferatu*, 167

nationalism and national identity, as factor in Gothic and tragic, 5, 19, 105, 108, 123, 179, 200, 216
negro, 111, 113. *See also* race; slave
Nietzsche, Friedrich Wilhelm, 46, 82
night, as setting for plots, 27, 65, 71, 73, 75–76, 78, 121, 126, 129, 189, 198, 203–5, 206–9, 215
nobility, as quality of epic protagonists, 16, 27
nobles: authors of tales, 104; characters

in tales, 83, 93; readers of tales, 204; transmitters of tales, 52–53
Nodier, Charles, 8, 65, 67, 69, 71–73, 75, 77–79, 181; "Aventures de Thibaud de La Jacquière," 77–79; *Infernalia*, 77
novela, novella and nouvelle, 2, 7, 8–10, 31–32, 34, 36–38, 52–53, 64, 95, 105, 130, 142, 160, 179, 191–92, 198, 202–3, 205–6, 209
novel, 2–3, 29, 37, 39, 105, 107, 123, 148, 161, 175, 177–79, 181–84, 186–90, 192, 195–97, 202, 213, 216

*oikos*, 12, 229. *See also* family; house
otherness and otherization, 10–11, 51, 199
Ottomans, 10, 110, 166–67, 169
Ovid, *Metamorphoses*, 60

pamphlets, 45–51, 53–55, 57, 59, 61, 63, 86, 146, 170. *See also* canards
parricide, 47, 49, 132. *See also* family; murder
pathos, 3, 17, 33, 92, 139. *See also* emotions; fear; pity
patriarchy, 47, 49, 108, 118, 126, 202, 219–20. *See also* family; father
Paul the Deacon, 129–30
Paulmy, Antoine-René de, 40, 44
Paynter, William, 25
Petrarch, 90
Phaedra, 3
phantom. *See* ghost
Phlegon of Tralles, 71
Pitton de Tournefort, Joseph, 169
pity, 18, 54, 57–60, 84, 92, 140. *See also* emotions; fear; pathos; reader
Plato, 18, 111
Platter, Thomas, 87
Plutarch, 33
Poe, Edgar Allan, 12, 201, 218, 225–35; "Fall of the House of Usher," 12, 225–35
poetics of tragedy, 2, 5, 16–18, 25, 38, 46
Polidori, John William, 160
Pomponazzi, Pietro 68
pornography, 106, 107, 114
possession, demonic, 124, 164
Potocki, Jean, 65, 67, 69, 71–73, 75, 77, 79

priests, 96, 169, 203, 205. *See also* Catholicism; monks
Protestants, 10–11, 10, 15, 33–34, 39, 68, 117, 120, 178, 197, 199, 213. *See also* Christianity
punishment, 33–34, 36–37, 49–50, 54–55, 82–83, 86–88, 92–93, 95, 97, 99, 110, 136, 221. *See also* revenge

race, 96–97, 105–10, 200, 212, 221
Racine, Jean, 6, 9, 17, 22–24, 46, 90; *Athalie*, 23; *Britannicus*, 3, 9; *Phèdre*, 23
Radcliffe, Ann, 11, 21, 25, 140, 148, 177, 179, 181–82, 185–86, 191, 195, 213; "On the Supernatural in Poetry," 21, 140; *The Romance of the Forest*, 177
Ranft, Michael, 165, 167
rape, 45, 74, 106, 108, 129, 148, 198, 204. *See also* sex; violence
reader: effect of story on, 33–35, 37, 49, 54, 57, 73, 89, 94–96, 108–9, 112, 150–51, 156, 182–83, 199, 203; expectations of, 30–31, 39, 61, 198, 217–18; interpretative role of, 66, 75–76, 78, 182, 201, 233
regicide, 129, 131, 137, 139–40, 145. *See also* murder
reincarnation, 59. *See also* resurrection
Rémy, Nicolas, 69–70, 72
resurrection, 92, 164. *See also* reincarnation
revenants. *See* ghosts,
revenge, 4, 9–11, 17, 22, 24, 30–32, 38, 58, 67, 111, 122, 129–40, 144–45, 147, 231, 234
Revolution, French, 179–83, 188, 199, 216
Richard, François, S.J., 165–66, 169
Richelieu, Amand-Jean du Plessis, cardinal, 189
Roberval, Jean François de, 38
romance (literary genre), 91, 198, 200–201, 203–4,
Romanticism, 62, 123–24, 148, 176, 203, 207
Rosamund, 9, 129–31, 135–4. *See also* Alboin
Rosset, François de, 8–9, 11, 40, 71–79, 89–91, 93–98, 100
Rotrou, Jean, 130
Rucellai, Giovanni di Bernardo, 130, 142, 144

Sade, Donatien Alphonse François, 11–12, 75, 114, 174–96, 214; *Aline et Valcour,* 179; *Les crimes de l'amour,* 179, 183–84; "Eugénie de Franval," 177, 190; *Idée sur les romans,* 179, 181, 183, 185; *Juliette,* 177, 190–91; *Justine,* 177, 179, 185, 189, 191; *The 120 Days of Sodom,* 12, 179, 187
Saint-Evremond, Charles le Marquetel de Saint-Denis, de, 17
Scarron, Paul, 105
Schelling, Friedrich, 5, 18
Schertz, Carl Ferdinand von, 162
Schiller, Friedrich, 1, 5–6, 19–20, 27; *Wallenstein,* 19
Schuster, Friedrich Wilhelm, 142
science, 124, 160, 165, 167, 171, 199, 202, 208; demonology and, 67–70; vampires and, 160–67
Scots, Mary, Queen of, 92
Seneca the Younger, 17, 226
sensation literature, 2, 30–33, 72, 109, 114, 150. *See also* canard; *histoires tragiques;* tabloid
sex, 47, 72, 74–78, 82–86, 91, 106–7, 109–10, 112, 140, 150, 153, 174, 178, 186, 188, 198, 200, 204, 208. *See also* incest; rape
Shakespeare, William, 1–2, 4, 19, 23, 25, 30, 46, 62, 118, 126, 132, 202–3, 206; *Hamlet,* 2, 4, 9, 11, 23–25, 30, 132; *Macbeth,* 3–4, 19, 118–20, 132; *Romeo and Juliet,* 2, 23, 25, 62
Shelley, Mary, 148, 202–3; *Frankenstein,* 198, 201–3, 209
sister, 38, 82–84, 86, 88, 90, 93–94, 97, 100, 191, 230, 232, 234. *See also* family
skeleton, 24, 33, 110–12, 185. *See also* skull
skepticism, 67–68, 71, 76, 78, 158. *See also* demonology; fantastic
skull, 9; used as drinking cup, 111, 129–30, 133, 135–40. *See also* skeleton
slavery, 22, 109, 111, 133, 212, 216, 221
son, 22, 55, 57–59, 61, 77–78. *See also* family
Sophocles, 1, 3, 16–17, 26; *Ajax,* 229; *Amphytrion,* 26; *Antigone,* 22; *Oedipus at Colonus,* 229
sorcerer and sorceresses. *See* witchcraft
Spain: publication of lurid tales in, 7, 10, 40, 105–8, 110; witch persecution in, 119–28

Spanish Inquisition, 120–24
spectacle: affective impact of, 21, 82–84, 86–88, 92, 95, 98, 111–12, 148, 219, 222; distinguished from plot, 54, 61
specter, 32, 71, 130, 133–34, 136, 138, 140. *See also* apparition; ghost
Steiner, George, 20
Stevenson, Robert Louis, *The Strange Case of Dr Jekyll and Mr Hyde,* 11, 197–203, 205–6, 208–9
Stoker, Bram, *Dracula,* 160–61, 167, 213. *See also* vampires
sublime, 5, 16, 19–20, 148, 158, 206
subterranean spaces, 10, 116, 185, 191, 198, 209, 232. *See also* burial
suicide, 31, 34, 65, 123, 139–40, 225
supernatural, 8, 11, 21, 66, 69, 75–76, 78, 130–32, 135–36, 138–40, 151, 153, 157, 164, 178, 183, 186–87, 198–99, 201–4
superstition, 10, 18, 69–70, 163, 166, 169, 199, 204, 218, 230
surrealism and the Gothic, 176–79
Swinburne, Algernon Charles, 142
Szondi, Peter, 5, 18

tabloid, 105–6, 108–9. *See also* canard; pamphlet
Taissonniere, Guillaume de la, 51–52
terror, 7, 18, 26, 92, 140, 180–81, 183–84, 189, 192, 199, 204, 208. *See also* emotion; fear; horror; pathos
Thyestes, 3, 16, 22, 232
Todorov, Tzvetan, 66–67, 79, 81, 192
torture, 10, 106, 108, 121, 148, 185, 191, 222. *See also* violence
tragedy, 1–7, 9–27, 33, 38, 46, 48, 51, 54, 59, 61–62, 88, 93, 95, 117, 129–33, 137–38, 140, 156–57, 192, 195, 202, 205; Aristotelian concepts of, 16–17, 24, 37, 46, 61, 92; French, 16, 24, 46, 129–41; Greek, 2–7, 12, 16–17, 19, 21–22, 24, 27, 51, 225–32; Idealist view of, 4–7, 16, 19–21; versus "drama," 4
tragic, concept of, 2–7, 16–21
tragic narratives. *See* canard; *histoires tragiques;* pamphlets

*Trauerspiel*, 1, 62

uncanny (*das Unheimliche*), 26–27, 32, 58, 200–201, 208, 218–19, 225, 235; and home 21, 200, 218–19, 225; and return or repetition, 22, 26–27, 201
usurpation, 130, 200, 202–4, 208–9. *See also* family

Valladier, André, 72
Valvasor, Johann, 163–65
vampirism and vampires, 10, 124, 128, 160–70
Vassilev, Kris, 88, 95
vengeance. *See* revenge
violence: as characteristic of tragedy and Gothic, 2–4, 6, 21–22, 46–48, 50, 53, 58–59, 61, 73, 106–8, 198–200, 202, 204–6, 208, 225–26, 228–31, 234; displaced to foreign locations, 10; as public spectacle, 82–101, 182–84; sexual, 47, 198, 204; within families, 2–4, 21–22, 59, 130–37, 149, 202, 225–30. *See also* murder; rape; torture
Vixouse, François-Xavier Pagès de, 181
Voltaire (François-Marie Arouet), 25, 158, 163, 166, 170, 174, 189

Walpole, Horace, 8, 10, 16, 20, 23–25, 27, 148, 179, 187, 197–99, 201–4, 206, 209, 235
Wilde, Oscar, 189; *The Picture of Dorian Gray*, 206
witchcraft, 9–10, 67, 117–18, 120–26, 163
wonder, aesthetic of, 8, 33–34, 48, 70, 72, 78, 109, 120, 182, 198

xenophobia. *See* foreignness, othering
Xylander, Wilhelm, 71

Zayas y Sotomayor, María de, 7, 104–13
Zopf, Johann Heinrich, 166

www.ingramcontent.com/pod-product-compliance
Lightning Source LLC
Chambersburg PA
CBHW030437300426
44112CB00009B/1049